- Outdoor Wine
- Frame Works
- Occiator
- MINUTE WINE
    → Snack Size
- Sweet smart bubble muscato
- VALUE ADD   VALUE OFF
- unique selling propsition (Blue Print)

- Adams Wine Statistics

- Agency Brand
- Fewer Reqd Drving Volume Growth
    - Bring more people in.

- DTC only option.

- Split Branns
    - Jacobsounslach. [CAB SAV, Mrlot, Gew]
    - Bunsen Family. (Pinot Whisp Gewrtz

    9+10

THE STRATEGY AND TACTICS OF PRICING

Fifth Edition

THE STRATEGY AND TACTICS OF PRICING
A GUIDE TO GROWING MORE PROFITABLY

Thomas T. Nagle
Monitor Group

John E. Hogan
Monitor Group

Joseph Zale
Monitor Group

Prentice Hall
Boston   Columbus   Indianapolis   New York   San Francisco   Upper Saddle River
Amsterdam   Cape Town   Dubai   London   Madrid   Milan   Munich   Paris
Montreal   Toronto   Delhi   Mexico City   Sao Paulo   Sydney   Hong Kong
Seoul   Singapore   Taipei   Tokyo

Editorial Director: Sally Yagan
Editor in Chief: Eric Svendsen
Acquisitions Editor: James Heine
AVP/Executive Editor: Melissa Sabella
Director of Marketing: Patrice Lumumba Jones
Marketing Manager: Anne Fahlgren
Marketing Assistant: Melinda Jensen
Project Manager: Renata Butera
Operations Specialist: Renata Butera
Creative Art Director: Jayne Conte
Cover Designer: Margaret Kenselaar
Full-Service Project Management: Nitin Agarwal
Composition: Aptara®, Inc.
Printer/Binder: Courier, Westford
Cover Printer: Courier, Westford
Text Font: Palatino

Credits and acknowledgments borrowed from other sources and reproduced, with permission, in this textbook appear on appropriate pages within text.

Library of Congress Cataloging-in-Publication Data
Nagle, Thomas T.
   The strategy and tactics of pricing / Thomas T. Nagle, John E. Hogan,
Joseph Zale.—5th ed.
      p. cm.
   ISBN-13: 978-0-13-610681-4
   ISBN-10: 0-13-610681-1
   1. Pricing.   2. Marketing—Decision making.   I. Hogan, John E., Ph.D.
II. Zale, Joseph.   III. Title.
   HF5416.5.N34 2010
   658.8'16—dc22

                                                                    2009047553

10
Prentice Hall
is an imprint of

www.pearsonhighered.com

ISBN 13: 978-0-13-610681-4
ISBN 10:   0-13-610681-1

BRIEF CONTENTS

Chapter 1   Strategic Pricing   1
Coordinating the Drivers of Profitability

Chapter 2   Value Creation   17
The Source of Pricing Advantage

Chapter 3   Price Structure   47
Tactics for Pricing Differently Across Segments

Chapter 4   Price and Value Communication   72
Strategies to Influence Willingness-to-Pay

Chapter 5   Pricing Policy   96
Managing Expectations to Improve Price Realization

Chapter 6   Price Level   118
Setting the Right Price for Sustainable Profit

Chapter 7   Pricing Over the Product Life Cycle   141
Adapting Strategy in an Evolving Market

Chapter 8   Pricing Strategy Implementation   158
Embedding Strategic Pricing in the Organization

Chapter 9   Costs   181
How Should They Affect Pricing Decisions?

Chapter 10   Financial Analysis   207
Pricing for Profit

Chapter 11   Competition   244
Managing Conflict Thoughtfully

Chapter 12   Measurement of Price Sensitivity   269
Research Techniques to Supplement Judgment

Chapter 13   Ethics and the Law   305
Understanding the Constraints on Pricing

CONTENTS

Preface   xiii

Chapter 1   Strategic Pricing   1
Coordinating the Drivers of Profitability
Cost-Plus Pricing   2
Customer-Driven Pricing   3
Share-Driven Pricing   4
What Is Strategic Pricing?   5
Value Creation   7
Price Structure   9
Price and Value Communication   11
Pricing Policy   12
Price Level   13
Implementing the Pricing Strategy   14
    Summary   15   •   Notes   16

Chapter 2   Value Creation   17
The Source of Pricing Advantage
The Role of Value in Pricing   18
How to Estimate Economic Value   21
    Competitive Reference Prices   21
    Estimating Monetary Value   23
    Monetary Value Estimation: An Illustration   26
    Estimating Psychological Value   32
    Psychological Value Estimation: An Illustration   32
    The High Cost of Shortcuts   36
Value-Based Market Segmentation   38
    Step 1: Determine Basic Segmentation Criteria   40
    Step 2: Identify Discriminating Value Drivers   41
    Step 3: Determine Your Operational Constraints
             and Advantages   41
    Step 4: Create Primary and Secondary Segments   42
    Step 5: Create Detailed Segment Descriptions   44
    Step 6: Develop Segment Metrics and Fences   44
    Summary   46   •   Notes   46

Chapter 3   **Price Structure   47**
Tactics for Pricing Differently Across Segments
Price-Offer Configuration   50
   Optimizing an Offer Bundle   51
   Designing Segment Specific Bundles   53
   Unbundling Strategically   54
Price Metrics   55
   Creating Good Price Metrics   56
   Performance-Based Metrics   60
   Tie-Ins as Metrics   61
Price Fences   63
   Buyer Identification Fences   64
   Purchase Location Fences   65
   Time of Purchase Fences   66
   Purchase Quantity Fences   68
      Summary   70   •   Notes   71

Chapter 4   **Price and Value Communication   72**
Strategies to Influence Willingness-to-Pay
Value Communication   73
   Adapting the Message for Product
      Characteristics   74
   Adapting the Message to Purchase Context   81
   The Buying Process   82
   Multiple Participants in the Buying Process   86
Price Communication   87
   Proportional Price Evaluations   87
   Reference Prices   88
   Perceived Fairness   90
   Gain–Loss Framing   91
      Summary   93   •   Notes   93

Chapter 5   **Pricing Policy   96**
Managing Expectations to Improve Price Realization
Policy Development   99
Policies for Responding to Price Objections   100
   The Problem with Ad Hoc Negotiation   100
   The Benefits of Policies for Price Negotiation   102
   Policies for Different Buyer Types   103

Policies for Dealing with Power Buyers   108

Policies for Managing Price Increases   110

Policies for Leading an Industry-Wide Increase   111

Policies for Transitioning from Low
One-Off Pricing   112

Policies for Dealing with an Economic Downturn   114

Policies for Promotional Pricing   115

Summary   117 • Notes   117

Chapter 6   Price Level   118

Setting the Right Price for Sustainable Profit

The Price-Setting Process   119

Defining the Price Window   121

Establishing an Initial Price Point   123

Pricing Objectives   125

Defining the Price-Volume Trade-off   129

Estimating Consumer Response   131

Communicate New Prices to the Market   137

Summary   140 • Notes   140

Chapter 7   Pricing Over the Product Life Cycle   141

Adapting Strategy in an Evolving Market

New Products and the Product Life Cycle   141

Pricing the Innovation for Market Introduction   143

Communicating Value with Trial Promotions   144

Communicating Value with Direct Sales   145

Marketing Innovations Through
Distribution Channels   146

Pricing New Products for Growth   146

Pricing within a Differentiated Product Strategy   147

Pricing within a Cost Leadership Strategy   148

Price Reductions in Growth   149

Pricing the Established Product in Maturity   150

Pricing a Product in Market Decline   153

Alternative Strategies in Decline   154

Summary   155 • Notes   156

Chapter 8   Pricing Strategy Implementation   158

Embedding Strategic Pricing in the Organization

Organization   160

Organizational Structure   161
Decision Rights   164
Pricing Processes   165
Motivation   166
Customer Analytics   168
Process Management Analytics   171
Performance Measures and Incentives   175
Managing the Change Process   178
Senior Management Leadership   178
Demonstration Projects   179
Summary   180   •   Notes   180

Chapter 9   **Costs   181**
How Should They Affect Pricing Decisions?
The Role of Costs in Pricing   181
Determining Relevant Costs   182
Why Incremental Costs?   183
Why Avoidable Costs?   186
Avoiding Misleading Accounting   189
Estimating Relevant Costs   191
Activity-Based Costing   196
Percent Contribution Margin
  and Pricing Strategy   197
Managing Costs in Transfer Pricing   199
Summary   204   •   Notes   205

Chapter 10   **Financial Analysis   207**
Pricing for Profit
Break-even Sales Analysis: The Basic Case   209
Break-even Sales Incorporating a Change
  in Variable Costs   212
Break-even Sales with Incremental
  Fixed Costs   213
Break-even Sales Analysis for Reactive Pricing   216
Calculating Potential Financial Implications   217
Break-even Sales Curves   220
Watching Your Baseline   223
Covering Nonincremental Fixed
  and Sunk Costs   224
Summary   232   •   Notes   232

Appendix 10A
Derivation of the Break-even Formula   233
Appendix 10B
Break-even Analysis of Price Changes   235

Chapter 11   Competition   244
Managing Conflict Thoughtfully
Understanding the Pricing Game   245
Competitive Advantage: The Only
Sustainable Source of Profitability   246
Reacting to Competition: Think Before You Act   251
How Should You React?   257
Managing Competitive Information   261
   Collect and Evaluate Information   261
   Selectively Communicate Information   263
When Should You Compete on Price?   266
   Summary   267   •   Notes   267

Chapter 12   Measurement of Price Sensitivity   269
Research Techniques to Supplement Judgment
Types of Measurement Procedures   270
   Uncontrolled Studies of Actual Purchases   271
   Experimentally Controlled Studies
     of Actual Purchases   276
   Uncontrolled Studies of Preferences and Intentions   282
   Experimentally Controlled Studies
     of Preferences and Intentions   288
Using Measurement Techniques Appropriately   294
   Using Judgment for Better Measurement   295
   Using Internet-Based Techniques   297
   Outside Sources of Data   298
   Selecting the Appropriate Measurement Technique   299
   Summary   300   •   Notes   301

Chapter 13   Ethics and the Law   305
Understanding the Constraints on Pricing
Ethical Constraints on Pricing   305
The Legal Framework for Pricing   308
   The Effect of Sarbanes-Oxley on Pricing Practices   309
Price-Fixing or Price Encouragement   310
   Horizontal Price-Fixing   311

Resale Price-Fixing or Encouragement   312
   Vertical Price-Fixing   312
   Direct Dealing Programs   314
   Resale Price Encouragement   314
Price and Promotional Discrimination   315
   Price Discrimination   315
   Defenses to Price Discrimination   317
   Promotional Discrimination   318
   Competitive Injury, Defenses,
     and Indirect Purchasers   319
Using Nonprice Variables to Support Pricing Goals   320
   Vertical Nonprice Restrictions   320
   Nonprice Incentives   322
Other Pricing Issues   322
   Predatory Pricing   322
   Price Signaling   322
     Summary   323 • *Notes   323*

Index   331

PREFACE

One purpose of this book is to change the common misperception that pricing is simply about calculating the "right" price for a product or transaction. In the years since the first edition was published in 1987, we have learned that pricing, if it is to be effective, cannot be so reactive and simplistic. Profitable pricing requires looking beneath the demand curve to understand and manage the monetary and psychological value that is a primary determinant of the purchase decision. Mastering the value proposition enables a firm (1) to segment prices to reflect differences in value and cost, (2) to communicate the value of offers to customers unfamiliar with the market, and (3) to create pricing policies for managing pricing issues fairly and consistently. In short, this book shows managers how to move from tactically "optimizing" prices in markets where they seemingly exercise little control to managing their markets strategically. When that happens, pricing becomes an integral part of a profitable growth strategy, rather than a blunt instrument to drive sales and market share.

The principles of strategic pricing, which were foreign to most business practitioners more than two decades ago, are now more widely accepted in principle. But most companies still struggle with the application. The changes in this fifth edition of our book reflect our attempts to address this need:

- A completely new chapter on "Pricing Strategy Implementation" identifies the challenges involved in embedding strategic pricing principles within an organization and describes how managers can lead a structured change process to build a commercial organization more consistently focused on value creation.
- The revised chapter on "Pricing Policy" provides a theoretically grounded framework to describe specific policies for managing price changes for a variety of situations, including raw material cost increases, demand recessions, and new product launches.
- The chapter on "Value Creation" for the first time addresses explicitly how to deal with value differently when it is driven by subjective psychological drivers (such as doing the right thing for the environment) rather than by tangible monetary drivers (for example, saving money on fuel).
- The chapter on "Value and Price Communication" has been substantially revised to describe how to communicate value in a wide variety of product and customer contexts. It demonstrates how to target communications to affect specific behaviors throughout the customer's buying process.
- The chapter on "Price Setting" has been expanded to provide a robust process for setting prices that can be widely applied both to consumer and business markets.
- Throughout the book, we have updated examples with more topical illustrations of current pricing challenges (such as iPhone pricing, new models for pricing music, and services pricing).

To complement this edition, we also introduce software from LeveragePoint Innovations Inc. for creating and communicating economic value estimations systematically. The trial software can be accessed at http://demo.leveragepoint .com/strategyandtacticsofpricing. While versions of the software that enable sharing require corporate contracts for access, versions for individual student and practitioner use are available without charge for three months. This software puts theory into practice and allows the reader to explore real-world scenarios.

ACKNOWLEDGMENTS

Over the years, this book has benefited from the influence and efforts of individuals too numerous to mention here. Nevertheless, we would be remiss in not acknowledging a few whose contributions have been either very large or new to this edition. Professor Gerald Smith's contributions to three prior editions of this book and the instructor's manuals are still reflected in the current ones. Michael Goldberg of Monitor Group was a diligent researcher, copy editor, and administrator without whose incessant prodding this edition would still be "in process." Georg Muller and Tony Seisfeld of Monitor Group and Paul Boni of Grail Research drew from their experience in pricing research to update our chapter on "Measurement of Price Sensitivity." Eugene Zelek of Freeborn and Peters once again shared his knowledge of pricing and the law to keep that chapter current. We would also like to thank our colleagues at Monitor Group who, since the previous edition, have taught us the concept of the buying process and the importance of aligning interventions at the most appropriate point in it. Our administrative assistant, Vivi Camin, diligently sought reprint permissions and recreated versions of diagrams and tables. Last, but certainly not least, we want to thank our colleagues at Monitor Group for their indulgence while we closeted ourselves to complete this edition, and to thank our families, which we neglected and to whom we now hope to make amends.

THE STRATEGY AND TACTICS OF PRICING

CHAPTER 1

Strategic Pricing
Coordinating the Drivers of Profitability

The economic forces that determine profitability change whenever technology, regulation, market information, consumer preferences, or relative costs change. Consequently, companies that grow profitably in changing markets often need to break old rules and create new pricing models. For example, Netflix changed the model for renting films from the daily rate at video stores to a time-independent membership model. Ryanair radically unbundled the elements of passenger air travel—charging separately for baggage, seat selection, in-person check in, beverages—enabling it to generate greater occupancy and more revenue per plane per day than its established European competitors. Producers of new online media created a new metric for pricing ads—cost per click—that aligns the cost of an ad more closely to its value than was possible in traditional media. Apple changed the market for music in part by pricing songs rather than albums.

Unfortunately, few managers, even those in marketing, have received practical training in how to make strategic pricing decisions such as these. Most companies still make pricing decisions in reaction to change rather than in anticipation of it. This is unfortunate given that the need for rapid and thoughtful adaptations to changing markets has never been greater. The information revolution has made prices everywhere more transparent, making customers increasingly price sensitive. The globalization of markets, even for services, has increased the number of competitors and often lowered their cost of sales. The high rate of technological change in many industries has created new sources of value for customers, but not necessarily led to increases in profit for the producers.

Still, those companies that have the capability to create and implement strategies that take account of these changes are well rewarded for their efforts. Our ValueScan survey, covering more than 200 companies in both consumer and business markets, found that firms developing and effectively executing value-based pricing strategies earn 31 percent higher operating income than competitors whose pricing is driven by market share goals or target margins.[1] Specific examples abound that illustrate the power of strategic pricing to reward innovation.

One prominent example is the iPhone. When Apple launched the iPhone, critics claimed that a price over $400 was way out of line when competitive products could be bought outright for half as much or obtained "free" with a two-year contract from a wireless service provider. Apple, however, understood that a hard-core group of technology "innovators" would easily recognize and place a high value on the iPhone's unique differentiation. By focusing on meeting that group's needs at a high price, Apple established a high benchmark for the value of its easy-to-use interface. When Apple later lowered the price to a still high $300, it seemed like a bargain in comparison to that benchmark, causing still more people to buy the phone. Having established a high value, the company now captures a dominant share at competitive prices while earning more than $1 billion per year from the sale of third-party "apps."

Wal-Mart is another company that has grown profitably by pricing strategically, but with the focus on where and how to discount prices. For example, Wal-Mart puts its deepest discounts on products, like disposable diapers, that drive frequent repeat visits by big spenders on other products. Since competitors with narrower product lines cannot justify an equally low price on a "loss leader," Wal-Mart can undercut them to generate more store traffic without triggering a price war that would otherwise undermine its strategy. As Wal-Mart illustrates, the measure of success at strategic pricing is not how much it increases price but how much it increases profitability.

This book will prepare you to understand the forces that determine the success of a pricing strategy, to develop strategies to address those forces proactively, and then to effectively implement tactics that enable you to profit from them. We offer no magic bullets that enable you to win higher prices than competitors while delivering no more in value. Many years of experience have convinced us, however, that applying the principles explained in these pages is an essential capability to earn profits commensurate with the value of one's products and services.

Before this goal can be achieved, managers in all functional areas must discard the flawed thinking about pricing that leads them into conflict and drives them to make unprofitable decisions. Let's look at these flawed paradigms so that we can discard them once and for all.

COST-PLUS PRICING

Cost-plus pricing is, historically, the most common pricing procedure because it carries an aura of financial prudence. Financial prudence, according to this view, is achieved by pricing every product or service to yield a fair return over all costs, fully and fairly allocated. In theory, it is a simple guide to profitability; in practice, it is a blueprint for mediocre financial performance.

The problem with cost-driven pricing is fundamental: In most industries it is impossible to determine a product's unit cost before determining its price. Why? Because unit costs change with volume. This cost change occurs because a significant portion of costs are "fixed" and must somehow be "allocated" to determine the full unit cost. Unfortunately, because these allocations depend on volume, and volume changes as prices change, unit cost is a moving target. To "solve" the problem of determining unit cost before determining price, cost-based pricers are forced to make the absurd assumption that they can set price without affecting volume. The failure to account for the effects of price on volume, and of volume on costs, leads managers directly into pricing decisions that undermine profits. A price increase to "cover" higher fixed costs can start a death spiral in which higher prices reduce sales and raise average unit costs further, indicating (according to cost-plus theory) that prices should be raised even higher. On the other hand, if sales are higher than expected, fixed costs can be spread over more units, allowing average unit costs to decline a lot. According to cost-plus theory, that would call for lower prices. Cost-plus pricing leads to overpricing in weak markets and underpricing in strong ones—exactly the opposite direction of a prudent strategy.

How, then, should managers deal with the problem of pricing to cover costs? They shouldn't. The question itself reflects an erroneous perception of the role of pricing, a perception based on the belief that one can first determine sales levels, then calculate unit cost and profit objectives, and then set a price. Instead of pricing reactively to cover costs and profit objectives, managers need to price proactively. They need to acknowledge that pricing affects volume, that volume affects costs, and that pricing strategy is in part about effectively managing the utilization of fixed costs.

Instead of asking whether the price covers fully allocated costs, a pricer should ask whether the change in price will result in a change in revenue that is more than sufficient to offset a change in total fixed variable costs. When the change in revenue minus the change in variable costs is positive, the firm is earning more revenue to cover its fixed costs. When the change in revenue minus change in variable costs is negative, the firm is earning less revenue to cover its fixed costs. In a later chapter on financial analysis of price changes, we describe shortcuts to calculate the change in volume necessary for any proposed price change.

CUSTOMER-DRIVEN PRICING

Many companies now recognize the fallacy of cost-based pricing and its adverse effect on profit. They realize the need for pricing to reflect market conditions. As a result, some firms have taken pricing authority away from financial managers and given it to sales or product managers. In theory, this trend is consistent with value-based pricing, since marketing and sales are that part of the organization best positioned to understand value to the customer. In practice, however, the misuse of pricing to achieve short-term sales objectives often undermines perceived value and depresses profits even further.

The purpose of strategic pricing is not simply to create satisfied customers. Customer satisfaction can usually be bought by a combination of over delivering on value and underpricing products. But marketers delude themselves if they believe that the resulting sales represent marketing successes. The purpose of strategic pricing is to price more profitably by capturing more value, not necessarily by making more sales. When marketers confuse the first objective with the second, they fall into the trap of pricing at whatever buyers are willing to pay, rather than at what the product is really worth. Although that decision enables marketers to meet their sales objectives, it invariably undermines long-term profitability.

Two problems arise when prices reflect the amount buyers seem willing to pay. First, sophisticated buyers are rarely honest about how much they are actually willing to pay for a product. Professional purchasing agents are adept at concealing the true value of a product to their organizations. Once buyers learn that sellers' prices are flexible, the buyers have a financial incentive to conceal information from, and even mislead sellers. Obviously, this tactic undermines the salesperson's ability to establish close relationships with customers and to understand their needs.

Second, there is an even more fundamental problem with pricing to reflect customers' willingness-to-pay. The job of sales and marketing is not simply to process orders at whatever price customers are currently willing to pay, but rather to raise customers' willingness-to-pay to a level that better reflects the product's true value. Many companies underprice truly innovative products because they ask potential customers, who are ignorant of the product's value, what they would be willing to pay. But we know from studies of innovations that the "regular" price has little impact on customers' willingness to try them. For example, most customers initially perceived that photocopiers, mainframe computers, and food processors lacked adequate value to justify their prices. Only after extensive marketing to communicate and guarantee value did these products achieve market acceptance. Forget what customers who have never used your product are initially willing to pay. Instead, understand the value of the product to satisfied customers and communicate that value to others. Low pricing is never a substitute for an adequate marketing and sales effort.

SHARE-DRIVEN PRICING

Finally, consider the policy of letting pricing be dictated by competitive conditions. In this view, pricing is a tool to achieve sales objectives. In the minds of some managers, this method is "pricing strategically." Actually, it is more analogous to "letting the tail wag the dog." Why should an organization want to achieve market-share goals? Because managers believe that more market share usually produces greater profit.[2] Priorities are confused, however, when managers reduce the profitability of each sale simply to achieve the market-share goal. Prices should be lowered only when they are no longer justified by the value offered in comparison to the value offered by the competition.

Although price-cutting is probably the quickest, most effective way to achieve sales objectives, it is usually a poor decision financially. Because a price cut can be so easily matched, it offers only a short-term market advantage at the expense of permanently lower margins. Consequently, unless a company has good reason to believe that its competitors cannot match a price cut, the long-term cost of using price as a competitive weapon usually exceeds any short-term benefit. Although product differentiation, advertising, and improved distribution do not increase sales as quickly as price cuts, their benefit is more sustainable and thus is usually more cost-effective.

The goal of pricing should be to find the combination of margin and market share that maximizes profitability over the long term. Sometimes, the most profitable price is one that substantially restricts market share relative to the competition. Godiva chocolates, BMW cars, Peterbilt trucks, and Snap-on tools would no doubt all gain substantial market share if priced closer to the competition. It is doubtful, however, that the added share would be worth forgoing their profitable and successful positioning as high-priced brands.

Strategic pricing requires making informed trade-offs between price and volume in order to maximize profits. These trade-offs come in two forms. The first trade-off involves the willingness to lower price to exploit a market opportunity to drive volume. Cost-plus pricers are often reluctant to exploit these opportunities because they reduce the average contribution margin across the product line, giving the appearance that it is underperforming relative to other products. But if the opportunity for incremental volume is large and well managed, a lower contribution margin can actually drive a higher total profit. The second trade-off involves the willingness to give up volume by raising prices. Competitor- and customer-oriented pricers find it very difficult to hold the line on price increases in the face of a lost deal or reduced volume. Yet the economics of a price increase can be compelling. For example, a product with a 30 percent contribution margin could lose up to 25 percent of its volume following a 10 percent price increase before it resulted in lower profitability. Effective pricers regularly evaluate the balance between profitability and market share and are willing to make hard decisions when the balance tips too far in one direction.

WHAT IS STRATEGIC PRICING?

The word "strategy" is used in various contexts to imply different things. Here we use it to mean the coordination of otherwise independent activities to achieve a common objective. For strategic pricing, that objective is profitability. Achieving exceptional profitability requires managing much more than just price levels. It requires ensuring that products and services include just those features that customers are willing to pay for, without those that unnecessarily drive up cost by more than they add to value. It requires translating the differentiated benefits your company offers into customer perceptions of a fair price premium for those benefits. It requires creativity in how you collect revenues so that customers who get more value from your differentiation pay more for it. It requires varying price to use fixed costs optimally and to discourage behavior that drives excessive service costs. It sometimes requires building capabilities to mitigate the behavior of aggressive competitors.

Although more than one strategy can achieve profitable results, even within the same industry, nearly all successful pricing strategies embody three principles. They are value-based, proactive, and profit-driven.

- *Value-based* means that differences in pricing across customers and changes over time reflect differences or changes in the value to customers. For example, many managers ask whether they should lower prices in response to reduced market demand during a recession. The answer: if customers receive less value from your product or service because of the recession, then prices should reflect that. But the fact that fewer customers are in the market for your product does not necessarily imply that they value it less than when they were more numerous. Unless a close competitor has cut its price, giving customers a better alternative, there may be no value-based reason for you to do so.

- *Proactive* means that companies anticipate disruptive events (for example, negotiations with customers, a competitive threat, or a techno-logical change) and develop strategies in advance to deal with them. For example, anticipating that a recession or a new competitive entry will cause customers to ask for lower prices, a proactive company develops a lower-priced service option or a loyalty program, enabling it to define the terms and trade-offs of the expected interaction, rather than forcing it to react to terms and trade-offs defined by the customer or the competitor.

- *Profit-driven* means that the company evaluates its success at price man-agement by what it earns relative to alternative investments rather than by the revenue it generates relative to its competitors. For example, when Alan Mulally took charge as Ford Motor Company's CEO in 2006, he declared that henceforth Ford would focus on selling cars profitably, even if that meant that Ford would become a smaller company. He cut Ford's 96 models to 20 and sold off its unprofitable Jaguar and Land Rover brands. When the recession appeared in late 2008, he quickly and relentlessly cut production—ending the long-standing policy at all the Big Three U.S. auto manufacturers to increase customer and dealer incentives to maintain production as long as possible.[3] Although Ford initially gave up market share, it was in the end the only one of the Big Three to avoid bankruptcy.

These three principles are evident throughout this book as we discuss how to define and make good choices. A good pricing strategy involves five distinct but very different sets of choices that build upon one another. The choices are represented graphically as the five levels of the strategic pricing pyramid (Exhibit 1-1), with those lower in the pyramid providing the necessary

EXHIBIT 1-1   The Strategic Pricing Pyramid

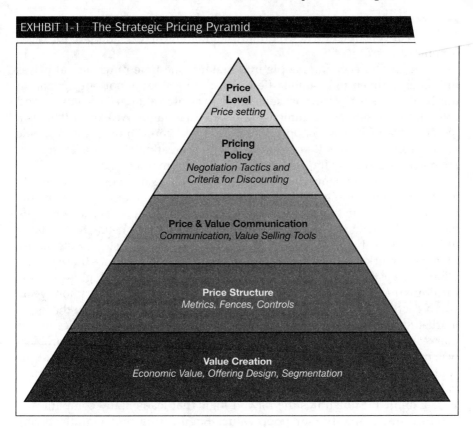

support, or foundation, for those above. Although the principles that underlie choices at each level are the same, implementing those principles in any given market requires creative application to the specifics of each product and market. Consequently, after briefly describing each choice here, the next five chapters will illustrate in greater detail the tools and tactics for making each choice well. Notice, however, that the choices fall into what, in large companies, are different functional domains staffed by different people. That is why senior management needs to be involved in pricing; not to set prices but to articulate goals for each set of choices that facilitate the implementation of a coherent strategy.

VALUE CREATION

It is often repeated that the value of something is whatever someone will pay for it. We disagree. People sometimes pay for things that soon disappoint them in use (for example, time-share condominiums). They fail to get "value for money," do not repeat the purchase, and discourage others from making the same mistake. Of greater importance for innovators, most people are unwilling to pay more for things that are new to them (such as acupuncture treatments or electronic books) despite the fact that in some cases growing numbers of consumers will eventually come to recognize and pay for those benefits.

Although deceiving people into making one-time purchases at prices ultimately proven to be unjustified is a strategy, that is not our agenda in this book. Ours is to show marketers how to create value cost-effectively and convince people to pay commensurate with that value. We expect that, as a result, those of you who apply these ideas will contribute to an economic system in which firms that are most adept at creating value for customers are most rewarded by improvement in their own market value.

Unfortunately, some companies that have the technology and capability to create value fail to convert that into value for customers. They make the mistake of believing that more, from a technological perspective, is necessarily better for the customer. One of us worked for a company making high-quality office furniture that was disappointed by its low share in fast-growing, entrepreneurial markets. The company wanted a strategy to convince those buyers what more established companies recognized already: that highly durable furniture that would hold its appearance and function for 20 or more years was a good investment. But it took a few interviews with buyers in the target market for the furniture maker to recognize the problem. Companies in this market expected either to be bought out in five years or be gone. The problem was not that customers did not recognize the differentiating benefits of the company's products. It was that the target market company did not see good value associated with those benefits.

Exhibit 1-2 illustrates the flawed logic that leads many companies to produce good quality, but poor value. Engineering and manufacturing departments design and make what they consider a "better" product. In the process, they make investments and incur costs to add features and services. Finance then totals these costs to determine "target" prices. Only at this stage does marketing enter the process, charged with the task of demonstrating enough value in these better products and services to justify premium prices to customers. Sometimes they get lucky; but often a much smaller share of the market sees enough value in the improvements to justify paying for them.

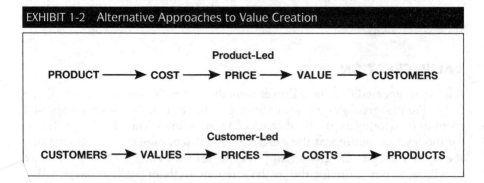

EXHIBIT 1-2   Alternative Approaches to Value Creation

Product-Led

PRODUCT ⟶ COST ⟶ PRICE ⟶ VALUE ⟶ CUSTOMERS

Customer-Led

CUSTOMERS ⟶ VALUES ⟶ PRICES ⟶ COSTS ⟶ PRODUCTS

When cost-based prices prove unjustifiable, managers may try to fix the process by allowing "flexibility" in the markups. Although this tactic may minimize the damage, it is not, fundamentally, a solution because the financial return on the product remains inadequate. Finance blames marketing and sales for cutting the price, and marketing blames finance for excessive costs. The problem keeps recurring as the features and costs of new products continue to mismatch the needs and values of customers. Moreover, when customers are rewarded with discounts for their price resistance, this resistance becomes more frequent even when the product is valuable to them.

Solving the problems of cost-based pricing requires more than a quick fix. It requires a complete reversal of the process—starting with customers. The target price is based on estimates of the value of features and services given the competitive alternatives and the portion of it that the firm can expect to capture in its price by segment. The job of financial management is not to insist that prices recover costs. It is to insist that costs are incurred only to make products that can be priced profitably given their value to the targeted customers.

Designing product and service offers that can drive sales growth at profitable prices has gone in the past two decades from being unusual to being the goal at most successful companies.[4] From Marriott to Boeing, from medical technology to automobiles, profit-leading companies now think about what market segment they want a new product to serve, determine the benefits those potential customers seek, and establish prices those customers can be convinced to pay. Value-based companies challenge their engineers to develop products and services that can be produced at a cost low enough to make serving that market segment profitable at the target price. The first companies to successfully implement such a strategy in an industry gain a huge market advantage. The laggards eventually must learn how to mange value just to survive.

The key to creating good value is first to estimate how much value different combinations of benefits could represent to customers, which is normally the responsibility of marketing or market research. We will describe how to estimate value in Chapter 2.

PRICE STRUCTURE

Once you understand how value is created for different customer segments, the next step in building a pricing strategy is to create a price structure. The most simple price structure is a price per unit (for example, dollars per ton or euros per liter) and is perfectly adequate for commodity products and services. The purpose of more complicated price structures is to reflect differences in the potential contribution that can be captured from different customer segments by capturing the best possible price from each segment, making the sale at the lowest possible cost, or both.

An airline seat, for example, is much more valuable for a business traveler who needs to meet a client at a particular place and time than it is for a pleasure traveler for whom different destinations, different days of travel, or even non-travel related forms of recreation are viable alternatives. Airline pricers have long employed complex price structures that enable them to maximize the revenue they can earn from these different types of customers. On Monday morning or Friday afternoon, they can fill their planes mostly with business passengers paying full coach prices, but they are likely to be left with many empty seats at those prices on Tuesday, Wednesday, and Thursday. While they could just cut their price per seat to fill seats at those "off-peak" times, they then would end up giving business passengers unnecessary discounts as well. To attract more price-sensitive pleasure travelers without discounting to business travelers, they create segmented price structures so that most passengers pay a price aligned with the value they place on having a seat.

On the Tuesday morning when this was written, you could fly from Boston to Los Angeles and return two days later for as little as $324—but with a nonrefundable ticket, a $100 charge for changes, a $15 checked baggage charge each way, and low priority for rebooking if flights are disrupted by weather or mechanical problems. For $514 you could get the very same seats on the very same flights, but with a refundable, changeable ticket and high priority rebooking in case of disruption—all things likely to be highly valued by a business traveler but barely missed by a pleasure traveler. Similarly, you could pay $934 for first-class roundtrip travel with a non-cancellable ticket and $150 change fee. Totally flexible and cancellable first-class travel would cost you $1901. With these different options, the airlines maximize the revenue from each flight by limiting the seats available at the discounted, non-cancellable prices to a number that they project could not be sold at higher prices.[5]

More recently, airline price structures are being designed to discourage behaviors that make some customers more costly to serve than others. The European carrier Ryanair has taken the lead in discounting ticket prices and in charging for everything else. If you don't print out your boarding pass before arriving at the airport, be prepared to pay an extra €5 to check in. Want to check a bag? Add €10. Want to take a baby on your lap? €20. Want to take the baby's car seat and stroller along? €20 each. To board the plane near the front of the line will cost you €3. Of course, you will pay for any food or drinks, but if you are short on cash you might be well advised to avoid them. The CEO recently reiterated his plan to charge for using the on-board lavatories on short flights, arguing that "if we can get rid of two of the three toilets on a 737, we can add an extra six seats."[6] Do you think this is pushing price structure complexity so far that it will drive away customers? We thought so too. But consider that in less than a decade Ryanair has risen to first place among European airlines in passengers carried, in revenue growth, and in market capitalization.[7]

Chapter 3 will describe in detail how to develop price structures that align prices with differences in value and cost across segments.

PRICE AND VALUE COMMUNICATION

Understanding the value your products create for customers and translating that understanding into a value-based price structure can still result in poor sales unless customers recognize the value they are obtaining. A successful pricing strategy must justify the prices charged in terms of the value of the benefits provided. Developing price and value communications is one of the most challenging tasks for marketers because of the wide variety of product types and communication vehicles. In some instances, marketers might employ traditional advertising media to convey their differential value, as was the case with the now famous "I am a Mac" ads created by Apple. The ads, featuring the actors Justin Long posing as a Mac and John Hodgman as a PC, highlighted common problems for PC owners not faced by Mac owners and are credited with making a major contribution to Apple's success in the late 2000s.[8] In other instances, value messages will be communicated directly during the sales process with the aid of illustrations of value experienced by customers within a market segment or with the aid of a spreadsheet model to quantify the value of an offering to a particular customer.[9]

The content of value messages will vary depending on the type of product and the context of the purchase. The messaging approach for frequently purchased *search goods* such as laundry detergent or personal care items will tend to focus on very specific points of differentiation to help customers make comparisons between alternatives. In contrast, messaging for more complex *experience goods* such as services or vacations will deemphasize specific points of differentiation in favor of creating assurances that the offering will deliver on its value proposition if purchased. Similarly, the content of value messages must account for whether the benefits are *psychological* or *monetary* in nature. As we explain in Chapter 4, marketers should be explicit about the quantified worth of the benefits for monetary value and implicit about the quantified worth of psychological benefits.

Price and value messages must also be adapted for the customer's purchase context. When Samsung, a global leader in cellular phone sets, develops its messaging for its new 4G (fourth generation) phones, it must adapt the message depending on whether the customer is a new cell phone user or is a technophile who enjoys keeping up with the latest technology. Samsung must also adapt its messages depending on where the customer is in their *buying process*. When customers are at the information search stage of the process, the value communication goal is to make the most differentiated (and value creating) features salient for the customer so that he or she weighs these features heavily in the purchase decision. For Samsung, this means focusing on its phones' big screens and high data-transfer speeds. As the customer moves through the purchase process to the fulfillment stage, the nature of messaging shifts from value to price as marketers try to frame their prices in the most favorable way possible. It is not an accident when a cellular provider describes its price in terms of pennies a day rather than one flat fee. Research has shown that reframing prices in smaller units comparable to the flow of benefits can have a significant positive effect on customer price sensitivity.[10]

As these examples illustrate, there are many factors to consider when creating price and value communications. Ultimately, the marketer's goal is to get the right message, to the right person, at the right point in the buying process. We show how to approach the challenge later in Chapter 4.

PRICING POLICY

Ultimately, the success of a pricing strategy depends upon customers being willing to pay the price you charge. The rationale for value-based pricing is that a customer's relative willingness-to-pay for one product versus another should track closely with differences in the relative value of those products. When customers become increasingly resistant to whatever price a firm asks, most managers would draw one of three conclusions: that the product is not offering as much value as expected, that customers do not understand the value, or that the price is too high relative to the value. But there is another possible and very common cause of price resistance. Customers sometimes decline to pay prices that represent good value simply because they have learned that they can obtain even better prices by exploiting the sellers' pricing process.

Telecommunications companies increasingly face this problem. In order to get people to consolidate their phone, Internet, and cable TV with one supplier, they offer attractive contracts (typically $99 per month) for new customers. After one year, the rate reverts to regular charges, which are higher by 20 percent or more. Because these offers have been advertised for some time, subscribers have learned that they can beat the system. At the end of one year, many simply sign up for one year with a new supplier for $99 per month. Thus, a program that was designed to induce people to learn about the high value of a supplier's service has become a program to enable aggressive shoppers to avoid paying prices that reflect that value.

Pricing policy refers to rules or habits, either explicit or cultural, that determine how a company varies its prices when faced with factors other than value and cost to serve that threaten its ability to achieve it objectives. Good policies enable a company to achieve its short-term objectives without causing customers, sales reps, and competitors to adapt their behavior in ways that undermine the volume or profitability of future sales. Poor pricing policies create incentives for customers, sales reps, or competitors to behave in ways that will undermine future sales or customers' willingness-to-pay. In the terminology of economics, good policies enable prices to change along the demand curve without changing expectations in ways that cause the demand curve to "shift" negatively for future purchases. Poor policies allow price changes in ways that adversely affect customer's willingness-to-pay as much or to buy as much in the future. Chapter 5 will describe good policies and alert you to the hidden risks of poor but commonly practiced pricing policies.

PRICE LEVEL

According to economic theory, setting prices is a straightforward exercise in which the marketer simply sets the price at the point on the demand curve where marginal revenues are equal to the marginal costs. As any experienced pricer knows, however, setting prices in the real world is seldom so simple. On the one hand, it is impossible to predict how revenues will change following a price change because of the uncertainty about how customers and competitors will respond. On the other hand, the accounting systems in most companies are not equipped to identify the relevant costs for pricing strategy decisions, often causing marketers to make unprofitable pricing decisions.

This uncertainty about marginal costs and revenues creates a dilemma for marketers trying to set profit-maximizing prices: How should they analyze pricing moves in the face of such uncertainty? There are many pricing tools and techniques in common use today such as conjoint analysis and optimization models that take the uncertain inputs and provide seemingly certain price recommendations. While these tools are invaluable aids to marketers (we show how to use them to maximum advantage in Chapter 6), they run the risk of creating a sense of false precision about the right price. There is no substitution for managerial experience and judgment when setting prices.

Price setting should be an iterative and cross-functional process led by marketing that includes several key actions. The first action is to set appropriate pricing objectives, whether that means to use price to drive volume or to maximize margins. McDonald's used a *penetration pricing* approach in 2008 to take significant share from Starbucks during a time when customers were increasingly price sensitive and willing to switch because of the recession. Once consumers tried McDonald's new premium coffees, they found that the taste was excellent, and many opted not to switch back. The second action is to calculate price-volume trade-offs. A 10 percent price cut for a product with a 20 percent contribution margin would have to result in a 100 percent increase in sales volume to be profitable. The same increase for a product with a 70 percent contribution margin would only require a 17 percent increase in sales to be profitable. We are frequently surprised by how many managers make unfortunate pricing decisions because they do not understand these basic financial considerations.

Once the price-volume trade-offs are made explicit for a particular pricing move, the next activity is to estimate the likely customer response by assessing the drivers of price sensitivity that are unrelated to value. Two coffee lovers might value a cup of Starbucks equally. Despite placing equal value on the coffee, the retiree on a fixed income will be much more price sensitive than the working professional with substantial disposable income. Conversely, both of those individuals may be made less price sensitive to the price of a Starbucks coffee relative to Dunkin' Donuts coffee, because the higher price is a signal that Starbucks is of superior quality. The marketer's job is to understand how price sensitivity varies across segments in order to better estimate the profit impact of a potential pricing move. As we explain in Chapter 6, there are a variety of tools to help accomplish this task while always remembering that it is better to be approximately right, rather than precisely wrong.

IMPLEMENTING THE PRICING STRATEGY

Over the past decade, pricing has risen in importance on the corporate agenda. Most top executives recognize the importance of price and value management for achieving profitable growth. Yet, given this strategic importance, it is surprising to us how many firms continue to organize their pricing activities so that pricing decisions are made by lower-level managers lacking the skills, data, and authority to implement tough new pricing strategies. This tactical orientation has financial consequences for the firm. Our research found that companies that adopted a value-based pricing strategy and built the organizational capabilities to implement the strategy earned 24 percent higher profits than industry peers.[11] Yet in that same research, we found that a full 23 percent of marketing and sales managers did not understand their company's pricing strategy or did not believe their company had a pricing strategy.

Implementing pricing strategy is difficult because it requires input and coordination across so many different functional areas: marketing, sales, capacity management, and finance. Successful pricing strategy implementation is built on three pillars: an effective organization, timely and accurate information, and appropriately motivated management. In most instances, it is neither desirable nor necessary for a company to have a large, centralized organization to manage pricing. What is required, however, is that everyone involved in pricing decisions understand what his role in the price-setting process is and what rights he has to participate. Whereas the pricing manager might have the right to set the price, sales management might have the right to consult on the pricing decision while senior management might have the right to veto the decision. Too often, these *decision rights* are not clearly specified, changing the pricing decision from a well-defined business process to an exercise in political power as various functional areas attempt to influence the offered price.

Once managers understand their role in the price-setting process, they must then be provided with the right data and tools to make the decisions assigned to them. In our research, when we asked managers about what would make the most improvement in their firm's pricing decisions, more than 75 percent answered, "Better data and tools." When one considers the data requirements for making organization-wide pricing decisions, this response is not surprising. Marketing managers need data on customer value and competitive pricing. Sales managers need data to support their value claims and defend price premiums. And financial managers need accurate cost data and volume data. Collecting these large volumes of data and distributing them throughout the organization is a daunting task that has led many companies to adopt sophisticated price management systems that can integrate with their data warehouses and ensure that managers get only the information they need. Not every firm needs to invest in dedicated systems to manage pricing data. However, everyone must address the question of how to get the right information into the right manager's hands in a timely fashion if they hope to keep their pricing strategies aligned with the ongoing changes occurring in most markets.

One last, important point about implementing a pricing strategy is the need to motivate managers to engage in new behaviors that support the strategy. All too often, people are offered incentives to act in ways that undermine the pricing strategy and reduce profitability. It is common for companies to send sales reps to training programs designed to help them sell on value, but when they return to work, they are paid purely to maximize top-line sales revenue. When sales reps or field sales managers are offered only revenue-based incentives, it is hard to imagine them fighting to defend a price premium if they think that doing so will increase their chances of losing the deal. But incentives can be developed that encourage more profitable behaviors.

A senior salesperson we know was recently promoted to regional sales manager for an area in which discounting was rampant. He began his first meeting by sharing a ranking of sales reps by their price realization during the prior quarter. He invited the top two reps to describe how they did those deals so profitably and the bottom two reps to describe what went wrong. He then facilitated an open discussion among the 30 reps on how challenges like those faced by the bottom two reps could be managed better in the future. At the end of the meeting, he told them that this exercise would be repeated every quarter. One month into the subsequent quarter, sales reps were asking to see where they stood in the rankings, suggesting that they were highly motivated to engage in productive behaviors to avoid a low ranking at the next meeting.

Summary

Pricing strategically has become essential to the success of business, reflecting the rise of global competition, the increase in information available to customers, and the accelerating pace of change in the products and services available in most markets. The simple, traditional models of cost-driven, customer-driven, or share-driven pricing can no longer sustain a profitable business in today's dynamic and open markets.

This chapter introduced the strategic pricing pyramid containing the five key elements of strategic pricing. Experience has taught us that achieving sustainable improvements to pricing performance requires ongoing evaluation of and adjustments to multiple elements of the pyramid. Companies operating with a narrow view of what constitutes a pricing strategy miss this crucial point, leading to incomplete solutions and lower profits. Building a strategic pricing capability requires more than a common understanding of the elements of an effective strategy. It requires careful development of organizational structure, systems, individual skills, and ultimately culture. These things represent the foundation upon which the strategic pricing pyramid rests and must be developed in concert with the pricing strategy. But the first step toward strategic pricing is to understand each level of the pyramid and how it supports those above it.

Notes

1. Source: ValueScan Survey, Monitor Group, Cambridge, MA, 2008.
2. In the past two decades, serious theoretical work has replaced simplistic, anecdotal guidelines for how to create a sustainably successful business. See Michael E. Porter, *Competitive Advantage* (New York: The Free Press, 1985); Gary Hamel and C. K. Parhalad, *Competing for the Future* (Cambridge, MA: Harvard Business School Press, 1994); Adrian Slywotzky and David Morrison, *The Profit Zone* (New York: Random House, 1997); Robert Kaplan and David Norton, *The Strategy-Focused Organization* (Cambridge, MA: Harvard Business School, 2001).
3. Andrew Clark, "Car Wars: How Alan Mulally Kept Ford Ahead of Its Rivals," *The Guardian*, May 11, 2009.
4. Peter F. Drucker, "The Information Executives Truly Need," *Harvard Business Review* (January–February 1995): 58.
5. The projection process for discounting is called "yield management" and is described in Chapter 9, Box 9–2.
6. "Ryanair Ready for Price War as Aer Lingus Costs Leap," *The Telegraph*, June 2, 2009.
7. Ryanair Full Year Results Analysts Briefing—June 2, 2009, www.ryanair.com/aboutus
8. The "I am a Mac" ads can be viewed on YouTube at the following link: http://www.youtube.com/watch?v=lgzbhEc6VVo
9. An example of a value communication tool for the sales process can be found at http://www.leveragepoint.com/valueManagement/index.html
10. J. T. Gourville, "Pennies-a-Day: The Effect of Temporal Reframing on Transaction Evaluation." *Journal of Consumer Research* 24, no. 4 (March 1998): 395–408.
11. John Hogan, "Building a World-Class Pricing Capability: Where Does Your Company Stack Up?" published by Monitor Group, April 2008.

CHAPTER 2

Value Creation
The Source of Pricing Advantage

Strategic pricing harvests the fruit of a company's investment in developing and delivering differentiated products and services to market. Each stage of the Strategic Pricing Pyramid, introduced in Chapter 1, plays a critical role in maximizing profitable and sustainable revenue. At the foundation of the pyramid, in what should be the first task of any strategic marketing organization, is gaining a deep understanding of how products and services create value for customers—the essential initial input to pricing strategy.

For many firms, the pricing harvest is less than bountiful because they fail to understand and leverage their potential to create value through their products, services, and customer relationships. They erroneously assume that merely adding features or improving performance will lead to profitable gains in price, volume, or both. But more and better features will not lead to greater profitability unless those features translate into higher monetary and/or psychological value for the customer.

An in-depth understanding of how your products create value for customers is the key that unlocks your organization's ability to improve pricing performance by enabling managers across the organization to make more profitable business choices. For example, salespeople armed with a clear value story supported by objective data are able to justify price premiums in the face of customers' aggressive purchasing tactics. In the marketing organization, understanding how value differs across segments provides the essential insight needed to make more profitable offer design and bundling choices. The product development group benefits from quantified estimates of customer value by enabling them to focus on features that customers will pay for rather than features the customers would simply like to have at no cost. Finally, understanding value enables the pricing organization to set profit-maximizing prices based on solid customer data instead of relying on internal cost data or market share goals.

These examples illustrate how a robust understanding of customer value creates profit improvement opportunities throughout the firm's internal value chain. But translating these opportunities into sustainable sources of differential profits is no simple task. Success requires effective processes to collect data, to estimate customer value, and to get that information into the hands of decision-makers. It requires new skills and tools to help managers make better pricing strategy choices in real time as they confront ever-shifting customer needs and competitive actions. Finally, it requires an organizational commitment to ensure that pricing decisions are made with an unswerving focus on long-term profitability. As a first step on that journey, in this chapter, we will define value and explain its role in pricing strategy, describe approaches to estimate value for different types of benefits, and show how value-based segmentation can enable a company to more profitably align what it offers with differences in what customers will pay.

THE ROLE OF VALUE IN PRICING

The term *value* commonly refers to the overall satisfaction that a customer receives from using a product or service *offering*. Economists call this *use value*—the utility gained from the product. On a hot summer day at the beach, for example, the use value of a cold drink is quite high for most people—perhaps as high as $10 for a cold soda or a favorite brand of beer. But because few people would actually pay that price, knowing use value is of little help to, say, a drink vendor walking the beach selling his wares.

Potential customers know that except in rare situations, they don't have to pay a seller all that a product is really worth to them. They know that competing sellers will usually offer a better deal at prices closer to what they expect from past experience—say $2.00 for a soda (economists refer to the difference between the use value of a product and its market price as *consumer surplus*). They might know that a half-mile up the beach is a snack shop where beverages cost just $1.50, and that a convenience store selling an entire six-pack for only $3.99 is a short drive away. Consequently, thirsty sun worshipers probably will reject a very high price even when the product is worth much more to them.

The value at the heart of pricing strategy is not use value, but is what economists call *exchange value* or *economic value*. Economic value depends on the alternatives customers have available to satisfy the same need. Few people will pay $2 for a cola, even if its use value is $10, if they think the market offers alternatives at substantially lower prices. On the other hand, only a small segment of customers insist on buying the lowest-priced alternative. It is likely that many people would pay $2.00 for a cola from the drink vendor strolling the beach despite the availability of the same product for less at a snack shop or convenience store because the seller is providing a *differentiated product offering* worth more than the alternatives to some segments. How much more depends on the economic value customers place on not having to walk up the beach to the snack shop or not having to drive to the convenience store. For some, the economic value of not having to exert themselves is high; they are willing to pay for convenience. For others who wouldn't mind a jog along the beach, the premium they will pay for convenience will be much less. To appeal to that jogger segment, the mobile vendor would need to differentiate the offering in some other way that joggers value highly.

Economic value accounts for the fact that the value one can capture for commodity attributes of an offer is limited to whatever competitors charge for them. Only the part of economic value associated with differentiation, which we call *differentiation value*, can potentially be captured in the price. Differentiation value comes in two forms: monetary and psychological, both of which may be instrumental in shaping a customer's choice but require very different approaches to estimate them.

Monetary value represents the total cost savings or income enhancements that a customer accrues as a result of purchasing a product. Monetary value is the most important element for most business-to-business purchases. When a manufacturer buys high-speed switching equipment for its production line from ABB, a global electrical equipment manufacturer, it gets products with superior reliability that minimize power disruptions. For many of ABB's customers, the benefit of fewer power disruptions has high monetary value because it translates into tangible cost savings associated with avoiding plant shutdowns.

Psychological value refers to the many ways that a product creates innate satisfaction for the customer. A Rolex watch may not create any tangible monetary benefits for most customers, but a certain segment of watch wearers derives deep psychological benefit from the prestige and beauty associated with ownership to which they will ascribe some economic worth. As the Rolex example illustrates, consumer products often create more psychological than monetary value because they focus on creating satisfaction and pleasure. However, some consumer products such as a hybrid car create both types of value, and it can be challenging to discern which is more important to the purchase decision. A Subaru owner in the market for a new car might focus on the monetary value derived from the fuel purchases that could be avoided by switching to a hybrid. Other customers will be motivated more by the psychological value derived from knowing that the hybrid is less damaging to the environment. Still others will gain satisfaction from the status associated with driving a "trendy" car. Regardless of the source of value, one thing is clear: a hybrid car has a premium economic value that drives a price premium over similar conventionally-powered cars because it provides demonstrable value in excess of the competing alternatives.

More formally, a product's *total economic value* is calculated as the price of the customer's best alternative (the *reference value*) plus the worth of whatever differentiates the offering from the alternative (the *differentiation value*). Differentiation value may have both positive and negative elements as illustrated in Exhibit 2-1. Total economic value is the maximum price that a "smart shopper," fully informed about the market and seeking the best value, would pay. Not every buyer is a smart shopper, however. Often product and

EXHIBIT 2-1   Economic Value

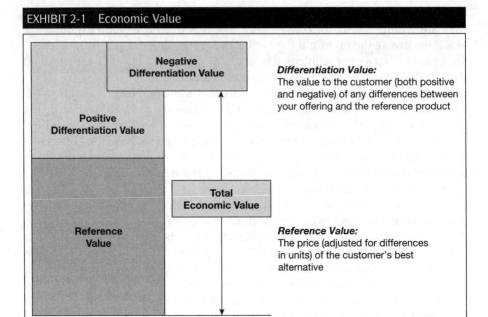

service users, and particularly purchasing agents buying on the users' behalf, may not recognize the actual economic value they receive from an offering. That is, the offering's *perceived value* to a buyer may fall short of the economic value if the buyer is uninformed. Therefore, it's critical that a company's sales presentations and marketing communications ensure that features likely to be important to the buyer—particularly competitively superior features—come to the buyer's attention. The need to communicate value is why the Toyota website contains easy-to-use calculators comparing fuel and emissions savings of the Prius hybrid car relative to other brands.[1]

One of the most critical factors driving customer choice and willingness-to-pay is the set of alternative products under consideration for purchase. From the marketer's perspective, these products represent the "next best competitive alternatives" or NBCA. Given the centrality of competitors' pricing in the purchase decision, economic value estimation begins by determining the *price* the competitor charges (not necessarily the NBCA's use value), which becomes the *reference value* in our model. For example, the reference value of a hotel room on a business trip is the price charged for the next-best hotel choice in town given the minimum lodging service level the traveler will accept. In the case of a new iPhone, the reference value would be the price of the comparable BlackBerry or other 3G phone under consideration.

In some cases, the reference product or service is not necessarily a specific competitive offering, but a self-designed solution that buyers might use to achieve their objectives. For example, most accounting software suppliers for years assumed that buyers would compare their wares to traditional double-entry bookkeeping methods. Software vendors designed products to automate double-entry accounting and its rigorous debit and credit data entry requirements. Intuit, however, learned that double-entry methods were the wrong reference process for the two-thirds of small-business bookkeepers who used their own simpler cash-based accounting solutions. Working closely with those customers to understand their need for simplicity, Intuit created QuickBooks, which quickly outsold competitors in the small-business market because it automated those simpler approaches.

Differentiation value is the net benefits that your product or service delivers to customers over and above those provided by the competitive reference product. Our soft drink vendor strolling right up to the customer's beach blanket provides convenience compared to a distant refreshment stand. The traveler's hotel of choice provides a free breakfast and free cocktail hour not available at the next-best hotel. Competing products in a category likely provide many sources of differentiation value. It's important that an effective value estimation concentrate on those value sources having the most differentiation "bang for the buck" for a customer or customer market segment. Whereas a free breakfast may not be an important value driver for a business executive on an expense account, it could be a crucial factor for a traveler booking a hotel for a family vacation. The degree to which a supplier differentiates its offer in terms of those needs will have the greatest impact on the price the marketer can successfully charge above the reference value.

HOW TO ESTIMATE ECONOMIC VALUE

Marketers have historically invested considerable effort to develop effective value propositions to represent their company and products. And few would argue that an effective value proposition, a concise statement of customer benefits, is an essential input to brand building and sales conversations. But a general statement of value is insufficient input to pricing decisions because it lacks the detail and quantification needed to shape strategy. In this section, we describe techniques that can be used to develop quantified estimates of customer value that, in turn, can be used to help set more profitable prices. We start with a discussion of how to collect and analyze competitive reference prices. Then we describe two approaches for quantifying monetary and psychological value and illustrate them with detailed examples.

Competitive Reference Prices

Identifying the next best competitive alternative to your product and gathering accurate reference prices, while conceptually simple, offers a number of challenges that often trip up pricing strategists. Some products, for example, may not have a single competing product that customers would consider a suitable alternative. Instead, customers might construct a basket of different products and services as a viable alternative. The "triple play" offered by communications companies such as Comcast, Time Warner, and Verizon gives price allowances to consumers who choose one vendor for phone, Internet connection and cable television service. Satellite TV companies can't offer this same bundle because of technical and regulatory limitations. Determining the reference price for these customers requires some analysis to estimate an aggregate price for a comparable basket of goods.

Another challenge to establishing competitive reference prices is gathering accurate price data and ensuring that it is comparable to the pricing for your product. You must ensure that competitive prices are measured in terms familiar to customers in the segment (for example, price per pound, price per hour) and are stated in the same units as your product. In some product markets such as groceries, competitive prices are readily available through data services such as IRI or by comparison shopping. In other categories, however, competitive prices are more difficult to obtain because of industry-wide practices of unpublished prices or because prices are negotiated individually with customers. In these instances, marketers must be creative in finding secondary sources of information by using techniques like polling the sales organization or interviewing customers. Secondary price data of this sort will invariably contain some bias and be less reliable than primary data obtained directly at that point of sale. Generally, though, it is possible to take imperfect competitive price data and treat it so that it becomes useful to a value estimation exercise.

Exhibits 2-2 and 2-3 provide an illustration of how secondary price data can be treated for use in a value estimation. The data in this example was

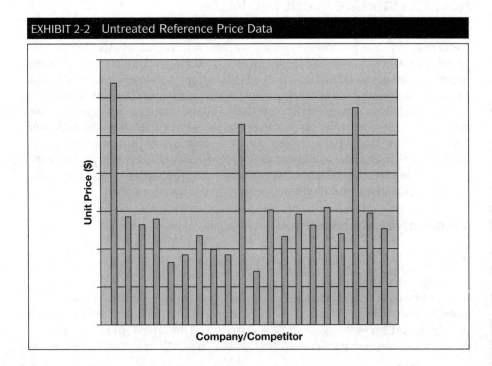

EXHIBIT 2-2   Untreated Reference Price Data

EXHIBIT 2-3   Adjusted Reference Prices

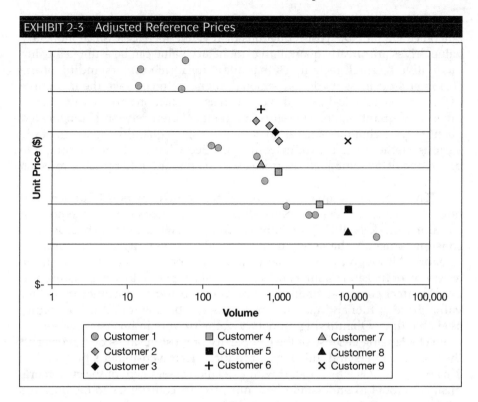

collected by a technology manufacturer in North America that had collected it as part of a competitive strategy assessment. When the data in Exhibit 2-2 was examined for use in a value estimation exercise, it seemed there was little coherence to how competitors were setting prices. After seeing the untreated data, one of the product managers noted that his suspicions were confirmed: the competitors were completely irrational in their pricing! Closer examination, however, revealed that much of the variation was due, not to irrational pricing, but to differences in volume and service levels. After the pricing data was adjusted for these factors, Exhibit 2-3 revealed much more consistent pricing behaviors that could be used as an input to the value estimation.

As this example illustrates, collecting reference prices is often more than just a data collection exercise. It requires some judgement and analysis to ensure that the data is ready to be incorporated into a value estimation calculation.

Estimating Monetary Value

After determining the competitive reference prices, the next step in value estimation is to gain a detailed understanding of customer value drivers and translate that understanding into quantified estimates that can be used to support pricing decisions. The distinct characteristics of monetary and psychological value drivers require different approaches to quantify. As we noted earlier, monetary value drivers are tied to the customer's financial outcomes via tangible cost reductions or revenue increases. Since monetary value drives are already quantitative, monetary value can be estimated using qualitative research techniques that allow for a rich understanding of the customer's business model or personal finances. In contrast, the intangible nature of psychological value drivers such as satisfaction and security are not inherently quantifiable. Therefore, marketers often rely on sophisticated quantitative techniques such as conjoint analysis to quantify the worth of the various elements of a product offering. (See Chapter 12 for a complete discussion of conjoint analysis, price experiments, and other pricing research techniques.)

The first step in quantifying monetary value drivers is to understand how the product category affects the customer's costs and revenues. In consumer markets, this is a relatively straightforward exercise because end consumers usually have few monetary value drivers for a given product category. Although there are many value-drivers for a hybrid car, with the exception of fuel and maintenance costs, most are psychological in nature and do not affect customer finances. Typical of most end consumer monetary value drivers, fuel and maintenance costs can be quantified using readily available data. Quantifying monetary value drivers in business markets is more challenging because of the complexity of most business operations and the need to understand fully how a product affects a customer's profitability. This complexity is why we start with a detailed assessment of the customer's business model to understand how our product contributes to the business customer's ability to create value for its own customers and to reduce its operating costs.

To illustrate this point, consider the example of Distributor Co., a technology distributor selling in a two-tier distribution system. Distributor Co. buys technology products such as servers, software and network components and re-sells them downstream to value-added resellers (hence the two-tier nature of the channel). The management team believed that all customers *valued* its technical service and support highly—a belief supported by high service usage across all segments. But an examination of its customers' business models revealed that this was not the case. One large segment of customers operated under a "systems integrator" business model that involved sourcing components from Distributor Co. and then installing and maintaining those components as an integrated system in their customer's businesses. For these customers, high quality technical support was essential to enable them to ensure proper installation and maintenance. In contrast, another segment operated with a "box-pusher" business model in which they might buy the exact same components purchased by a systems integrator, box them up, and resell them as a packaged solution for the customer to install. For the box-pushers, technical support was not essential to their business success because they relied on low prices, minimal inventory costs, and quick turnaround to make their business successful. Interestingly, the box-pushers consumed significant amounts of technical service even though it was not integral to their business model because Distributor Co. included it for free as part of its customer value proposition. When Distributor Co. started charging for technical support, usage by the box-pushers dropped dramatically because of the low monetary value in their business model. This pricing move improved profits in two ways: it reduced cost-to-serve for the box-pushers that didn't value technical support and increased margins earned from the systems integrators, for whom technical support was integral to their business model.

Once the mechanisms for value creation are understood in terms of the customer's business model, the next step is to collect specific data to develop quantified estimates. In-depth customer interviews are the best source of information. Very different from survey or even focus group methods, in-depth interviews probe the underlying economics of the customer's business model and your product's prospective role in it. The goal is to develop *value driver algorithms*, the formulas and calculations that estimate the differentiated monetary worth of each unit of product performance (Exhibit 2-4).

In-depth interviews require a different skill set than many qualitative research methods. Rather than striving for statistical precision, validity, and reliability, the price researcher seeks approximations about complex customer processes that might defy accurate, to-the-decimal-point calculations. It's critical, as a wise adage goes, to accept being approximately right lest you be precisely wrong in disregarding an important driver of value that seems too difficult to quantify. Therefore, the in-depth interview provides a foundation for developing value algorithms and collecting some initial data points to turn those algorithms into quantified estimates of customers' monetary value drivers.

EXHIBIT 2-4   Examples of Value Driver Algorithms for Equipment Manufacturer

Cost Drivers	Algorithm
Reduction in mounting costs	(Current mounting costs) × (Percent reduction in mounting costs)
Reduction in procurement costs	(Reduction in procurement costs)/(Number of units ordered)
Reduction in defective board handling costs	((Reduced number of defective boards) × (Cost per board))/(Number of units ordered)

Revenue Drivers	Algorithm
New contracts	(Number of contractors as a percent of upgrade business) × (Percent of business a customer wins due to lower cost bids) × (Average contribution per contract)
Increased throughput	(Percent increase in throughput per measurement) × (Dollar contribution per measurement) × (Average number of measurements)

Once the differential value algorithms have been determined, the final step is to sum the reference value and the differentiation value to determine the *total monetary value*. There are several guidelines for estimating monetary value that will enable you to simplify the process and avoid common errors. First, consider only the value of the *difference* between your product and the next best competitive alternative (NBCA) product. The value of any benefits that are the same as those delivered by the NBCA is already determined by competition and incorporated into the reference value. You can charge no more for it than the price of the NBCA product, regardless of its use value to the customer. Second, measure the differentiation value either as costs saved to achieve a particular level of benefit *or* as extra benefits achieved for an identical cost. Don't add both; that's double counting. Finally, do not assume that the percentage increase in value is simply proportional to the percentage increase in the effectiveness of your product. Although your part might last twice as long as a competitor, it does not follow that your value is only twice as large. An essential part, for which the competitior charges only $10, might save tens or hundreds of thousands of dollars if it requires shutting down a customer's production line half as frequently to replace it. Would you charge only $15 (a 50 percent premium) for such performance? Of course not!

Monetary Value Estimation: An Illustration

GenetiCorp (a disguised name) creates innovative products that accelerate the process of genetic testing. Monetary value estimation determines the financial impact that those breakthroughs actually deliver to different types of institutional customers.

One GenetiCorp product, Dyna-Test, synthesizes a complementary DNA strand from an existing DNA sample, significantly reducing DNA molecule degradation and enhancing the precision of a DNA analysis. Dyna-Test preserves sample integrity much longer than does its primary competitor, EnSyn, thus improving DNA test yields and accuracy in a variety of applications. For example, criminal investigators use DNA to match hair, blood, or other human samples. Hospitals and medical professionals use DNA to diagnose diseases. Pharmaceutical manufacturers use DNA analyses to target genes susceptible to new drug treatments. In all applications, test failures can be costly. For criminal investigators, getting a "fuzzy picture" in a criminal investigation may produce a false-negative result, requiring a retest that might take several weeks. Retests for investigators are problematic because tissue sample sizes in criminal cases are very limited, often precluding repeated tests. Similarly, for a pharmaceutical company, getting a fuzzy picture when analyzing a DNA strand may cause drug researchers to miss their true target, the genetic portion of the DNA suspected of triggering a disease.

Unfortunately, when it first marketed Dyna-Test, GenetiCorp did not have a clue about its product's monetary value. It set prices based on a high markup over costs and then discounted those prices under pressure from purchasing organizations that could buy large volumes. To improve its profits, GenetiCorp decided to learn what its product is really worth to customers: Dyna-Test's reference value (the price of what the customer considers the best alternative product) plus its positive and negative differentiated values (the customer use value of the attributes that distinguish Dyna-Test from the next best alternative). Buyers will pay no more than the reference value for features and benefits that are the same as the competing product's. When multiple competitors offer customers the same benefits, those benefits are commoditized; a customer need not pay anything close to a product's worth because it can get the product elsewhere. A product earns a price premium over the reference value only for the extra performance—the differentiated value—it alone delivers. The sum total of reference and differentiated values is the monetary value estimate.

Dyna-Test has more than one monetary value driver because different types of users have different reference alternatives and receive different use value from Dyna-Test's distinguishing features. Let's examine the value estimation components in two different market segments, commercial researchers and nonindustrial markets.

Commercial researchers in pharmaceutical and biotech firms most often consider EnSyn the best alternative to Dyna-Test. EnSyn sells for $30 per test kit; that's the product category's reference value for such users. To determine Dyna-Test's differentiation value, GenetiCorp studied the five primary drivers of Dyna-Test's positive differentiation value among commercial researchers.

Value Driver 1—Yield Opportunity Costs: Dyna-Test provides a greater yield of full-length cDNA, the compound DNA structures used for analysis, which is extremely valuable. With more full-length cDNA to work with, drug researchers can reduce the number of experiments needed to find the relevant portions of DNA, saving an average of a week's valuable research time, according to GenetiCorp's customer interviews.

GenetiCorp studied its pharmaceutical industry customers' business models and found the annual revenue from a successful commercial drug ranges from $250 million to $1 billion. GenetiCorp used a conservative estimate of $400 million in revenue for one drug, which, with a 75 percent contribution margin, generated $300 million in annual profit contribution. The cost of developing a typical drug was approximately $590 million. These contribution and cost estimates yield an average net present value of $41 million a year profit for a successful drug over a 17-year patent life. But it takes 500 target tests on average to finally identify the gene sequence leading to a successful new drug, so each target test eventually is worth $82,000. With a 260-day work-year (approximately 2,100 hours), the value of a target test is $39 per hour. If using Dyna-Test saves the researcher an additional week that can be devoted to another new drug, the value of those additional 40 hours is $1,560.

Value Driver 2—Yield Labor Savings: Dyna-Test's cDNA yield superiority over EnSyn also produces more efficient laboratory staff work.

Customer interviews indicated that using Dyna-Test saved 16 hours of processing labor compared to using EnSyn. Because laboratory personnel receive an average of $24 per hour, labor savings from Dyna-Test are about $384.

Value Driver 3—Quality Control Labor Savings: Prior to Dyna-Test, researchers frequently checked test-chemical batches for quality, sterility, and reproducibility, adding two hours to a test. However, Dyna-Test maintained uniform quality and performance over several years, assuring researchers that they could eliminate these quality-control checks. In interviews, customers said "I am confident with Dyna-Test because it is a quality and tested product" or "Dyna-Test has been around long enough; you know it works. If someone says they ran the experiment with Dyna-Test it must be right." High quality produced two hours of customer cost savings totaling $48.

Value Driver 4—Sample Size Opportunity Costs: Using traditional methods, analyzing a DNA sample usually requires using some "starter" sample material at the outset. Often, the amount of original sample material is very small; gathering more on an emergency basis might take about three weeks of lost research time. But the Dyna-Test kit has a two-step system that reduces the need for starter samples, making available more testable original sample material and freeing researchers from the search for more. Using the value per week of Dyna-Test usage, GenetiCorp estimated the opportunity cost of searching for new material at $4,680 ($3 \times \$1,560$) per project. But because such emergency searches happened only about 10 percent of the time, the likely opportunity cost averages to $468.

Value Driver 5—Sample Size Labor Savings: Similar to Driver 4, gathering additional emergency starter material requires researchers to repeat the entire analytical test—an extra 16 hours of research labor time—about 10 percent of the time. But with the Dyna-Test kit yielding more usable material and with labor costing $24 per hour, the value of using Dyna-Test on this dimension is $38 ($24 \times 16 \times 0.1$).

In sum, for pharmaceutical and commercial biotechnology firms, the estimated total economic value of Dyna-Test is calculated by adding together the reference value of $30, plus the estimates of differentiated value associated with each value driver, yielding a total estimated economic value of $2,528. In other words, purchasing the new Dyna-Test kit instead of the EnSyn kit would produce $2,528 in cost reductions and new product profit gains for a commercial researcher . Exhibit 2-5 illustrates the monetary value estimation for that industrial buying segment.

Nonindustrial markets such as academic institutions and government laboratories estimate economic value in a similar fashion. Their reference value is also the $30 price of the EnSyn test kit; however, the most price-sensitive

EXHIBIT 2-5   Monetary Value Estimation for Dyna-Test Industrial Buyers

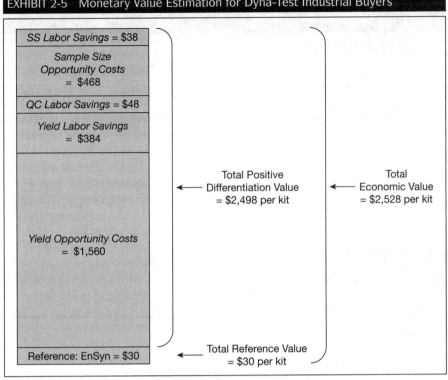

among them simply have lab assistants—essentially free student labor—make DNA test products from scratch. Their differentiating value drivers are similar to those of industrial customers, but modified to reflect the business model in this market, which has a different research environment and economic reward structure.

Value Driver 1—Yield Opportunity Costs: The yield opportunity cost avoided by using Dyna-Test is $1,055, somewhat less than for commercial researchers because of the lower economic rewards from breakthroughs in primary research.

Value Drivers 2, 3, 4, and 5:   The yield labor savings of $231, quality control savings of $29, sample size opportunity cost avoided of $317, and sample size labor savings are also less because of the reduced cost of labor within university systems.

Thus, the estimated total economic value of Dyna-Test for academic laboratories is calculated by adding the reference value of $30 plus the estimates for each value driver, yielding a total monetary value estimate of $1,685. Exhibit 2-6 illustrates the relationships.

Remember that the economic value derived from monetary value estimation is not necessarily the perceived value that a buyer might actually

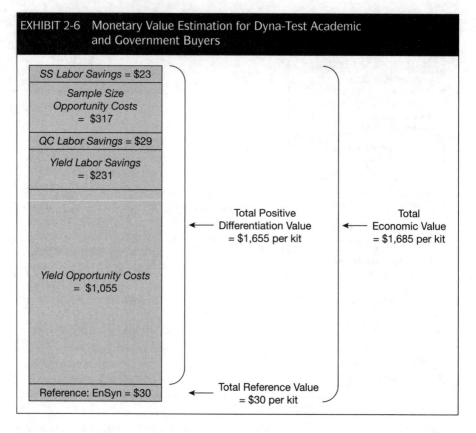

EXHIBIT 2-6   Monetary Value Estimation for Dyna-Test Academic and Government Buyers

place on the product. A customer might not know about a reference product and won't be influenced by its price. A buyer might be unsure of a product's differentiating attributes and may be unwilling to invest the time and expense to learn about them. If the product's price is small, the buyer may make an impulse purchase without really thinking about its economic value. Similarly, brand image and equally unquantifiable factors can influence price sensitivity, reducing the impact of economic value on the purchase decision, as in the case of Rolex watches. Ultimately, a product's market value is determined not only by the product's economic value, but also by the accuracy with which buyers perceive that value and by the importance they place on getting the most for their money.

This limitation of monetary value estimation is both a weakness and a strength. It is a weakness because economic value cannot indicate the appropriate price to charge. It only estimates the maximum price a segment of buyers would pay if they fully recognized the product's value to them and were motivated to purchase. It is a strength, however, in that it indicates whether a poorly selling product is overpriced relative to its true value or is under-promoted and unappreciated by the market. The only solution to the overpricing problem is to cut price. A better solution to the perception problem often is maintaining or even increasing price while aggressively educating the market. That is what GenetiCorp did with Dyna-Test. After previously cutting price to meet the demands of its apparently price-sensitive buyers, GenetiCorp raised prices two- to fivefold, at the same time launching an aggressive marketing campaign. While customer purchasing agents expressed dismay, sales continued growing because even the new prices represented but a small fraction of the value delivered. Profits increased significantly in the following year as purchasers learned about Dyna-Test's superior economic value to their institutions and accepted, sometimes grudgingly, the need to pay for that value.

GenetiCorp's experience also shows how value can vary among market segments. To determine a pricing strategy and policy for a product, you must determine the economic value delivered to all segments and the market size of each. With that information, you can develop an *economic value profile* of the entire market and determine which segments you can serve most profitably at which prices. Exhibit 2-7 profiles the economic value and market potential for each Dyna-Tech market segment.

Monetary value estimation is an especially effective sales tool when buyers facing extreme cost pressures are very price sensitive. For example, since health-care reimbursement systems began giving hospitals and doctors financial incentives to practice cost-effective medicine, pharmaceutical companies have been forced to add cost and performance evidence to their traditional claims about a drug's clinical effectiveness. Some now offer

EXHIBIT 2-7   Monetary Value Profile for Dyna-Test

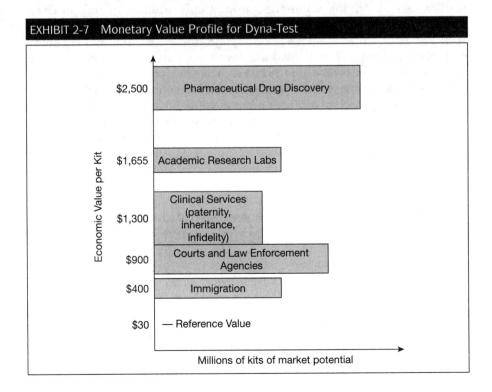

purchasers elaborate tests to show that greater effectiveness is worth a higher price. Johnson & Johnson's invention of the medicated arterial stent, for instance, initially appeared expensive at $1,300 per stent. J&J successfully countered customer resistance by demonstrating that dramatically reducing the probability of an artery reclogging was worth at least $3,500 per treatment in avoided surgery and hospital costs.

Estimating Psychological Value

Psychological value drivers such as satisfaction and security, by virtue of their subjective nature, do not lend themselves to estimation via qualitative research techniques like in-depth interviewing. Instead, pricing researchers must rely on a variety of quantitative techniques to estimate the worth of a product's differentiated features. The most widely used of these techniques is *conjoint analysis*—a technique developed in the late 1970s and early 1980s that can discern the hidden values that customers place on product features. The basic approach is to decompose a product into groups of features and then provide customers with a series of choices among various feature sets to understand which they prefer. In recent years, marketing researchers have extended the basic conjoint techniques so that virtually any type of consumer choice can be tested including choices involving different brands, budget constraints, and even purchasing environments.

Using conjoint analysis makes it possible to estimate the value of different feature sets in driving willingness-to-pay and, ultimately, the purchase decision. For example, a flat screen TV can be described in terms of attributes such as size of screen, number of pixels, and brightness. In a conjoint study, each of these attributes is divided into levels that can be tested. For instance, screen size might be broken into 36 inches, 42 inches, and 52 inches as a means to estimate the relative value placed on greater screen size. Similarly, conjoint is a common approach to estimating brand value because it enables brand to be treated as any other attribute. Treating brand as another attribute in the choice decision allows us to understand how customers might value a 36-inch Sony TV relative to a 42-inch Samsung model. Regardless of the attributes tested, the value estimates derived from a conjoint study can then be used as an input to a variety of pricing decisions.

Psychological Value Estimation: An Illustration

Sport Co. (disguised name), a leading sporting goods manufacturer, has developed a revolutionary golf club named the "Big Drive." The new design has led to significant increases in distance and accuracy for both beginning and advanced players. The question facing the management team was how to set prices given that there were many different types of golfers who would be potential customers. Beginning players found the club appealing because it was much more forgiving of poorly hit balls compared to traditional clubs. However, the management team believed that beginners would be relatively price sensitive and unwilling to pay a premium price for the technology.

More advanced players concerned about improving performance found the added distance of the Big Drive very appealing, and qualitative research indicated they would be willing to pay a substantial premium for the club. Knowing that there were multiple segments with different value drivers and willingness-to-pay created a quandry for Sport Co. management—how should they set prices to maximize profits?

The approach involved several steps. The first was to identify the different segments that might be interested in the new club and profile them based on actionable descriptors. This segmentation work uncovered four unique segments:

- *Innovators:*   Frequent golfers highly focused on performance. They tend to have higher incomes and purchase clubs through their local pro shop after extensive consultation with the club pro and friends.
- *Value Seekers:*   Casual players who play from 5–10 times during the season. They have moderate income and purchase from major retailers such as the Sports Depot or Golf Warehouse. Value seekers are thrifty, but they will pay a premium for added performance.
- *Lost Players:*   This is a large segment of occasional players who have largely drifted away from the game. They do not purchase significant amounts of golf equipment, but they can be drawn back to playing if a new innovation creates enough buzz to capture their attention.
- *Budget Shoppers:*   These players range widely in ability and frequency of play, but they have budget constraints that limit the amount they can spend on equipment. They typically buy new equipment through discount stores such as Wal-Mart and online outlets.

Having identified the key segments, the next step was to identify the attributes of the club that each segment found appealing so that they could be tested in the conjoint study. Of the extensive list of attributes that were tested, three were noted most commonly by all segments: distance, straightness, and consistency. These attributes were then tested along with some other features of the offering such as warranty in a conjoint survey of 670 golfers.

The results of the conjoint study provided the needed inputs to develop a segmented pricing strategy. For example, the study provided actionable data on consumer willingness-to-pay for various attributes such as a warranty, as shown in Exhibit 2-8. The initial hypothesis was that a warranty was not a key driver in the purchase decision; potential purchasers were more focused on the performance attributes of the club. The data revealed that the initial hypothesis was not correct, because consumers across all segments were willing to pay a premium for a one-year warranty. Interestingly, extending the warranty from one to two years did not lead to a similar increase in willingness-to-pay.

The results also provided key insights into the value derived by different market segments that, in turn, informed the channel pricing strategy. The data in Exhibit 2-9 shows the differences in willingness-to-pay between the Innovator and Budget Shopper segments based on the conjoint

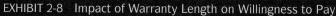

EXHIBIT 2-8   Impact of Warranty Length on Willingness to Pay

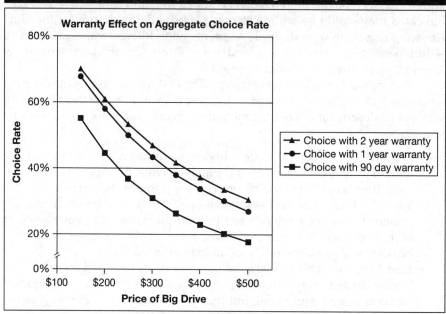

results. The profit-maximizing price for the innovators was $425, which would lead to approximately 40,000 unit sales. As expected, the optimal price point for budget shoppers was considerably less at $275. This difference in the value (and hence willingness-to-pay) created a dilemma for Sport Co.: If they set the optimal price for the innovator segment, they would lose many of the budget consumers, who represent nearly 30 percent of the market. This challenge of setting prices when value differs widely across segments is a common one that we will address in detail in Chapter 3. In this instance, the quantified value estimates of the different segments combined with a detailed understanding of segment buying patterns and value drivers enabled the team to make a solid business case for a two-tier pricing strategy. With some minor modifications to the club design, aesthetics, and brand, Sport Co. was able to introduce a lower-performance model aimed at budget shoppers and sold through discount retailers. At the same time, they introduced the premium model aimed at Innovators and Value Buyers to be sold at a higher price in pro shops and high-end sporting goods outlets.

It was possible to generate reliable estimates of psychological value for the "Big Drive" because the key benefits of distance and accuracy are ones with which golfers have prior experience. They know what it feels like to hit the best ball off the tee in their foursome and can imagine what they might pay for that feeling. Where conjoint and other similar survey research techniques can fall short is when the differentiating benefits are innovative. The research subject in that case must guess what the benefits are and how satisfying they might be. Most people, even those deeply familiar with the

EXHIBIT 2-9   Impact of Warranty Length on Willingness to Pay

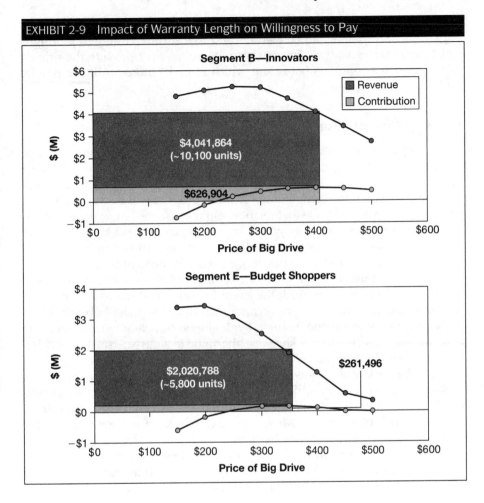

technology, are not good at inferring the benefits of innovation. In 1977, the founder and CEO of the world's second largest computer company at the time asserted publicly, "There is no reason anyone would ever want a computer in their home." But Steve Jobs did imagine the benefits and set prices for the Apple computer that sparked the growth of the home computer industry.

As the GenetiCorp and Sport Co. examples illustrate, the approach and data used to estimate monetary and psychological values differ substantially, with each having some advantages over the other. While both approaches yield quantified value estimates that are essential to effective pricing strategy, the qualitative approach used for monetary value enables the price-setter to make an explicit linkage between a product's differentiated features, the benefits those features create for customers and the value associated with each benefit. The importance of this feature–benefit–value linkage will become clear in later chapters where we discuss bundling and value communication choices. Quantitative approaches such as conjoint analysis are appealing because they enable the pricing researcher to perform a wide variety of statistical analyses that can be readily used to test different offering designs and competitive scenarios. In each case, however, they provide the pricing manager with a solid fact base from which to make more profitable pricing choices.

The High Cost of Shortcuts

When setting prices, there are no shortcuts for understanding the economic value received by the customer. Many companies, nonetheless, shortchange themselves by assuming that if their differentiated product is "x" percent more effective than the competition, then the product will be worth only "x" percent more in price. While that relationship makes sense superficially, closer examination reveals how wrong it is. If you had cancer and knew of a drug that was 50 percent more effective than the competition's in curing your disease, would you refuse to pay more than a 50 percent higher price? Of course not. Suppose you were planning to paint your house and discovered a paint sprayer that lets you finish the job in half the usual time—a doubling of your productivity. Would you pay no more than twice the price of a brush? Obviously not, unless you're some rare individual who can paint twice as fast with two brushes simultaneously. Otherwise, the value to a busy person of the painting time saved by the sprayer is much greater than the price of a second brush.

As these examples show, the value-based price premium one can charge is often much greater than the percentage increase in an offering's technical efficiency. The total economic value of a differentiated product is proportional to its technical efficiency *only* when a buyer can receive the benefits associated with a superior product simply by buying more of the reference product. In our example, that would be the case only if using 50 percent more of the competitive cancer drug or painting with two brushes at the same time would produce the same increase in efficiency as using the superior products. Because of this misunderstanding, many companies committed to value-based pricing have been misled into believing that they cannot price to capture their value if their ratio of price-to-use value would exceed that of their competitors.

At the center of this misconception is the popular concept of customer value modeling (CVM), which emerged from the total quality management movement when companies tried to measure and deliver superior quality at a competitive price. Marketers and a variety of value consultants have applied CVM in many contexts, including early criteria for the Malcolm Baldrige National Quality Award, largely because it is easy to implement. CVM relies on customers' subjective judgments about price and product attribute performances. It assumes that customers seek to purchase the products that give them the greatest perceived benefit—which might be quantified in monetary terms, but need not be—per unit price. Avoiding the translation of relative attribute performance into hard-dollar estimates, CVM is analytically simpler than economic value estimation, particularly for pricing consumer products with their heavily psychological values.

The fact is, however, that CVM underestimates the value of the more differentiated products in a market and overestimates the value of the less differentiated products. CVM methods define value differently than does economic value estimation. CVM rates each competitive supplier's relative strength on each product attribute, weighing each attribute by customer estimates of importance, according to customer and prospect surveys. Then CVM calculates the average relationship between perceived quality and price, creating what is variously called a "fair-value line," a "value equivalence line," "indifference line," or other term for the presumed linear relationship between price and perceived quality. A point on the line putatively indicates a "fair" balance of price for quality. For a given price, a product with less than fair perceived quality is disadvantaged and stands to lose market share, say CVM theorists, while a product offering more than fair quality will gain share.

There are flaws in this thinking. First, customers don't pay for average differential benefit estimates; they pay for the *worth* of the benefits they receive. That is, they mentally convert benefits into monetary terms so that they can judge how much more they should pay for the extra value received from a more expensive product. If it's worth more than the price premium charged, they buy it.

Second, CVM fails to distinguish between the value of common benefits that are priced as commodities and the value of the unique benefits associated with a differentiated offering. Total economic value—what the customer *really* gets from the offering in monetary and psychological terms—does not have a single linear relationship to price. One of the two components of economic value, the reference value, usually is much less than the use value of the benefits delivered by the reference product. The reference value is the *price* a customer pays for the next best alternative offering—like the price of the second paintbrush, the price of the EnSyn DNA test kit, or the price of a soda at the refreshment stand. Benefits offered by more than one supplier become commodity benefits; customers can get them from more than one source. Competition among suppliers drives the price for those benefits below their use value, making the price-to-use value ratio of the reference product lower than one-to-one.

In contrast, differentiation value, the second component of total economic value, is the *extra* use value a product delivers compared to the reference product. The differentiation value, expressed in monetary terms, is equivalent to the price premium the differentiated supplier could charge as a fair price. It's fair because the customer gets just what she's paying for in additional value, no more and no less. The price premium-to-differentiation value ratio is one-to-one. In other words, the relationship between price and economic value is a function of two different price-to-quality ratios, not the single average ratio hypothesized in a CVM model.

This difference is significant because the larger the proportion of differentiation value in a product's total economic value delivered, the more the truly fair price to the customer—the economic value estimation price—can exceed the CVM-hypothesized "fair-value line" price.[2] Pricing your highly

| | | | Total | | CVM | |
Product	Reference Value	Diff. Value	Monetary Value	Value-Based "Fair" Price	"Fair" Price	Difference
					Avg. price / value = .61	
Widget A	$40	$0	$80	$40	$49	($9)
Widget B	$40	$20	$100	$60	$61	$1
Widget C	$40	$30	$110	$70	$67	$3
Widget D	$40	$40	$120	$80	$73	$7

EXHIBIT 2-10   Impact of Warranty Length on Willingness to Pay

differentiated product at the supposed "fair-value line" level will be hazardous to your bottom line!

The simple example in Exhibit 2-10 illustrates the difference between economic value estimation and customer value modeling (CVM). For simplicity, let's assume that all widget customers have complete information about the respective benefits they can receive from suppliers A, B, C, and D. Perceived quality, therefore, equals economic value in this example. The overall "fair-value line" (FVL) represents the CVM-determined average relationship of price to economic value delivered, in this case a ratio of 0.61. The reference value is $40, the most that any supplier can charge for commoditized everybody-offers-them benefits, even though the use value of reference product A is $80. The low reference price forces the average price-to-value relationship designated by a single CVM FVL into a slope that's less than 1.0, implying that a dollar's worth of price produces only 61 cents additional value. More accurate might be a curvilinear FVL, or a linear FVL representing only differentiation values. Even better would be curves showing accelerating and decelerating marginal value at different price levels. But to figure all that out requires the harder work of calculating economic value estimation in the first place. Sadly, there are no shortcuts for profitable strategic pricing.

Note how the fair economic value estimation price exceeds the fair CVM price as the differentiation value of the product grows. Were widget D priced at the fair-value CVM price of $73, its manufacturer would be leaving $7 per unit, nearly 9 percent of the value widget D creates, on the table. (As we shall see in later chapters, how much of widget D's $40 differentiation value the manufacturer actually receives is a matter of price negotiation.)

VALUE-BASED MARKET SEGMENTATION

Market segmentation is one of the most important tasks in marketing. Identifying and describing market subgroups in a way that guides marketing and sales decision-making makes the marketing and pricing process much more efficient and effective. For example, customers who are relatively price insensitive, costly to serve, and poorly served by competitors can be charged more than customers who are price sensitive, less costly to serve, and are served well by competitors. At many companies, however, segmentation strategy focuses on customer attributes that are not useful for pricing decisions, creating customer groupings that do not adequately describe differences in purchase motivations among customers and prospects, or classify them in a way that's meaningful for making pricing decisions.

Consultants and market researchers abound who peddle various segmentation-modeling schemes. Often those plans emphasize the obvious, such as statistical differences in personal demographics or company *firmographics* (customer size, standard industrial classification, and so forth). While the results seem clear and sometimes coincidentally differentiate buying motivations, those segmentations seldom assist pricing decisions, especially for setting different prices that maximize profit from different segments. More useful are value-based segmentation models that facilitate pricing commensurate with actual value perceived and delivered to customers. Only then can a marketer ensure that each different customer subgroup is paying the most profitable price that the marketer can charge. Charging the entire market a single price risks undercharging some segments, causing foregone profit to you, and overcharging others, costing you additional foregone profit since those customers buy from other suppliers.

Significant differences between value-based segmentation and other methods are especially critical for pricing. First, most segmentation criteria correlate poorly with different buyers' motivations to pay higher or lower prices. Both plumbers and personal-injury lawyers consider online advertising to be very important, for example. They advertise to attract customers who have an immediate, unexpected, and high-value need. Google could charge both groups the same advertising rates, but the lawyer can afford to pay more than the plumber because of the greater value of each legal client. Simply raising ad prices across the board would eventually price plumbers out of the market and into less expensive media leading to lower profits. But Google has developed an ingenious bidding mechanism that allows customers to pay whatever price reflects the value to them. The trade-off, of course, is that the lower you bid the less prominent your ad or webpage will be displayed. By enabling the customer to make price and value trade-offs via the bidding mechanism, Google has successfully aligned prices with value and improved the profitability of their advertising business.

Second, even needs-based segmentations give priority only to those differences that are important to the customer. They miss the other half of the story, those customer needs that have the greatest operational impact on the seller's costs to serve those needs. The seller's costs and constraints are also important to pricing decisions, as we will see below, because our goal is not just sales and market share, but profitability. Finally, the customer in-depth interviews required for value-based segmentations also uncover *why* customers find certain product benefits appealing—or would find them appealing were they sufficiently informed. Such knowledge reveals opportunities to develop new products and services and can reveal flawed strategies based on less comprehensive research.

That is a lesson International Harvester Company (IH), in a classic example, learned the hard way. For years, IH classified farmers according to surveys of farmer "benefit perceptions," particularly IH's equipment reliability compared to that of archrival John Deere. Farmers consistently rated Deere equipment as "more reliable," so IH invested heavily to ensure that an IH tractor could not possibly break down more frequently than a Deere tractor. Still, Deere kept leading the reliability rankings by a wide margin. IH marketers understood the true situation only when they conducted in-depth interviews. Asking farmers about repair problems revealed that what was important to farmers was the downtime caused by breakdowns. IH customers viewed a breakdown as a "big deal" to be avoided because of the days of lost productivity waiting for repairs. Deere customers viewed Deere's equivalent reliability as much less of a problem because Deere's extensive, service-oriented dealer network stocked spare parts and offered loaner tractors, getting a farmer working again in less than a day. IH's benefit segmentation had missed the mark. A value segmentation would have revealed that Deere served a different segment of farmers—those driven by the value of a total-service solution, which perfectly fit Deere's strengths.

To conduct a value-based segmentation, we recommend a six-step process.

Step 1: Determine Basic Segmentation Criteria

The goal of any market segmentation is dividing a market into subgroups whose members have common *criteria that differentiate their buying behaviors*. A simple example illustrates the concept. A business marketer of, say, an industrial grinding machine could segment customers in terms of their industries, their applications for which they use the marketer's product, or the total value they receive from the product. A segmentation done by industry using industrial classification criteria would not indicate, however, whether customers use the grinders in similar ways. A segmentation based on application criteria would account for different ways of using the grinders, but would not indicate if the grinder is more important to one segment's business model than to another's. Only a segmentation based on the value delivered by the grinder would reveal, for instance, that customers in one segment consider grinder use a small part of assembly line costs, while in another segment the grinder delivers much more value by performing a finishing step that allows the grinder buyer to earn a price premium from its customers. In our tractor marketing example, had IH chosen rapid service needs as its segmentation criterion, it would have seen that it could not match Deere's field service capabilities. Had IH done its homework, it would have realized that it needed to try and outweigh its service shortcomings with other offering attributes—which would be tough with farmers for whom downtime is very costly—or concentrate on other segments that put relatively more emphasis on attributes where IH excels.

Choosing appropriate segmentation criteria starts with a descriptive profile of the total market to identify obvious segments and differences among them. In consumer markets, basic demographics of age, gender, and income provide obvious discriminators. Enterprise firmographics such as revenue, industry, and number of employees clearly separate firms into nominally homogenous groups. Inputs for this basic analysis can include existing segmentation studies, industry databases, government statistics, and other secondary sources. Outputs include buying patterns, customer descriptions, a preliminary set of current customer needs, and a provisional list of unmet customer needs. You should be able to design first-pass segmentation maps based on those outputs. Along the way, check if those preliminary maps look sensible to salespeople and sales managers. Though your eventual pricing strategy will rely on value-based segmentation, communications and sales strategies are likely to be heavily dependent on those obvious customer characteristics on which media choices and sales territory assignments are based.

Step 2: Identify Discriminating Value Drivers

Having preliminary segmentations in hand, you identify those value drivers—the purchase motivators—that vary the most among segments but which have more or less homogenous levels within segments. This allows you to zero in on what's most important to each customer segment. The GenetiCorp example earlier in this chapter determined that segments classified by obvious firmographics—commercial and nonindustrial research institutions—also differed on several cost-reduction and profit-enhancement value drivers. Never assume for pricing purposes that preliminary segmentations based on obvious criteria will coincidentally yield effective discrimination on value criteria. Commercial and nonindustrial medical laboratories probably have similar needs, for instance, and derive similar value from an undifferentiated product such as laboratory glassware.

In-depth interviews probing how and why buyers choose among competitive suppliers provide the additional input required. Industry experts, distributors, and salespeople can provide supplemental information for double checking the value perception patterns revealed by the interviews. The outputs of this step include a number of useful building blocks for value-based market segmentation, including a list of value drivers ranked by their ability to discriminate among customers (statistical cluster analysis of quantitative data is a useful tool here), an explanation of why each driver adds value, and whether customers in each segment recognize that value. The list should also include the value the customer will receive if your product or service offering satisfies unmet needs.

Step 3: Determine Your Operational Constraints and Advantages

In this step, you examine where you have operational advantages. Which value drivers can you deliver more efficiently and at lower cost than others? Also, which drivers are constrained by your resources and operations? Experience, capital spending plans, personnel capabilities, and overall company strategy are among the inputs to this step. Use the discipline of activity-based costing (a fascinating diagnosis of your own business, but a topic beyond the scope of this book) to build a *customer behavior spectrum* mapping your true costs serving different customers. Will some require more on-site service than others? Which have shorter decision-making cycles? Those factors contribute to customer profitability, value delivery, and the price you can charge for bundled and unbundled offering features. You should also examine competitive strengths and weaknesses on key drivers as closely as you can.

With these data, you can cross-reference and compare lists of customer needs served and unserved, the seller's advantages and resource limitations, and competitors' abilities. Where do you have sustainable competitive advantages, and where do rivals hold the upper hand? Which customers can you, therefore, better serve than can competitors, and which are likely to be beyond your reach, assuming that prospective customers are well-informed?

Step 4: Create Primary and Secondary Segments

This step combines what you've learned so far about how customer values differ and about your costs and constraints in serving different customers. Unless you're comfortable with multivariate statistical analyses accounting for several value drivers simultaneously, you'll find it most convenient to segment your marketplace in multiple stages, value driver by value driver. The number of stages depends on the number of critical drivers that create substantial differences in value delivery among customer groups. In theory, your primary segmentation is based on the most important criterion differentiating your customers. Your secondary segmentation divides primary segments into distinct subgroups according to your second most important criterion. Your tertiary segmentation divides second segments based on the third most important criterion, and so on.

In practice, however, the deeper your successive segmentations, the more unmanageable the number of segments you identify. It doesn't make sense to split hairs by segmenting according to drivers with less than critical discriminating power. Minor differences among such subsegments will have little impact on pricing policies.

Also, your primary segmentation should account for your company's capabilities and constraints as well as customer needs. A primary value segmentation that recognizes such a "strategic overlap" discriminates on what is likely to be the most important differentiator among customers: the needs that have the most impact on the seller's operational constraints and whether those needs can be satisfied profitably, if at all. Your secondary segmentation, therefore, will use the value driver that varies the most among the subsegments within each primary segment.

The example in Exhibit 2-11 illustrates the process for an industry-leading commercial printing company serving catalog marketers. Catalog companies have a variety of printing needs. Some are primarily concerned with brand image and ensuring that their direct marketing integrates well with their other sales channels such as retail stores. Others have unique needs, such as the ability to tailor catalogs to particular segments of a market by varying the "signatures" (groups of printed pages) bound into different parts of the print run. In this industry, print timing appears to be the major value differentiator. Some catalog companies insist on firm printing dates demanded by their business models, while others are more willing to let the printer determine when their jobs run. The strategic overlap is the cost-to serve implication that results from the printer having only a finite number of presses and so many hours in the day, which limits the ability to commit to a firm print time.

Exhibit 2-11 shows a primary segmentation based on the strategic overlap of customer scheduling needs and printer operational capabilities. Two primary segments emerge: buyers needing precise timing and those who are willing to relinquish timing control for a break on price. Within the "customer-controlled scheduling" primary segment, three secondary segments have different needs for special service:

- A "brand focus" segment requires custom services and tailored solutions.
- "Consistency" segment customers, more value-driven and concerned with their own margins, insist on getting high quality print every time but expect standard services such as proofing, binding, and trimming.
- A "unique equipment" segment has special needs such as odd trim sizes, small print orders, and customer-tailored binding, yet still wants control of the print scheduling process.

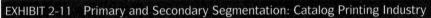

EXHIBIT 2-11   Primary and Secondary Segmentation: Catalog Printing Industry

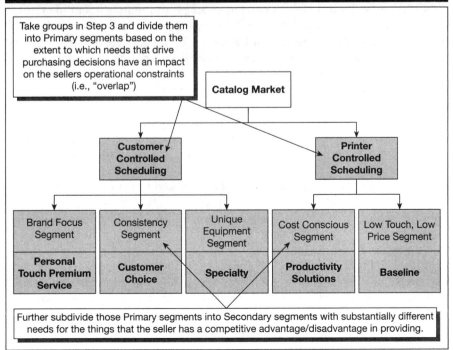

The printer originally treated customers able to be flexible in their scheduling like all other customers, assigning them firm print dates even as they demanded and negotiated lower prices. Value-based segmentation revealed that these buyers would be willing to trade some flexibility in scheduling for reduced prices. The printer could schedule their jobs for off-peak demand periods when capacity otherwise would be idle. These secondary segments differed by the services they would trade for a lower price:

- A "cost conscious" segment responded to service options that enabled them to deliver copy in to meet consistently a fixed time window for printing.
- The "low-touch, low-price" segment accepted bare-bones service, including a flexible print time and direct internet to press transactions, in return for even lower prices.

Step 5: Create Detailed Segment Descriptions

Value-based segmentation variables can look fine to the price strategist, but segments should be described in everyday business terms so that salespeople and marketing communications planners know what kinds of customers each segment represents. Exhibit 2-12 lists the needs and typical firmographics of the customer-controlled scheduling segment's three sub-segments. It also lists specific catalog publishers within each segment.

Step 6: Develop Segment Metrics and Fences

This is the next logical step in pricing strategy and management, a step we cover in greater detail in Chapter 3. Here, it's important to recognize that segmentation isn't truly useful until you develop the metrics of value delivery to market segments and devise *fences* that encourage customers to accept price policies for their segments.

Metrics are the basis for tracking the value customers receive and how they pay for it. For example, car rental companies once used a distance-based value metric and charged customers for the mileage traveled, in addition to the time used. Over time, competition forced rental companies to drop mileage charges. Time alone has become the market-recognized value metric. Sellers define discounts such as weekly and monthly rental rates on time bundles.

Fences are those policies, rules, programs, and structures that customers must follow to qualify for price discounts or rewards. For example, minimum volume requirements, time-based membership requirements, bundled purchase requirements, and so on keep prices paid and the value delivered to customers in line. Some fences can also force customers to pay higher prices regardless of the seller's costs; the notorious Saturday night stay requirements for reduced airline fares are a good example. Until competition forced airlines to drop the requirement, Saturday night stays effectively separated business travelers, who, presumably, could afford higher fares, from price-sensitive pleasure travelers.

EXHIBIT 2-12   "Associate More Detailed Descriptions for Easier Identification"

	CUSTOMER CONTROLLED		
Segment	Brand Focus	Consistency	Unique Capability
Needs	• Maintain brand image across channels • Custom services tailored to customer needs • Proactive problem resolution development • High Maintenance • Full service bundled solutions	• Margin Management • Expects big 3 standard services, managed by the customer's staff • Precision Printer Performance • Moderate Maintenance • Needs Print/Bind, Dist—will provide won PMT • Paper supply options	• Products that are distinct to the end-user • Advanced targeting techniques to drive demand • Product longevity requires longer catalog shelf life
Representative Catalogs	• Coldwater Creek • Spiegel • Eddie Bauer • William Sonoma	• J Crew • Brylane • Fingerhut • Brooks Brothers	• Viking • Bon Marche • Quill • Industrial Catalogs
Key Demographics	• Large Print Order Quantities • Mid-size Catalogs • Prints 1-4 or > 12 times per year • Uses high quality paper grades • Mostly Saddle Stitched	• Small to Medium Print Order Quantities • Mostly Short Cut-off/ Standard Trim Sizes • Medium Sized Catalogs • Mostly Saddle Stitched	• Small Print Order Quantities • Smaller sized catalogs • Must have Supplied Component Parts • Catalogs carry numerous store brands • Higher percentage of B2B catalogs

Choose metrics and fences that establish and enforce premium prices for high value segments, and allow feature repackaging and unbundling to appeal to low-value and low-cost-to-serve segments. As we shall see later in this book, the result is a menu of prices, products, services, and bundles that reflect different value received for different prices paid.

Identifying value-based segments, the metrics of pricing offerings, and the fences that maintain a price structure allow a marketer to expand its profit margins by aligning its prices, service bundles, and capacity utilization with the different value levels demanded by different customers. That's a win-win balance for sellers and buyers; everyone gets something. But, as we will see in later chapters, just how much either side wins depends on how much of the differential value created in a transaction each side captures. That's when policies to facilitate value-based price negotiations become important.

Summary

The foundation of a profitable pricing strategy begins with a complete understanding of the economic value the product delivers to buyers because, ultimately, value is the primary determinant of willingness-to-pay. This foundational understanding of value contributes to a com- prehensive pricing strategy in a number of ways. First, it provides insight into how willingness-to-pay differs across segments. As the commercial printing company example illustrates, a value-based segmentation can inform not only pricing, but offering design as well. Second, understanding value is the only way to develop effective communications campaigns to increase customer's willingness-to-pay. Although a hot beachgoer probably recognizes the value of a cold drink delivered to her blanket, most customers are not so well informed, and it is the job of the seller to get the value message across. Finally, value can and should be one of the key inputs to the price setting decision because, as we demonstrated in Chapter 1, building a pricing strategy on other metrics such as market share or costs leads to less profitable results.

Notes

1. http://www.toyota.com/sem/prius .html?srchid=K610_p2665505
2. For additional related discussion of this "proportional value-proportional price" argument, see Gerald E. Smith and Thomas T. Nagle, "Pric- ing the Differential," *Marketing Management*, May/June 2005; and Gerald E. Smith and Thomas T. Nagle, "A Question of Value," *Marketing Management*, July/August 2005.

CHAPTER 3

Price Structure
Tactics for Pricing Differently Across Segments

After developing products or services that create value, a marketer must then determine how most profitably to capture that value in both volume and margin. The challenge in doing so is that customers value products differently because of different abilities to pay, different preferences, and different intended uses. Moreover, the timing of customers' needs, the speed of their payments, and the level of service and support they require can drive significant differences in the cost to serve them. When a company tries to serve all customers with one price, or a standard markup in the case of distributors and retailers, it is forced to make large tradeoffs between volume and margin—enabling some customers to acquire the product for much less than they would be willing to pay for it, while others are excluded even though the lower price that they would pay is sufficient to cover variable costs and make a positive contribution to profit.

Except for pure commodities, such as ethanol or pork bellies, a single price per unit is rarely the best way to generate revenues. Realizing a company's profit potential created by the differentiation in its features or services requires creating a structure of prices that aligns with the differences in economic value and cost to serve across customer segments. The goal of that structure is to mitigate the tradeoff between winning high prices for low volume and high volume for low prices. The goal is to capture more revenue from sales where value or cost to serve is higher, while accepting lower revenue where necessary to drive still profitable volume.

To illustrate the huge benefits of a well-defined segmented price structure, suppose that a supplier faced five different segments, all willing to pay a different price to get the benefits they sought from a product (see Exhibit 3-1). Segment 1 with sales potential of 50,000 units is willing to pay $20 for the firm's product. Segment 2 with sales potential of 150,000 units is willing to pay $15, and so on. What price should the firm set? The right answer in principle

EXHIBIT 3-1 The Incremental Contribution from Price Segmentation

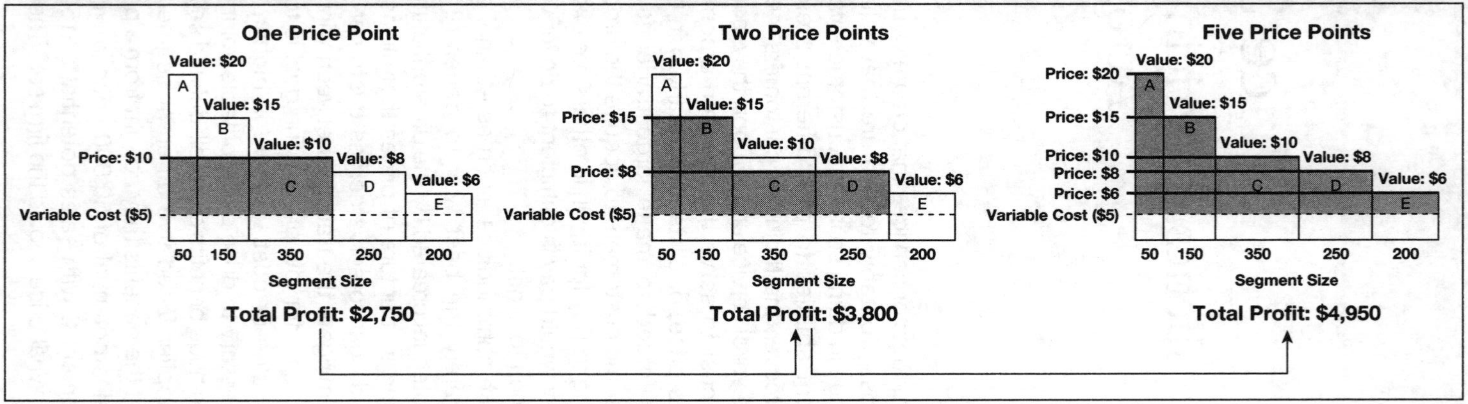

One Price Point

Value: $20
Value: $15
Value: $10
Value: $8
Value: $6

A
B
C
D
E

Price: $10

Variable Cost ($5)

Segment Size
50 150 350 250 200

Total Profit: $2,750

Two Price Points

Value: $20
Value: $15
Value: $10
Value: $8
Value: $6

A
B
C
D
E

Price: $15
Price: $8

Variable Cost ($5)

Segment Size
50 150 350 250 200

Total Profit: $3,800

Five Price Points

Value: $20
Value: $15
Value: $10
Value: $8
Value: $6

A
B
C
D
E

Price: $20
Price: $15
Price: $10
Price: $8
Price: $6

Variable Cost ($5)

Segment Size
50 150 350 250 200

Total Profit: $4,950

is whatever price maximizes profit contribution. If you calculate the profit contribution at each of the five prices assuming a variable cost of $5 per unit, the single price that produces the maximum contribution ($2,750) is $10.

However, a single-price strategy clearly leaves excess money on the table for many buyers who are willing to pay more: those willing to pay $20 and $15. These high-end buyers perceive significantly greater value from purchasing this product, relative to other buyers. At the price of $10, they are enjoying a lot of what economists call "consumer surplus." The firm would be better off if it could capture some of this surplus by charging higher prices to these buyers. The second problem is that the supplier leaves nearly half of the market unsatisfied, even though it could serve those customers at prices above the $5 per unit variable cost.

For industries with high fixed costs, serving those additional customers is often very profitable and, when they constitute large amounts of volume, can be essential for a company's survival. Railroads could not maintain, let alone expand, their costly infrastructures without a segmented price structure. Railroad tariffs are designed to reflect the differences in the value of the goods hauled. Coal and unprocessed grains are carried at a much lower cost per carload than are manufactured goods, resulting in a much lower contribution margin per carload. Still, the large volumes of coal and grain transported enables that low-priced business to make a substantial contribution to a railroad's high fixed cost structure. If railroads were required to charge all shippers the tariff for manufactured goods, they would lose shippers whose commodities would no longer be competitive on a delivered cost basis and so would lose that profit contribution. On the other hand, if railroads had to charge all shippers the tariff currently charged for a carload of unprocessed grain, their systems would reach capacity before they generated enough contribution to cover their fixed costs and become profitable. Freight railroads survive and prosper by leveraging their capacity to serve multiple market segments at value-based prices for each segment.

Even companies that serve only the premium end of a market often find that it is risky to limit themselves to that segment when they could be leveraging some common costs to serve other segments as well. In his book, *The Innovator's Dilemma*, Clayton Christensen cites numerous examples of companies that failed to meet demand from the lower-performance, lower-margin segment of a market that they dominated. Invariably, someone eventually addressed that need and used it as a base to partially support the fixed costs investments necessary to enter higher margin segments.[1] For years, Xerox owned the high end of the copier market. It lost that dominant position only after companies that had entered at the bottom of the market developed service networks of sufficient size to support the higher-priced equipment bought by customer segments, such as copy, centers that require quick service to minimize downtime.

How many segments with different price points should a supplier serve? To return to our illustration, Exhibit 3-1 shows that if the firm were to set two price points serving two general price segments—high-end buyers willing to pay $15 or more, and mid-level buyers willing to pay $8 or more—it could increase profit contribution by 40 percent. But if the supplier could charge separate prices to each of the five market segments, it could increase profit contribution by 80 percent relative to the single price strategy. In principle, more segmentation is always better. In practice, however, the extent of price segmentation is limited by the ability of the seller to enforce it at an acceptable cost.

Segments for pricing are easier to define conceptually than to maintain in practice because customers whom you intend to charge a higher price have an incentive to undermine the structure. They will not freely identify themselves as members of a relatively price-insensitive segment simply to help the seller charge them more, but will try to disguise themselves as customers who qualify for a lower price. Distributors, too, can undermine a segmented pricing strategy by buying the product for delivery to a customer entitled to a lower price but then actually sell to segments that will pay more and pocketing the difference for themselves. This is a huge problem for companies in the European Union because distributors in countries where prices are lower will ship products to one where prices are higher, which often happens simply due to changes in currency values. European law prohibits attempts by national governments to restrict such "parallel trade" even between two European Union countries that have different currencies. Thus, the manufacturer without a segmentation strategy can lose sales in the low-value country due to shortages, while losing margin to competition with "parallel traders" into the high-value countries.

So how can sellers charge different prices to different customers and for different applications? The answer is by creating a segmented price structure that varies not just the price, but also adjusts the offer or the criteria to qualify for it. A segmented price structure is one that causes revenues to vary with differences in the two key elements that drive potential profitability: the economic value that customers receive and the incremental cost to serve them. There are three mechanisms that one can use to maintain such a segmented structure: **price-offer configuration, price metrics**, and **price fences**. Each is appropriate for addressing different reasons for the existence of value-based segments.

PRICE-OFFER CONFIGURATION

When differences in the value of an offer across segments is caused by differences in the value associated with features, services, or both, a seller can segment the market by configuring different offers for different segments. Using offer design to implement segmented pricing requires minimal enforcement of the segments because customers self-select the offers that determine their prices. The segmented pricing of airline seats described in Chapter 1 is based partially on offer design, with passengers freely choosing whether they want the price that includes the ability to cancel or change flights freely, or want to forgo that feature in return for a much more discounted price. To

EXHIBIT 3-2   The Financial Benefits of Price Segmentation

	A	B	C	D	E	Total
Optimal price by Segment	$20	$15	$10	$8	$6	
Sales Potential (000)	50	150	350	250	200	1,000
Variable Cost of Production	5	5	5	5	5	
Segmentation "Fence" Cost	1	1	1	1	0	
Gross Contribution (000) and Incremental Cost to Segment:						Net Contribution
1 Price ($10)	$250	$750	$1,750	0	0	**$2,750**
2 Prices ($15, $8)	$500	$1,500	$1,050	$750	0	**$3,250**
– Incremental Cost to Segment	50	150	350	0	0	
5 Prices ($20, $15, $10, $8, $6)	$750	$1,000	$1,750	$750	$200	**$4,150**
– Incremental Cost to Segment	50	150	350	250	0	

Adapted from Richard Harmer. "Strategies for Segmented Pricing," The Pricing Institute 6th Annual Conference (Chicago, March 22–25, 1993).

determine whether it would be profitable to add another offer combination to the menu of choices, you would need to create a spreadsheet analogous to the one in Exhibit 3-2. With that spreadsheet, you could analyze whether the additional offer combination costs more to administer than the incremental profits it would contribute. The right number of price points depends in each case on the sizes of the customer segments, the value and cost-to-serve differences between them, and the cost inefficiency from a proliferation of offers.

To create an effective price structure, one must first determine which features and services the firm should price *à la carte*, leaving customers to customize their own offers and which features and services to bundle into packages. There are multiple arguments against pricing all individual features and services separately. A single price for a bundle of features and services reduces transactions costs for both customers and sellers. The costs to make and deliver most products and services increase with the number of variations allowed, although technology is reducing the cost of mass customization. Lastly, research has shown that people are less sensitive to the cost of value-added features and services when bundled as a single expenditure.[2]

Optimizing an Offer Bundle

By creating more than one bundled option designed to appeal to different segments, a marketer can get most of the benefits described above along with the financial rewards of segmentation. Auto manufacturers, for example, put features together in the "sport package" or the "luxury edition" that have a single price for that bundle of options, while cable TV operators create different bundles focused on families, sports enthusiasts, and movie buffs. Since very few buyers would want just one element of the bundle without putting any value on the others, few sales are lost relative to the bundling efficiencies achieved.

Adding to the benefits of bundling, sellers can often earn more profit by pricing a bundle than they could by pricing the individual elements when a particular relationship exists among the features included in the bundle. Bundling is profit enhancing when it is possible to bundle features and services that create high value for some significant customer segments but more moderate value for another. A simple *à la carte* price for one feature or service that optimized profitability from one segment would necessarily over or under price other segments. Bundling, however, can facilitate more profitable, value-based pricing to each segment. The following example illustrates the principle when the same features can be priced profitably for more than one segment, but the most profitable price level for different segments is not the same.

Musical entertainment can provide an ideal opportunity for profitable bundling, where the "features" valued differently by different segments are the different types of performances. In Boston, where the authors live, one can buy tickets in a series that includes a few headline performers—such as Green Day, Jay-Z, or Kenny Chesney—as well as some lesser-known but often more "innovative" performers such as Kings of Leon or Solja Boy. The challenge is that there are two large customer segments to which these concerts appeal.

There is a large general entertainment segment that views music as just one entertainment option. People in this segment are willing to pay a lot to hear great headline performers, so revenue from them is maximized at a high ticket price (say $60 per ticket). However, they need to be induced to try a concert that is more innovative (no more than $25 per ticket). Without their support, it is unlikely that innovative concerts could attract a large enough audience to justify offering them.

Fortunately, since Boston is home to multiple music schools and music aficionados, there is a smaller segment that is willing to pay as much or more to see new, innovative performers as to see headliner performers. However, because much of this segment consists of students and musicians, they are more price sensitive to the headline performers whose music they have already experienced. The challenge is to maximize income from these two segments combined.

Based upon past research and experimentation, assume that the concert promoters believe that the ticket prices in Exhibit 3-3 represent roughly the acceptable price that would optimize price and attendance by each segment alone at each concert type. Unfortunately, if prices were set at $60 per ticket for headline performances, much of the music aficionado segment would be priced out, leaving some seats empty. Even more importantly for the survival of the concert series, if the innovative performances were priced at $40 per ticket, the large general entertainment segment would fail to show, and so those performances would probably not be viable. Charging $40 per ticket for "headliners" and $25 for "innovations" would fill the halls for both types of

EXHIBIT 3-3 Revenue Optimizing Pricing by Segment for Musical Performances

Concert Segment	"Must See" Performances	Innovative Performances
Music Aficionados	$40	$40
General Entertainment Segment	$60	$25

concerts but would leave a lot of potential revenue on the table. Each segment would be underpriced for some type of concert for which the revenue optimizing price was higher.

Because of this reversal of preference ("headliners" are valued more by the general segment while "innovations" are valued more by the aficionado segment), it is possible to price tickets more profitably as a bundle. After establishing single ticket prices of $60 for headliners concerts and $40 for innovative concerts, the promoter can offer a series of headliner and innovative performances at a discount from those prices that fill the halls. Since the music aficionado segment would pay up to $80 for one headliner plus one innovative performance and the general entertainment segment would pay $85 for the same combination, the series promoter could maximize revenue at $80 for the pair (or $160 for 4, or $240 for 6, so long as the subscriber must choose a specified number of concerts of each type to make up a series). The venues can then be filled and generate more revenue per patron from each bundle of concerts than would be possible with single ticket pricing only (totally only $65 for a pair). The magic behind this is that the different segments are paying the additional $15 per pair of performances for different reasons. Giving them both a reason to pay more within the same bundle facilitates the capture of that value without forgoing volume.

In practice, there are often more than two segments, segments of very different sizes, and more than two types of products to bundle. Maximizing contribution requires building a spreadsheet or employing complex optimization model to evaluate bundling alternatives.[3] The principle, however, is the same for bundling features in auto packages, items to include in the four-course dinner special, items in a vacation package, or spots for advertising at different times on a television network. The key is to bundle elements that are valued differently by different segments so long as the incremental revenue earned from inducing more customers to buy an element of the bundle exceeds the incremental cost to supply it. In principle, one could maximize revenue from three segments with one bundle containing three different elements, each valued most highly by one of the segments.

Designing Segment Specific Bundles

Bundling can also facilitate segmented pricing, thus increasing profitability, when different customer segments have different price sensitivity for a "core" product or service (for example, lodging at a popular vacation spot). When it is possible to find features or services that one segment values highly and another does not (for example, access to a pro-quality golf course or a "kids' club" where children can be left safely and entertained), it is easy to design segment-specific pricing by bundling. The golfer evaluates the sum of the room cost plus the golf cost in figuring the cost of the vacation. If the golfer values lodging at this location by $100 per night more than the family, he will pay up to $100 more per day for greens fees than he would at an equal quality course in a less desirable location. (Assuming, of course, that no cheaper but equal quality course is available near this location.) Since the family did not come to play golf, they are unaffected by high greens fees.

As rewarding but often overlooked is the potential for bundling value-added features and services to attract customer segments that require a lower price to win their patronage. Although they pay a lower price, their purchase volume may, nevertheless, be profitable, especially during off-peak periods or economic downturns when excess capacity would otherwise remain unused. Simply cutting prices to win their business would, however, make it difficult to continue charging other customer segments a higher price and could "cheapen" the image of the brand. Bundling a "free" or low-cost service or feature specifically preferred by this segment, however, can improve the value proposition for that segment without having to cut the offer price explicitly.

For example, the resort hotel could charge a higher price for the room but bundle the "kids' club" free for one child with each paying adult, admit children free at the breakfast buffet, or provide a shuttle and discount tickets to nearby family-friendly entertainment. Since the golfers would find none of this worthwhile, the attraction to the buyer and the added cost to the seller are limited to the targeted segment. Similar bundles exist in business-to-business markets. Companies that cannot discount prices to small businesses without facing demands for lower prices from larger customers may offer their price-sensitive small business customers low-cost financing, free software for better inventory management, or anything else that they would value but that large company customers would not want.

There is an alternative to adding a feature that raises the value of the discounted offer to only the low-price segment. That is to add a feature to the lower cost offer that kills value for the higher-priced segment without affecting the value to the discount segment. Dick Harmer, a former colleague of ours, gave this practice the memorable name "selective uglification." Chemical companies often do not have separate lines for making "food grade" and cheaper "industrial grade" chemicals. They simply add something for the "industrial grade" that makes it no longer acceptable for food manufacturers and consumers. The Saturday night stay requirement for a discount airline ticket is another example, since it has no affect on the pleasure traveler who wants the trip to include the weekend anyway, but deters most business travelers.

Unbundling Strategically

While bundling can be a profit-enhancing strategy for segmentation, it often has the opposite effect when variable cost services are bundled simply to differentiate an offering. For example, a business-to-business equipment company might try to convince customers to pay more for its machines by bundling the promise of faster warranty repair service and free delivery anywhere, and a business-to-consumer airline might hope to charge more for its tickets because they include free baggage handling and agent assistance with reservations. Such price-offer structures often undermine rather than enhance profits and can be fatal to companies that cling to them in competitive markets.

The problem arises when the cost to provide the bundled service to customers can be widely different. Customers who have a high need for the bundled services gravitate to the companies that offer them for "free." As companies gain share among these high-cost service users, the average cost to deliver the bundle increase. If they try to add the increasing average service cost to the price, they begin losing sales to customers who are not high service users. If they avoid raising the price of the bundle to reflect the increasing cost of the service, the increasing cost erodes their margins.

Unless the cost to deliver a service is trivial relative to the overall value of the offer, bundling optional services "free" will undermine profitability. Unbundling them with per use fees or limiting the use of them, as many airlines are doing for baggage handling or for using an agent to make reservations, is in fact strategically essential when facing intense competition. Where customers have come to expect the service to be included, companies can unbundle the price structure without upsetting customers by offering rebates for forgoing use. For example, one company whose customers had become accustomed to placing orders on short notice for "free" raised its prices but, at the same time, offered a discount of more than the price increase for orders to be shipped within seven days. That enabled it to avoid disrupting relationships with customers already paying a premium for its quick service while enabling it to match competitive prices when necessary.

PRICE METRICS

Not all differences in value across segments reflect differences in the features or services desired. Value received is sometimes not even related to differences in the quantity of the product consumed, necessitating a price metric unrelated to quantity of product or service provide. For example, in the field of health care, both government and private payers are resisting paying for health care on a "fee for service" basis since delivery of more days in the hospital or more tests is often indicative of poor treatment choices, not better patient outcomes. Both payers and health care providers, like Kaiser Permanente and Mayo Clinic, that have a proven ability to deliver care more cost effectively than their peers, have benefited from adopting more value-based price metrics: either a "capitation" price that covers all services required by a patient during a year or a price per illness or procedure that covers all services required to treat a condition to a satisfactory outcome. By adopting such metrics, health care providers that can do that more cost-effectively can avoid the difficult problem of having to convince payers to pay more per service to reflect the value of better treatment. It is much easier to make the case that they can get patients "back on their feet" for no more than the cost per patient of less effective providers.

The example just described involved changing from a feature-based to a benefit-based price metric. *Price metrics* are the units to which the price is applied. They define the terms of exchange—what exactly will the buyer receive per unit of price paid. There are often a range of possible options. For example, a health club could charge per hour of use, per visit, per an "annual membership" for unlimited access, or per some measure of benefit (inches lost at the waist or gained at the chest). The club might also vary those prices by time of day (low for a midday membership, higher for peak-time membership) or by season of the year to reflect differences in the opportunity cost of capacity. Finally, it might have a multi-part metric: an annual membership with an additional hourly charge for use of the tennis courts. These reflect the common categories of price metrics: per unit, per use, per time spent consuming, per person who consumes, per amount of benefit received.

The problem with most price metrics is that they are adopted by default or tradition. For example, initially software companies charged a price per copy installed on one "server" machine. In most cases, that led to a poor alignment with value. A few creative vendors recognized that when more users accessed the software, the buyer was getting more value. Consequently, they changed the price metric from a price "per server" to a price "per seat," resulting in customers paying more when they had more users accessing the software. When this "per seat" metric proved much more profitable for the computer-aided design and financial analysis companies that adopted it, other software companies copied it. For many of their applications, however, the number of users still aligned poorly with value, leaving many customers underpriced while pricing others out of the market. The most thoughtful among them created still better price metrics. Leaders in manufacturing software replaced "price per seat" with "price per production unit." Storage management software suppliers replaced "price per server" with a "price per gigabit of data moved." Each time a company discovers a better metric than its competitors, it gains margin from existing customers, incremental revenue from customers formerly priced out of its markets, or both.

Creating Good Price Metrics

There are five criteria for determining the most profitable price metrics for an offering (Exhibit 3-4). The first criterion for a good price metric is that it tracks with differences in value across segments. While offer design facilitates different pricing differently based upon what people chose to buy, a price metric not based upon units of purchase can facilitate different pricing for the same offer. For example, it often makes more sense to price drug per day of therapy rather than per milligram of the drug—as Eli Lilly did when it launched the antidepressant Prozac. Someone who requires only a 10-milligram dose gets no less value than someone who requires a 30-milligram dose to control the disease. Consequently, the company charged the same amount per pill regardless

EXHIBIT 3-4   Criteria for Evaluating Price Metrics

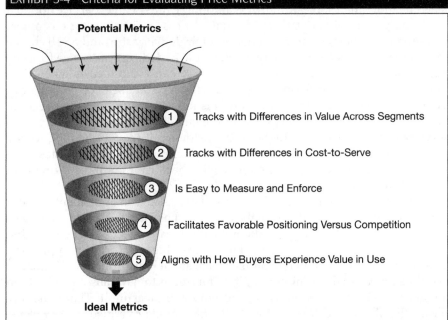

Potential Metrics

1. Tracks with Differences in Value Across Segments
2. Tracks with Differences in Cost-to-Serve
3. Is Easy to Measure and Enforce
4. Facilitates Favorable Positioning Versus Competition
5. Aligns with How Buyers Experience Value in Use

Ideal Metrics

of the quantity of active ingredient it contained. Second, a good metric tracks with differences in the cost to serve across customer segments. When customers' behavior influences the incremental cost to serve them and those costs are significant, a profit-maximizing price metric needs to reflect that as well. The cost to deliver a service is significant if it exceeds the cost of measuring, monitoring, and charging for differences in its usage. Marketers are often reluctant to charge for services, even when costs are significant, because they fear that they will become uncompetitive relative to others who do not charge for them. In fact, the opposite is the case.

Giving services for "free" attracts customers who are relatively higher users of them. Customers who want to minimize their inventories will gravitate to suppliers who offer free rush orders. Customers with a lot of employee turnover resulting in poor equipment maintenance will gravitate to equipment suppliers who offer unlimited and quick on-site service. Customers who require only minimal amounts of service will, in similar fashion, gravitate to competitors offering little or no service but lower prices. As a result, marketers often find that they have differentiated their companies into lower profitability by improving their service offerings because they lack an appropriate metric to capture the value and discourage excessive use of services.

By adding charges for services, at least for those customers who are excessively costly to serve, companies are able to keep their core product prices competitive and avoid attracting a mix of customers who are costly to serve. As their markets have become more competitive, software suppliers added charges for formerly "free" online telephone support. Banks have added charges for small account holders to use a teller, or to access a teller machine more than some authorized amount. United Parcel Service added a $1.75 charge for delivery to a residential address, a $5 charge for customers who don't put their account number on their delivery slip, and a $10 charge for a wrong address. These charges reflect the added cost of service for such packages, and the tendency for customers to cause those costs when they don't have to pay for them. Suppliers with separate service charges can price more competitively for the core business (the software, the checking account, the package delivery) to win the customers who are lower cost to serve, while still attracting higher cost customers if they are willing to pay for the higher service levels that they demand. In fact, companies with unbundled service can offer better service because they have a financial incentive to do so.

A third criterion for a good metric is that it is easy to implement without any ambiguity about what charge the customer has incurred. Profit-sharing or performance-based pricing are theoretically ideal ways to achieve the first two criteria for a good metric—tracking with value and cost. But in practice, these methods often end in rancorous debate about how profit or performance should be measured. At minimum, it is important to have absolute clarity in advance about what the metric is and who will measure it. That generally means that the metric must be objectively measured or verified.

We once helped to create a value-based metric at a company whose lubricant enabled manufacturers to cut through difficult materials more quickly with less wear on their tools. The company's product was an easy sell at launch when potential customers were operating at maximum capacity. Cutting materials faster increased capacity at this stage in the production process, enabling many customers to increase revenues without additional capital cost. But when a recession hit, the value associated with increased capacity fell to zero. The value created by the company's product was reduced to the savings in labor costs and machine wear.

In theory, the price could be adjusted to reflect the customer's capacity utilization. However, whenever price depends upon the customer voluntarily reporting information that will lead to a higher price, the potential for conflicts and misinformation is almost always too high. Fortunately we found a published industrial sales index that seemed to track well with the customers' capacity utilization. The company continued to charge a price per pound for its product, but in return for lower pricing during the recession, the customers accepted automatic price adjustments monthly based upon the level of an industry sales index.

The fourth criterion for evaluating a price metric is how the metric makes your pricing appear in comparison with competitors' pricing, and the impact of that on the perceived attractiveness of your offer. A new, hosted voice-recognition software that enabled a call center to process more callers without as much need for human intervention promised to create huge differential economic value for purchasers. Unfortunately, the traditional metric for pricing and evaluating hosted call center software was a price per minute of use. Since voice-recognition software processes callers faster, minutes using traditional call center software were not comparable to minutes using the voice-recognition software. A value-based price using that per-minute metric would need to be at least three times the price per minute for traditional software—inviting resistance from purchasers.

To overcome that, the company adopted a new metric: "cost per call processed." That metric naturally required conversion of the competitors' cost-per-minute metric into a cost-per-call metric. While the new software was still more expensive, its percent price premium was much smaller when framed in terms of cost per call than in terms of a cost per minute (see Exhibit 3-5). Moreover, the differentiation value of the avoided operator intervention was much more dramatic when framed in terms of cost per-call rather than cost per-minute basis. The total cost per call was less with the new software, despite being higher on a per-minute basis. While the favorable economics of the new software was exactly the same using either metric, the per-call basis of comparison made the sales effort a lot easier.

The fifth and final criterion for evaluating a price metric is how the metric aligns with how buyers experience the value in use of the product or service. The better the alignment—how a price metric fits the timing and magnitude of the customers' expenditure—the more attractive the offer. Movie renters get value from watching a DVD once, not from the amount of time they have it in their possession. Netflix changed the metric for film rentals when it recognized that the decline in the cost of making disks no longer required incentives for renters to return the disk quickly. By replacing the rental metric based on time ($3.95 per day) with a metric based on the number of films "out at-a-time" ($8.99 per month for one DVD at a time, $13.99 per month for two, and so forth), Netflix eliminated the inconvenience of having to acquire the movie shortly before watching it and return it shortly thereafter. That made the Netflix metric more compelling than the video store

EXHIBIT 3-5   Hosted Call Center Software

	Traditional Caller-Response Software	Natural Voice-Recognition Software	Percent Difference
Call Length	7.2 minutes	4.4 minutes	−39%
"Price" of software per minute	0.90	$1.55	+72%
"Price" of software per call	$6.48	$6.82	+5%
% of calls requiring human intervention	47%	12%	
Cost of Operator Intervention	$3.50	$3.50	
Total cost per minute	$1.13	$1.65	+46%
Total cost per call	$8.14	$7.26	−11%

metric for a large share of the video rental market, which Netflix won over amazingly quickly.

In some cases, it is not possible to achieve all of these criteria with one metric, but they can be achieved with a multi-part metric. Mobile telephone service providers charge a fixed monthly fee, capturing the value of simply having access to a phone when needed, plus charges for the amount of different services consumed (calls, text messages, Internet time). Amusement parks sometimes have an entry fee plus a ticket charge for each ride. Banks charge a monthly fee for an account, plus additional charges for transactions. Each of these structures is designed to strike a balance between service cost recovery, encouraging use that drives volume with pricing that is seen as aligned with value, and capturing more profit from those customers who are getting more value.

Performance-Based Metrics

An ideal price metric would tie what the customer pays for a product or service directly to the economic value received and the incremental cost to serve. In a few cases, called "performance-based" pricing, price structures can actually work that way.[4] Attorneys often litigate civil cases for which they are paid their out-of-pocket expenses plus a share of the award if they win, rather than for hours worked. Internet ads are usually priced based on the number of "click-throughs" rather than the traditional metric for advertising: cost "per thousand" exposure. Systems that control the lights, heating, and cooling within office buildings are sometimes installed in return for contracts that share the energy cost saving, rather than charges for the equipment installed. In each case, the price metric naturally charges customers differently for the same product or service based on differences in the value they receive.

Most importantly, performance-based pricing has the effect of shifting the performance risk from the buyer to the seller. General Electric (GE) used bundling to reduce risk when it launched a new series of highly efficient aircraft engines, its GE90 series. These engines promised greater fuel efficiency and power that could make them much more profitable to operate. The catch was a high degree of uncertainty about the cost of maintenance. Some airlines feared that these high-powered engines might need to be over-hauled more frequently, thus easily wiping out the financial benefits from operating them. This undermined GE's ability to win buyers at the price premium that power and fuel efficiency would otherwise justify.

Rather than accept a lower price to account for a buyer's perceived risk, GE absorbed the risk by changing the price metric. Instead of selling or leasing an engine alone, GE effectively rented aircraft engine for a fee per hour flown that included all costs of scheduled and unscheduled maintenance. Without the uncertainty of maintenance cost, GE90 engines quickly became popular despite a price premium. In most cases, however, "performance-based pricing" is simply impractical. It requires too much information and too much trust that the buyer will actually report the information accurately. It also leaves the buyer uncertain regarding the cost of a purchase until after it is used. In practice, therefore, marketers must design profit-driven price structures by finding measures that only roughly predict the value a customer will receive and the costs to serve. Often the difference between a good and a great pricing strategy lies in finding, or creating, such measures.

Tie-Ins as Metrics

A very common challenge for a company that sells capital goods is that the value of owning them can vary widely across segments based upon how intensely they are used. For example, a company that makes a uniquely efficient canning machine might like to sell it both to salmon packers in Alaska, who will use it intensely for only a couple months each year, as well as to fruit and vegetable packers in California, who will use it to can crops all year round. One option would be to put a meter on the machine to record every time that machine went through one cycle. That, in fact, is how Xerox priced its copiers at launch, leasing them at a price based upon machine usage and refusing to sell them outright.

For the canning machine manufacturer that did not expect to have service people at the client site on a regular basis, the idea of a usage-based lease was not practical. What was practical was a "tie-in sale" that contractually required purchasers of the canning machine to use it only with cans sold by the seller at a premium price. Thus, the true cost of the machine was not just its low explicit price but also the net present value of the price premiums paid for the tied-in cans. Since buyers who used the machine more intensely must buy more of the tied-in product to use it, they effectively paid more for the asset.

"Tie-in" sales like those that tied purchase of cans contractually to purchase of the machine were quite common until 1949, when the federal courts decided that such contracts were not enforceable under U.S. antitrust law because of their impact on the otherwise freely competitive market for the tied commodity.[5] But although contractual tie-ins are no longer enforceable, companies still frequently use technological design to tie a unique consumable to an asset. For example, Hewlett-Packard (HP) led the industry in the development and manufacture of inkjet printers. HP strategically priced the printer—the asset—low to make the up-front cost competitive with much lower-quality printers. The replacement ink cartridge—the consumable—was designed with proprietary technology to fit uniquely with the asset and carried a remarkable wholesale margin of 60 percent. The key to HP's pricing success is that its pricing allowed it to earn some profit from its superior printers from the many light users who bought them and its high-priced ink. But HP could earn much more from heavy users who need to replace their printer cartridges more frequently. This tie-in strategy enables HP's inkjet division to maintain a 50 percent market share and profit per dollar sales ratio that is twice that of the company in general.

In service-based companies, tie-in contracts are frequently used to reduce the cost for new buyers to try their services. Wireless phone providers offer a digital telephone for a nominal fee, and sometimes free, if the buyer agrees to purchase a long-term service contract to use the company's wireless network for 12 or 24 months. Satellite entertainment companies offer households a satellite dish and receiver unit for a greatly reduced price when buyers agree to subscribe to a higher-priced entertainment package of channels for a minimum of 12 or 24 months. These packages can be particularly effective for low-knowledge buyers, who perceive significant risk in investing in a new and little-known technology—and then developing them into loyal buyers who become accustomed to the firm's technology and programming.

Value-Based Pricing Finances Hamlet's Castle

The seeds of value-based pricing were planted centuries ago with the first documented use of value-based pricing metrics to improve profitability. The use occurred in the 15th century when Erik of Pomerania, King of the United Kingdom of Scandinavia, summoned to Copenhagen a group of merchants from the powerful German Hanseatic League, which at the time dominated nearly all trade in northern Europe. He informed them that henceforth, he intended to levy a new toll: Every ship wishing to sail past Elsinore, whether on its way out of or into the Baltic, would have to dip its flag, strike its topsails, and cast anchor so that the captain might go ashore to pay the customs officer in the town a toll of "one English noble."

Nobody challenged the right of the King of all Scandinavia to impose a toll of this kind. After all, mere barons who owned castles on the banks of the Rhine, the Danube, and other major European waterways had for centuries forced all passing ships to pay a similar toll. However, its relative heaviness, combined with the obligation to cast anchor at Elsinore in order to hand over the money, made it highly unpopular. Erik foresaw that if he also established a proper town at Elsinore, sea-captains, after paying their toll and then waiting for a favourable wind, would welcome an opportunity to replenish stocks of water, wine, meat, vegetables, and whatever else they needed. In other words, even if they had to pay toll, calling in at Elsinore could have its attractions— all he had to do was provide them.

Elsinore's fortunes changed in 1559 with the accession to the throne of Frederik II, aged 25. He was young, ambitious, and entertained imperialistic ideas about reconquering Sweden and restoring the Nordic Union. [Consequently,] he declared war, and it dragged on for seven years. Like all wars, it was a severe drain on Denmark's finances. By 1566 the situation was so serious that Frederik II and his councillors decided as a last resort to enlist the help of a man with special talents named Peder Oxe. Oxe was acknowledged to be a financial wizard, which was just what Frederick needed.

Erik of Pomerania's toll fee of one English noble per ship had long been regarded by skippers and shipowners as grossly unfair. After all, ships were of so many different sizes, carried so many different cargoes, and according to nationality, had various interests and affiliations. But the system had also been proving increasingly disadvantageous from the Danish king's point of view. The first four or five kings after Erik of Pomerania had therefore continually tried to introduce amendments of one kind or another, and these in turn made it necessary to introduce various special concessions. Some nationalities were exempted completely and others enjoyed preferential treatment in certain respects.

By this time, the basic toll had been raised from one to three nobles per ship, but it was still far from being a satisfactory system. Peder Oxe realized that the only answer lay in a radical reform of the whole basis upon which the [tolls] were calculated. Henceforth, instead of a simple toll per ship, payment must be made, he suggested, on the basis of the cargo carried: to start with, two rix-dollars 'per last' [a 'last' being approximately two tons of cargo]. Soon this was changed to an even subtler and more flexible system: a percentage of the *value* of each last of cargo.

The King held the right of pre-emption, that is to say an option to buy, if he so chose, all cargoes declared. This royal prerogative encouraged the captain of a ship to make a correct declaration. Naturally, if he thought the King might be interested in buying his cargo, he was tempted to put a high value on it. However, in doing so, he ran the risk that His Majesty might be totally disinterested, in which case he would have to pay a duty calculated on this high valuation. Conversely, if he played safe and declared a low value in the hope of getting away with paying a low duty, the King might decide to buy the whole consignment which could leave the captain seriously out of pocket.

Summoning Peder Oxe to reorganize the levying of the Sound Dues proved to be a masterful stroke: Within a few years the King's income from this source practically tripled. At the age of thirty-eight, Frederik II married his fifteen-year-old cousin, Sophie of Mecklenburg, and in 1574 embarked on what was to become the major architectural project of his life: the building of a new castle at Elsinore.

Abridged from *Hamlet's Castle and Shakespeare's Elsinore* by David Hohnen (Copenhagen: Christian Ejlers, 2000)

PRICE FENCES

Sometimes value differs between customer segments even when all the features and measurable benefits are the same. Value can differ between customer segments and uses simply because they involve different "formulas" for converting features and benefits into economic values. The difference may be tied to differences in income, in alternatives available, or in psychological benefits that are difficult to measure objectively. Unless there is a good "proxy" metric that just happens to correlate with the resulting differences in value, the seller needs to find a price *fence*: a means to charge different customers different price levels for the same products and services using the same metrics.

Price fences are fixed criteria that customers must meet to qualify for a lower price. At theaters, museums, and similar venues, price fences are usually based on age (with discounts for children under 12 years of age and for seniors) but are sometimes also based on educational status (full-time students get discounts), or possession of a coupon from a local paper (benefiting "locals" who know more alternatives). All three types of customers have the same needs and cost to serve them, but perceive a different value from the purchase. Price fences are the least complicated way to charge different prices to reflect different levels of value. Unfortunately, while simple to administer, the obvious price fences sometimes create resentment and are often too easy for customers to get over whenever there is an economic incentive to do so. Thus, finding a fence that will work in your market usually requires some creativity.

Buyer Identification Fences

Occasionally pricing goods and services at different levels across segments is easy because customers have obvious characteristics that sellers can use to identify them. Barbers charge different prices for short and long hair because long hair takes more time to cut. But, during nonpeak hours, barbers also cut children's hair at a substantial discount, despite the fact that children can be more challenging and time consuming. The rationale in this case is entirely to drive business with a discount for a more price-sensitive segment. Many parents view home haircuts as acceptable alternatives to costly barber cuts for their children, even though they would never bear the risk of letting their spouses cut their own hair. For barbers, simple observation of the customer segment, children, is the key to segmented pricing.

Issuers of credit cards resort to far more sophisticated, proprietary models to anticipate the price sensitivities and costs to serve for different types of consumers. Some are more sensitive to the annual fee, some to the interest rate, and others to the frequent flyer miles they can earn. On the cost side, some consumers are more likely to default or to use their card only infrequently, thus generating fewer fees from retailers for processing charges. Finally, the companies can see from consumers' credit reports what competitive cards they hold and can estimate their annual fee and interest rates, thus determining the "reference value" of the next best competitive alternative (NBCA). Based upon these analyses, credit card companies very finely segment their potential customer base and send out different offers that optimize the expected profitability of each segment. The metrics are the same, but the levels vary depending on which metric the issuer can use most cost effectively to capture the most value.

Rarely is identification of customers in different segments straightforward. Yet, management can sometimes structure price discounts that induce the most price-sensitive buyers to volunteer the information necessary to identify them. Many service providers, from hotels and rental car companies to theaters and restaurants, offer "seniors" discounts to those who will show an American Associations of Retired Persons (AARP) card, Medicare card, or some other ID that confirms their eligibility. College students qualify for discounts on various types of entertainment because their low incomes and alternative sources of campus entertainment make them, as a group, price-sensitive shoppers. Seniors and students readily volunteer their identification cards to prove that they are members of the price-sensitive segment. Members of the less price-sensitive segment identify themselves by not producing such identification.

Even schools and colleges charge variable tuitions for the same education based on their estimates of their students' price sensitivities. Although the official school catalogs list just one tuition, it is not the one most students pay at private colleges. Most receive substantial discounts called "tuition remission scholarships" obtained by revealing personal information on financial-aid applications. By evaluating family income and assets, colleges can set tuition for each student that makes attendance attractive while still maximizing the school's income.

Deal proneness is another form of self-induced buyer identification—especially through the use of coupons and sales promotions, a frequent tool of consumer marketers. Coupons provided by the seller give deal-prone shoppers a way to identify themselves.[6] Supermarkets and drug stores put coupons in ads circulars because people who read those ads are part of the segment that compares prices before deciding where to shop. Packaged-good and small appliance manufacturers print coupons and rebate instructions directly on the packages, expecting that only price-sensitive shoppers will make the effort to clip them out and use them for future purchases.[7]

Often a buyer's relative price sensitivity does not depend on anything immediately observable or on factors a customer freely reveals. It depends instead on how well informed about alternatives a customer is and on the personal values the customer places on the differentiating attributes of the seller's offer. In such cases, the classification of buyers by segment usually requires an expert salesperson trained in soliciting and evaluating the information necessary for segmented pricing.

The retail price of an automobile is typically set by the salesperson, who evaluates the buyer's willingness to pay. Notice how the salesperson takes a personal interest in the customer, asking what the customer does for a living (ability to pay), how long he has lived in the area (knowledge of the market), what kinds of cars she has bought before (loyalty to a particular brand), where she lives (value placed on the dealer's location), and whether she has looked at, or is planning to look at, other cars (awareness of alternatives). By the time a deal has been put together, the experienced salesperson has a fairly good idea how sensitive the buyer's purchase decision will be to the product's price. (Note: If you want to get the best price, show the sales rep your printout from the Internet of the wholesale cost of the car and its features, and offer $200 more. You will save yourself and the sales rep a lot of time.)

Purchase Location Fences

When customers who perceive different values buy at different locations, they can be segmented by purchase location. This is common practice for a wide range of products. Dentists, opticians, and other professionals sometimes have multiple offices in different parts of a city, each with a different price schedule reflecting differences in the target clients' price sensitivity. Many grocery chains classify their stores by intensity of competition and apply lower markups in those localities where competition is most intense. Colorado ski resorts use purchase location to segment sales of lift tickets. Tickets purchased slope side are priced the highest and are bought by the most affluent skiers, who stay in the slope-side hotels and condos. Tickets are cheaper (approximately 10 percent less) at hotels in the nearby town of Dillon, where less affluent skiers stay in cheaper, off-slope accommodations. In Denver, tickets can be bought at grocery stores and self-serve gas stations for larger discounts (approximately 20 percent less). These discounts attract locals, who know the market well and who are generally more price-sensitive because the ticket price represents a much higher share of the total cost for them to ski.

A clever segmented pricing tactic common for pricing bulky industrial products such as steel and coal is *freight absorption*. Freight absorption is the agreement by the seller to bear part of the shipping costs of the product, the amount of which depends upon the buyer's location. The purpose is to segment buyers according to the attractiveness of their alternatives. A steel mill in Pittsburgh, for example, might agree to charge buyers the cost of shipping from either Pittsburgh or from Gary Indiana, where its major competitor is located. The seller in Pittsburgh receives only the price the buyer pays, less the absorbed portion of any excess cost to ship from Pittsburgh. This enables the Pittsburgh supplier to cut price to customers nearer the competitor without having to cut price to customers for whom his Chicago competitors have no location advantage. The Chicago competitor probably uses the same tactic to become more competitive for buyers nearer Pittsburgh.

Trade barriers between countries once made segmentation by location viable even for products that were inexpensive to ship. As trade barriers have declined around the world, and especially within the European Union, the tactic has become less effective. For example, automobiles used to be sold throughout Europe at prices that varied widely across borders. German luxury cars sold in Britain were often 20 percent more expensive than when sold just across the channel in Belgium. Now, brokers in Britain will survey the continent for cars, which people can fly to pick up and drive home—or have the broker bring it back for them. To fight back, some makers of German luxury brands, which are cheaper in Germany than in some other countries where they carry a more premium image, have used their warranties to enforce location fences. A car bought in Germany and imported to Britain cannot get warranty service in the United Kingdom without paying an additional charge for warranty transfer.

Time of Purchase Fences

When customers in different market segments purchase at different times, one can segment them for pricing by time of purchase. Theaters segment their markets by offering midday matinees at substantially reduced prices, attracting price-sensitive viewers who are not employed during the day at times when the theater has ample excess capacity. Less price-sensitive evening patrons cannot so easily arrange dates or work schedules to take advantage of the cheaper midday ticket prices. Restaurants usually charge more to their evening patrons, even if they cater to peak crowds at lunch, because demand (in the United States, but not in Europe) is more price sensitive for the midday meal. Why? There are more numerous inexpensive substitutes for lunches than there are for dinners. A Big Mac or a brown bag, acceptable for lunch, is generally viewed as a poor substitute for a formal dinner as part of an evening's entertainment.

Priority pricing is one example of segmenting by time of purchase. New products in a retail store are offered at full price, or sometimes premium surcharges over full price in the case of extreme excess demand. Over time, as product appeal fades in comparison to newer competitive alternatives, buyers discount the product's value until they are willing to pay only a fraction of its original price for leftover models. This is a common tactic in the retail fashion and automobile industries, where customers with high incomes and low price sensitivity pay premium prices for the latest styles and models and can choose from a full inventory of sizes and colors. Over time, as inventories age and the availability of sizes and colors declines, prices are reduced in successive rounds of promotions to appeal to more price-sensitive buyers who are willing to wait for the opportunity to buy high-quality, but less trendy, inventory and with less certainty of obtaining their preferred size or color.

Priority pricing also applies in business-to-business purchases. A favorite strategy of Intel is to introduce a leading-edge semiconductor at a premium price, and then discount its existing semiconductor product lines. Leading-edge original equipment manufacturer (OEM) computer manufacturers that produce and sell the fastest and latest computers to innovative professional buyers with low price sensitivity pay the price premium for the latest chip technology. More price-sensitive buyers who are willing to accept slightly outdated technology are then offered older-model computers equipped with Intel's now older semiconductors at lower prices.

Predictable, periodic sales offering the same merchandise at discounted prices can also segment markets. This tactic is most successful in markets with a combination of occasional buyers who are relatively unfamiliar with the market, and with more regular buyers who know when the sales are and plan their purchases accordingly. Furniture manufacturers employ this tactic with sales every February and August, months when most people usually would not think about buying furniture. However, people who regularly buy home furnishings, and who are more price sensitive because of the reference price and total expenditure effects, know to plan their purchases to coincide with these sales.

Time is also a useful fence when demand varies significantly with the time of purchase but the product or service is not storable. The problem plagues airlines, hotels and restaurants, electric utilities, theaters, computer time-sharing companies, beauty salons, toll roads, and parking garages. Unable to move supplies of their products from one time to another, their only option is to manage demand. One way of doing so is with peak-load pricing, the implementation of which we will discuss in Chapter 8 when we explain how and when to adapt pricing to changes in the cost of capacity.[8]

Pricing for travel through the Eurotunnel between England and France is an interesting application of segmented pricing for a product with fixed capacity. The channel tunnel allows transport of an automobile and its occupants for a flat price between Folkestone, England, and Calais, France. Prices that allow travel at whatever time of day you choose are twice as high as during the off-peak evening and night periods. This reflects the opportunity cost of limited capacity. More interesting is the fact that rates increase with the time elapsed between the outbound and the return trips. Roundtrip use of the tunnel for a two-day, one-night visit from the United Kingdom to France costs from £44 per auto while roundtrip use for a three- to seven-day visit costs from £78 per auto for use of the tunnel at the same times of day. Clearly, this has nothing to do with cost or available capacity, so what drives it? The answer is that the value of having your own car with you on the trip, versus having to rent one after traveling by plane or train, increases with the length of the stay.[9]

Purchase Quantity Fences

When customers in different segments buy different quantities, one can sometimes segment them for pricing with quantity discounts. There are four types of quantity discount tactics: *volume discounts, order discounts, step discounts,* and *two-part prices.* All are common when dealing with differences in price sensitivity, costs, and competition.[10] Customers who buy in large volume are usually more price sensitive. They have a larger financial incentive to learn about all alternatives and to negotiate the best possible deal. Moreover, the attractiveness of selling to them generally increases competition for their business. Large buyers are often less costly to serve. Costs of selling and servicing an account generally do not increase proportionately with the volume of purchases. In such cases, volume discounting is a useful tactic for segmented pricing.

Volume discounts are most common when selling products to business customers. Steel manufacturers grant auto companies substantially lower prices than they offer other industrial buyers. They do so because auto manufacturers use such large volumes they could easily operate their own mills or send negotiators around the world to secure better prices. Volume discounts are based on the customer's total purchases over a month or year rather than on the amount purchased at any one time. At some companies, the discount is calculated on the volume of all purchases; at others, it is calculated by product or product class. Many companies give discounts for multiple purchases of a single model but, in addition, give discounts based on a buyer's total expenditure on all products from the company.

Although less common, some consumer products are volume discounted as well. Larger packages of most food, health, and cleaning products usually cost less per ounce, and canned beverages cost less in twelve-packs than in six-packs. These differences reflect both cost economies for suppliers and the greater price sensitivity for these products by large families. Warehouse food stores, such as Wal-Mart, Costco, Sam's, and BJ's often require consumers to buy in large-quantity packages to qualify for discounted prices.

Often sellers vary prices by the size of an order rather than by the size of a customer's total purchase volume. *Order discounts* are the most common of all quantity discounts. Almost all office supplies are sold with order discounts. Copier paper, for example, can be purchased for about $20 per case of about 10 reams, but purchased individually it costs several dollars per ream. The logic for this is that many of the costs of processing an order are unrelated to the size of it. Consequently, the per-unit cost of processing and shipping declines with the quantity ordered. For this reason, sellers generally prefer that buyers place large, infrequent orders, rather than small frequent ones. To encourage them to do so, sellers give discounts based on the order quantity. Order discounts may be offered in addition to volume discounts for total purchases in a year, because volume discounts and order discounts serve separate purposes. The volume discount is given to retain the business of large customers. The order discount is given to encourage customers to place large orders.

Step discounts differ from volume or order discounts in that they do not apply to the total quantity purchased, but only to the purchase beyond a specified amount. The rationale is to encourage individual buyers to purchase more of a product without having to cut the price on smaller quantities for which they would pay a higher price. Thus, in contrast to other segmentation tactics, step discounting may segment not only different customers, but also different purchases by the same customers. Such pricing is common for public utilities, from which customers buy water and electricity for multiple uses and place a different value on it for each use.

Consider, for example, the dilemma that local electric companies face when pricing their product. Most people place a very high value on having some electricity for general use, such as lighting and running appliances. The substitutes (gaslights, oil lamps, and hand-cranked appliances) are not very acceptable. For heating, however, most people use alternative fuels (gas, oil, coal, and kerosene) because of their lower cost. Utilities would like to sell more power for heating and could do so at a price above the cost of generating it. They do not want to cut the price of electricity across the board, however, since that would involve unnecessary discounts on power for higher-valued uses.

One solution to this dilemma is a step-price schedule. Assume that the electric company could charge a typical consumer $0.06 per kilowatt-hour (KWH) for general electricity usage but that it must cut its price to $0.04 per KWH to make electricity competitive for heating. If the company charged the lower price to encourage electricity usage for heating, it would forgo a third of the revenue it could earn from supplying power for other uses. By replacing a single price with a block-price schedule, $0.06 per KWH for the first block of 100 KWH and $0.04 for usage thereafter, the company could encourage people to install electric heating without forgoing the higher income it can earn on power for other purposes. To encourage people to use electricity for still more uses, such as charging their car batteries during off-peak hours, utilities often

EXHIBIT 3-6   Step-Price Schedule for Electricity

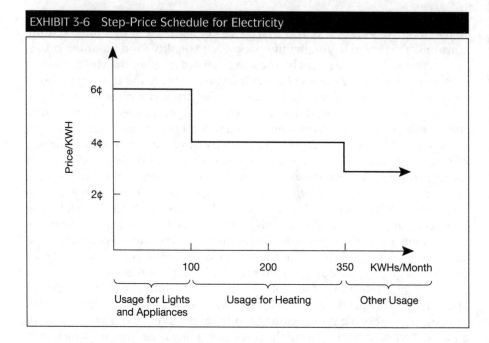

add another step discount for quantities in excess of those for general use and heating. Exhibit 3-6 illustrates a step-price schedule for an electric utility.

Given the clear increase in profit from offering step discounts, effectively moving along an individual customer's demand curve, why do most companies still offer each individual customer volume at only one price? The answer is that segmenting different purchases by each customer is possible only under limited conditions. It is profitable only when the volume demanded by individual buyers is significantly price sensitive.

Summary

Designing an optimal price structure that effectively segments your market and maximizes your profitable sales opportunities is clearly among the most difficult, but potentially rewarding, aspects of pricing strategy. For companies that are launching an offering with differentiated benefits or employing a business model with a different cost structure, creating a new price structure that aligns with those differences is usually necessary to capture the profit potential associated with them. Even without such a change, a company that can incrementally improve the price structure can gain profitable incremental volume. The principles of price structure discussed in this chapter, and the examples cited to illustrate them, can serve as a guide to a better basis for collecting revenues across segments. There is no simple formula. Each case requires creativity to find the best means to implement those principles within your market. It is, however, one of the most important activities that a marketer can do to improve profitability, since the investment required is small relative to other marketing investments, and the payoff is often very large.

Notes

1. Clayton M. Christensen, *The Innovator's Dilemma* (Cambridge MA: Harvard Business School Press, 1997, 44–46).
2. Daniel Kahneman, Jack L. Knetsch, and Richard H. Thaler, "The Endowment Effect, Loss Aversion, and Status Quo Bias," Journal of Economic Perspectives, 5, no. 1 (Winter 1991): 193–206.
3. Gary D. Eppen, Ward A. Hanson, and R. Kipp Martin, "Bundling—New Products, New Markets, Low Risk," *Sloan Management Review* 32, no. 4 (Summer 1991): 7–14, describes a model for optimizing very complex bundles.
4. For a complete treatment of performance-based pricing, see Benson P. Shapiro, "Performance-Based Pricing is More Than Pricing," Harvard Business School Note 9-999-007, February 25, 2002.
5. United States v. American Can Company (Northern District court of California, 1949).
6. See Narasimhan Chakravarthi, "Coupons as Price Discrimination Devices—A Theoretical Perspective and Empirical Analysis," *Marketing Science* 3 (Spring 1984): 128–147; Naufel J. Vilcassim and Dick R. Wittink, "Supporting a Higher Shelf Price Through Coupon Distributions," *Journal of Consumer Marketing* 4, no. 2 (Spring 1987): 29–39.
7. See the discussion in Chapter 5 of the framing effect to understand why rebates may influence purchases by customers who do not ultimately redeem them.
8. In addition to Chapter 8 of this book, also see Romarao Desiraju and Steven Shugan, "Strategic Service Pricing and Yield Management," *Journal of Marketing* 63, no. 11 (January 1999): 44–56.
9. www.eurotunnel.com
10. For an in-depth discussion of the motivations for quantity discounting, see Robert J. Dolan, "Pricing Structures with Quantity Discounts: Managerial Issues and Research Opportunities," Harvard Business School working paper, 1985.

CHAPTER 4

Price and Value Communication

Strategies to Influence Willingness-to-Pay

In Chapter 2, we argued that developing an effective pricing strategy requires understanding and quantifying the value of your offer in order to set profit-maximizing prices across segments. Yet even the most carefully constructed value-based pricing strategy will fail unless your offer's value, and how it differs from that of competitors' offers, is actually understood by potential customers. Customers who fail to recognize your differential value are vulnerable to buying inferior offerings at lower prices supported by loosely defined performance claims. The role of value and price communications, therefore, is to protect your value proposition from competitive encroachment, improve willingness-to-pay, and increase the likelihood of purchase as customers move through their buying process.

In our research, we have found that business managers rated "communicating value and price" as the most important capability necessary to enable their pricing strategies. Ironically, the same study found that the ability to communicate value is also one of the weakest capabilities in most sales and marketing organizations. In retrospect, these results are not surprising because effective value and price communications require a deep understanding of customer value (which most firms lack) combined with a detailed understanding of how and why customers buy (another shortcoming) to formulate messages that actually influence purchase behaviors.

When Amazon.com launched the Kindle e-book reader in October 2007, sales grew rapidly even though Amazon broke from conventional wisdom by not supporting the product launch with a traditional advertising campaign. Amazon management understood that an innovative product like their electronic book reader would quickly generate buzz that would build awareness of it in the marketplace. But, although advertising on television and in print media could reinforce awareness, it would do little to motivate customers who knew of the product but were unwilling to invest in such a radical departure from traditional books. The challenge facing Amazon management was how to help customers overcome the perceived risk that the value of being able to order and read books electronically might not justify the $400 price tag.

Amazon had to communicate the value of the new book reader to customers in a clear and compelling way to overcome the perceived risk—something that advertising alone could not accomplish. Their solution was as innovative as the product. For a fraction of the cost of a traditional advertising campaign, Amazon established a "Meet a Kindle Owner" program in major cities across the United States. Under the program, customers could meet current Kindle owners and try out the reader for themselves. The combination of positive word of mouth from Kindle enthusiasts and the ability to experience the product firsthand was enough to overcome doubts about the Kindle's value and has led to robust sales growth that has surpassed many analysts' projections, a clear demonstration of the power of effective value communications.

As the Kindle example illustrates, efffective price and value communications can have a significant impact on purchase intent and willingness-to-pay. The challenge for marketing and sales managers is how to develop effective value messages for different types of products *and* differences in the buying process that customers employ. It would be absurd to use the same communication approach for breakfast cereal as for computer data servers. Similarly, the approach must vary depending on whether the customer is a first-time buyer in the category or an experienced user, or whether the buyer is an individual, a family, or large corporation. McDonald's, which understands the customer's buying process well, targets many of its messages toward children because they are key influencers in the final choice for a family meal. Top salespeople in business markets also understand the need to adapt messages to different people inside a customer's organization because of the variety of roles that managers have in the buying process.

The purpose of this chapter is to explain how to develop value-based messages to reflect key product characteristics such as the nature of the benefits (psychological versus monetary) and the type of good (search versus experience). We also discuss how to adapt the message for important purchase characteristics such as the stage of the buying process or the number of individuals involved in the purchase decision. Finally, we show how to communicate prices in a way that can have a positive influence on a customer's willingness-to-pay.

VALUE COMMUNICATION

Value communication can have a great effect on sales and price realization when your product or service creates value that is not otherwise obvious to potential buyers. The less experience a customer has in a market or the more innovative a product's benefits, the more likely it is that the customer will not recognize nor fully appreciate the value of a product or service. For example, without an explicit message from the seller, a business buyer might not realize that a nearby distribution center offering shorter delivery times could reduce or eliminate the cost of carrying inventories. An unsophisticated buyer might not recognize how quickly inventoried items depreciate. Properly informed, the customer would see how much money faster delivery saves, justifying a price premium.

Adapting the Message for Product Characteristics

The first step in developing a value message is determining which customer perceptions to influence. We start with an understanding of the value drivers that are deemed most important to a customer segment. The goal is to help the customer recognize the linkages between a product's most important differentiated features and the salient value drivers. Two product characteristics determine how you should try to influence buyer perceptions of key value drivers: the target customer's *relative cost of search* for information about the differentiating attributes of your offering and the *type of benefits sought*— monetary or psychological.

Relative cost of search is the financial and nonfinancial cost, *relative to the expenditure in the category, that a customer must incur* to determine differences in features and benefits across alternatives. The size of the expenditure is important because investing even five minutes comparing product alternatives may be too much to make a more informed choice about a $5.00 purchase, but spending an hour researching alternatives before spending $5,000 would seem merely prudent. Several other factors determine the relative cost of search, including search characteristics of the product and the customer's expertise in the category. The relative search cost is low when the customer can easily determine product differences before purchase. Such products, called *search goods*, allow buyers to find information and choose among them prior to purchase. Examples include commodity chemicals, desktop computers, home equity loans, cosmetics, and digital cameras. The objective nature of search goods means that value messages can be quite definitive about the linkage between product features and the value drivers they impact. This concept of explicitly linking product features to benefits is illustrated by GE's "Energy Smart" campaign in which each package of GE flourescent bulbs contains a claim about the savings a consumer could earn through reduced power consumption when she uses the bulb (Exhibit 4-1).

In contrast, *experience goods* have differentiating attributes that are more difficult to evaluate across brands, requiring the customer to invest substantial time and effort to evaluate the products before purchase. Examples include most services such as management consulting, auto repair, and investment advice, as well as some products such as pharmaceuticals and home entertainment systems. The nature of experience goods makes it more difficult for marketers to establish clear linkages between features and the expected benefits. Consequently, instead of making explicit linkages between features and the associated value drivers, marketers of experience goods will

EXHIBIT 4-1   Economic Value Messages for a Search Good

focus on broader assurances of value intended to reduce the perceived risk of purchase and to increase awareness of the potential benefits.

The relative cost of search declines significantly for expert customers with extensive knowledge about the product category. A technophile can read the feature specifications for a personal computer and quickly infer how it will perform various tasks. A more typical buyer, however, would have to try different brands to make the same inferences. As a result, less sophisticated buyers often develop strategies to lower search costs such as purchasing a brand name or relying on the advice of an expert. The endorsement of an expert can be very powerful, even in business markets. For example, Kaiser Permanente, a western U.S. health maintenance organization, has a reputation for being a well-informed buyer of the most cost-effective medical products. The company often tests drugs and devices itself and will not buy a more expensive product without economic justification. Consequently, when other hospitals and health maintenance organizations (HMOs) learn that Kaiser Permanente has adopted a more expensive product or service, they assume that its price premium is cost-justified.

The relative cost of search diminishes as a customer's expenditure for the product increases. The relative cost of search is high for an individual buying an automobile because so much of the car's performance cannot be determined

EXHIBIT 4-2   Different Product Types Require Different Communication Strategies

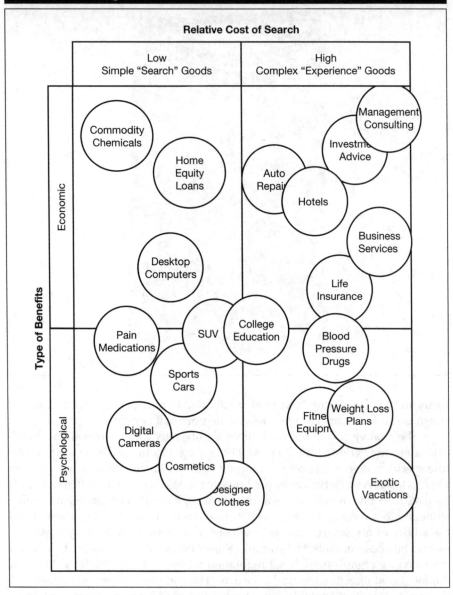

prior to purchase. However, for a fleet buyer planning to purchase 2,000 cars, the relative cost to evaluate different brands, including buying one of each and trying it for three months, is not prohibitive.

The content of value messages for high cost-of-search products, such as those on the right-hand side of Exhibit 4-2, should differ from those for low cost-of-search products in the left-hand column. High cost-of-search products are often more complex, and the value derived tends to be more uncertain prior to purchase. Personal services are one example. How can a hair salon communicate the value of its services to new customers? Unlike grocery stores, which frequently offer free samples for search goods such as packaged foods, a salon cannot offer free trials because the cost would be prohibitive. Although advertising might help new customers to become aware of the salon and its location, it would be difficult to craft an ad to clearly demonstrate the differential value relative to competitors, because the quality of a haircut can only be assessed after it has been purchased. Instead of using direct feature-benefit linkages, sellers of experience goods design value messages to reduce the uncertainty associated with their product's benefits. This can be done in a variety of ways such as relying on expert endorsements, using a high price to signal high value, providing money-back guarantees, or leveraging a known brand image to create an assurance that the customer will get high value following his purchase. Community banks have long used feature-benefit associations by focusing their messages on their key differentiators from national banks, such as personal service and understanding the needs of the local community. Advertising messages, for example, might display a happy family at a picnic in an ad related to home mortgages, parents with a graduate in cap and gown communicating the value of college loans, or a couple enjoying a vacation associated with their retirement account.

One of the most effective ways to influence value perceptions for experience goods is to subsidize trial. Health clubs offer free trial memberships. Suppliers of baby products pay hospitals to give away samples of baby formula to new parents. New brands of food products often spend significantly to induce trial with coupons, trial sizes, and free samples in addition to advertising. Their messages strive to increase buyer confidence that the product, when tried, will deliver enough psychological value to justify the choice. The challenge for marketers is to ensure that the discounts provided to induce trial do not undermine pricing to existing customers. This is why, advertisements for new trial promotions such as those used by companies such as Verizon, Comcast, and others showcase the performance, value, and packaging of their cable TV, Internet, and telephone services are accompanied by numerous restrictions in the fine print.

Type of benefits sought also influences communication strategy. Measurable monetary benefits such as profit, cost savings, or productivity motivate many purchases and translate directly into quantified value differences among competing brands. But, for other purchases, especially consumer products, psychological benefits such as comfort, appearance, pleasure, status, health, or personal fulfillment play a critical role in customer choice. Although the value of both psychological and monetary value drivers can be quantified, the way in which that data should be used in market communications differs. For goods in which monetary value drivers are most important to the customer, value quantification should be a central part of the message because the data calls attention to any gaps between the customer's *perceptions* of value and the *actual* monetary value of the product.

Exhibit 4-3 shows an example of a value-based selling tool used by sales people to develop customer-specific monetary value estimates with the

EXHIBIT 4-3   Spreadsheet Value Communication Tool

Variable	ENTER AMOUNTS HERE
ENTER these Inputs:	
Help Desk and/or Customer Service	
Total customers in impacted service area	4000
Average no. of trouble calls per day - normal	150
Avg. no. of trouble calls per day - outage incident	200
Duration of outage or network congestion - days	60
Average call duration in minutes	3.8
Help Desk wages & benefits - hourly	$ 11.50
Management Time	
No. Managers needed to resolve incident	1
Percent of Management time required	15%
Management loaded salary and benefits	$ 75,000
Other Costs	
Percent calls unresolved or receive bill credits	50%
Average billing credit (1 month)	$ 17.95
Percent impacted calls that are long distance	100%
Avg. cost per minute for 800 calls to help desk	$ 0.07
General	
Number of users per port	10
Calculation:	
Total ADDITIONAL man hours cust. service	190
Total cost for additional help desk & cust. service labor required	$ 2,185
Total cost for management time	$ 1,875
Total billing credits	$ 26,925
Total 800 call costs	$ 798
Avg. cost per call (less mgt. expense)	$ 9.97
TOTAL COST SAVINGS TO CUSTOMER (per outage incident)	$ 31,783
Estimated number PRI in impacted service area	17
COST SAVINGS PER PRI	$ 1,870

customer in the course of a sales call. Notice that the data and assumptions, derived from the value estimation model, are well documented and quite detailed. While inexperienced salespeople sometimes fear that they will be challenged if they make value claims, more experienced salespeople relish the opportunity to engage in give-and-take conversations about precisely how much value their product creates. Only in that context can a salesperson justify a price premium that might otherwise seem unacceptable to a business buyer who is not the actual user of the product.

When the important value drivers for a purchase decision are pyschological rather than monetary, it is best to avoid incorporating quantified value estimates into market communications, because value is subjective and will vary from individual to individual. However, one should not conclude that subjective values, such as those that a customer might reveal in a conjoint research study, cannot be influenced by communication. There are two ways to do this. One is to focus the message on high-value benefits that the customer might not have been thinking about when considering the differentiating features of the product. The second is to raise perceptions of the product's performance benefits that cannot be easily judged prior to experiencing them. Batteries all look and feel the same, even after one begins to use them. Not until they are entirely consumed can one actually know the life, and even then one would have no comparison unless two brands were bought and used side-by-side. Exhibit 4-4 shows the storyboard for a Duracell commercial. The advertisement is effective in clearly specifying the linkage between the Duracell battery's key differentiating feature of longer life with the benefits that might bring to a variety of customers. Notice that the ad does not mention price or estimates of monetary value its goal is to establish Duracell's differentiation.

In many cases, you may need to communicate both economic and psychological benefits for the same product to the same customers. Hybrid car buyers may want to feel good about protecting the environment, a psychological benefit a manufacturer could promote by reporting the car's reduced pollution ratings while showing it driving through unspoiled scenery. However, the price premium that buyers will pay for a hybrid car also depends on how much money they expect to save from improved gas mileage, an economic benefit the company could communicate by comparing the car's fuel efficiency with that of non-hybrid models.

Another example of combining financial and psychological value messages occurred when Johnson & Johnson had to justify a substantial price premium for its new and unique drug-coated coronary stent, used to keep clogged arteries open. J&J priced its stent at $3,500—250 percent higher than traditional uncoated stents and well in excess of the cost of the drug used to coat the stent. Such aggressive pricing aroused critics in the medical professions and in the public press, who accused the company of price gouging and challenged J&J to reconcile the value of the new product with its price. J&J did so by explaining the economic benefits to medical professionals. Stent implantation surgery costs more than $30,000, including the cost of the stent. But in

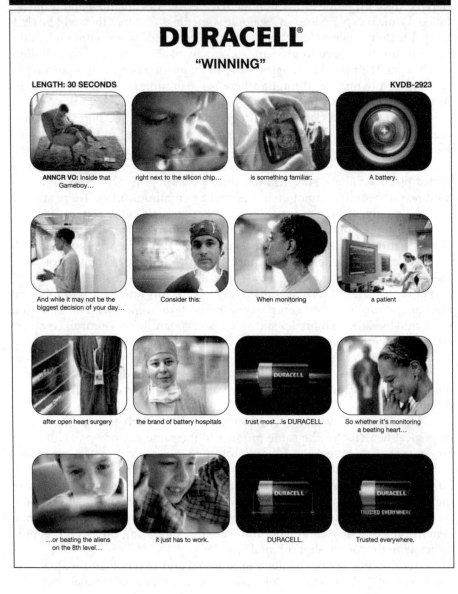

DURACELL®

"WINNING"

LENGTH: 30 SECONDS   KVDB-2923

ANNCR VO: Inside that   right next to the silicon chip...   is something familiar: A battery.
Gameboy...

And while it may not be the   Consider this: When monitoring   a patient
biggest decision of your day...

after open heart surgery   the brand of battery hospitals   trust most...is DURACELL.   So whether it's monitoring
a beating heart...

...or beating the aliens   it just has to work.   DURACELL.   Trusted everywhere.
on the 8th level...

20 percent of cases, an uncoated stent reclogs in less than a year, requiring a repeated procedure at another $30,000 cost. With J&J's new drug-eluting stent reducing the likelihood of reclogging, the surgery repeat rate fell to around 5 percent. Thus, the objective differentiation value from the smaller reclogging rate was $4,500: the 15 percent rejection rate difference multiplied by the cost of a second surgical procedure. In addition, patients received substantial psychological value in avoiding the risk and discomfort of a repeat procedure,

a benefit J&J emphasized to the public. The combination of economic and psychological justification enabled J&J to not only win a larger reimbursement from payers when surgeons used its drug-eluting stent but also to defuse the initial hostility and resistance to its price.

Adapting the Message to Purchase Context

Value-based communications must not only be adjusted for product characteristics such as cost of search and benefit type, but also for the customer's purchase context. Consider the challenge facing Lenovo, a leading maker of netbook computers. Netbooks are small computers with limited computing power designed to provide inexpensive access to the Internet and basic home office functions such as word processing. The value drivers for Lenovo's netbooks are well understood. Their light weight and small size make them highly portable for travelers or students. They are exceedingly reliable because of their simple design and the fact that they run only mature operating systems such as Microsoft's Windows XP.

Given the relatively clear linkage between product attributes and customer value drivers, crafting a value message would seem to be a straightforward exercise. But consider how the message would have to be adjusted depending on the specifics of the purchase context. Suppose the target customer was a long-time laptop buyer who was thinking about replacing his five-year-old Dell computer. Since this customer has not been in the market for a new computer since before netbooks were introduced, he might not even know what a netbook is, much less that Lenovo is a leading manufacturer. At this stage of his search, the communication objective is not to demonstrate the superior value of Lenovo's products, it is simply to make him aware of the benefits of netbooks that could make them a preferable option. This might be accomplished by purchasing numerous search terms on Google such as "new laptops," "laptop comparisons," or "laptop performance"—so that text ads for Lenovo netbooks appear next to search results for those terms—and then providing a link to a site describing the latest innovations in personal computing such as the advent of netbooks.

Having learned of netbook computers as a potential option for replacing his Dell laptop, the customer is ready to gather basic information about various alternatives so that he can narrow his options to a manageable set. The goal at this stage of the buying process is to create some assurances that Lenovo's product is differentiated and worthy of further investigation. This might be accomplished with messages describing the numerous awards the product has won or the high ratings it receives from third-party sites such as CNET.

It is not until the customer has progressed from awareness and through consideration of the product that he is ready to receive and process detailed product-related value messages. So, once again, the Lenovo marketing managers must be ready to adapt market communications to detail the superior performance of their computer versus other netbooks as well as versus full-sized laptops. This might be accomplished through product comparison tools on the Lenovo website or by working with channel partners to promote differentiated features of the product. Finally, after progressing through a number of steps in his buying process, the customer may be ready to think about price-value tradeoffs and to make a purchase.

The Buying Process

The Lenovo example illustrates the need to adapt value messages as customers move through the stages of their buying process. In some instances, such as for frequently purchased goods such as grocery items, the buying process is relatively short, and and the only opportunity to communicate value might be at the shelf front through label comparisons and point-of-sale displays. For purchases involving more complex, higher involvement goods such as computers, vacations, or automobiles, the buying process can be quite lengthy and involve extensive search and evaluation of information. In either case, the challenge is the same: how to adapt the value messages to influence customers' learning about goods as they move through the stages of the buying process.

Exhibit 4-5 illustrates the four basic stages of the buying process: *origination, information gathering, selection,* and *fulfillment* and describes the customer's learning process at each stage. **Origination** is the stage at which the customer becomes aware of a need and begins the search for a suitable offering to satisfy it. Origination of the buying process can be initiated in a variety of ways. Consider the example of a new car purchase. A customer might initiate a buying process because:

- Her 10-year-old car has broken down for the second time in a month
- A neighbor has just purchased a new convertible, and it seems like a fun idea to buy something more exciting than the customer's current sedan

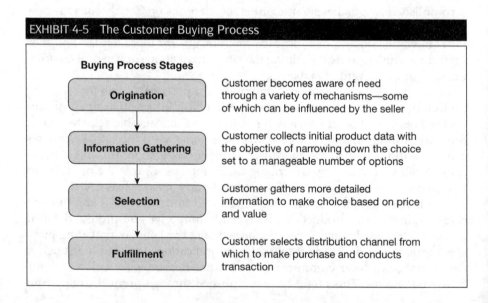

EXHIBIT 4-5   The Customer Buying Process

Buying Process Stages

Origination — Customer becomes aware of need through a variety of mechanisms—some of which can be influenced by the seller

Information Gathering — Customer collects initial product data with the objective of narrowing down the choice set to a manageable number of options

Selection — Customer gathers more detailed information to make choice based on price and value

Fulfillment — Customer selects distribution channel from which to make purchase and conducts transaction

- The family is expecting their first child, and they need more space and are concerned about safety
- The owner just lost her job and can't afford to make payments on her current car

The objective for value communications at the origination stage is to use value as a lever to encourage customers to consider a purchase within the category. Hyundai Motors did this admirably during the 2008–09 recession. At a time when North American new car sales had dropped by more than 50 percent, Hyundai developed a promotional campaign that boosted sales of its cars by 38 percent. The "Hyundai Assurance" campaign enabled a customer to purchase a new car and then return it with no penalty if he subsequently lost his job in the next year. It encouraged tens of thousands of customers to initiate a buying process for a new car because it was actually less risky than continuing payments on an existing car. In this case, Hyundai identified an emerging value driver (uncertainty about future income), developed a promotion to address the need, and then invested heavily in communicating the program to consumers.

The next stage of the buying process, **information gathering**, is a critically important stage for complex goods with a high cost of search. Historically, distribution channels were central to the search for information as customers turned to salespeople to explain their products and facilitate product comparisons. The prominent role of salespeople gave sellers considerable power to communicate value and influence the purchase decision. In recent years, however, the balance of power has shifted toward the customer because of the explosion of data available from websites and social networking channels. Instead of relying on potentially biased messages from the seller, customers can, with little effort, gather information from objective third parties and current users.

The ready access to information reduces the cost of search and places a greater burden on the seller to provide accurate and relevant information to the customer. The communication objective at this stage of the buying process is to increase the salience of the value drivers upon which your product has an advantage. Kodak has done an admirable job of highlighting critical value drivers in its advertising for computer printers (Exhibit 4-6). Most customers are well aware of the traditional pricing model for printers in which the printer is sold at a low price (often near cost) and the replacement ink cartridges are sold at a premium. By highlighting the high quality and low prices of its ink cartridges, Kodak encourages customers to consider the total cost of owership, including the price for ink. The greater the weight customers put on the cost of ink cartridges, the more they are likely to choose Kodak's printer over a competitor's.

Selection, the next stage in the buying process, involves winnowing the alternatives to a manageable number in order to conduct a more detailed product evaluation that ultimately leads to choice. The communication objective is to create awareness of your brand and its superiority in terms of the

EXHIBIT 4-6 Kodak Printer Ad

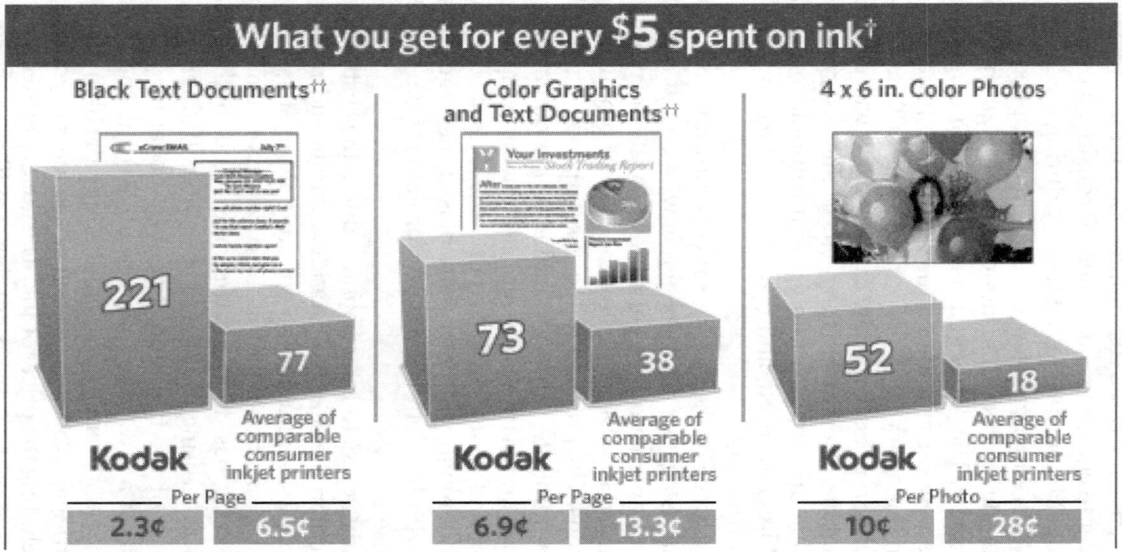

What you get for every $5 spent on ink†

Black Text Documents††

Color Graphics and Text Documents††

4 x 6 in. Color Photos

Black Text Documents
Per Page
Kodak: 221 — 2.3¢
Average of comparable consumer inkjet printers: 77 — 6.5¢

Color Graphics and Text Documents
Per Page
Kodak: 73 — 6.9¢
Average of comparable consumer inkjet printers: 38 — 13.3¢

4 x 6 in. Color Photos
Per Photo
Kodak: 52 — 10¢
Average of comparable consumer inkjet printers: 18 — 28¢

most salient value drivers. When it launched the Scion in 2008, Toyota did an excellent job of facilitating awareness of the car's advantages durng the selection stage. The Scion is a small, boxy vehicle targeted at 20-something first-time car buyers. Toyota recognized that this segment valued individuality and designed the Scion so that it could be configured in tens of thousands of ways by changing bumpers, lights, and a host of other options. But Toyota did not stop at simply providing a product that met the needs of its customers; it communicated those benefits through a highly interactive website containing visualization and design tools that enabled potential customers to customize their own vehicle and see precisely how their new car would look. Because Toyota adopted a fixed-price policy for the Scion (a departure from its other models), customers could explore different car configurations to stay within their budget while getting a car made just for them.

The final stage of the buying process, **fulfillment**, involves the selection of a purchase channel and then actual purchase. The value communication goal at this stage is to justify the price by using value to create a favorable framing for the price. For goods in which monetary value drivers are most relevant, marketers can use quantified estimates of value to frame price as a discount from value received instead of a premium over a competitor's price. Framing price in this way focuses on what a customer gains by purchasing your product (the discount from value) instead of what they lose (additional price over competition) and can have a powerful psychological influence on the purchase decision.

For goods in which psychological value drivers are most relevant to the customer, the goal is to develop messages that clearly demonstrate high value relative to price. This can be done through a variety of means, such as benchmarking against other products with well-understood value propositions. Exhibit 4-7 shows such an approach for a nutritional supplement called

EXHIBIT 4-7   Glucofast Ad

It's Time to Invest in Your Healthy Future . . .A serving of Glucofast™ costs **less than a cup of coffee at the single bottle price.** *What else can you do that will so greatly affect the quality of your life?*

Glucofast that helps to stablize blood sugar levels for diabetics. While the value of such a product could be quite high, the intangible nature of the value drivers makes comparison to price difficult. The company cleverly reframed the value by comparing it to the cost of a cup of coffee, implying that any reasonable person would naturally want better health for less than she spends for a hot drink.

Multiple Participants in the Buying Process

The buying process frequently involves more people than just the customer, since others participate by providing information, facilitating search, and influencing the purchase decision. Multiple participants are, in fact, the norm for purchases of high involvement goods characterized by complex offerings and, often, higher prices. Multiple participants are also common in most business markets, where purchasing is managed by professional procurement managers using sophisticated information systems and aggressive negotiation tactics. The addition of individuals to the buying process complicates the job of value communications because it forces marketers to adapt and deliver multiple messages at different points in the buying process.

To illustrate how value communications can be adapted for multiple individuals in the buying process, we turn to the example of a chemical company attempting to sell the value of a new chemical additive for a steel mini-mill. Suppose that the chemical provided an incremental $18 per ton in monetary value for the steel producer. However, the $18 is an aggregate, company-level estimate that is not equally relevant to the different stakeholders in the customer organization (see Exhibit 4-8). For example, the marketing manager may appreciate the total value estimate, but he is impacted directly only by the fact that the chemical additive enables him to penetrate new market segments. The melt shop foreman will value the reduced scrap rate, worth $2 per ton, but he will be less pleased about the $5 cost created by the additional process steps needed to incorporate the additive into the steel slurry. In the

EXHIBIT 4-8 Distribution of Value Across Organization

	Marketing Manager	R&D Manager	Melt-Shop Foreman	Finish Mill Supervisor	Procurement Agent
Reduces Scrap Costs		+	+		
Reduces Labor Costs				−	
Additional Process Steps			+		
New Market Entry	+				

Adapted from Leveragepoint Innovations, Inc. website: http://www.leveragepoint.com/lpi/index.html

end, the melt shop foreman may be negatively disposed toward the product because it lowers his organization's financial performance even though the overall value is positive. Finally, note the value impact for the procurement agent is neutral because her functional area has no operational involvement with the additive; she is only involved in negotiating the price.

The need to adapt marketing communications to the product and the customer's context makes creating effective value communications more challenging today than ever before. It is not sufficient to adapt the *content* of the message to the customer's learning needs at different stages of the buying process. You must also ensure that it is delivered to the right person at the right time in the buying process. Accomplishing this task requires meaningful insight about *what* value is created, *how* that value is generated across the organization, and *when* the participants in the buying process are ready to receive the value messages. Our research shows that successful value communications requires close coordination beween marketing and sales—a trait lacking in many of the organizations we surveyed. For those companies that make the investment to strategically communicate value, the return, in the form of more profitable pricing, can be substantial.

PRICE COMMUNICATION

Although it is easy to understand how value can be influenced, particularly the perceived value of psychological benefits, prices would seem to be hard data that are relatively easy to compare and communicate. But research over the years has repeatedly shown that people do not necessarily evaluate prices logically. Customers can perceive the same price paid in return for the same value differently depending on how it is communicated. We will examine four aspects of price perception and their implications for price communication: *proportional price evaluations, reference prices, perceived fairness*, and *gain-loss framing*.

Proportional Price Evaluations

Buyers tend to evaluate price differences proportionally rather than in absolute terms. For example, one research study asked customers if they would leave a store and go to one nearby to save $5 on a purchase. Of respondents who were told that the price in the first store was $15, some 68 percent said they would go to the other store to buy the product for $10. Of respondents who were told that the price in the first store was $125, only 29 percent would switch stores to buy the product for $120. Similar studies have replicated this effect, including research with business managers as respondents. When the $5 difference was proportionally more—33 percent of the lower price—it was more motivating than when it was proportionally a small part, 4 percent of the higher price.

Psychologists call the tendency to evaluate price differences proportionately the Weber-Fechner effect. It has clear implications for price communication.

For example, auto companies increased the motivational power of their rebate promotions when they offered the option of free financing instead of a fixed-dollar rebate only. Despite the fact that the present value of the interest saved was no more, and often less, than the value of the fixed-dollar rebate, free financing proved more popular. Why? Because eliminating 100 percent of the financing cost motivated consumers more than a 5 percent discount on a $20,000 car. Similarly, hotel chains have found it more effective to offer "free breakfast" or "free Internet access" with their rooms rather than offer a slightly lower price.

An important implication of the Weber-Fechner effect is that price change perceptions depend on the percentage, not the absolute difference, and that there are thresholds above and below a product's price at which price changes are noticed or ignored.[1] A series of smaller price increases below the upper threshold is more successful than one large increase. Conversely, buyers respond more to one large price cut below the lower threshold than to a series of smaller, successive discounts. For example, one full-service brokerage house raised its commissions every six months over a three-year period with little resistance from customers. Seeing this success, its competitor tried to match these increases in one large step and received intense criticism.

Reference Prices

A *reference price* is what a buyer considers a reasonable and fair price for a product. Reference prices are a critical issue in product line pricing decisions as illustrated in Exhibit 4-9 in which subjects in a controlled experiment were asked to choose among different models of microwave ovens. Researchers asked half the subjects to choose between two models (Emerson and Panasonic); the other half chose from among three models (Emerson, Panasonic I, and Panasonic II). Although 13 percent of the subjects were drawn to the top-end model, the Panasonic II, the largest impact from adding that third-model choice was on the Panasonic I, which gained 17 additional share points when

EXHIBIT 4-9 Reference Price Effects of a High-End Product		
	Choice%	
Microwave Oven Model	**Group 1 (n = 100)**	**Group 2 (n = 100)**
Panasonic II (1.1 cubic feet; regular price $199.99; saleprice 10% off)	—	13
Panasonic I (0.8 cubic feet; regular price $179.99; saleprice 35% off)	43	60
Emerson (0.5 cubic feet; regular price $109.99; saleprice 35% off)	57	27

Source: Itamar Simonson, and Amos Tversky, "Choice in Context: Tradeoff Contrast and Extremeness Aversion," *Journal of Marketing Research*, 29 (August 1992), 281–295.

it became the mid-priced choice. The implications of product-line pricing are clear. Adding a premium product to the product line may not necessarily result in overwhelming sales of the premium product itself. It does, however, enhance buyers' perceptions of lower-priced products in the product line and encourage low-end buyers to trade up to higher-priced models.

Another way in which marketers can influence reference prices is by suggesting potential reference points. For example, buyers' reference prices can be raised by stating a manufacturer's suggested price, a higher price charged previously ("Was $999, Now $799!"), or a higher price charged by competitors ("Their price $999, Our price $799!"). Research indicates that advertisements suggesting reference prices are very effective in influencing consumer durable product purchases (video cameras), particularly among less knowledgeable buyers who rely more on price to determine quality when making buying decisions.[2] Other studies have found that providing buyers with a suggested reference point enhances perceptions of value and savings, even if the advertised reference point is exaggerated.[3] Although buyers may discount or question the credibility of such claims, the claims still favorably influence perceptions and behaviors.[4]

Precisely how a product vendor presents pricing information is important. The order in which customers see pricing data influences their thinking about reference prices. In seminal research on this effect, two groups of experimental subjects saw the same sets of prices for a number of products in eight product classes. One group saw the prices in descending order (from the highest to the lowest); the other group saw them in ascending order (from the lowest to the highest). Researchers then asked each subject how much the same individual product in each product class was priced "high" or "low" relative to its value. From those judgments, the researchers calculated average reference prices for each product. The result: subjects who saw the prices in descending order formed higher reference prices than those who saw them in ascending order, even though both groups saw the same set of prices.[5] When forming their reference prices, buyers apparently give greater weight to the prices they see first.

These results clearly have important implications for price communication. In personal selling, this reference price effect implies that a salesperson should begin a presentation by first showing products above the customer's price range, even if the customer ultimately will choose from among cheaper products. This tactic, known as "top-down selling," is common for products as diverse as automobiles, luggage, and real estate. Direct-mail catalogs take advantage of this effect by displaying similar products in the order of most to least expensive. Within a retail store, the order effect has implications for product display. It implies, for example, that a grocery store might sell more low-priced (but high-margin) house brands by *not* putting them at eye level where they would be the first to catch the customer's attention. It may be preferable to have consumers see more expensive brands first and then look for the house brands.

Finally, promotional deals such as coupons, rebates, and special package sizes can influence reference prices strategically. Some marketers have argued that new products should be priced low to induce trial and thus build a market of repeat purchasers, after which the price can be raised. But if the low initial price lowers buyers' reference prices, it may actually affect repeat sales adversely. This is the result that some researchers have found. In one well-controlled study,[6] five new brands were introduced to the market in two sets of stores. During an introductory period, one set of stores sold the new brands at a low price without any indication that this was a temporary promotional price; the control stores sold the new brands at the regular price. As expected, the brands sold better during the introductory period where they were priced lower. During the weeks following the introduction, however, both sets of stores charged the regular price. In all five cases, sales during the post-introductory period were lower in the stores with the low initial price than in the control stores. Moreover, total sales for the introductory and post-introductory periods combined were greater in the control stores than in the stores where the low price initially stimulated demand. This and other studies showing similar results demonstrate the importance of discounting tactics. The seller should clearly establish a product's regular price and then promote the discount as a temporary price cut. Otherwise, initially low promotional prices designed to build an audience for product trials can establish low reference prices that will undermine the product's perceived value at regular prices later on.

Perceived Fairness

The concept of a "fair price" has bedeviled marketers for centuries. In the Dark Ages, merchants were put to death for exceeding public norms regarding the "just price." Even in modern market economies, putative "price gougers" often face press criticism, regulatory hassles, and public boycotts. Consequently, marketers should understand and attempt to manage perceptions of fairness. But what is fair? The concept of fairness appears to be totally unrelated to issues of supply and demand.[7] Naturally assumptions about the seller's profitability influence perceived fairness, but not entirely. Oil companies have often been accused of gouging, even when their profits were below average. When Hurricane Katrina disrupted gasoline supplies in the American south, gas station owners who raised prices were soundly criticized as "price gougers" even though they had only enough supply to serve those who wanted the product at that price. In contrast to the situation faced by oil companies, popular forms of entertainment (Disney World, for example, or state lotteries) are very profitable and expensive, yet their pricing escapes widespread criticism.

As these examples illustrate, research shows that perceptions of fairness are more subjective, and therefore, more manageable, than one might otherwise think.[8] Buyers apparently start by comparing what they think is the seller's likely margin now to what the seller earned in the past, or to what others earn in similar purchase contexts. In a famous experiment, people imagined that they were lying on a beach, thirsty for a favorite brand of beer, and that a friend was walking to a nearby location and would bring back beer if the price was not too high. Researchers asked the subjects to specify the maximum amount that they would pay. Subjects did not know that half of them had been told that the friend would patronize a "fancy resort hotel" while the other half had been told that the friend would buy from "a small grocery store." Although these individuals would not themselves visit or enjoy the amenities of the purchase location, the median acceptable price of those who expected the beer to come from the hotel—$2.65—was dramatically higher than the median acceptable price given by those who expected it to come from the grocery store—$1.50.[9]

Presumptions about the seller's motive influence customers' perceived fairness judgments. A seller justifying a higher price with a "good" motive (for example, funding employee health insurance, improving service levels) makes the price more acceptable than does a "bad" motive (for example, exploiting a market shortage to increase stockholder profits). Research suggests that companies with good reputations, such as Disney, are much more likely to get the benefit of the doubt about their motives. Those with unpopular reputations (for example, oil companies) are likely to find their motives suspect.[10]

Finally, perceptions of fairness seem to be related to whether the price is paid to maintain a standard of living, or is paid to improve a standard of living. People consider products that maintain a standard to be "necessities," although humanity has probably survived without them for most of its history. Charging a high price for a necessity is generally considered unfair. For example, people object to what they perceive as high prices for life-saving drugs because they feel that they shouldn't have to pay to be healthy. After all, they were healthy last year without having to buy prescriptions and medical advice. People react similarly to rent increases. Yet, the same individuals might buy a new car, jewelry, or a vacation without objecting to equally high prices or price increases.[11]

Fortunately, perceptions of fairness can be managed. Companies that frequently adjust prices to reflect supply and demand or to segment buyers with different price sensitivities are careful to set the "regular" price at the highest possible level, rather than at the average or most common price. This enables them to "discount" when necessary to move product during slow times (a "good" motive), rather than have to increase prices when demand is strong (a "bad" motive).[12] Similarly, because buyers believe that companies should not have to lose money, it's often best to blame price increases on rising costs to serve customers. Buyers believe that is fair, such as when petroleum prices increase. Landlords who raise rents should announce property improvements at the same time. Innovative companies raise prices more successfully when they are launching a new product and say that they are recovering development costs.

Gain–Loss Framing

A final consideration in price communication involves how the price is presented to customers, who tend to evaluate prices in terms of gains or losses from an expected price point.[13] How they frame those judgments affects the attractiveness of the purchase. To illustrate this effect, grounded in *prospect theory*, ask yourself which of the following two gasoline stations you'd be more willing to patronize, assuming that you deem both brands to be equally good and you would always pay with a credit card.

- Station A sells gasoline for $2.20 per gallon, but gives a $0.20 per gallon discount if the buyer pays with cash.
- Station B sells gasoline for $2.00 per gallon, but charges a $0.20 per gallon surcharge if the buyer pays with a credit card.

Of course, the economic cost of buying gasoline from either station is identical. Yet, most people find the offer from station A more attractive than the one from station B. The reason is that people place more psychological importance on avoiding "losses" than on capturing equal size "gains." Also, both the gains and losses of an individual transaction are subject, independently, to diminishing returns, as one would expect from the Weber-Fechner effect we discussed earlier: A given change has less psychological impact the larger the base to which it is added or subtracted.

In our gas station example, cash buyers prefer A, where they receive the psychological benefit of earning a discount, a "gain" to them. Paying the same $2.00 net price per gallon at station B, which offers no explicit discount, does not provide a psychological benefit. Credit card buyers also prefer station A, mainly because station B's credit card surcharge creates a "loss," a negative psychological benefit to be avoided. Paying the same $2.20 net price per gallon at station A, which requires no explicit surcharge, does not provide a psychological benefit, positive or negative.

Buyers otherwise indifferent to paying by cash or credit will not be indifferent to stations A or B despite the sellers' economic value equivalence; such buyers would always pay cash to get the lowest price but would likely choose A to get the psychological satisfaction unavailable at B. Prospect theory has many implications for price communication:

- To make prices less objectionable, make them opportunity costs (gains forgone) rather than out-of-pocket costs. Banks often waive fees for checking accounts in return for maintaining a minimum balance. Even when the interest forgone on the funds in the account exceeds the charge for checking, most people choose the minimum balance option. People find it less painful to pay for things such as insurance or mutual funds with payroll deductions instead of buying them outright.

- When a product is priced differently to different customers and at different times, set the list price at the highest level and give most people discounts. This type of pricing is so common that we take it for granted. Colleges, for example, charge only a small portion of customers the list price and give everyone else discounts. To those who pay at or near the full price, the failure to receive more of a discount (a gain forgone) is much less objectionable than if they were asked to pay a premium because they are not star students, athletes, or good negotiators.

• *Unbundle gains and bundle losses.* Many companies sell offerings consisting of many individual products and services. For example, a printing company not only prints brochures but also helps design the job, matches colors, schedules the job to meet the buyer's time requirements, and so on. To maximize the perceived value, the seller should identify each of these as a separate product or service and promote the value of each one explicitly ("Look at all you get in our Deluxe Package!"), unbundling the gains. However, rather than asking the buyer to make individual expenditure decisions, the seller should identify the customer's needs and offer a package price to meet them ("One price brings it all to you"), bundling the loss. If the buyer objects to the price, the seller can take away a service, which will then make that service appear as a stand-alone "loss" that will be hard to give up.

Strategists who think only in terms of objective economic values might find these principles far-fetched. One might argue that buyers in these cases could easily think of the same choices as entirely different combinations of "gains" and "losses." That is precisely the point that prospect theorists make: Buyers can frame the same transactions in many different ways, each implying somewhat different behavior. Researchers have shown that changing how people think about their gains and losses in otherwise identical transactions consistently alters their behavior.

Summary

How customers respond to your pricing is determined by more than the value delivered by your product and the price you charge. It is also influenced by how they evaluate your product and your price. If you leave those judgments to chance, you are likely to be paid much less or sell much less than you could. Most customers lack the time or the incentive to fully inform themselves about their alternatives and to evaluate the information they do have. If you want them to recognize your value, you have to make the process easier for them by supplying them with information about your offer and what you think it should mean to them.

You also need to actively manage how you communicate the price to minimize adverse feelings about paying it. By controlling the visibility of price differences, the formulation of references, and the perceptions of fairness, you can reduce negative reactions to your pricing without reducing your overall margins.

Notes

1. Kent B. Monroe and Susan M. Petroshius, "Buyers' Perceptions of Price: An Update of the Evidence," in *Perspectives in Consumer Behavior,* 3rd ed., ed. H. Kassarjian and T. S. Robertson, (Glenview, IL: Scott Foresman, 1981, 43–55).

2. Gerald E. Smith and Lawrence H. Wortzel, "Prior Knowledge and Effectiveness Suggested Frames of Reference in Advertising," *Psychology and Marketing* 14(2) (March 1997) 121–43.

94   Chapter 4 • Price and Value Communication

3. Joel E. Urbany, William O Bearden, and Dan C. Weilbaker, "The Effect of Plausible and Exaggerated Reference Prices on Consumer Perceptions and Price Search," *Journal of Consumer Research*, 15 (June 1988): 95–110.
4. See Eric N. Berkowitz and John R. Walton, "Contextual Influences on Consumer Price Responses: An Experimental Analysis," *Journal of Marketing Research* 17 (August 1980): 349–358; Albert J. Della Betta, Kent B. Monroe, and John M. McGinnis, "Consumer Perceptions of Comparative Price Advertisements," *Journal of Marketing Research* 18 (November 1981): 415–427: Cynthia Fraser, Robert E. Hite, and Paul L. Sauer, "Increasing Contributions in Solicitation Campaigns: The Use of Large and Same Anchorpoints," *Journal of Consumer Research* 15 (September 1988): 284–287: Mary F Mobley, William O. Bearden, and Jesse E. Teel, "An Investigation of Individual Responses to Tensile Price Claims," *Journal of Consumer Research* 15 (September 1988): 273–279; James G. Barnes, " Factors Influencing Consumer Reaction to Retail Newspaper Sale Advertising," Proceedings, Fall Educators' Conference (Chicago: American Marketing Association, 1975): 471–477; Edward A. Blair and E. Laird Landon, Jr., "The Effects of Reference Prices in Retail Advertisements," *Journal of Marketing*, 45, no. 2 (Spring 1981): 61–69; John Liefeld and Louise A. Heslop, "Reference Prices and Deception in Newspaper Advertising," *Journal of Consumer Research* 11 (March 1985): 868–876. See also Robert E. Wilkes, "Consumer Usage of Base Price Information," *Journal of Retailing* 48 (Winter 1972): 72–85; Sadrudin A. Ahmed and Gary M. Gulas, "Consumers' Perception of Manufacturers' Suggested List Price," *Psychological Reports* 50 (1982): 507–518; Murphy A. Sewall and Michael H. Goldstein, "The Comparative Advertising Controversy: Consumer Perception of Catalog Showroom Reference Prices," *Journal of Marketing* 43 (Summer 1979): 85–92.
5. Albert J. Della Betta and Kent Monroe, "The Influence of Adaptation Levels on Subjective Price Perceptions," in *Advances in Consumer Research*, 1973, Proceedings of the Association for Consumer Research, vol. 1, ed. Peter Wright and Scott Ward (Urbana, IL: ACR, 1974, 359–369.).
6. A. Door et al., "Effect of Initial Selling Price on Subsequent Sales," *Journal of Personality and Social Psychology* 11 (1969): 345–350.
7. Daniel Kahneman, Jack L. Knetsch, and Richard H. Thaler, "Fairness As a Constraint on Profit Seeking: Entitlements In the Market," *American Economic Review* 76, no. 4 (September 1986): 728–741.
8. Joel Urbany, Thomas Madden, and Peter Deckson, "All's Not Fair in Pricing: An Initial Look at the Dual Entitlement Principle," *Marketing Letters* 1, no. 1 (1990): 17–25; Marielza Matins and Kent Monroe, "Perceived Price Fairness: A New Look at an Old Construct," *Advances in Consumer Research*, vol. 21 (Provo, UT: Association for Consumer Research 1994, 75–78).
9. Richard Thaler, "Mental Accounting and Consumer Choice," *Marketing Science* 4 (Summer 1985): 206.
10. Margaret C. Campbell, "Perceptions of Price Unfairness: Antecedents and Consequences," *Journal of Marketing Research* 36 (May 1999): 187–199.
11. Daniel Kahneman, Jack L. Knetsch, and Richard H. Thaler, "The Endowment Effect, Kiss Aversion, and Status Quo Bias," *Journal of Eco-*

nomic Perspectives, 5, no. 1 (Winter 1991): 203–204.

12. Campbell, *op. cit.*

13. Daniel Kahneman and Amos Tversky, "Prospect Theory: An Analysis of Decision Under Risk," *Econometrica* 47 (March 1979): 263–291; Daniel Kahneman and Amos Tversky, "The Psychology of Preferences," *Scientific American* 246 (January 1982): 162–170; Daniel Kahneman and Amos Tversky, "Choices, Values, and Frames," *American Psychologist* 39, no. 4

(April 1984): 341–350; Amos Tversky and Daniel Kahneman, The Framing of Decisions and Psychology of Choice," in *New Directions for Methodology of Social and Behavioral Science: Question Framing and Response Consistency,* no. 11 (San Francisco: Jossey-Bass, March 1982); Amos Tversky and Daniel Kahneman, "Advances in Prospect Theory: Cumulative Representation of Uncertainty," *Journal of Risk and Uncertainty* 5, no. 4 (1992).

CHAPTER 5

Pricing Policy
Managing Expectations to Improve Price Realization

How should a company respond when a key customer announces that its next contract will be determined by a "reverse auction"? How should it respond when some of its customers are experiencing an economic downturn and ask for help? How should it deal with customers who resist a price increase necessitated by increased costs that all suppliers are experiencing? Responding to such challenges with ad hoc "price exceptions" rewards those customers who are the most aggressive negotiators, and ultimately alienates a company's best customers. Those aggressive customers slow the sales process with increasing requests for "exceptions" that have to be sold internally. And they preclude any ability to exercise price leadership since it is difficult for competitors to adapt their strategies to prices that are neither consistent nor predictable.

A better solution to this challenge is to treat each request for a "price exception" as an opportunity to create a pricing policy that precludes the need for such requests in the future. *Pricing policies* are rules or habits, either explicit or cultural, that determine how a company varies its prices when faced with factors other than value and cost that threaten its ability to achieve its objectives. Some companies enforce rules regarding who in the organization has the authority to approve discounts: a sales rep up to 5 percent, his regional manager 15 percent, the vice president of sales 25 percent. Although these rules are often called "pricing policies," they are not. They are personnel policies designed to mitigate the adverse consequences of undefined policies. Pricing policies would state explicitly the criteria that, say, a regional sales manager should use when deciding whether or not to exercise his authority to grant a 10 percent discount. Such a policy would be applied the same way by all sales managers to all similar requests for exceptions.

A customer's purchase behavior is influenced by more than just the price and the product or service that the seller offers. It is also influenced by the expectations that the seller has created. Past experience, a buyer's own and that of others about which he has become aware, drives expectations about what conditions are necessary to get a good price, and those expectations in turn drive the buyer's future purchase behavior.

For example, a retail consumer may believe that a new fall fashion is well worth the price asked for it in September but still not buy it if she expects that the store, following its past behavior, will soon have a 20 percent off promotion when the price will be even better. A retail pricing policy of predictable discounting trains many retail consumers to wait for "the sale price." To change that expectation, some retailers adopt and publicize an "everyday low price" policy, while others maintain regular discounting but offer "30-day price protection" enabling the customer to receive a credit for the difference between the regular and the sale price within 30 days of purchase. Changing the expectation that waiting is rewarded encourages more people to buy at the offered price, thus reducing the need to discount the price later. The same dynamic plays out—only more so—when businesses sell products and services to business customers who have more ways to influence the prices they receive through their purchase behavior.

The behavior of sellers too is driven by expectations inferred from past experience. The seller's most recent experience in the example above is that sales go up a lot during a period of discounts, but fall increasingly short of expectations during the weeks before discounting. If the seller forms expectations based only on that experience, he is likely to become even more aggressive in the discounting—perhaps starting the discount even a week earlier in the quarter to take advantage of customers' increasing "price sensitivity." For sellers to see the value in creating something like a 30-day price guarantee, they need to see the whole picture (as illustrated by Exhibit 5-1). Rather than simply reacting to past customer behavior, they

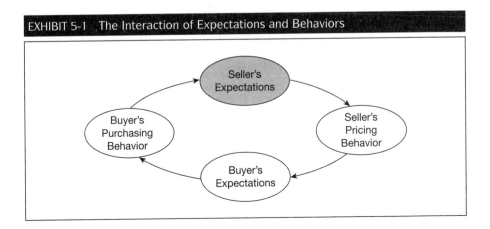

EXHIBIT 5-1   The Interaction of Expectations and Behaviors

need to look forward to understand how a systematic change in their behavior (for example, a new policy) could affect customers' expectations in a way that would affect their future behavior.

The difference between tactical pricing and strategic pricing is the difference between reacting to past customer behavior and acting to influence future customer behavior. If a seller or buyer understands only that half of the process that involves her own expectations or behaviors, it is impossible to be strategic. Unfortunately, in many business-to-business markets, where high-volume repeat purchasers negotiate their prices, buyers are ahead of sellers in thinking strategically (Exhibit 5-2). Under the rubric of "strategic sourcing," they have developed systematic and sophisticated policies for managing suppliers' expectations, while sellers often understand little about how expectations are formed in the buying organization. Buyers have goals and a long-term strategy for driving down acquisition costs, while suppliers rarely have comparable long-term strategies for raising or at least preserving margins.

For example, buyers often adroitly separate discussion of terms and service levels from the discussion of price—often leaving them off the request-for-proposal (RFP) to make all suppliers more comparable during a

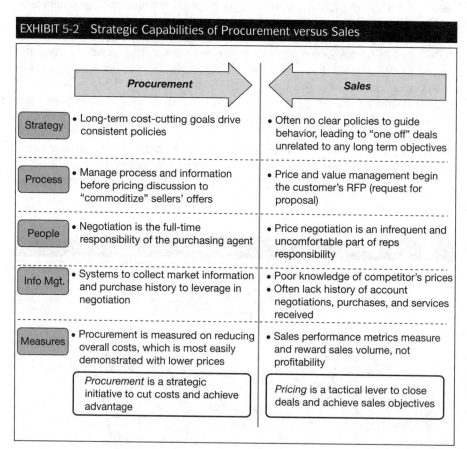

EXHIBIT 5-2   Strategic Capabilities of Procurement versus Sales

	Procurement	Sales
Strategy	• Long-term cost-cutting goals drive consistent policies	• Often no clear policies to guide behavior, leading to "one off" deals unrelated to any long term objectives
Process	• Manage process and information before pricing discussion to "commoditize" sellers' offers	• Price and value management begin the customer's RFP (request for proposal)
People	• Negotiation is the full-time responsibility of the purchasing agent	• Price negotiation is an infrequent and uncomfortable part of reps responsibility
Info Mgt.	• Systems to collect market information and purchase history to leverage in negotiation	• Poor knowledge of competitor's prices • Often lack history of account negotiations, purchases, and services received
Measures	• Procurement is measured on reducing overall costs, which is most easily demonstrated with lower prices	• Sales performance metrics measure and reward sales volume, not profitability
	Procurement is a strategic initiative to cut costs and achieve advantage	*Pricing* is a tactical lever to close deals and achieve sales objectives

bidding process. They then pick a supplier who can meet their high service requirements, which are specified only after the bidding process. Sellers, on the other hand, often lack the corresponding ability to unbundle services to meet just the specs in the RFP, which would enable them to charge individually for better terms and services over-and-above those specified.

Buyers have full-time professionals to negotiate prices who are separate from those who specify or use the product, while the seller's counterpart is a rep whose main job is customer service. The purchasing professional is rewarded for cutting acquisition costs or establishing conditions that increase future leverage, while the typical sales professional is rewarded simply for making the sale. The purchasing professional usually has access to a database of information about all the offers and counteroffers that the supplier has made to his company in the past, and often about the pricing and terms that other companies have done. A new sales rep usually knows only what is in the previous contract and on the invoices.

POLICY DEVELOPMENT

The process for developing good policies involves treating each request for a price exception as a request to create or to change a policy that could be applied repeatedly in the future. The more requests, the more likely it is that a policy, or the more fundamental price structure, is in need of review. In the beginning, if the firm has few clearly defined or consistently followed policies, a lot of potential deals will end up as requests for price exceptions. As new, well-thought-out policies are put in place, customers and sales reps will learn that ad hoc exceptions to policies will not be granted. The only requests for "special pricing" that should be considered are those involving situations not already covered by a policy. Creating the policies is not the responsibility of sales reps or local sales managers, since they do not have the perspective on the overall market or the authority to make the changes required to remedy this imbalance. It is the responsibility of management at a market level.

Putting a "no exceptions" stake in the ground is a key to making pricing decisions that are profit enhancing. Most discount proposals, whether to reduce price to win business or to increase price to exploit tight supply, have an immediate reward that is obvious but a corresponding cost that is delayed, diffused over more accounts, and less transparent. In contrast, pricing by policy forces companies to consider the impact on the entire market when making a pricing decision. It should involve asking whether it makes sense to establish a policy that the proposed pricing option could be offered to all customers like this one and still be profitable. Making the decision a policy question forces decision makers to think through the broader and longer-term implications of the precedents they are setting.

Pricing policies cover more than just discounting. They include the company's pattern for passing along changes in raw materials costs (such as requiring that all long-term contracts allow for adjustments versus adjusting only after a fixed-price contract expires) and its pattern for inducing product trials.

Pricing policies also deal with how a company will respond to low price offers made to its customers by a competitor. Any pattern creates expectations for how the company will deal with such issues in the future, and thus can change customers' future buying behavior. Policies also influence how your sales reps sell and which ones succeed. Who is most rewarded at the company: the sales rep who sells at high margins by understanding customers well enough to communicate value, or the rep who drives big volume at a few accounts by understanding his company's management well enough to make the case internally for price exceptions?

Ideally, policies are transparent, are consistent, and enable companies to address pricing challenges proactively. If your policies are transparent, customers need not engage in threats and misinformation to learn the trade-offs you are willing to make. Airlines have transparent pricing rules that none of us like (low prices only when purchased well in advance, charges for making changes, no transfer of tickets to another passenger), but we accept them because we know what they are. Consistency communicates that it is impossible to "game the system" by contacting multiple points in the company to find the best deal. Communicating policies proactively is much less contentious than telling a customer reactively that a proposal of theirs has, after some delay for review, been rejected.

Analyzing pricing challenges and developing policies to deal with them is an ongoing process, one that is generally the responsibility of a pricing staff overseen by a group of managers with collective responsibility to preserve or improve profitability. Over time, a company's policies can become a source of competitive advantage—creating expectations that drive better behavior on the part of customers, competitors, and sales reps and empowering sales reps to offer creative solutions more quickly and with less wasted effort selling their ideas internally. Still, building that set of policies takes time, and policy-based pricing will lose organizational support if few of the initial applications produce positive results. To avoid that problem, the remainder of this chapter will identify the common challenges that call for policy-based solutions and describe successful policies that we have seen for dealing with each of them.

POLICIES FOR RESPONDING TO PRICE OBJECTIONS

The most common, and therefore, most important domain for policy development falls into the arena of responding to price objections from customers with whom pricing involves a process of negotiation. The lack of policies for dealing with price objections is not only a challenge for companies that sell directly. Consumer goods manufacturers face just as much price pressure from powerful retailers—such as Wal-Mart, Carrefour, Home Depot, and Staples—as they do from consumers who switch to alternatives because of price.

The Problem with Ad Hoc Negotiation

To illustrate the problem created in price negotiation by non-existent or poorly enforced pricing policies, think about how the process commonly plays out badly for the seller. Imagine that to cover the increased costs of raw materials, your company announces a 5 percent price increase. When sales reps attempt to get their next orders at those higher prices, purchasing agents confront them with the assertion that the increase is unacceptable. How each sales rep responds to that resistance is critical to the success of this and any future price increases. Unfortunately, most companies lack consistent policies for how to respond, so that the mistakes of even a few can leave the company worse off than if it never even attempted the increase. The reason is that the response will create an expectation among the company's customers about how to get a better price.

Let's look first at what happens when a company has poorly defined or unenforced pricing policies. Imagine that when confronted by the purchasing agent, the sales rep looks flustered and says only that he cannot change any pricing without the approval of his manager. This simple statement will make all future negotiations much more difficult. The sales rep has told the purchasing agent (1) that his company makes price concessions to some customers and (2) that to get one, or at least to get one at the highest level, requires resisting until a sales manager is involved. In short, by communicating that it makes exceptions, the company and the sales rep have lost their price integrity. Given that lack of integrity, the purchasing agent realizes that either she must figure out how to exploit it or she will be paying higher prices than other buyers pay. A purchasing agent's worst nightmare is that someone discovers that a competitor is buying the same product from the same supplier for less than she was able to negotiate.

Buyers exploit a lack of price integrity by adopting defensive negotiation tactics. These usually involve purchasing policies that shift the negotiation from one where the seller manages the buyer's expectations to one where the buyer manages the seller's expectations. The expectation that the purchasing agent wants to create is that the buying company views the seller's product or service as essentially a commodity for which there are easy, cheaper substitutes. Creating this expectation involves minimizing direct contact between sales reps and users who could acknowledge the value of differences. It also involves creating at least the impression of a highly competitive market for the customer's business.

We have seen many cases where a company lost market share at an account because it became more flexible in negotiating price exceptions. Once customers learn that their price is dependent upon creating substitutes, they qualify second and third sources for their business and solicit lower bids with promises of a higher share. Of course, they give their preferred supplier a "last look" chance to match those lower bids to retain a larger share. And every time the preferred supplier matches, it reinforces the value of maintaining competitive suppliers and minimizes the expectation that the supplier's differentiation has a justifiable economic value.

Seeing this erosion of market share causes sellers to believe that their products and services have become more commoditized. Because they fear additional sales loss, they discount more and often cut expenditures for the differentiation that customers appear not to appreciate. If the company lacking price integrity is the market leader, the damage from a lack of price integrity is compounded. Competitors never know the real price against which they are competing, since there is no consistency. Their information about what you are offering on any particular deal comes from the purchasing agent who has an incentive to under-represent the prices and forgets to mention restrictive terms to qualify for them. As a result, competitors will on average imagine that the leader is pricing lower than it is, and so they will price lower than necessary to win sales.

The Benefits of Policies for Price Negotiation

Now consider the impact on expectations when the same scenario is managed with strong pricing policies that maintain price integrity. Your company has announced a 5 percent price increase to cover rising raw materials costs. When confronted by the purchasing agent, the sales rep knows that his company will back him in holding firm on the increase, even at the cost of a sale. He confidently explains to the purchasing agent why all suppliers will face the same cost increases and so cannot maintain their same quality and service levels without passing it along. Many purchasing agents will still refuse to accept the result at that point unless the firm's price integrity has already been proven in the past. Some may only be bluffing. Others may be prudently planning to check what other suppliers are doing before deciding to accept the increase. Others, however, may be operating under a mandate to keep total costs from increasing.

Although your price increase is creating a problem for these buyers, it is the seed of an opportunity to change their behavior by changing their expectations. The sales rep who works for a company with pricing policies can be armed with more than just the confidence that he can lose the sale. He can also be empowered with pre-approved value trade-offs and discount policies that in a policy-free company would require review by someone higher up. The sales rep can build credibility with the customer by offering the customer win-win, or at least win–not lose trade-offs. If the purchasing department could get the multiple users in the company to place one consolidated order each month rather than many smaller orders, the sales rep explains, his company can cut the buyer's shipping costs. If the purchaser would buy a wider variety of products from the seller under a multi-year contract, it would be possible to reach the volume threshold for end-of-year rebates exceeding 5 percent. If the purchaser would allow the seller's technical people to talk with the users, they might be able to suggest some process improvements to cut waste by more than enough to offset the price increase.

To take advantage of these trade-offs, the purchasing agent would need to change purchasing behavior. To make the trade-offs, she would need to bring actual users into the decision process to evaluate them. If the policies are well designed, she will learn either that savings can come from working with this supplier rather than by threatening him, or that she already has the best deal available for her company. Once she develops the expectation that the best way to minimize cost is to work with her sales rep and that there is no reward to be had from deceiving him, she will become more open with information that enables the seller to identify other trade-offs that could be mutually beneficial. As buyers come to trust the process, there is no need for the seller to maintain multiple suppliers simply to gain leverage in price negotiations. This does not mean that the process will be free of conflict, anger, or occasional threats. But it will force the interactions toward a focus on value.

Regaining the ability to capture value in negotiated pricing requires more than training the sales force on "SPIN selling" or any other sales program. Value-based sales tactics need to be backed by a pricing process that is consistent with those same principles. Unless a company is selling a unique product to each customer, pricing should not be driven by a series of requests for one-off price approvals from the sales force, since the sales force then becomes little more than a conduit for strategies designed by the customers. Changes in price should be driven by consistent policies designed to achieve the seller's market-level objectives. When the policies are aligned with those objectives and clearly articulated for the sales force, the sales reps (as well as distributors and channel partners) are empowered and motivated to sell on value rather than on price.

Policies for Different Buyer Types

Given the growing power of some buyers, and the increasing transparency of pricing to all buyers, any profitable and sustainable solution for dealing with price objections must be codified in policies. But what policies? The answer to this question depends upon the type or types of buyers from whom you are encountering the objection. Exhibit 5-3 illustrates four general types of buyers, who differ in the importance to them of differentiation among suppliers.

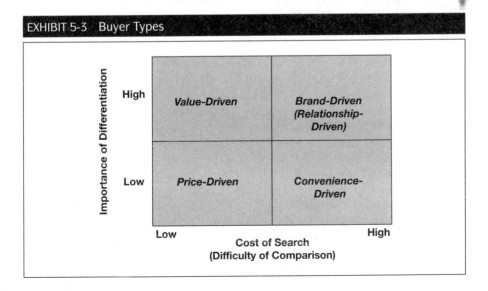

EXHIBIT 5-3 Buyer Types

within the product class (for example, how important is durability or immediate availability when buying office furniture), and the cost of search among suppliers relative to the potential savings. You need policies that enable your company to respond appropriately to price objections driven by the different motivations of these different types of buyers.

Value buyers purchase a disproportionate share of sales volume in most business-to-business markets. They have sophisticated purchasing departments that consolidate and buy large volumes, and they can afford the cost to search and evaluate many alternatives before making a purchase. They are trying to manage both the benefits in the purchase to get all the features and services that are important to them, as well as to push down the price as low as possible. The policies that the sales rep needs to deal with value buyers are ones that empower him or her to make trade-offs, while at the same time offering a defense against pressure on price alone.

The key to creating value-based policies is to understand every way in which your product or service might add more value to the customer than the product or service of a competitor, and every way that a change in a customer's behavior could add more value to you. Then create a set of pre-approved trade-offs. For example, if a source of your value is higher quality service that competitors do not offer, you need to find a way that the service can be unbundled even if that is not the way you prefer to deliver your product. It may not even save you any money to unbundle it. But it gives the sales rep a low-cost alternative to walking away or simply giving in on the price without any cost to the buyer for the concession. With that lower cost option, the rep can call the bluff of purchasing agents at companies that do in fact value your differentiation. If too many buyers are actually taking the low service, lower price option, it is time for management to reconsider whether the service differentiation is really worth what they think it is.

The other option is to think of things the customer can do for you that would justify a discount. For example, could you create an end-of-year rebate based upon the customer buying more broadly from your product line, increasing volume by at least 20 percent, establishing a regular steady order that will not be changed less than seven days before the shipping date? Each of these illustrates a principle that we call *give-get negotiation*. The policy for dealing with value-driven buyers is that no price concession should ever be made that does not involve getting something from the other side. The price concession need not be fully covered by any cost savings to the seller, but it should eliminate any differentiation that the buyer claims not to value. This principle, which if the sales reps are empowered with pre-approved trade-offs can be established at the moment when the purchaser raises the price objection, educates the buyer that there is always a cost to price concessions. That cost puts a limit on the buyer's willingness to pursue price concessions indefinitely. Once purchasers understand these new rules of the game, it also creates an incentive for them to think of new trade-offs that they might propose (for example, partnering on developing a new product) that would warrant consideration by the seller's management as a new policy.

The fear that too many companies have is that if they adopt give-get tactics rather than simply concede to price objections with an ad hoc deal, they will lose too many value-driven customers. The problem with this thinking is that if you never test it, you never know whether the objections are driven by a lack of value or simply the expectations they you have created that objections are rewarded with concessions. Moreover, because value buyers know their market, they sometimes do not even give you the benefit of a price objection. You just lose their business because your product or service levels are beyond what they need.

By proposing trade-offs, you can learn from the research what value buyers are thinking. By listening to how they respond to proposed trade-offs, you can gauge whether the problem is that you are offering too much or that you are uncompetitive for the same things. If your proposed trade-offs are rejected and you lose business, then your prices may not be competitive. In that case, it is better to lower your price proactively by policy than to wait for each customer to object. Price integrity is worth more in the long run than the extra revenue you can earn for a while from the customers who are slowest to recognize that you no longer offer a good value.

Brand buyers (also known as *relationship buyers*) are those for whom differentiation, particularly of the type that is difficult to determine prior to purchase, is valuable but the cost to evaluate all suppliers to determine the best possible deal is just too high. Perhaps the buyer is new to the market and just lacks the experience to make a good judgment. The buyer will buy a brand that is well-known for delivering a good product with good service without considering cheaper but riskier alternatives. Other times, the buyer may have had positive past experience with a current supplier and the cost to evaluate another supplier versus any potential savings is too high; consequently, the buyer becomes "loyal" to the seller.

A price objection from a relationship buyer, or a customer satisfaction survey showing a decline in brand buyers' belief that the company offers fair value for money versus competitors, is something to take very seriously. It can signal one of two things: that the brand buyer has been disappointed by the supplier relative to expectations or has learned something about market prices that leads him to expect that the price he is paying for security is excessive. A price concession is never a good response in the first case and may not be in the latter.

If the issue is a disappointment, it is important to understand the nature of it and make recompense, rather than giving a price concession going forward; such a concession signals to this customer that it is reasonable to expect such disappointment in the future, and the adjusted price reflects that less-than-adequate result. A client of ours in the printing industry failed to print and ship the client's catalog when promised which, since the catalog was for seasonal merchandise, represented a serious breach of trust. The customer opened the catalog bid to other printers for the next year and the sales rep, having been berated by the customer, felt certain that the only way to keep the account was to slash the price. After understanding the high value that this customer placed on the quality and technical relationship that they had built up over many years with the printer's technical personnel, we proposed a different approach.

The president of the printer went to see the president of this mid-size catalog company to express personally that what happened reflected an unacceptable misunderstanding of how important the promised mail date was to their business. He explained how, because the client was not one of the largest in the printing plant, their job had been given lower priority when problems arose. The president explained that they now realized what a poor policy that was for sequencing jobs. The president indicated that if given another chance, his company would put together a proposal by which the client could purchase the right to be, during the weeks of time-sensitive print runs, the top priority job in the plant. The deal would involve a sizable financial guarantee from the printer that its job would ship exactly as promised. By way of apology and to prove its commitment, the printer would give the client a large credit that would offset all of the cost of this service in the first year of a new three-year contract.

A few days later, the sales rep and the vice president of sales arrived with the proposal, including the option to "own" their desired time on the presses for what amounted to a 24 percent premium over the already high rate this customer had been paying. The proposal also gave the customer the promised credit to compensate for the prior year's failure. After some further negotiation that slightly increased the size of the credit, the customer accepted the deal and expressed appreciation that the printer was finally giving their relationship the respect that they felt it deserved. Allowing this customer to negotiate a larger credit was acceptable because it was based upon the value lost by the past failure while still preserving the policy that the price the customer would pay reflected the value going forward.

Of course, if this buyer's objection were driven not by any disappointment in the service but by a belief that it was already being exploited on the price, the solution would have needed to be very different. One way to avoid that problem is to understand the value you are delivering and have a policy to never let the price premium for the relationship buyer exceed that value. As important is the need to ensure that the buyer recognizes the added value that you are delivering. The key to doing that is to track all the value-added services that the customer gets and associate a quantifiable value to them. For example, a company can itemize differentiating features and services with prices for each on its invoice. Then, at the bottom, show a credit for the sum of those charges reflecting the fact that they are covered in the all-inclusive price.

Price buyers are the polar opposite of brand buyers. They genuinely are not looking for a feature or service that exceeds some level that they specify in advance. The clearest symptom of a price buyer is the "sealed bid" or "reverse auction" purchasing process. The buyer commits in writing to the specification of an acceptable offer and is distinctly unwilling to invest time in hearing about the value of an offer that exceeds those specs. He wants a proposal that simply communicates your capability to achieve the specs and your price. If managed appropriately, price buyers can be useful as a place to unload excess inventory, to fill excess capacity, or generate incremental profitability, but only if the risks are recognized and managed.

The only successful policy for dealing with price buyers is the following: strip out any and every cost that is not required to meet the minimum specification, create a "fence" if necessary to ensure that the product does not compete with product you have sold through more lucrative channels, and make no long-term investment or commitment. Branded pharmaceuticals companies have traditionally ignored developing markets such as India and China because of low prices, but rapid growth in those markets has caused big pharma to take a new look at how they could generate incremental revenue from patented drugs. They have done so by licensing reputable local suppliers to make local versions, without the use of the brand name or distinctive shape and often combined with local ingredients that would not be accepted in higher-priced Western countries. The companies earn incremental revenue from these price-buyer markets with minimal investment. Moreover, minimizing their investments in the market enables them to withdraw if their patents are not respected.

Sometimes value buyers, and even relationship buyers, will masquerade as price buyers in an attempt to extract reactive concessions from their preferred supplier. They hold a reverse auction, for example, that is widely open and they share the prices among the bidders with the goal to get their existing supplier to reduce its price. There are a number of tip-offs to look for to determine if this is a sham. One is that the buying company still spends a lot of time evaluating the differences among suppliers before the bid. Second is that its RFP is vague about the details of product and service specifications. Third is a lack of commitment to buy from the lowest price bidder who meets the specs. If any of these happen, then there is reason to believe that the buyer is not really ready to make the final decision solely on price.

There are two common policies that expose value and relationship buyers disguised as price buyers. One is to adopt and publicize a policy never to respond with a bid unless minimum acceptable product and service specifications are fully defined, enabling you to infer which lower quality bidders will be excluded and to understand exactly what the buyer is willing to give up. The other approach, recommended only when the volume at stake is very large, is to submit a bid that you can deliver profitably within the ill-defined spec but is explicit in stating the lower quality or service levels that reflect the "gives" you expect from the buyer in return for a lower price. If the customer wants what they have gotten from you in the past—such as the ability to place rush orders, to order shipments that are less than one truck load, and to demand higher-quality specs—you will enforce firm policies that will trigger unspecified additional charges for those services. Either of these policies by a supplier with an existing relationship will usually result in a return to more traditional give-get negotiations.

A common error that we see in dealing with genuine price buyers is the attempt to make them into value buyers by offering them a "promotional" price. The argument is that by giving a proven price buyer more quality or service than they have paid for, particularly when the users could really benefit from it, these customers will see what they have been missing and be willing to pay more in the future. In practice, exactly the opposite occurs. If price buyers learn that they can get priority service or superior quality when they really need it without paying for it, they have no incentive to ever change their policy of price buying. A better strategy is to let the price buyer know that you can deliver a much higher level of quality and service. When the price buyer needs a rush order or technical support because the low-priced bidder shipped defective product or failed to ship at all, a strategic pricer should have a policy to fill the order, but only at the highest list or spot price, perhaps including charges for a rush order, services, or anything else out of the ordinary. When the buyer has seen the cost of not dealing with a higher quality supplier, the seller may offer the customer a contract retroactively that would cover those services going forward at prices equal to what other buyers pay. If the price buyer declines the offer, at least you will have earned a good profit as an emergency supplier.

Convenience buyers don't compare prices; they just buy from the easiest source of supply. Convenience buyers are value, loyal, or price buyers in categories where they spend more or buy more frequently, but will pay a price that is much more than the economic value defined in the market for a relatively small or infrequent purchase. They expect to pay a premium for convenience so price objections from them are rare.

Policies for Dealing with Power Buyers

A subset of value buyers is what we call *power buyers*, who control so much volume that they have the power to deliver or deny huge amounts of market share. They expect to get better prices than any other buyer because of that power. As one supplier reported being told by a big box purchasing agent, "We expect your price to us to cover your costs. Earn your profits from somebody else." The worst of these was General Motors, which bankrupted most of its suppliers before bankrupting itself. In contrast, retail power buyers—such as Wal-Mart, Home Depot, and Staples—have increased their market share profitably over the past twenty years and are still expanding into new product lines. Power buyers have also arisen in the market for hospital supplies as integrated hospital networks and as "buying groups" of independent hospitals. *Buying groups* are not really buyers, but associations of buyers that increase their power to negotiate deals collectively by refusing to buy from suppliers that have not signed a contract with the group. Dealing with power buyers reactively is risky; a seller is almost certain to suffer a decline in profitability as a result.

So how can a seller deal with power buyers proactively? First, stay realistic. The effect of power buyers is to reduce the value of brands. Many companies that were seduced by the big volume of power buyers have lost their profitability as a result. Their mistake was to think of power buyer volume as purely incremental, leading them to cut ad hoc deals without thinking about the effect on the overall market. If a brand has enough value to consumers that they will go to a store that has it rather than accept another brand from a store (or a buying group) that does not, then the brand has value to the power buyer beyond the margin on that product. The brand can draw store traffic. Retailers competing with the big-box stores pay more than the power buyers precisely because the brand can draw a buyer to them. For example, Benjamin Moore paints have high value to local hardware stores and home centers not just because they have high customer loyalty, but also because they are not available at Home Depot or Lowe's.

Still, in many markets, power buyers control so much volume that one cannot grow without them. For brands without broad customer recognition and preference, the broad distribution and access to volume that power buyers offer may be the key to profitable growth. Even companies such as Procter & Gamble with strong brands have found dealing with power buyers profitable, but not on their terms. Here is how others have made the choice to deal with power buyers and still preserved profitability.

MAKE POWER BUYERS COMPETE.   Many companies with strong brand preference miss a big opportunity by framing the strategic issue poorly. They ask themselves whether they should continue with their traditional retail channel, targeting customers who are less price-sensitive, or sell to power buyers with their high volumes at lower margins. This misses a third option: sell to one power buyer in a segment exclusively giving it a pull advantage over competing power buyers. Martha Stewart certainly got higher margins from Kmart because of her exclusive contract than she would have gotten from selling Martha Stewart products to all big chains.

QUANTIFY THE VALUE TO THE POWER BUYER.   There are many ways that a brand can bring differential value to a big-box retailer. Even if the retailer already has someone as a customer, the brand can drive store visit frequency. Disposable diapers are very valuable to Wal-Mart because their bulk requires frequent visits from a high-spending demographic group. A large manufacturer that is capable of serving power buyers everywhere it operates also reduces acquisition costs for such buyers.

ELIMINATE UNNECESSARY COSTS.   The most difficult challenge to manage is trying to serve both high-volume power buyers who are unwilling to pay for your pull marketing efforts, and non-power buyers who value your brand because you support its marketing. One option is to specialize in serving only power buyers, enabling the company to eliminate costs of marketing and distribution. Shaw Industries, the largest carpet supplier in North America, squeezed costs from fiber production, carpet manufacture, and distribution by totally aligning itself to sell massive volume though Home Depot, Lowe's, and large retail carpet buying groups.

SEGMENT THE PRODUCT OFFERING.   There is no need to offer exactly the same product through a power buyer and through traditional channels where there is a conflict. Although John Deere sells products through Home Depot, it does not sell exactly the same products as through distributors. In the case of some packaged goods, only large sizes are available though Wal-Mart, Target, and other big-box retailers. These steps obviously do not entirely prevent the potential cannibalization, but they do reduce it.

RESIST "DIVIDE AND CONQUER" TACTICS.   Power buyers get their power from their ability to deny a brand or product line any volume through their stores or buying group. The key to their success is to structure the discussion as being about the pricing of each of the manufacturer's products individually. As a result, they maximize the competition for each product line and minimize any negotiating benefit that the supplier gets from offering a full line. Thus a large hospital buying group will tell a medical products manufacturer with nine product lines that there will be nine separate buying decisions, occurring at different times, for each product line. The implication for the seller is that, in the absence of the best price for each, it could end up with a few orphaned products that are excluded from the buying group's distribution channel.

If you have a product line with some strong brands, you do not need to react passively to purchasing policies that undermine your advantages; proactively set policies of your own. When a large medical products company was confronted with these divide and conquer tactics, it simply returned multiple bid forms for each product with different prices, adding a line to the top margin of each specifying the conditions under which those prices would apply. The lowest applied only if all the manufacturer's products were approved by the buying group, while the highest would apply if only a subset were approved. The hospital buying group hated this tactic, but the seller maintained its policy, explaining how the value of the channel to it was vastly reduced without complete acceptance of its product line. Recognizing the cost of losing all the seller's products, some of which had large market share among members, the buying group approved all the products.

Perhaps the most important thing to remember in dealing with power buyers is to be emotionally prepared for them to be bullies who have seen intimidation tactics succeed. If you are confident of the value you offer and you are willing to unbundle differentiation that you know the customer values, be prepared for the fact that someone high up in purchasing may become furious. He may demand to speak to your CEO and threaten unspecified consequences of a damaged relationship with his company. If and when that happens, remember that power buyers who do not need you do not get mad; they can easily get others to supply them. They get mad because they are frustrated that they are not going to get the lop-sided deal that they expected.

POLICIES FOR MANAGING PRICE INCREASES

One of the most difficult discussions to have with a customer involves telling them that you will increase their prices. One of our clients in the New York metro area actually had a customer in the habit of throwing things—particularly shoes—at sales reps who proposed pricing that he did not like. Other customers would quietly ignore the increase when placing an order but, when paying bills, adjust them to reflect the old prices and return the invoice with a check marked "paid in full." As a result of being cowed by such antics, this company typically realized on average less than half the amount of the increases, with customers who already paid lowest prices being the ones who avoided paying more. There are two very different occasions that call for increases, and well-designed policies can help to make all of them more successful.

Policies for Leading an Industry-Wide Increase

The most important increase to achieve quickly is the one that results from a large, sustained increase in variable cost of production or a shortage of industry capacity. These should be the easiest price increases since all suppliers are facing the same problem. There is no real alternative for the customers, regardless of how difficult the increase may prove for them. Problems arise, however, from poorly designed policies that fail to manage expectations. Good policies can influence expectations in ways that help such increases get a better reception.

Even when customers realize that a price increase is ultimately inevitable, none wants to be the first to take it. They do not want to be the first to tell their customers that their prices are increasing, or the first to tell their investors that their margins have declined because of rising prices. That means that they need to trust that their competitors are all taking the same hit. The only way to get the first large customers to go along is to make them confident that doing so will not put them at a competitive disadvantage. Your policy must be that you will not back off the increase for anyone without doing so for everyone who is a customer in the same industry.

There are a few things you can do to create the expectation that taking the increase will not put them at a competitive disadvantage. First, before you announce the increase, let it be known publicly why the increase is necessary for the industry as a whole based upon costs that the industry is incurring or demands on capacity. Listen carefully for similar sentiments that all of your major competitors recognize the same need before proceeding. Second, announce the size and effective date of the increase, stating exactly which product lines are increasing by how much. Explain the cause and effect relationship (for example, energy accounts directly or indirectly for X percent of costs and that translates into Y percent price increases). The public announcement reinforces that this is an across-the-board increase and insulates your sales reps from any personal responsibility for it.

Third, if customers are fearful that their competitors will not have to take the increase or will not take it as quickly, empower them to give your most important customers a transition guarantee. If you are the supplier to their competitors, you guarantee that if you agree to a lesser or delayed increase with any of their major competitors for the same product and service, they will get the same concession retroactively. If they are concerned that a competitor who is served by one of your competitors will not get the increase, you might agree that you will delay their increase until the effective date of a competitor's increase. All of these will help create the impression that the cost increase problem is one that you are willing to solve together in a way that recognizes their legitimate business needs as well as yours. Because it is easier for any individual customer to accept the increase given these conditions, it is more likely that all will ultimately accept it.

Under no circumstances should you back off on the full increase for customers who are more resistant while leaving loyal customers to take it, a common practice. Although such a policy can generate greater return in the immediate quarter, it reinforces that resistance pays and outrages good customers whenever they learn that they have been taken advantage of. On the other hand, if a major competitor fails to initiate a comparable price increase, a general rollback may be necessary. If so, contact your customers proactively to let them know that you are protecting them by temporarily suspending the increase out of concern for their competitiveness. The increase will automatically be reinstated when it can be accomplished without putting them at any disadvantage. This builds trust with your customers, keeps the price increase agreement with them in play, while letting your competitor realize that there is nothing to gain from delay.

Finally, there are situations where you can safely make concessions for good customers, but only ones that involve the timing, not the fact, of the inevitable increase. For example, you can build loyalty by being sympathetic that they may have some fixed price commitments yet to be met. For volumes necessary to fulfill those contracts, you can legitimately agree to share the pain. Thus a customer receives the concession near term by agreeing to the increase going forward.

Policies for Transitioning from Low One-Off Pricing

In markets where volume comes mostly from repeat purchasers, it is difficult to transition from poor policies to good ones all at once. Customers have already developed expectations that they can get rewards from certain behaviors. They will continue those behaviors for a while until their expectations change. The change takes time within the seller's own company, too; marketing and sales management needs that time to develop good policies, and the plans to carry them out. We have seen the move to policy-based pricing fail when management implements a rigid fixed-price policy of no more discounting without a plan for the transition.

To minimize the risk of transition and create time to test new policies for managing price variation consistently, one needs to begin with policies for managing the transition. Chapter 8, on pricing strategy implementation, describes a technique called *price banding* that enables managers to estimate how much of the price variation is illegitimate, both on an aggregate and a per account basis. The first policies should focus on managing the outliers: "outlaws" who now enjoy prices much lower than other customers for the same products, service levels, and commitments, and the "at-risks" who are paying more than can be justified relative to the average.

The first step is to identify the outlaws and how they got that way. The reason to start here is because they are the least profitable accounts, so there is less at risk if they take their business elsewhere. These outlaw accounts pull down other customers over time—either as a result of information leaking into the market about their pricing or because their competitive advantage in purchasing enables them to take share from others who buy at a higher price. If an outlaw is in a unique industry or different market from other customers and the low price reflects low value and low cost-to-serve, then an amendment is called for in your price structure that articulates objective criteria to qualify for the price and defines fences necessary to keep it from undermining your general price level. When there is no logical rationale for the low prices these accounts pay, an effective fence means to make an outlaw and others like him legitimate. That requires figuring out how the outlaw got such pricing in the first place and creating a policy to correct that mistake. If the original reason for such low pricing no longer exists (for example, a service mistake in the past led management to allow a discount to compensate, or the price reflected expectations of volume that never materialized), the customer needs to be confronted with that reality. Most importantly, the customer needs to be contacted by someone above the sales rep (the level dependent upon the size of the customer) to communicate that, while the customer has gotten a much better deal than others in the past, top management is unwilling to continue pricing that is unfair to other customers and unhealthy for the supplier.

With the bad news delivered unequivocally by management, the sales rep is now free to initiate a give-get negotiation in an attempt to save the account. He can contact the customer to learn if there might be some trade-offs they would consider, to mitigate the size of the mandated increase. Various concessions on the part of the customer consistent with those made by other customers could reduce some costs. With the ability to use a second or third source as a bargaining chip now unnecessary, the buyer might even be willing to sign up for an exclusive supply contract to qualify for a discount that would reduce the impending increase.

Finally, the firm may create a policy authorizing a period of transition to a legitimate pricing level in steps. An outlaw buyer who agreed to either an exclusive contract or minimum "must take" volumes under a long-term contract (say 18 months), would then be allowed to take the necessary price increases in steps: one-third of the increase becoming effective immediately, one-third in six months, and the last third in 12 months. What makes this effective is that the purchasing agent will be able to argue that he precluded an average increase over the contract that would have been twice as large as originally proposed and pushed realization of most of it to the back end. What is important to the seller is that by the end of the contract, the buyer will be purchasing at a price comparable to what other customers pay.

Of course, some of these outlaws will be genuine price buyers who may not accept any increase. Walking away from such customers, and publically acknowledging it as a good business decision, signals your resolve externally and internally. It will communicate a newfound commitment to doing business only with good business partners, and put others who may be masquerading as price buyers on notice that there is a potential cost. Unless your industry has excess capacity, it might also strain your competitor's capacity with low margin business. If that makes it more difficult to serve some of their higher margin customers well, if only during a transition period, it gives you the chance to win some more profitable volume.

POLICIES FOR DEALING WITH AN ECONOMIC DOWNTURN

Pricing policies are most likely to be abandoned when the market enters a recession and sales turn down. Revenue then seems much more important than preserving profitability in the future. But unmanaged price-cutting in a recession not only undermines price levels that you will want to sustain in the later recovery, it can trigger a price war that makes all competitors worse off while still in the downturn. Fortunately, if a company thoughtfully manages pricing by policy though the downturn, it can minimize the damage in both the short and long run.

First, you must enforce a firm policy not to use price to take market share from close competitors during the downturn since they can easily respond with price cuts of their own. (But you can and should retaliate selectively against price-based moves by close competitors, as explained in Chapter 11 on managing price competition.) Safeway, which initiated a supermarket price war in 2009, increased its share of revenue but tanked its share of profits. Smarter competitors, such as Winn-Dixie, promoted their high-margin house brands to help thrifty shoppers cut costs, and weathered the recession with much less damage to themselves and their markets.[1]

In business markets, the value that some products can justify is tied to the health of their customer's markets. For example, the value of a page of advertising in a magazine or space at a trade show is related to the size of the market for the product being advertised. In 2009, the return from advertising real estate was not what it was in 2008. In such markets, particularly when variable costs are low, sellers sometimes "index" their pricing for customers willing to make long-term commitments, with the index tied not to their costs but to market conditions in their customer's market. Such a policy supports customers and maintains volume while times are difficult while establishing an automatic mechanism for price increases when customers can better afford them. An alternative is to unbundle elements of your product or service that the customer can no longer afford (such as, new product development and technical support), even though they value them. The point in all these cases is that these price discounting options can be designed to expire when they are no longer needed and do not directly threaten competitors.

But what can a company do to gain volume during a downturn when demand from its current customers is shrinking but taking share will only trigger a price war that will shrink the market further? As discussed in Chapter 3 on price structure, there are various ways to attract a new, more price sensitive segment, without cutting price to most of your existing customers. Moreover, when you have excess capacity, the cost to serve a new segment is minimal. Although you want to maintain policies that protect margins in the market where you are invested for long-term growth, you have nothing to lose from price competition, even of the ad hoc variety, in markets from which you hope to gain incremental business only short term. For those markets only, a policy of one-off pricing to fill excess capacity can be worth pursuing if the business can be carefully fenced.

For example, one high-end chain of hotels in Europe, which would never consider serving tour groups in good times, approached tour companies catering to small groups of high-income travelers with some very good deals. They brought in both incremental revenue and introduced their chain to a market segment of people they would want to have as nightly guests, while still enabling themselves to exit the tour segment in better times. Our commercial printer client approached direct mail advertisers accustomed to accepting poor quality from printers who use inferior presses. For mail circulars and newspaper inserts only, they offered better quality that nearly matched what advertisers were paying already. The low-end competitors could not match the offer, and the company won some incremental contribution that kept its press operators employed during some lean months.

POLICIES FOR PROMOTIONAL PRICING

A discount to induce product trial is a legitimate means to gain sales, but poorly managed can have the effect of depressing margins. For search goods, the discount is the incentive for the customer to investigate the supplier's offer. For experience goods, it is the incentive to take the risk of what could turn out to be a disappointing purchase. The size of the promotional discount necessary to induce trial can be mitigated by policy. A liberal returns policy if the customer is unsatisfied is one way to take away the risk of trying a product at full price. Bowflex does not discount its unique, high-end exercise equipment. But it combines direct-to-customer value communication with a money-back guarantee requested within the first six weeks of delivery. If product performance is measurable objectively, a performance-based rebate policy can accomplish the same thing. Rebating is becoming a common means for pharmaceutical and medical device companies to win acceptance of higher-priced products with as yet unproven differentiating benefits. When Valcade, a cancer treatment, was deemed not cost-effective and rejected for payment by the British National Health Service (NHS), the company did not agree to reduce its price. Instead, it came back with a new offer to guarantee effectiveness without lowering its premium price. The company would refund the entire cost of the drug for any patient who did not show adequate improvement after an initial period of treatment. The effect of this policy on the net average price remains to be seen, but the guarantee won approval for payment within the NHS and created potential for the company to earn higher profits if justified by superior performance.[2] By putting money on the line, the company raised expectations both within the NHS and with other payers and clinicians that the product probably will produce the superior treatment outcomes that the company claimed, which will increase its market share.

For consumer products, promotional pricing is one of the most important issues for which a company needs pricing policies and a process for reviewing their effectiveness. Even companies that have established brands with large market shares face the problem that a high percentage of buyers will leave the market or, particularly in the case of food products, will become "fatigued" and look for something different. Consequently, manufacturers must constantly win new customers to maintain a fixed market share. Promotional discounts are often a very cost-effective way to educate consumers, particularly for frequently purchased consumer products, which are usually experience goods.

The easiest way to induce trial with little additional cost of administration is simply to offer the product at a low price for a time, say one week each quarter. For frequently purchased products sold through retailers, the sales increases resulting from such "pulsed" promotions are usually huge—easily justifying the deal if looked at in isolation. But there are various reasons why a company might want to ban such promotions as a policy. First, there is some evidence that when a product is bought at a promotional price, it depresses willingness-to-pay for the product in the future. Second, both consumers and retailers will stock up on the product when promoted, giving the appearance of a big increase in volume that simply depresses sales in later periods. There are categories, usually among food products, for which stocking up is a good thing. The more inventory people have of sodas and snack foods, for example, the more they consume. For most products, however, stocking up at promotional prices simply reduces the average price that customers pay while educating them to wait for the discount.

Consequently, a policy of limiting the availability of promotional discounts and targeting them to prospective buyers is often advisable. One way to do this is with coupons. Coupons have the advantage of limiting the ability of already loyal customers to stock up. With new scanner technology, retailers offer manufacturers the ability to print coupons on cash register receipts for customers who have bought competing products, or a combination of items that indicate that they might be good prospects for something that the manufacturer wants them to try. Rebates can be offered on the item but be limited to one per family.

Many service companies are in need of more disciplined policies for pricing to induce trial. Cable TV companies offer large discounts to sign up new subscribers for a year, as do newspapers and magazines and mobile telephone services. The problem in many of these cases is that, at the end of the discount period, they have to go back to the customer and ask for a much higher price to continue the service. A high percentage of those customers balk, knowing that either they can win an incentive from another supplier to try that supplier's product for awhile, or can wait a week or two and sign up for another incentive from the same supplier who just tried to raise their price. None of this should be surprising given what we have learned from the study of experimental economics.[3] Once someone spends 6 or 12 months enjoying a service at one price, renewing it at a higher price is viewed as a "loss" to be resisted. No services company should ever use a discount on the service price as its means to induce trial. Instead, it should create an inducement that maintains the integrity of the price and builds the habit of paying it. For example, a far better inducement to purchase is a "free" gift for signing up—such as the choice from a list of new best sellers for signing up for a magazine, or $300 in pay-per-view credits for signing up for a year of cable TV. After the initial commitment, the incentive is gone but the customer is paying the monthly cost that reflects the value. As a result, there is no perception of "loss" that drives away subscribers at the back end.

Summary

Good policies cannot magically make pricing of your product or service profitable, but poor ones can certainly undermine your ability to capture prices justified by the value of what you offer. Good policies lead customers to think about the purchase of your product as a price-value trade-off rather than as a game to win at your expense. As such, they are an essential part of any pricing strategy designed to capture value and maintain ongoing customer relationships.

Notes

1. "Winn-Dixie CEO: Supermarket Pricing Rational, No Price War," *Dow Jones News Wire*, May 12, 2009.
2. "NICE Responds to Velcade NHS Reimbursement Scheme" *PMLive .com*, June 7, 2007.
3. Daniel Kahneman, Jack L. Knetsch, and Richard H. Thaler, "The Endowment Effect, Loss Aversion, and Status Quo Bias," Journal of Economic Perspectives 5, no. 1 (Winter 1991): 193–206.

■ ■ ■ ■ ■

CHAPTER 6

Price Level

Setting the Right Price
for Sustainable Profit

Price setting is challenging, requiring the collection and analysis of information about the company's business goals and cost structure, the customer's preferences and needs, and the competition's pricing and strategic intent. Even the best marketers struggle to synthesize these data into coherent, profit-maximizing prices. The price setting task is all the more challenging because of its importance to the organization—there are few decisions that have greater impact on financial performance. Whereas a good pricing decision can improve profits dramatically, a poor one can invoke a competitive response that quickly devolves into a price war that destroys profits for all.

Given the importance and complexity of pricing decisions, one might expect firms to invest heavily in the pricing function to ensure that managers have the right data and effective decision-support tools. Yet our research has found this is often not the case. In a benchmarking survey, 74 percent of managers indicated they often make pricing decisions with insufficient data; another 65 percent cite a lack of decision-support tools. Given this lack of data and tools, it's not surprising that managers often take shortcuts that undercut their profits and increase their customers' ability to negotiate lower prices.

For example, a biomedical device manufacturer we know has focused primarily on costs and to a lesser degree, value, when setting prices. The company knows that many of its products are differentiated, but it has not invested enough time and effort in value estimation to know how much that differentiation is worth to customers. As a result, its published prices tend to be quite high relative to the competition and the customer's willingness-to-pay. On the surface, theirs might seem like a prudent approach because it ensures the company never "leaves money on the table" when negotiating final prices. Over time, however, the differentiation value of many of its products

118

has eroded as competitors introduced new, higher-performing products. The resulting price pressure led to ad hoc discounting, which undercut the company's reputation for price integrity. Customers have learned that published prices are only a starting point for negotiation and that the way to get better prices is to negotiate harder. Now, after several years of reduced price realization and lower profits, the company has correctly concluded that it must add discipline to its pricing process to set prices that are defensible to customers.

In this chapter, we present a three-stage price setting process that integrates the relevant customer, competitor, and cost data in a way that enables marketers to set more profitable price levels. The process is designed to be efficient and adaptable to most products, services, and market contexts. It integrates data on value estimation and segmentation, non-value price sensitivity drivers, costs, strategic objectives, and market response analysis in a way that can be supported by the organization and understood by customers.

THE PRICE-SETTING PROCESS

The goal of the price-setting process shown in Exhibit 6-1 is to set profit-maximizing prices by capturing the appropriate amount of differential value in each of the served segments. In following the process, we advise managers to evaluate the return on their time invested at each stage to ensure each analysis provides enough actionable information to materially affect the final price decision. For example, a key question when establishing the price window is the amount of effort to invest in assessing the value of a product or service. For mature products with little differentiation and whose benefits are well understood by the customer, marketers would not learn enough actionable information to justify a full value assessment using the monetary estimation process or a conjoint study described in Chapter 2. They would be better served by relying on past experience and readily available data to form a rough estimate of customer value as a means of setting a price ceiling. When pricing a more differentiated product, however, the insight gained from thorough value estimation can substantially improve the price setting choice.

The process is grounded in the premise that prices should be set at the segment level to reflect value differences and to maximize profitability as described in Chapter 3. For companies that have historically used a "one size fits all" approach to pricing, this segmented approach can be a significant change. It requires managers to think less about what price will sell the most products and more about how to use price to capture the different values they create. The first step in the process is to set an initial price window defined by a price ceiling and floor for each segment. This band provides the "guardrails" for the organization to ensure that no matter what kind of price pressures are confronting managers, the final price will not inadvertently trigger unexpected reactions from competitors and customers.

The second step in the process involves determining the amount of differential value to be captured with price. A common mistake made by novice

EXHIBIT 6-1. Overview of the Price Setting Process

Define Price Window	Set Initial Price	Communicate Prices to Market
Set initial price range based on differential value and relevant costs	Determine amount of differential value to be captured with price	Develop communication plan to ensure prices are perceived to be fair
Key Questions	Key Questions	Key Questions
• What is the appropriate price ceiling for this product?	• Is the price point consistent with my overall business objectives?	• What is the best approach to communicate price changes to customers?
• How should I incorporate reference prices into my price window?	• What are the non-value related determinants of price sensitivity?	• What are the considerations for implementing significantly higher prices?
• What is the role of costs in setting my initial price range?	• What are the price-volume tradeoffs and what is their impact on profitability?	

pricing strategists is to always seek to capture the maximum amount of differential value possible. For these managers, strategic pricing becomes a mechanism for raising prices and little else. But true strategic pricing requires a more insightful approach to price setting that discerns when it is more profitable to allow the customer to keep more value as a purchase incentive. Small companies vying for sales volume to bring their costs down, for example, might appropriately price their offerings to capture less value so they can increase market share. Similarly, first-time customers may feel that a purchase is more risky than long-time buyers and, hence, may be legitimately more price sensitive and merit a lower price. The price-setting process outlined in Exhibit 6-1 accounts for these factors as well as others to ensure that the price maximizes profitability.

Having arrived at a preliminary price point through the analytics in steps one and two, the final step is to communicate new prices to the market. This requires careful consideration to ensure the prices are perceived to be fair even when they represent a premium to past prices or prices offered by less differentiated competitors.

Defining the Price Window

The price window is set for each segment and is defined by the ceiling, the highest allowable price point, and the floor, the lowest allowable price point. We begin the price setting process by establishing the price window for each segment and then, in step two, narrow that window based on strategic objectives for the segment and potential customer responses to the new prices. The price points for the price ceiling and floor will differ depending on whether the product is positively or negatively differentiated as shown in Exhibit 6-2.

In both cases, the price ceiling is determined by the economic value created for customers. If the price were set higher than the economic value, then customers would be better off buying the competitor's product even though they might very much want (or need) some of the differentiated value of your offering. Suppose you were pricing a product with a total economic value of $140 comprised of a $100 reference price and $40 of net differential value as shown below. A customer buying your product at a price of $150 would find themselves with a net benefit loss of $10. The same customer would have a net gain of $10 if they purchased from your competitor, even though they would have to forgo some of the differential value offered by your product.

	Your Product	Competitor Product
Reference Price	100	150
Pos. diff. value	60	20
Neg. diff. value	(20)	(60)
Total Economic Value	140	110
Price	150	100
Net Benefit	−$10	$10

EXHIBIT 6-2 Defining Price Windows

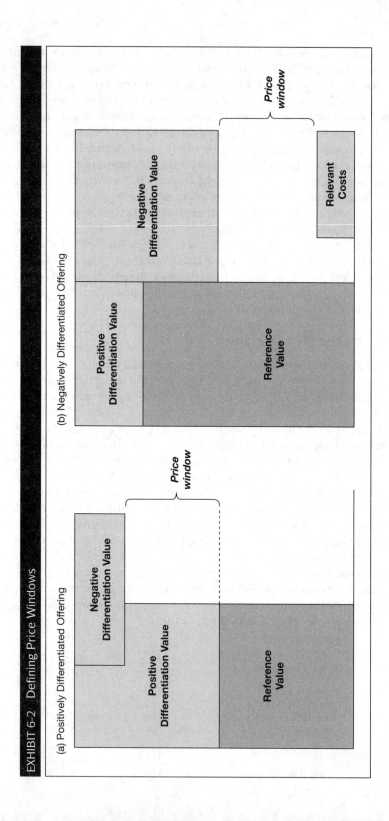

(a) Positively Differentiated Offering

(b) Negatively Differentiated Offering

The price floor for a positively differentiated product is determined by the competitor's reference price because it represents an important tipping point for competitive response. Suppose that we chose to set our price for the product in the previous example at $90, which is $10 below the reference value. We can see the implications for such a move by calculating the economic value of the competitor's product, as illustrated below. By pricing below the competitive reference price, we have placed the competitor in an untenable position in which their product creates negative economic benefit for customers—a situation they can reverse in the short term only by cutting the price. Indeed, if their price ceiling is their total economic value, then you could expect a cut in excess of 50 percent as your competitor tries to stave off significant volume loss.

	Competitor Product
Reference Price	90
Pos. diff. value	20
Neg. diff. value	(60)
Total Economic Value	50
Price	100
Net Benefit	−$50

As this example illustrates, the price floor for a negatively differentiated product cannot be the competitive reference value because that would place the floor above the price ceiling defined by the economic value (see graphic illustration on right side of Exhibit 6-2). The limiting factor for a negatively differentiated product is the relevant costs of the offering that are defined as those that determine the profit impact of prices. We define these costs and discuss their role in pricing in depth in Chapter 9 and, thus, will not repeat that discussion here. Instead, it is sufficient to point out that the price window for negatively differentiated products is lower than those that are positively differentiated, and it is important to allow those offerings to maintain lower prices in order to maintain stable market prices.

Establishing an Initial Price Point

Once the price window has been defined for different customer segments, the next step is to determine where, within that window, the initial price should be set. The decision should not be driven by altruism but rather by judgment about what will yield long-term, sustainable profits. Leaving more of the economic value "on the table" can, other things equal, induce customers to migrate to a new product or service more quickly. They will not first need to fully understand the value if they can see that it is much greater but the price is only a little more. Moreover, the seller saves the cost of having to educate customers and the low price, and quick market uptake discourages competitive entry. On the other hand, if the product's differentiation is likely to be sustainable for a long time, setting price significantly below value to drive sales may require forgoing a lot of potential margin over the long term. Unless value is initially established and paid by the early adopters, it can be difficult if not impossible to raise prices to value-based levels later on.

There are three considerations when determining where in the price window to set the initial price:

1. *Alignment with Overall Business Strategy:*   Pricing is but one element of the firms marketing and sales strategy and it is important that price levels reinforce the overall business strategy. When Jeff Bezos founded Amazon.com in 1995, his goal was to grow market share quickly in the retailing sector before any competitor could enter and duplicate the company's business model. His pricing strategy was to undercut traditional retailers so much that customers would be willing to switch their purchases to the new Internet channel. Although Amazon.com creates significant differential value through quicker search, greater selection, and customer reviews, a premium pricing strategy intended to capture that value would not have advanced the company's mission.

2. *Price-Volume Trade-offs:*   The inability to establish fences between different segments will force a seller to make trade-offs between price and volume. The financial impact of these trade-offs is determined primarily by a firm's cost structure. If a firm's costs are primarily variable (as in grocery retailing and personal service businesses), its percent contribution margin (the amount of each sale that contributes to fixed costs and profit), will tend to be low as well. As a result, small decreases in price require large increases in volume to be profitable. In contrast, if costs are primarily fixed (as in software, pharmaceuticals, and publishing), the percent contribution margin will tend to be high. As a result, small decreases in price will require much smaller increases in volume to improve profits because each additional sale adds significant contribution to profit. These concepts, and the calculations to support them, are developed further in Chapters 9 and 10. However, it is essential that the underlying economics of the price volume trade-off be understood at this stage of the price setting process.

3. *Customer Response:*   Perhaps the most challenging question when setting prices is "how will customers respond to the new prices?" There are many non-value related factors that can affect the degree to which price influences a customer's purchase decision. If the expenditure is small for the segment of customers, or if someone else is paying the bill, then a seller can win sales even while pricing to capture a high share of the economic value to that segment. This is why small impulse purchases such as candy bars and gum are rarely, if ever, discounted. On the other hand, if customers feel the price is unfair, even when justified by value, they will tend to be highly price sensitive and less likely to buy. The amount of differential value that can be captured depends upon how successful marketers are identifying and mitigating those non-value factors that drive price sensitivity.

Understanding each of these three factors in detail enables a manager to determine the extent to which price should be used to capture value or to drive volume in each segment. We discuss each of these factors in more detail below.

Pricing Objectives

Few decisions that marketers make influence customer behaviors as much as pricing. That is why it is essential that price levels be set in a way that supports and advances the broader marketing objectives of the firm. When Microsoft dropped prices on its Windows operating system by as much as 40 percent in 2009, the move was consistent with the company's long-held goal of maintaining and growing market share. The critical question for Microsoft managers was whether the price cuts would result in higher profits over the long-term. It is easy to envision scenarios in which competitor response limits any volume gains from the price cuts, thereby reducing profitability. If Microsoft's primary business objective was to increase profitability and market share, it might have been better served by maintaining a premium pricing strategy, even at the expense of some lost volume.

To be useful, pricing objectives must be set relative to some reference point. Given the strategic importance of customer value to the overall pricing strategy, we define pricing objectives in terms of the percentage of value captured with price. This decision should be driven by judgments about what will yield long-term, sustainable profitability. As noted earlier, a low price will, other things equal, induce customers to migrate to a new product or service more quickly. On the other hand, if the product's differentiation is likely to be sustained, a low price established to drive sales means foregoing considerable margin over the long run because it is difficult, if not impossible, to raise prices later. There are three options for setting prices: skimming the market, penetrating the market, and neutral market pricing. Let's examine the conditions under which each option is appropriate.

OPTION 1: SKIM THE MARKET Skim pricing (or skimming) is designed to capture high margins at the expense of large sales volume. By definition, skim prices are high in relation to what most buyers in a segment can be convinced to pay. Consequently, this strategy optimizes immediate profitability only when the profit from selling to relatively price-insensitive customers exceeds that from selling to a larger market at a lower price. In some instances, products might reap more profit in the long run by setting initial prices high and reducing them over time—the "sequential skimming" strategy we discuss below—even if those high initial prices reduce immediate profitability.

Buyers are often price insensitive because they belong to a market segment that places exceptionally high value on a product's differentiating attributes. For example, in many sports a segment of enthusiasts will often pay astronomical prices for the bike, club, or racquet that they think will give them an edge. You can buy a plain aluminum canoe paddle for $35. You can buy a

Bending Branches Double Bent paddle (wood laminate, 44 ounces) for $149. Or you can buy the Werner Camano paddle (graphite, 26 ounces) for $249. The Werner Camano not only makes canoeing long distances easier but also signals that one belongs to a select group that has a very serious commitment to the sport.

Of course, simply targeting a segment of customers who are relatively price insensitive does not mean that they are fools who will buy at any price. It means that they can and will pay fully for the exceptionally high value they place on perceived differentiating benefits. Thus skim pricing generally requires a substantial commitment to communicate the benefits that justify a high price. If effective value communications are neither practical nor cost-effective, then the firm must limit its pricing to reflect what it can communicate or to what potential customers are likely to believe from what they can observe.

The competitive environment must be right for skimming. A firm must have some source of competitive protection to ensure long-term profitability by precluding competitors from providing lower-priced alternatives. Patents or copyrights are one source of protection against competitive threats. Pharmaceutical companies cite their huge expenditures on research to justify the skim prices they command until a drug's patent expires. Even then, they enjoy some premium because of the name recognition. Other forms of protection include a brand's reputation for quality, access to a scarce resource, and pre-emption of the best distribution channels.

A skim price isn't necessarily a poor strategy even when a firm lacks the ability to prevent competition in the future. If a company introduces a new product at a high price relative to manufacturing cost, competitors will be attracted by the high margin even if the product is priced low relative to its economic value. Pricing low in the face of competition makes sense only when it serves to deter competitors or to establish a competitive advantage. If a low price cannot do either, the best rule for pricing is to earn what you can while you can. If and when competitors enter by duplicating the product's differentiating attributes and, thus, undermine its competitive advantage, the firm can then reevaluate its strategy.

Sequential skimming can be a more appropriate strategy for products and services with low repurchase rates. The market for long-lived durable goods that a customer purchases infrequently, or products that most buyers would purchase only once, such as a ticket to a stage play, can be skimmed for only a limited time at each price. Skimming, in such cases, cannot be maintained indefinitely, but its dynamic variant, sequential skimming, may remain profitable for some time.

Sequential skimming, like the more sustainable variety of skimming, begins with a price that attracts the least price-sensitive buyers first. After the firm has "skimmed the cream" of buyers, however, that market is gone. Consequently, to maintain its sales, the firm must reduce its price enough to sell to the next most lucrative segment. The firm continues this process until it has exhausted all segments with profitable volume potential. In theory, a firm could sequentially skim the market for a durable good or a one-time purchase by lowering its price in hundreds of small steps, thus charging every segment the maximum it would pay for the product. In practice, however, potential buyers catch on rather quickly and begin delaying their purchases, anticipating further price reductions. To minimize this problem, the firm can cut price less frequently, thus forcing potential buyers to bear a significant cost of waiting. It can also launch less attractive models as it cuts the price. This is the strategy Apple followed when it introduced the iPod. The fist iPod was priced at $399. Rather than follow a traditional sequential pricing strategy and cut the price some time after launch, Apple introduced the iPod mini and the iPod shuffle with more limited functionality and lower price points. Over time, Apple has increased the functionality and value for each of its products while generally maintaining the price points. This variant to sequential skimming has been described as "pushing down the stack" and is used frequently in other technology markets such as semiconductors and cellular phones.

OPTION 2: PENETRATE THE MARKET   *Penetration pricing* involves setting a price low enough to attract and hold a large base of customers. Penetration prices are not necessarily cheap, but they are low relative to perceived value in the target segment. Hyundai, for example, used a sustained penetration pricing strategy to enter the U.S. market in which the company offered high value in the form of reliability, 10-year warranties, and well-appointed interiors at prices far below those of Japanese makers such as Toyota or Honda. Similarly, Target and Trader Joe's stores have positioned themselves as offering the same or better value as their competitors at lower prices.

Penetration pricing will work only if a large share of the market is willing to change brands or suppliers in response to lower prices. A common misconception is that every market will respond to lower prices, which is one reason why unsuccessful penetration pricing schemes are so common. In some cases, penetration pricing can actually undermine a brand's long-term appeal. When Lacoste allowed its "alligator" shirts to be discounted by lower-priced mass merchants, high-image retailers refused to carry the product and longer and traditional Lacoste customers migrated to more exclusive brands.

Of course, not all buyers need to be price sensitive for penetration pricing to succeed, but enough of the market must be adequately price sensitive to justify low pricing. Warehouse clubs such as Sam's, Costco, and B.J.'s Wholesale Club have used penetration pricing to target only buyers willing to purchase in large quantities. Charter vacation operators sell heavily discounted travel to people who do not mind inflexible scheduling. Discount retail stores such as T.J. Maxx, Marshall's, and Trader Joe's target those price-sensitive customers willing to shop frequently through limited and rapidly changing stocks to find a bargain. Some wholesalers of sheet steel use penetration prices to attract the high-volume buyers, who require no selling or service and who buy truckload quantities.

To determine how much volume one must gain to justify penetration pricing, a manager must also consider costs. Conditions are more favorable for penetration pricing when incremental costs (variable and incremental fixed) represent a small share of the price, so that each additional sale provides a large contribution to profit. Because the contribution per sale is already high, a lower price does not represent a large cut in the contribution from each sale. For example, even if a company had to cut its prices 10 percent to attract a large segment of buyers, penetration pricing could still be profitable if the product had a high contribution margin. In order for the strategy to pay with a 90 percent contribution margin, the sales gain would need to exceed only 12.5 percent. The lower the contribution per sale, the larger the volume gain required before penetration pricing is profitable.

Penetration pricing can succeed without a high contribution margin if the strategy creates sufficient variable cost economies, enabling the seller to offer penetration prices without suffering lower margins. The price sensitivity of target customers enables penetration-priced retailers to vary the brands they offer depending on who gives them the best deal, thus increasing their leverage with suppliers. The penetration prices of Save-A-Lot grocers (a division of Supervalu Inc.) enables them to maintain such high turnover, high sales per square foot, and high sales per employee that they can offer rock-bottom prices and still earn higher profits than traditional grocers do.[1] To cite a manufacturing example, as personal computer users became more knowledgeable buyers, manufacturers such as Dell and Gateway leveraged the economies of mail-order distribution to sell high-quality products to knowledgeable buyers using penetration pricing. Competitors who distributed through retail stores could not match their prices.

For penetration pricing to succeed, competitors must allow a company to set a price that is attractive to a large segment of the market. Competitors always have the option of undercutting a penetration strategy by cutting their own prices, preventing the penetration pricer from offering a better value. Only when competitors lack the ability or incentive to do so is penetration pricing a practical strategy for gaining and holding market share. There are three common situations in which this is likely to occur:

1. When the firm has a significant cost advantage and/or a resource advantage so that its competitors believe they would lose if they began a price war
2. When the firm has a broader line of complementary products, enabling it to use one as a penetration-priced "loss leader" in order to drive sales of others
3. When the firm is currently so small that it can significantly increase its sales without affecting the sales of its competitors enough to prompt a response

As telecom markets have opened to competition in most developed countries, new suppliers have successfully used penetration pricing to capture market share. The low variable costs of carrying a call or message make such a strategy desirable. Regulatory constraints and the unwillingness of large, established competitors to match the lower prices of new entrants on their large installed base of customers has made the strategy successful in many markets. Many telecom managers would question whether the heavy reliance on penetration strategies was a wise choice over the long term because it conditioned consumers to seek deals and may have accelerated the decline in prices for the entire market.

OPTION 3: NEUTRAL MARKET PRICING *Neutral pricing* involves a strategic decision not to use price to gain market share, while not allowing price alone to restrict it. Neutral pricing minimizes the role of price as a marketing tool in favor of other tactics that management believes are more powerful or cost-effective for a product's market. This does not mean that neutral pricing is easier. On the contrary, it is less difficult to choose a price that is sufficiently high to skim or sufficiently low to penetrate than to choose one that strikes a near perfect balance.

A firm generally adopts a neutral pricing strategy by default because market conditions are not sufficient to support either a skim or penetration strategy. For example, a marketer may be unable to adopt skim pricing when buyers consider the products in a particular market to be so substitutable that no significant segment will pay a premium. That same firm may be unable to adopt a penetration pricing strategy because, particularly if it's a newcomer to the market, customers would be unable to judge its quality before purchase and would infer low quality from low prices (the price–quality effect) or because competitors would respond vigorously to any price that undercut the established price structure. Neutral pricing is especially common in industries where customers are quite value sensitive, precluding skimming, but competitors are quite volume sensitive, precluding successful penetration.

Although neutral pricing is less proactive than skimming or penetration pricing, its proper execution is no less difficult or important to profitability. Neutral prices are not necessarily equal to those of competitors or near the middle of the range. A neutral price can, in principle, be the highest or lowest price in the market and still be neutral. Sony TVs are consistently priced above competitors, yet they capture large market shares because of the high perceived value associated with their clear screens and reliable performance. Like a skim or penetration price, a neutral price is defined relative to the perceived economic value of the product.

DEFINING THE PRICE-VOLUME TRADE-OFF

The second factor that must be understood when determining where to set price levels is the relationship between changes in price and volume. Economic theory indicates that profit-maximizing prices are found at the point on the demand curve where marginal revenue is equal to marginal cost. While this price-setting theory is elegant and clear, setting prices in practice is considerably more difficult. Identifying marginal revenues is challenging because revenues are dependant on multiple factors such as the relative size of the increase (for example, is it a significant portion of the customers' expenditure?), the visibility of the price increase in the market, and competitor response, to name a few. Although marketers have many techniques available to them for estimating customer response (which we discuss later in this chapter), all of them have some uncertainty associated with their estimates.

Just as estimating customer response is challenging, many marketers struggle to determine the relevant costs for a pricing decision. One might think that determining the relevant costs for pricing would be straightforward given the ubiquity of sophisticated enterprise software systems and data warehouses in use today. As we explain in more detail in Chapter 9, relevant costs are those that are incremental (not average) and avoidable (not sunk). In practice, identifying relevant costs can be challenging because much of the data available to marketers is averaged (for example, the average labor rate) or loaded with non-avoidable costs such as corporate overhead.

This point is illustrated by the experience of one of this book's authors when he was starting his first job as a pricing analyst for a global manufacturing firm. On his first big pricing project, he went to the director of corporate pricing to ask where he could find the cost data for the product. The director showed him where to find the data and then told him ". . . you need to understand that our system will spit out a cost number for any product you are interested in . . . but that number is created for accounting purposes and has almost no relationship to the relevant cost of the product because it is fully loaded with overheads." Needless to say, it was a rude awakening for an idealistic analyst well versed in theory but inexperienced in the workings of the real world.

Rather than attempting to determine marginal revenues and costs, we advocate that marketers follow a sequence of steps to first understand the financial trade-offs between price and volume and then analyze the market to estimate consumer response. Rather than attempt to answer the impossible question of "How will sales change following this price change," we suggest that managers focus on a more useful pair of questions to guide their pricing choice:

- How much volume could I afford to lose before a particular price increase would be unprofitable?
- How much volume would I have to gain in order for a particular price decrease to improve my profitability?

These are more useful questions because they provide directionally sound guidance about profit-maximizing prices without a detailed volume estimate. Instead of developing future volume and profit estimates with a false sense of precision, it is better to gain a definitive understanding of the price-volume trade-offs using a simple, yet powerful, break-even analysis.

Incremental break-even analysis can be implemented on a spreadsheet and easily combined with both data and managerial judgment to make price adjustments that improve profitability. Although similar in form to the break-even analyses commonly used to evaluate investments, incremental break-even analysis for pricing is quite different in practice. Rather than evaluating the price and volume required for the product to achieve overall profitability, incremental break-even analysis focuses on the *change* in volume required for

EXHIBIT 6-3 ⋮ Incremental Percent Break-Even Sales Changes

		Contribution Margin									
		5%	10%	20%	30%	40%	50%	60%	70%	80%	90%
% Change in Price	35%	-88%	-78%	-64%	-54%	-47%	-41%	-37%	-33%	-30%	-28%
	25%	-83%	-71%	-56%	-45%	-38%	-33%	-29%	-26%	-24%	-22%
	15%	-75%	-60%	-43%	-33%	-27%	-23%	-20%	-18%	-16%	-14%
	5%	-50%	-33%	-20%	-14%	-11%	-9%	-8%	-7%	-6%	-5%
	0%	0%	0%	0%	0%	0%	0%	0%	0%	0%	0%
	-5%	NA	100%	33%	20%	14%	11%	9%	8%	7%	6%
	-15%	NA	NA	300%	100%	60%	43%	33%	27%	23%	20%
	-25%	NA	NA	NA	NA	167%	100%	71%	56%	45%	38%
	-35%	NA	NA	NA	NA	700%	233%	140%	100%	78%	64%

NA indicates "Not Achievable"

a price change to *improve* profitability. Using only the size of the price change and the contribution margin of the product as inputs, the break-even % sales change demonstrates the degree to which volume is required to make the price change profitable, as illustrated in Exhibit 6-3. This exhibit shows how much unit volume must change for a given price change to produce an equivalent profit, depending on the product's contribution margin before the price change. (We will describe incremental break-even analysis in more detail in Chapter 10.)

One of the benefits of the break-even sales change approach is practicality. Very few pricing decisions are made with the luxury of knowing in advance how competitors and customers will respond to them. Even the most statistically rigorous research techniques (discussed in Chapter 12) rely either on making inferences from past data or rely on customer responses to surveys of their intentions, neither of which is highly reliable. Most managers must make decisions with less quantitative information than that. Incremental break-even analysis enables managers to deal with the judgments they must make despite that uncertainty. In our experience, managers who report that they have no idea what their customers' demand curve looks like, or even how much more customers would buy if prices were 10 percent lower, can and will estimate comfortably the probability that sales will change by more than the break-even number. Fortunately, that is all the information they need to conclude whether or not the decision is directionally correct.

ESTIMATING CONSUMER RESPONSE

Once the price-volume trade-offs are understood, the next consideration is to estimate how consumers are likely to respond to a potential price change in order to balance the potential profit impact against the risks.

One of the major drivers of how consumers respond to new prices is the degree to which factors other than value influence willingness-to-pay. People casually call this "price" sensitivity, but it is really sensitivity to the price-value trade-off. If the expenditure is small or if someone else is paying the bill (for example, expenses for business travelers), then a new competitor or established player can win sales even while capturing a high percentage of the value provided. Conversely, if customers believe prices to be unfair, even when justified by value, they will be highly sensitive to the price-value trade-off. Researchers have identified a wide variety of factors influencing price-value sensitivity, which we have summarized in Exhibit 6-4.

EXHIBIT 6-4   Price Sensitivity Drivers

Size of expenditure: **Buyers are more (or less) price sensitive when expenditures are relatively large (or small).**
- How significant is the expenditure for the product in monetary terms (for B-to-B) or as a portion of income (for B-to-C)?

Shared costs: **Buyers are less price sensitive when some or all the purchase price is paid by others.**
- Does the buyer pay the full cost of the product? If not, what portion of the cost does the buyer pay?

Switching costs: **Buyers are less sensitive to the price of a product the greater the added cost (both monetary and non-monetary) of switching from their current supplier (if any)?**
- To what extent have buyers already made investments (both monetary and psychological) in dealing with one supplier that they would need to incur again if they switched suppliers?
- For how long are buyers locked in by those expenditures?
- Have customers invested heavily in product-specific training that would have to be repeated if they chose to switch?

Perceived risk: **Buyers are less price sensitive when it is difficult to compare suppliers and the cost of not getting the expected benefits of a purchase are high.**
- How difficult is it for buyers to compare the offers of different suppliers?
- Can the attributes of a product be determined by observation (search goods), or must the product be purchased and consumed to learn what it offers (experience goods)?
- Is the product new or innovative to a segment of customers, requiring some radical change in how they consume it?
- Is the product highly complex, requiring specialized skill to evaluate its differentiating attributes?
- Are the prices of different suppliers easily comparable, or are they stated in ways that make comparisons difficult?

Importance of end-benefit: **Buyers are less price sensitive when the product is a small part of the cost of a benefit with high economic or psychological importance.**
- How economically or psychologically important is the end-benefit that buyers seek from the product?
- How price sensitive are buyers to the cost of that end-benefit?
- What portion of the end-benefit does the price of the product account for?

Price-quality perceptions: **Buyers are less sensitive to a product's price to the extent that price is a proxy for the likely quality of the purchase.**
- Is a prestige image an important attribute of the product?
- Is the product enhanced in value when its price excludes some consumers?
- Is the product of unknown quality with few reliable cues for ascertaining quality other than price?

Perceived fairness: **Buyers are more sensitive to a product's price when it is outside the range that they perceive as "fair or reasonable".**
- How does the product's current price compare with prices people have paid in the past for similar products?
- Can any price difference be justified based upon a plausible cost difference?

Price framing: **Buyers are more sensitive when they perceive the price as a "loss" rather than as a forgone "gain". They are more price sensitive when the price is paid separately than when paid as part of a bundled price.**
- Do customers see the price as something they pay to avoid loss of some benefit (e.g., insurance), or to achieve the gain of a benefit?
- Is the price paid as part of a larger cost or does it stand alone?
- Is the price perceived as an out-of-pocket cost or as an opportunity cost (e.g., a payroll deduction)?

Marketers must understand which of these price sensitivity drivers are relevant for their particular products in order to influence them favorably through price and value communications. One of the major differences between tactical and strategic pricing is that tactical pricing assumes that price sensitivity is a constant that cannot be influenced. That assumption, which often is made implicitly, simplifies price setting by reducing it to a measurement task. But experienced marketers understand that this simplification comes at a cost, because thoughtful price and value communications can decrease price sensitivity and support higher prices with less adverse volume impact than would have been expected.

In some instances, it is beneficial to perform research to estimate which of the sensitivity drivers are most important for a particular product and purchase context. In other cases, it is sufficient to estimate customer response at a more aggregate level and use managerial judgment to identify which factors can be influenced through communications. These aggregate approaches, ranging from the most sophisticated and costly to the least effective but easy to implement are: controlled price experiments, purchase intention surveys, structured inferences, and incremental implementation.

A thoughtful choice from among these options involves trade-offs between the cost to implement and the quality of data gained to aid in making the pricing decision.

Price experimentation involves testing new prices on a controlled sample of customers before rolling the price change out to the entire market. After we helped a large business-to-business distributor restructure its pricing into three different service options, it had to reset price points for various products in its line. The distributor did so by experimentally rolling out the new price structure to approximately 180 of its more than 1,000 value-added resellers (VARs). The rest of its value-added resellers served as a control group. After three weeks, a second round of price adjustments, some up and some down, were made based on the degree to which sales exceeded or fell short of the break-even sales changes for each product category. After a final iteration a few weeks later, the profit improvement from the new structure and levels was clear and the new pricing was rolled out to the entire market.

Price experimentation is most useful when the cost of implementing the change is low and useful comparisons can be made between the experimental and control groups. The online environment is ideally suited to price experiments because the cost to implement new prices is minimal and it is difficult for some customer to realize they are seeing different prices than others. This ability to customize prices at the individual customer level is invaluable to the ability to conduct price experiments. However, it carries the risk of customer backlash if customers discover they are not being treated the same as others. Amazon.com found this out when customers discovered that the price they were charged to purchase a DVD varied depending on the data stored in a cookie on the customer's computer. Although Amazon was simply trying to discover the profit maximizing price points for various types of DVDs, customers viewed the practice as exploitive and put enough pressure on the company so that it chose to discontinue the experiment.

Purchase intention surveys can be used when price experimentation is impractical, as is the case for many large, infrequently purchased products (such as automobiles and enterprise software) that don't lend themselves to experimentation. In those cases, surveys of various types and sophistication can be used to uncover customer product preferences at various price points. By comparing differences in responses at different price points, and by adjusting for historical biases in responses, researchers can infer how customers would respond if faced with those price differences in actual purchase situations. Chapter 12 describes the benefits and costs of alternative survey techniques.

Structured inference by managers is an approach that leverages managerial market knowledge combined with appropriate analysis to arrive at a sound price point. Structured inferences can range from the highly formal and statistical to the purely judgmental. In all cases, the idea is to use results that managers have seen in the past to estimate the likelihood that they will achieve the necessary break-even sales changes under new conditions. For example, in one case we built a model for a chain of newspapers that in the past

Amazon.com Tests "Free" Price Point in Online Experiment

In August 2009, Amazon.com launched an online price experiment for its Kindle electronic book reader in which select books were made available for download at no charge. While Amazon has long given away public domain titles such as *Pride and Prejudice* and *The Adventures of Sherlock Holmes*, this experiment involved titles by best-selling authors such as James Patterson, Joseph Finder, and Greg Keyes.

Some critics of the approach raised concerns that the zero price point would lower customers' reference prices and impact willingness-to-pay for other titles not included in the experiment. But Amazon is testing very specific hypotheses about how the unusual price point will affect buying behaviors. For example, the James Patterson novel titled *The Angel Experiment* is the first in his "Maximum Ride" series targeted at young adults. Amazon is testing whether customers who get the first book free will then be willing to pay for subsequent books in the series. In addition to follow-on sales, Amazon is testing whether customers who download free products purchase other, unrelated products.

Some industry watchers, such as Chris Anderson, author of the book *Free*, argue that this experiment is indicative of a sweeping trend in which all digital content will be sold at no charge, with marketers making money from ancillary services and products. We do not have a crystal ball to predict where price-setting trends will ultimately land. However, it is clear that an increasing number of marketers are experimenting with new pricing models in response to changing market conditions.[2]

had initiated multiple price changes at different locations. By pooling data and controlling statistically for differences in demographics and market conditions across geographies and time, we were able to create rough models that predicted the impact of future price changes accurately enough to justify additional profitable price changes. After each change, the publisher added the new data generated to the database, which management could use to make inferences about the effect of future price changes.

When companies lack historical data on their own products, as is common for new product launches, they often look for surrogate information about the impact of price differences in other geographic markets, or on similar products in the same market. For example, pharmaceuticals companies look for "analogs" when launching a new product to get some idea of how much of the value they might successfully capture. They look at what happened, both in their same category and ones they deem similar, when earlier drugs were launched with price premiums reflecting their value, and compare that to the market penetration gained by drugs priced closer to parity. Such analysis reveals that the ability to capture value varies widely depending on the category of disease being treated and the type of differentiation offered.

Incremental implementation can work when none of the other methods for estimating customer response are practical or reliable enough to produce confident inferences. This approach often works well for products for which price changes are not very costly to make or reverse. In this approach, managers simply test customer response by making limited price changes in a series of small steps. The goal is to gradually arrive at a profit-maximizing price point while minimizing the risk of a pricing blunder that could have long-term negative effects. For example, a maker of distinctive pre-manufactured homes slowly repositioned its brand from being a cheaper alternative to being a premium-priced product with distinctive value in design and reliability. During that period, it raised prices a few percentage points more each year than the prices of similar traditional homes and tracked the effect on its sales relative to the industry. When the changes no longer improved profits, the manufacturer stopped making them.

Simulations provide a means to explore systematically the effects of competitor reactions to customer responses to a price change. Simulations combined with an appropriate decision framework provide a deeper understanding of the upside potential of a price change as well the potential downside risks. They also provide a powerful tool to compare different pricing strategies and develop action plans to manage identifiable risks. By performing thousands of simulated "runs" of the strategy, it is possible to estimate the distribution of potential outcomes for each strategy. To illustrate, Exhibit 6-5 shows a risk profile for a skim pricing strategy. Using this analysis, managers can make informed, thoughtful decisions about the trade-offs between the risk and the potential gain of alternative strategies. Instead of assuming away uncertainty, the analytic approach accounts for risk in a way that facilitates more effective decision making.

EXHIBIT 6-5   Risk Analytic Output from Profitability Analysis

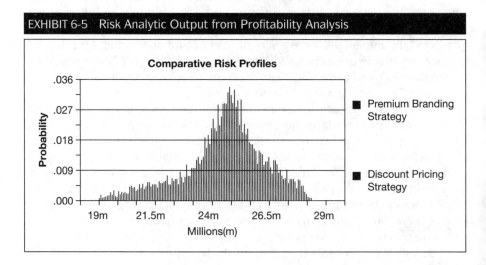

COMMUNICATE NEW PRICES TO THE MARKET

The final task in setting the price level is to ensure that new prices are communicated to the market. The most important consideration when communicating price changes to customers is that they understand the rationale for the change and believe it to be fair. Perceived fairness is one of the most powerful factors driving price sensitivity. Done correctly, communicating fairness can have dramatic effects. For example, a well-known medical device manufacturer successfully implemented a 40 percent price increase for one of its key products by carefully communicating why such a large increase was fair. The company recognized that it had made a tactical mistake by not raising prices annually along with industry practice, so it notified customers three months in advance of the increase to allow them to plan for the new prices. Not surprisingly, some customers "bought forward" at the lower prices, loading up before the price increase. But, giving them an option for dealing with the change made the company's decision seem fair and reasonable.

Dynamic Pricing Models

The last several years have witnessed a growing trend to set prices with sophisticated dynamic pricing models with data extracted from company enterprise resource planning (ERP) systems or from monitoring Internet purchase patterns.[3] Dynamic pricing models, defined as those that update prices frequently based on changing supply or demand characteristics, are not new. Utilities and other capacity-constrained service providers have long used temporal pricing models to encourage customers to buy in off-peak hours to balance capacity utilization. Airlines have used "revenue management" systems for decades, pricing airline seats to maximize the revenues from individual flights. One of the main benefits of dynamic pricing models is that they enable companies to price discriminate on a very granular level (often for individual customers) and it is more effective for managing perishable inventories than entirely manual systems.

Three factors have fueled the rapid growth of dynamic pricing systems, with the first being the increased availability of data. The widescale adoption of enterprise data management systems from companies such as SAP and Oracle have given managers access to tremendous amounts of transaction data that can be used to spot purchase patterns and estimate price elasticities. Initially, companies built customized analytical pricing applications to leverage the new data (as exemplified by the airlines revenue management systems). These systems were credited with generating billions in incremental revenues but were very costly to develop and maintain, making the costs prohibitive for widespread adoption.

The prohibitive development costs led to the second factor driving the adoption of dynamic pricing models: the emergence of price analytic software that can be customized to a particular market context and data sources. These software applications from companies such as Zilliant and Vistaar as well as many smaller firms can be integrated with existing ERP platforms and are based on sophisticated algorithms for estimating price sensitivity. Dynamic pricing software can be an invaluable tool to marketers—especially in firms with many products and a high transaction frequency that generates the data necessary to create reliable elasticity estimates.

The final factor driving adoption of dynamic pricing models is the increasing use of the Internet as a distribution channel. The transactional environment created by Internet purchases is well suited for price experiments and estimating elasticities. Moreover, it has enabled other types of dynamic pricing models such as auctions that have created new ways for sellers to capture value. Auction sites such as eBay and Onsale.com have been running auctions successfully for more than a decade for a wide spectrum of products ranging from cars to electronics. More recently, stalwart computer manufactures such Sun Microsystems and IBM have been selling increasing numbers of servers via auctions with good success.[4]

Dynamic pricing models are an exciting development in the pricing field that will enable firms to consistently segment prices based on estimates of willingness-to-pay. Nevertheless, it is essential to understand the limitations of these models. Regardless of the timeliness of the data, these models are based on historical purchase data that may not be indicative of future behaviors. This temporal data issue is particularly relevant in turbulent markets where past behavior is not a good predictor of future behavior. During the recession in 2008 and 2009, many marketers found that their pricing systems produced recommendations that were inconsistent with the rapidly evolving market conditions. That is why it is essential to ensure that final pricing choices are made by experienced managers who understand the market and can make pricing choices *informed* by the pricing system, not *dictated* by it.

To further communicate fairness, the company's letter to customers noted it had not taken an increase in eight years and the new price was still less than what it would have been had they increased prices in line with the medical device price index. Finally, the sales force met with each major account to explain that, prior to the price increase, the product was not generating sufficient returns to fund continued research and development (R&D). This was important to hospitals and doctors who relied on the company, a technology leader, to bring innovative solutions to market. Moreover, it communicated the inherent fairness of the price change by explaining that much of the additional profit would be invested in R&D and returned to customers in the form of new products rather than end up in executive and shareholder pockets.

Just as there are different reasons for price changes, there are different approaches to communicating fairness. In some instances, rising raw material costs requires a price increase. In such situations, customers are concerned about whether the vendor is being opportunistic by raising prices more than is justified and whether all customers are being treated equally. To communicate fairness in these situations, first send a letter, e-mail, or press release to all customers simultaneously that explains why across-the-board price increases are necessary. Tie the increase clearly to the cost increase (for instance, "Energy prices have increased 24 percent; energy accounts for 10 percent of the price you pay, so prices must increase by 2.4 percent") and be prepared to provide documented evidence. Where possible, index your prices to an objective measure of raw material costs such as a published commodity price index. Customers, and competitors, too, are more likely to accept a price increase if they know that prices will come back down when costs are lower. Indexed pricing is especially useful in times of significant price spikes because indices can be adjusted monthly or weekly depending on the frequency of raw material price changes.

Second, avoid being opportunistic by attempting to gain share by compromising on the increase. It can be tempting to waive a 5 percent increase for customers willing to give you 20 percent more volume, particularly in industries with excess capacity. But such an action is shortsighted because your competitors cannot afford to lose volume any more than you can. Although being opportunistic may lead to a short-term volume increase, it will surely invoke a competitive response and send a clear message to customers that the rationale for the price increase was not legitimate.

Finally, be prepared to play hardball with competitors who are opportunistic about the increase and cut deals like the one just described. Your ability to pass along cost increases will be undercut if even one credible supplier does not go along with it. Combined, these tactics send a clear message to customers that the price increase is fair and will be evenly enforced.

Another situation that requires communicating fairness occurs when a company increases prices after underpricing its products relative to the value delivered. This occurs frequently when companies begin to assess the economic value of their products for the first time and discover that they have an opportunity to increase price if they communicate value more effectively. The fairness issue stems from the fact that the company wasn't charging for value in the first place, so why start charging for it now? This is a legitimate question, the answer to which should be that over time, all prices will be adjusted to align with value. In some cases, this will mean lower prices and in others, higher prices.

To ensure that customers do not think that price increases are being forced on them, offer them options on how they can adjust to the new prices. For example, when large customers resist the price change, offer them the ability to "earn" lower prices by increasing the share of their total spend that they spend with you. Alternatively, be prepared to unbundle the core offering from services and other value-adds in order to provide a lower-value option at the old price. Whichever approach the company adopts, it is critical that customers pay for the value received. By providing choices for how that happens, you increase the perception of fairness and improve the odds that the price change will be successful.

Summary

Despite the sophisticated tools and analytics available to marketers, price setting ultimately comes down to using informed judgment to find a price that balances costs, customer value, and competitor responses. The process we have described in this chapter when followed by managers well informed about their markets and basic pricing knowledge, will lead to sustainable and profitable prices.

Notes

1. "To Find Growth, No-Frills Grocer Goes Where Other Chains Won't," *Wall Street Journal*, vol. CCXLVI, no. 42, August 30, 2005, 1.
2. "Amazon Experiments with Free EBook Offerings," *RedOrbit.com*, August 7, 2009. http://www.redorbit. com/news/technology/1734074/ amazon_experiments_with_free_eb ook_offerings/
3. W.J. Reinartz, "Customizing Prices in an Online Market," *European Business Form* 6 (2001): 35–41.
4. Y. Narahari, C.V. Raju, K Ravikumar, and Sourabh Shah, "Dynamic Pricing Models for Electronic Business," *Sadhana* 30 (April/June 2005).

CHAPTER 7

Pricing Over the Product Life Cycle
Adapting Strategy in an Evolving Market

Products, like people, typically pass through predictable phases. A product is conceived and eventually "born;" it "grows" as it gradually gains in buyer acceptance, eventually it "matures" as it attains full buyer acceptance, and then it ultimately "dies" as it is discarded for something better. There are, of course, exceptions to this process. Death sometimes comes prematurely, dashing expectations before they even begin to materialize; youth sometimes extends inordinately, deceiving the unwary into thinking it can last forever. Still, the exceptions notwithstanding, the typical life pattern affords managers a chance to understand the present and anticipate the future of most products. Such understanding, anticipation, and preparation make up a firm's long-run strategic plan. Profitable pricing is the bottom line measure of that plan's success.

The market defined by the introduction of a new product evolves through four phases: development, growth, maturity, and decline, as Exhibit 7-1 illustrates.[1] In each of its phases, the market has a unique personality. Accordingly, one's pricing strategy must vary if it is to remain appropriate, and one's tactics must vary if they are to remain effective.

NEW PRODUCTS AND THE PRODUCT LIFE CYCLE

New products play an integral, albeit frequently misunderstood, role in the product life cycle. Every product life cycle begins with the launch of an innovative new product. When the Apple iPod first hit store shelves in 2002, it transformed the way that consumers purchased, stored, and consumed music. Today, the market for portable music players with electronic storage

141

EXHIBIT 7-1   Sales and Profits Over the Product's Life from Inception to Demise

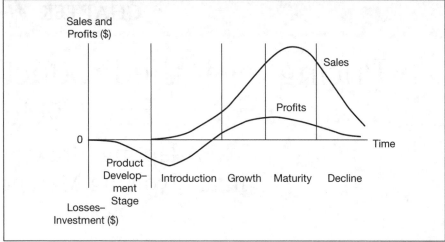

capacity is in the growth stage of the product life cycle with few signs of reaching maturity any time soon. Whereas all product life cycles begin with the launch of a new product, the converse is not always true—not all new products start a new life cycle. Companies frequently launch new products at the maturity stage to refine their differentiation relative to the many competitors in the market. Even when a new product provides a completely new benefit, it may not be an innovation from the standpoint of buyers. For example, drugs are so readily accepted as cures in our culture that new ones are generally adopted with little hesitation by both doctors and patients. Similarly, most new consumer packaged goods products and business manufacturing products represent incremental improvements to existing products in a mature product category. This distinction between innovative new products early in the life cycle versus incremental improvements to existing products in mature markets is an important one because the focus for pricing strategy changes depending on the stage.

Understanding the unique aspects of pricing new products, regardless of their stage in the life cycle, is crucial for a number of reasons. First, new products represent a primary source of organic volume and profit growth, and avoiding pricing mistakes can have both short and long-term impact on financial performance. If priced too high at launch, a new product will fail to achieve the volume necessary to maintain short-term profitability. Conversely, if priced too low, a new product *may* achieve its volume targets while failing to deliver sufficient profits. The latter scenario, pricing too low at launch, can have long-term implications for future profit growth because existing products are the primary reference price for future products. As we explained in Chapter 6, customers with a low reference price will frame the purchase as a loss, leading to greater price sensitivity and lower willingness-to-pay.

A second reason that new product pricing is especially important is that it represents an opportunity to redefine the process and considerations that determine what and how customers purchase. Customers are less knowledgeable about new products and, hence, must educate themselves about new features, benefits, and, ultimately, the value that the product might deliver. This lack of knowledge represents an opportunity and a challenge for marketers. The opportunity stems from the fact that customers are more receptive to new value communications, price metrics, policies, and price points. As a result, new product launches represent one of the best opportunities to introduce value-based pricing to a market because customers are prepared for, and even expecting, change. The challenge stems from the fact that customers perceive higher risk, which makes them reluctant to purchase even what promises to be a good value.

PRICING THE INNOVATION FOR MARKET INTRODUCTION

An innovation is a product that is unique and so new that buyers find the concept somewhat foreign. It does not yet have a place in buyers' lifestyles or business practices. The first automobiles, vacuum cleaners, and prepackaged convenience foods initially had to overcome considerable buyer apathy grounded in a lack of awareness of the benefits offered. The first business computers had to overcome skepticism bordering on hostility from managers who thought using a keyboard was beneath them. Today, innovations from acupuncture to Zipcars have encountered similar consumer reluctance, despite their legitimate promise of substantial value. An innovation requires buyers to alter the way they evaluate satisfying their needs. Consequently, before a product can become a success, its market must be developed through the difficult process of buyer education.

By definition, most customers know little about an innovative product and how it might meet their needs in new ways. Hence, successful launches of innovations hinge upon the effectiveness of the education process that customers undergo. An important aspect of that educational process is called information diffusion. Most of what individuals learn about innovative products comes from seeing and hearing about the experiences of others.[2] The diffusion of that information from person to person has proved especially influential for large-expenditure items, such as consumer durables, where buyers take a significant risk the first time they buy an innovative product. For example, an early study on the diffusion of innovations found that the most important factor influencing a family's first purchase of a window air conditioner was neither an economic factor such as income nor a need factor such as exposure of bedrooms to the sun. The most important factor was social interaction with another family that already had a window air conditioner.[3] This finding has been replicated in dozens of markets ranging from consumer electronics to business computers.

Recognition of the diffusion process is extremely important in formulating pricing strategy for two reasons. First, when information must diffuse through a population of potential buyers, the long-run demand for an innovative product at any time in the future depends on the number of initial buyers. Empirical studies indicate that demand does not begin to accelerate until the first 2 percent to 5 percent of potential buyers adopt the product.[4] The attainment of those initial sales is often the hardest part of marketing an innovation. Obviously, the sooner the seller can close those first sales, the sooner she will secure long-run sales and profit potential.

Second, "early adopters" are not generally a random sample of buyers. They are people particularly suited to evaluate the product before purchase. In many cases, they are also people to whom the later adopters, or "imitators," look for guidance and advice. However, even early adopters know little about how attributes or major attribute combinations should be valued. Value communications and effective promotional programs can, therefore, readily influence which attributes drive those initial purchase decisions and how those attributes are valued. Identifying the early adopters and making every effort to ensure that their experience is positive is an essential part of marketing an innovation.[5]

What is the appropriate strategy for pricing an innovative new product? To answer that question, it is important to recognize that consumers' price sensitivity when they first encounter an innovation bears little or no relationship to their long-run price sensitivity. Both early and late adopters are relatively price insensitive because they lack a reference for determining what would constitute a fair or bargain price. A small number of early adopters will try the product once based on the promise of value almost regardless of price, while later adopters will not try it at any price until they learn from the experience of others.

Given the problem of buyer ignorance, the firm's primary goal in the market development stage is to define the product's worth through effective price and value communications as described in Chapter 4. Thus it is important to consider the value message that various list price strategies send to the market. If the seller plans a skim-pricing strategy, the list price should be near the relative value that early adopters will experience. If the seller plans a neutral strategy, the list price should be near the relative value for the more typical potential user. The seller of an innovation should not set a list price for market penetration, however, since the low price sensitivity of uninformed buyers will make that strategy ineffective and may, due to the price–quality effect, damage the product's reputation. In addition to using list price, marketers must consider other value communication approaches.

Communicating Value with Trial Promotions

Deciding what the list price should be and what price first-time buyers actually pay are entirely separate questions. Determining the actual price for early adopters depends on the relative cost of different methods for educating buyers about the product's benefits. If the product is frequently purchased, has a low incremental production cost, and its benefits are obvious after just one use, the cheapest and most effective way to educate buyers may be to let them sample the product. For example, satellite operators Sirius and XM built interest in their product through aggressive discounts for placement in rental vehicles with either a low or no cost of trial (satellite radio was typically included in the regular rental fee).

Not all innovative products can be economically promoted by price-induced sampling, however. Many innovations are durable goods for which price-cutting to induce trial is rarely cost-effective. A seller can hardly afford to give the product away and then wait years for a repeat purchase. Moreover, many innovative products, both durables and nondurables, will not immediately reveal their value when sampled once. Few people who sampled smoke alarms, for example, would find them so satisfying that they would yearn to buy more and encourage their friends to do the same. And many innovations (for example, Web-enabled cell phones) require that buyers learn skills before they can realize the product's benefits. Without a marketing program to convince buyers that learning those skills is worth the effort and strong support to ensure that they learn properly, few buyers will sample at any price, and fewer still will find the product worthwhile when they do. In such cases, price-induced sampling does not effectively establish the product's worth in buyers' minds. Instead, market development requires more direct education of buyers before they make their first purchases.

Communicating Value with Direct Sales

For innovations that involve a large dollar expenditure per purchase, education usually involves a direct sales force trained to evaluate buyers' needs and to explain how the product will satisfy them. The first refrigerators, for example, were sold door-to-door to reluctant buyers who did not yet know they needed such an expensive device. The salesperson's job was to help buyers imagine the benefits that a refrigerator offered, beyond those that an ice chest was already capable of providing. Only then would those first buyers abandon tradition to make a large capital expenditure on new, risky technology. Business buyers are equally skeptical of the value of new innovations. In the 1950s, most potential users of airfreight service thought they had no need for such rapid delivery. American Airlines built the market for this new innovation by offering free logistics consultation. American's sales consultants showed potential buyers how this high-priced innovation in transportation could replace local warehouses, thereby actually saving money.[6] They taught the shippers how to see their distribution problems differently, from a perspective that revealed the previously unrecognized value of rapid delivery by American's planes.

When the innovation is more complicated than refrigeration or airfreight, even a convincing evaluation of buyers' needs may leave them too uncertain about the product's benefits to adopt it. For example, in the early 1990s enterprise software was considered quite a risky purchase because of the high degree of uncertainty about the ability to integrate the software into the company's IT architecture to do the billing, payroll, and production scheduling that the salesperson claimed it could do. SAP, a market leader in enterprise software, increased the business adoption rate of their software by mitigating this source of uncertainty. SAP did so by providing new customers access to successful installations and by partnering with integration firms to ensure successful implementation. The result was that sales of SAP's enterprise software increased ninefold in the mid-nineties.

Neither American Airlines nor SAP priced their products cheaply despite their desire for rapid sales growth. Instead, they educated their markets, showing why their products were worth the price, and they aided buyers' adoption to minimize the risk of failure. They funded these high levels of education and service with the high prices buyers paid for the perceived value of the products. DuPont has employed this same high-price, high-promotion strategy in introducing numerous synthetic fabrics and specialty plastics. Apple employed it in developing the market for personal computers and storable digital music devices and successful innovators in alternative energy are using it today.

Marketing Innovations Through Distribution Channels

Not all products have sufficiently large sales per customer to make direct selling practical. This is particularly true of innovative products that are sold indirectly through channels of distribution. However, the problem of educating buyers and minimizing their risk does not go away when the product is handed over to a distributor. It simply makes the need to rely on an independent distribution network problematic. The innovator must somehow convince the distributors who carry the product to promote it vigorously. One way to do this is with low wholesale pricing to distributors. The purpose of the low wholesale prices is not for distributors to pass the discounts on to consumers. The purpose is to leave distributors and retailers with high margins, giving them an incentive to promote the product with buyer education and service. While that works whenever distribution is relatively exclusive, there is the risk whenever distribution is less restricted that competition will simply cause the extra margin to be passed on in price discounts, thus losing the promotional incentive. One way to maintain distribution margins is to refuse to deal with distributors or retailers that discount during the innovation stage. This strategy of resale *price maintenance* has become easier in the United States as a result of recent legal rulings, but the rules are tricky. The rules at the time of this edition are described in Chapter 13, but they should be confirmed with legal counsel before proceeding. Alternatively, a company can allow discounting but pay incentive fees for stocking the product, for co-op advertising, for in-store displays, for premium shelf space, and for on-site service and demonstration. They may also offer incentives directly to the middleman's salespeople for taking the time to understand and promote the product.

PRICING NEW PRODUCTS FOR GROWTH

Once a product concept gains a foothold in the marketplace, the pricing problem begins to change. Repeat purchasers are no longer uncertain of the product's value since they can judge it from their previous experience. First-time buyers can rely on reports from innovators as the process of information diffusion begins. In growth, therefore, the buyer's concern about the product's utility begins to give way to a more calculating concern about the costs and benefits of alternative brands. Unless a successful innovation is unusually well protected from imitation, the market is ripe for the growth of competition. As competition begins to break out in the innovative industry, both the original innovator and the later entrants begin to assume competitive positions and prepare to defend them. In doing so, each must decide where it will place its marketing strategy on the continuum between a pure differentiated product strategy and a pure cost leadership strategy.[7]

With a differentiated product strategy, the firm focuses its marketing efforts on developing unique attributes (or images) for its product. In growth, the firm must quickly establish a position in research, in production, and in buyer perception as the dominant supplier of those attributes. Then, as competition becomes more intense, the uniqueness of its product creates a value effect that attenuates buyers' price sensitivity, enabling the firm to price profitably despite increasing numbers of competitors. Apple created such a reputation during the growth stage of computers with its user-friendly graphical interface, proprietary operating system, and distinct product designs. As a result, Apple has always carried a premium relative to Windows-based machines with similar capabilities. Intel did this for its chips, creating a customer perception that a computer was more reliable with "Intel inside." Paccar's heavy-duty trucks carry a premium from the reputation the company built for exceptional reliability and style.

With a cost leadership strategy, the firm directs its marketing efforts toward becoming a low-cost producer. In growth, the firm must focus on developing a product that it can produce at minimum cost, usually but not necessarily by making the product less differentiated. The firm expects that its lower costs will enable it to profit despite competitive pricing. The high share winner in the market for more efficient batteries, necessary for all-electric cars and to store power from wind farms, will almost certainly be the one that is able to drive down manufacturing costs faster than its competitors.

Pricing within a Differentiated Product Strategy

A differentiated product strategy may be focused on a particular buyer segment or directed at multiple segments. In either case, the role of pricing is to collect the rewards from producing attributes that buyers find uniquely valuable. If the differentiated product strategy is focused, the firm earns its rewards by skim pricing to the segment that values the product most highly. For example, Godiva (chocolate), BMW (automobiles), and Gucci (apparel) use skim pricing to focus their differentiated product strategies. In contrast, when the differentiated product strategy is more broadly aimed at multiple segments, companies should set neutral or penetration prices and earn rewards from the sales volume that its product can then attract. Procter & Gamble (consumer packaged goods), Toyota (automobiles), and Caterpillar (construction equipment) use neutral pricing to sell their differentiated products to a large share of the market.

Penetration pricing is also possible for a differentiated product. This is common in industrial products where a company may develop a superior piece of equipment, computer software, or service, but price it no more than the competition. The price is used to lock in a large market share before competitors imitate, and therefore eliminate, the product's differential advantage. Although the Windows operating system is clearly a unique product, Microsoft used penetration pricing to ensure that its product became the dominant architecture and default standard for software application programmers. Penetration pricing is less commonly successful for differentiated consumer products, since buyers who can afford to cater to their desire for the attributes of differentiated products can often also afford to buy them without shopping for bargains.

Pricing within a Cost Leadership Strategy

Like the differentiated product strategy, a cost leadership strategy can also be either focused or more broadly based. If a firm is seeking industry-wide cost leadership, penetration pricing often plays an active role in the strategy's implementation. For example, when the source of the firm's anticipated cost advantage depends on selling a large volume, it may set low penetration prices during growth to gain a dominant market share. Later, it maintains those penetration prices as a competitive deterrent, while still earning profits due to its superior cost position. Wal-Mart uses this strategy successfully to achieve substantial cost economies in distribution and high sales per square foot. Even when the source of the cost advantage is not a large volume but a more cost-efficient product design, a firm may set low penetration prices to exploit that advantage. Japanese manufacturers used penetration pricing to exploit their cost advantages and dominate world markets for TV sets after extensively redesigning the manufacturing production process with automated insertion equipment, modular assembly, and standardized designs.

At this point, a definite word of warning is in order. Much of the business literature implies that penetration pricing is the only proper strategy for establishing and exploiting industry-wide cost leadership. That literature is dangerously misleading. If a market is not particularly price sensitive, penetration pricing will not enable a firm to gain enough share to achieve or exploit a cost advantage. In this case, neutral pricing is the most appropriate pricing strategy and can still be consistent with the successful pursuit of cost leadership. The marketing histories of many cost leaders (for example, Honda in electric generators and R. J. Reynolds in cigarettes) confirm that industry-wide cost leadership is attainable without penetration pricing. The battle for the dominant share and cost leadership in those markets and many others is fought and won with weapons such as cost-efficient technological leadership, advertising, and extensive distribution. In many cases, the battle is won even against competitors with lower prices.

Penetration pricing is not always appropriate when cost leadership is based on a narrow customer focus. If the focused firm's cost advantage depends directly on selling to only one or a few large buyers, penetration pricing may be necessary to hold their patronage. For example, suppliers that sell exclusively to Wal-Mart or to the auto industry enjoy lower costs of selling and distribution but usually have to charge penetration prices to retain that business. When, however, the firm's cost advantage is derived simply from remaining small and flexible, neutral pricing is compatible with focused cost leadership. For example, specialized component assembly is often done by small contract manufacturers that are cost leaders because their small size enables them to maintain non-union labor, low overhead, and flexibility in accepting and scheduling orders. Since those cost advantages do not depend on maintaining a large volume of orders, and since the buyers that those companies serve are more concerned about quality and reliability than about price, their pricing strategy is usually neutral. When an order requires an especially fast turnaround and the buyer has little time to look for alternatives, those same manufacturers will occasionally even skim price their services.

Price Reductions in Growth

The best price for the growth stage, regardless of one's product strategy, is normally less than the price set during the market development stage. In most cases, new competition in the growth stage gives buyers more alternatives from which to choose, while their growing familiarity with the product enables them to better evaluate those alternatives. Both factors will increase price sensitivity over what it was in the development stage. Moreover, even if a firm enjoys a patented monopoly, reducing price after the innovation stage can speed the product adoption process and enable the firm to profit from faster market growth.[8] Such price reductions are usually possible without sacrificing profits because of cost economies from an increasing scale of output and accumulated experience.

Pricing in the growth stage is not generally cutthroat. The growth stage is characterized by a rapidly expanding sales base. New firms can generally enter and existing ones expand without forcing competitors' sales to contract. For example, sales of Apple's iPhone continue to grow despite loss of some market share to new entrants in the smart phone category. Because new entrants can grow without forcing established firms to contract, the growth stage normally will not precipitate aggressive price competition. The exceptions occur in the following situations:

1. Production economies resulting from producing greater volumes are large and the market is price-sensitive. Consequently, each firm sees the battle for volume as a battle for long-run survival (as often occurs in the electronics industry).
2. Sales volume determines which of competing technologies becomes the industry standard (as occurred in the market for digital music players).
3. Growth in production capacity jumps ahead of the growth in sales (as occurred in the cell phone market), creating excess capacity.

In the cases above, price competition can become bitter as firms sacrifice short-term profit during growth to ensure their viability in maturity.

Whether or not pricing competition becomes intense, the most profitable pricing strategies in growth are usually segmented. The logic for this is simple. In the introduction phase, all customers are new to the market and technology is simple. In growth, customers naturally segment themselves between those who are new to the market and those who are knowledgeable and experienced purchasers. For laptop computers, the experienced buyers usually purchase on line, and so get better pricing than less experienced buyers who require the help of in-store staff to select and configure the product.

In addition, different groups of customers emerging during the growth stage may receive different levels of value or have different costs-to-serve. Innovative pharmaceuticals are a case in point. Companies target the highest value application (called an "indication") with the greatest unmet need to launch their innovation. This enables them to win regulatory approval quickly and win sales at the highest price. Often, however, they follow with additional indications to drive growth that involve selling against cheaper drugs. The challenge is to design discounting options for contracting with different types of payers (such as insurers and governments). Those that can and would limit use of the drug to only the highest value indication must pay the highest price. Those that will enable use of the drug across many indications without restriction qualify for a lower price. Those that man-date use of the drug over competitive alternatives (such as Veterans Affairs hospitals) get the best price. Although prices may be much lower and thus less profitable for the last type, the ability to avoid having to convince every indi-vidual doctor to prescribe the drug dramatically cuts the cost of sales.[9]

PRICING THE ESTABLISHED PRODUCT IN MATURITY

A typical product spends most of its life in maturity, the phase in which effec-tive pricing is essential for survival, even as latitude in pricing is far more lim-ited. Without the rapid sales growth and increasing cost economies that characterize the growth phase, earning a profit in maturity hinges on exploit-ing whatever latitude one has. Many products fail to make the transition to market maturity because they failed to achieve strong competitive positions with differentiated products or a cost advantage in the growth stage.[10] Firms that have successfully executed their growth strategies are usually able to price profitably in maturity, although rarely as profitably as at the height of in-dustry growth.

In the growth stage, the source of profit was sales to an expanding mar-ket. In maturity, that source has been nearly depleted. A maturity strategy predicated on continued expansion of one's customer base will likely be dashed by one's competitors' determination to defend their market shares. In contrast to the growth stage, when competitors could lose share in an expand-ing market and suffer only a slower rate of sales increase, competitors that lose share in a mature market suffer an absolute sales decline. Having made capacity investments to produce a certain level of output, they will usually de-fend their market shares to avoid being overwhelmed by sunk costs.[11] Pricing latitude is further reduced by the following factors that increase price competition as the market moves from growth to maturity:

1. The accumulated purchase experience of repeat buyers improves their ability to evaluate and compare competing products, reducing brand loyalty and the value of a brand's reputation.
2. The imitation of the most successful product designs, technologies, and marketing strategies reduces product differentiation, making the various brands of different firms more directly competitive with one another. This homogenizing process is sometimes speeded up when product standards are set by government agencies or by respected independent testing agencies such as Underwriters Laboratories.
3. Buyers' increased price sensitivity and the lower risk that accompanies production of a proven standardized product attract new competitors whose distinctive competence is efficient production and distribution of commodity products. These are often foreign competitors but may also be large domestic firms with years of experience producing or marketing similar products.

All three of these factors worked to reduce prices and margins for photocopiers during the early 1980s and for personal computers and peripherals during the 1990s, as those markets entered maturity.

Unless a firm can discover a marketing strategy that renews industry growth or a technological breakthrough that enables it to introduce a more differentiated product, it must simply learn to live with these new competitive pressures.[12] As we will discuss in Chapter 11 on competition, effective pricing in maturity focuses not on valiant efforts to buy market share but on making the most of whatever competitive advantages the firm has to sustain margins. Even before industry growth is exhausted and maturity sets in, a firm does well to seek out opportunities to improve its pricing effectiveness to maintain its profits in maturity, despite increased competition among firms and increased sophistication among buyers. Fertile ground for such opportunities lies in the following areas:

UNBUNDLING RELATED PRODUCTS AND SERVICES

The goal in the market development stage is to make it easy for potential buyers to try the product and experience its benefits. Consequently, it makes sense to sell everything needed to achieve the benefit for a single price. During the early years of office automation, IBM sold the total office solution, bundling hardware, software, training, and ongoing maintenance contracts. In growth, it makes sense for the leading firms to continue bundling products for a different reason: the bundle makes it more difficult for competitors to enter. When all products required for a benefit are priced as a bundle, no new competitor can break in by offering a better version of just one part of that bundle.

As a market moves toward maturity, bundling normally becomes less a competitive defense and more a competitive invitation. As their number increases, competitors more closely imitate the differentiating aspects of products in the leading company's bundle. This makes it easier for someone to develop just one superior part, allowing buyers to purchase other parts from the leading company's other competitors. If buyers are forced to purchase from the leading company only as a bundle, the more knowledgeable ones will often abandon it altogether to purchase individual pieces from innovative competitors. Unless the leading company can maintain overall superiority in all products, it is generally better to accommodate competitors in maturity. This is accomplished by selling many buyers most of the products they need for a benefit rather than selling the entire bundle to ever fewer of them. An example of this tactic can be seen in the desktop computer industry, when experienced buyers seeking increased performance and customized configurations chose to satisfy their unique performance needs by purchasing options provided by innovative specialized suppliers. To avoid losing part of their sales, the dominant manufacturers were forced to unbundle the packages they had offered successfully during growth.

IMPROVED ESTIMATION OF PRICE SENSITIVITY

Given the instability of the growth stage of the life cycle, when new buyers and sellers are constantly entering the market, formal estimation of buyers' price sensitivity is often a futile exercise. Estimates of price-volume trade-offs during growth frequently rely on qualitative judgments and experience from trial-and-error experimentation. In maturity, when the source of demand is repeat buyers and when competition becomes more stable, one may better gauge the incremental revenue from a price change and discover that a little fine tuning of price can significantly improve profits. The techniques for making such estimates of price sensitivity are outlined in Chapter 12.

IMPROVED CONTROL AND UTILIZATION OF COSTS

As the number of customers and product variations increases during the growth stage, a firm may justifiably allocate costs among them arbitrarily. New customers and new products initially require technical, sales, and managerial support that is reasonably allocated to overhead during growth, since it is as much a cost of future sales as of the initial ones. In the transition to maturity, a more accurate allocation of incremental costs to sales may reveal opportunities to significantly increase profit. For example, one may find that sales at certain times of the year, the week, or even the day require capacity that is underutilized during other times. Sales at these times should be priced higher to reflect the cost of capacity.

More important, a careful cost analysis will identify those products and customers that are simply not carrying their weight. If some products in the line require a disproportionate sales effort, that should be reflected in the incremental cost of their sales and in their prices. If demand cannot support higher prices for them, they are prime candidates for pruning from the line.[13] The same holds true for customers. If some require technical support disproportionate to their contribution, one might well implement a pricing policy of charging separately for such services. While the growth stage provides fertile ground in which to make long-term investments in product variations and in developing new customer accounts, maturity is the time to cut one's losses on those that have not begun to pay dividends and that cannot be expected to do so.[14]

EXPANSION OF THE PRODUCT LINE
Although increased competition and buyer sophistication in the maturity phase erode one's pricing latitude for the primary product, the firm may be able to leverage its position as a differentiated or as a low-cost producer to sell peripheral goods or services that it can price more profitably or by establishing charges for "discretionary" services. Although car rental margins are slim because they are easy to compare, the rental companies earn highly profitable margins from sales of the related add-ons: insurance, GPS systems, child safety car seats, and fuel purchase options. Credit card companies make money on the over-limit and late payment charges, the foreign currency fees, and the fees charged to retailers, even when they barely break-even on the annual fee and the interest charges that drive a consumer's choice of a card.

REEVALUATION OF DISTRIBUTION CHANNELS
Finally, in the transition to maturity, most manufacturers begin to reevaluate their wholesale prices with an eye to reducing dealer margins. There is no need in maturity to pay dealers to promote the product to new buyers. Repeat purchasers know what they want and are more likely to consider cost rather than the advice and promotion of the distributor or retailer as a guide to purchase. There is also no longer any need to restrict the kind of retailers with whom one deals. The exclusive distribution networks for Apple, HP, and even IBM have given way to low-service, low-margin distributors such as discount computer chains, off-price office supply houses, warehouse clubs, and even direct sales websites. The discounters who earlier could destroy one's market development effort can in maturity ensure one's competitiveness among price-sensitive buyers.

PRICING A PRODUCT IN MARKET DECLINE

A downward trend in demand driven by customers adopting alternative solutions characterizes a market in decline. The effect of such trends on price depends on the difficulty the industry has in eliminating excess capacity. When production costs are largely variable, industry capacity tends to adjust quickly to declining demand and there will be little or no effect on prices. When production costs are fixed but easily redirected, the value of the fixed capital in other markets places a lower boundary on prices. When an industry's production costs are largely fixed and sunk because capital is specialized to the particular market, the effects of market decline are more onerous. Firms in such industries face the prospect of a fatal cash hemorrhage if they cannot maintain a reasonable rate of capacity utilization. Consequently, each firm scrambles for business at the expense of its competitors by cutting prices. Unfortunately, since the price cuts rarely stimulate enough additional market demand to reverse the decline, the inevitable result is reduced profitability industry-wide. The goal of strategy in decline is not to win anything; for some it is to exit with minimum losses. For others the goal is simply to survive the decline with their competitive positions intact and perhaps strengthened by the experience.

Alternative Strategies in Decline

There are three general strategic approaches that can be adopted in a declining market: retrenchment, harvesting, or consolidation. In most declining markets, each of these strategies will be adopted by various competitors. The conventional camera market, which went into decline in the late 1990s and early 2000s, is a good case in point. A retrenchment strategy involves either partial or complete capitulation of some market segments to refocus resources on others where the firm has a stronger position. The firm deliberately forgoes market share but positions itself to be more profitable with the share it retains. Kodak adopted a retrenchment strategy in which it intentionally exited the broad conventional camera market while maintaining a position in the conventional disposable camera market as long as it remained viable.

Not all firms that forgo market share in a declining market do so as a deliberate strategic decision. Some are forced to sell out to satisfy creditors or for other reasons. Retrenchment, in contrast, is a carefully planned and executed strategy to put the firm in a more viable competitive position, not an immediate necessity to stave off collapse. The essence of a retrenchment strategy is liquidation of those assets and withdrawal from those markets that represent the weakest links in the firm's competitive position, leaving it leaner but more defensible. In the case of Kodak, it leveraged its name recognition to sell inexpensive digital cameras that feed its Kodak Gallery, which extends the life of some of its traditional products such as prints and photographic paper. Given that capacity to make those products is sunk, the incremental revenue they represent is likely to be highly profitable.

In contrast to retrenchment, a harvesting strategy is a phased withdrawal from an industry. It begins like retrenchment with abandonment of the weakest links. However, the goal of harvesting is not a smaller, more defensible competitive position but to exit the industry entirely. The harvesting firm does not price to defend its remaining market share but rather to maximize its income. The harvesting firm may make short-term investments in the industry to keep its position from deteriorating too rapidly, but it avoids fundamental long-term investments, preferring instead to treat its competitive position in the declining market as a "cash cow" for funding more promising ventures in other markets. Polaroid was forced into a rapid harvesting strategy that ultimately led to the demise of the company in 2002 because it failed to respond to the emergence of digital photography technologies in time.

A consolidation strategy is an attempt to gain a stronger position in a declining industry. Such a strategy is viable only for a firm that begins the decline in a strong financial position, enabling it to weather the storm that forces its competitors to flee. A successful consolidation leaves a firm poised to profit after a shakeout, with a larger market share in a restructured, less-competitive industry. Consolidation is the approach adopted by Nikon and Canon that recognized that the high-end market for art photography is likely to remain viable for many years. Although most of their product development investments are focused on the growing digital market, they recognize that the art market is likely to remain viable for years and have restructured their business to enable them to continue to serve those markets profitably.

The lesson from the camera industry is that there are strategic choices that can improve even the worst phases of life cycles, but the choice is not arbitrary. It depends on a firm's relative ability to pursue a strategy to successful completion, and it requires forethought and planning. For any of the strategic choices during the decline phase, timing, foresight, and creativity are crucial for successful implementation. It is crucial that companies in declining markets act decisively. The sooner managers face market realities, the more time they have to craft strategies appropriate for their firms.

Summary

The factors that influence pricing strategy change over the life of a product concept. The market defined by a product concept passes through four phases: development, growth, maturity, and decline. Briefly, the changes in the strategic environment over those phases are as follows:

MARKET DEVELOPMENT
Buyers are price insensitive because they lack knowledge of the product's benefits. Both production and promotional costs are high. Competitors are either nonexistent or few and not a threat since the potential gains from market development exceed those from competitive rivalry. Pricing strategy signals the product's value to potential buyers, but buyer education remains the key to sales growth.

MARKET GROWTH
Buyers are increasingly informed about product attributes either from personal experience or from communication with innovators. Consequently, they are increasingly responsive to lower prices. If diffusion strongly affects later sales, price reductions can substantially increase the rate of market growth and the product's long-run profitability. Moreover, cost economies accompanying growth usually enable one to cut price while still maintaining profit margins. Although competition increases during this

phase, high rates of market growth enable industry-wide expansion, which generally limits price competition. However, price cutting to drive out competitors may occur if market share in growth is expected to determine which competing technology becomes the industry standard, or if capacity outstrips sales growth.

MARKET MATURITY

Most buyers are repeat purchasers who are familiar with the product. Increasing homogeneity enables them to better compare competing brands. Consequently, price sensitivity reaches its maximum in this phase. Competition begins to put downward pressure on prices since any firm can grow only by taking sales from its competitors. Despite such competition, profitability depends on having achieved a defensible competitive position through cost leadership or differentiation and on exploiting it effectively. Common opportunities to maintain margins by increasing pricing effec-

tiveness include unbundling related products, improved demand estimation, improved control and utilization of costs, expansion of the product line, and reevaluation of distribution channels.

MARKET DECLINE

Reduced buyer demand and excess capacity characterize this phase. If costs are largely variable or if capital can be easily reallocated to more promising markets, prices need fall only slightly to induce some firms to cut capacity. If costs are largely fixed and sunk, average costs soar due to reduced capacity utilization, while price competition increases as firms attempt to increase their capacity utilization by capturing a larger share of a declining market. Three options are available: retrench to one's strongest product lines and price to defend one's share in them, harvest one's entire business by pricing for maximum cash flow, or consolidate one's position by price-cutting to drive out weak competitors and capture their markets.

Notes

1. See Theodore Levitt, "Exploit the Product Life Cycle," *Harvard Business Review* 43 (November–December 1965): 81–94; John E. Smallwood, "The Product Life Cycle: A Key to Strategic Market Planning," *MSU Business Topics* (Winter 1973): 29–35; and George Day, "The Product Life Cycle: Analysis and Applications," *Journal of Marketing* 45, no. 4 (Fall 1981): 60–67. For a criticism of the life cycle concept, especially when applied to individual brands, see Nariman K. Dhalla and Sonia Yosper, "Forget the Product Life Cycle Concept," *Harvard Business Review* 54 (January–February 1976): 102–112.

2. See Everett M. Rogers and F. Floyd Shoemaker, *Communication of Innovations*, 2nd ed. (New York: The Free Press, 1971); Frank M. Bass, "A New Product Growth Model for Consumer Durables," *Management Science* 15 (January 1969): 215–227.

3. William H. Whyte, "The Web of Word of Mouth," *Fortune*, 50 (November 1954), pp. 140–143, 204–212.

4. Rogers and Shoemaker, *op. cit.*, pp. 180–182.

5. See Everett M. Rogers, *Diffusion of Innovations* (New York: The Free Press, 1962), Chapters 7 and 8; Rogers and Shoemaker, *op. cit.*, Chapter 6; Gregory S. Carpenter and Kent Nakamoto, "Consumer Preference Formation and Pioneering Advantage," *Journal of Marketing Research*, 26 (August 1989), pp. 285–298.

6. Theodore Levitt, *The Marketing Mode* (New York: McGraw-Hill, 1969), pp. 7–8.

7. Porter, *Competitive Strategy*, pp. 34–41.

8. See Abel P. Jeuland, "Parsimonious Models of Diffusion of Innovation, Part B: Incorporating the Variable of Price," University of Chicago working paper (July 1981).

9. For examples of such contracts, see Thomas Nagle, "Money-back guarantee and other ways you never thought to sell your drugs" *Pharmaceutical Executive*, April 2008.

10. See Hall, "Survival Strategies," pp. 75–85.

11. This problem can even result in a period of intensely competitive, unprofitably low pricing in the maturity phase if, as sometimes happens, the industry fails to anticipate the leveling off of sales growth and thus enters maturity having built excess capacity.

12. See Porter, *op. cit.*, pp. 247–249, for a discussion of the problems faced by firms that do not acknowledge the transition to maturity.

13. See Philip Kotler, "Phasing Out Weak Products," *Harvard Business Review*, 43 (March–April 1965), pp. 107–118.

14. Theodore Levitt, "Marketing When Things Change," *Harvard Business Review*, 55 (November–December 1977), pp. 107–113; Porter, *op. cit.*, pp. 159, 241–249.

CHAPTER 8

Pricing Strategy Implementation
Embedding Strategic Pricing in the Organization

Few challenges cause more anxiety for senior executives than the implementation of pricing strategies. Even after investing the time and energy to develop a comprehensive plan addressing price structure, segmentation, value communication, policies and price levels, those leaders often find that much of their organization can be remarkably resistant to changing their behaviors. As one senior executive, we know, remarked: "Given the attention we pour into pricing our products, why do the outcomes seem like a random walk?" This executive is not alone. Our research shows that more than 60 percent of sales and marketing managers are frustrated by their organization's ability to improve pricing performance over time. And more than 75 percent were unsure what they should be doing to drive more effective execution of the organization's pricing strategy.

Given such a seemingly straightforward task, why do so many organizations struggle to implement and maintain pricing strategies? Although there are many answers to this question, several factors account for the majority of the challenge. First, the inherently cross-functional nature of pricing provides many opportunities for the strategy to "come off the tracks" because there is often no clear ownership of, and responsibility for, pricing outcomes. Even when a company has a pricing function formally tasked with setting and managing prices, final decisions are often made by product managers, salespeople, or senior management negotiating with aggressive channel partners and customers. Even with years of experience, these managers often struggle to defend price points when negotiating with professional procurement organizations or when facing a competitive price cut.

A second reason that pricing strategies fail is that conflicted motivations of decision-makers translate into inconsistently applied pricing policies. Compensation plans that reward managers on revenues alone encourage ad hoc discounting and reactive pricing. Even well-intentioned sales representatives find it difficult to fight for an additional percentage point of price when that might increase the probability of losing a deal and the associated compensation. Marketers are often incented on maintaining or growing market share, which can often be accomplished most quickly through price promotions. Finance executives are often evaluated on achieving a target margin percentage, which leads them to argue against low-margin/high-volume opportunities that could increase return on investment even at the expense of return on sales. Operations executives often focus on maintaining capacity utilization even when that drives down market prices and reduces profits for all. In our experience, allowing pricing to be run by managers with conflicted incentives such as these is one of the most common reasons that pricing strategies are inconsistently implemented.

Another reason for inconsistent application of pricing strategies is that managers often do not have the necessary information and tools to make profitable pricing decisions. The advent of enterprise-wide data systems has led to an explosion of pricing data that overwhelms many managers. Often the problem is not how to get the right data, but how to translate that data into actionable information through the use of appropriate analytics. The list of possible analytics that could be used in support of pricing strategy development is much greater than the small number needed to answer any particular question. The challenge is to understand which ones are most helpful and how to get them into the hands of the appropriate decision makers. This data challenge is one of the primary drivers behind the increasingly rapid adoption of price management systems from companies such as Vendavo and Zilliant, among others. These systems can be instrumental in analyzing pricing data to deliver managerial insights across large organizations. It is not necessary for every company to have a computerized price management system to support the pricing strategy. What is necessary, however, is that managers have the right data and tools in hand to make more consistent and more profitable pricing decisions.

These common problems with incentives and information provide a good starting point for understanding what is needed to make pricing strategies stick. Implementing pricing strategy decisions requires properly addressing *organizational* issues related to how decisions are made and enforced as well as *motivational* issues that encourage managers to engage in more profitable behaviors (see Exhibit 8-1).

Organization covers the entire structure of the pricing function. It includes ownership of the decisions and the process by which those decisions are made and implemented. *Motivation* involves using principles, data, and analytics and performance metrics and incentives that encourage the right behaviors by both the organization and the individual. Even the best organizational structure will not lead to higher profits unless managers are motivated to

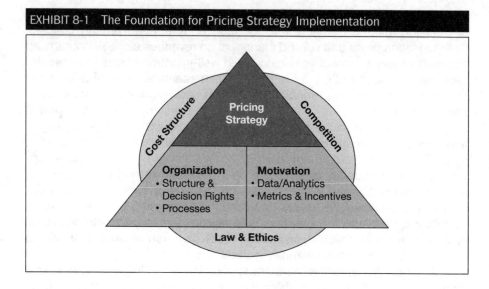

EXHIBIT 8-1   The Foundation for Pricing Strategy Implementation

change old ways in favor of more profitable behaviors. Strategic pricing requires marketing to shift from promoting features to understanding value and building price and offering structures. It requires salespeople to shift from negotiating price to selling value. It also requires operations to shift from improving the efficiency of current service operations, to designing a service organization that delivers differential value to customers. These are major changes to long-held ways of working that can be understandably uncomfortable. It is essential, therefore, to provide meaningful reasons and incentives for managers to participate actively in the new pricing processes.

Effectively addressing these key elements of implementation, represented by the lower sections of the triangle in Exhibit 8-1, will go a long way toward embedding the pricing strategy within the organization. The top part of the triangle in Exhibit 8-1 represents the elements of pricing strategy that have been detailed in the previous chapters. Combining the management actions outlined in this chapter with an understanding of the opportunities and constraints presented by the company's cost structure, its market competition, and the legal and ethical context in which it operates can lead to a pricing strategy and supporting activities that ensure consistent implementation and profitable results.

ORGANIZATION

The organization of the pricing function has a major impact on the quality of pricing decisions as illustrated by a chemical company we know that struggled for years to maintain price levels even in periods of limited supply. Historically, the company's management team had used price to maximize capacity utilization, which led them to over extend their product portfolio as they continually launched products to fill ever-smaller market niches. After years of subpar results, the company dropped their volume-driven strategy in favor of a value-based approach intended to improve margins while maintaining sufficient volumes to keep costs in line. The management team wisely recognized that the current organization would struggle with the transition to a new strategy because it involved new choices that would be difficult for many to make. So they decided to reorganize the pricing function to better support the new strategy.

The first step was the creation of small pricing committees within each business unit that were tasked with managing pricing policies and execution. Historically, major pricing decisions were managed centrally from corporate headquarters. The management team realized that each business unit operated in unique markets requiring distinct pricing policies and a decentralized decision-making approach. Endowing the business unit pricing committees with decision rights and holding them accountable for profit improved outcomes substantially as a result of market specific pricing policies and choices. The second step was to form a corporate-supported pricing council composed of representatives from the pricing committees at the business units. The council, which met on a quarterly basis, did not have a formal role in decision-making. Instead, its role was to act as a vehicle for sharing best practices and providing support to the pricing committees as they built credibility and influence. The end result of the new pricing strategy and organizational structure was an impressive $250 million profit improvement beyond the projected baseline.

Organizational Structure

Designing an organizational structure for the pricing function involves establishing formal reporting relationships for the managers responsible for managing the pricing process. It is important to recognize that no single organizational design will work for every company and market situation. The key is to ensure that structural choices are aligned with the strategic goals and activities of the business. What is the right role for a pricing function? While the specific answer will differ depending on the market context, we have identified four alternative roles for the pricing group (Exhibit 8-2) reflecting different levels of ownership of pricing decisions and processes.

The *expert resource* role can be effective with a centralized pricing function supporting multiple divisions where each unit operates in distinct markets. The expert resource role is especially helpful when the business units work with similar types of data yet operate in different market contexts where they face different competitors, incur different costs, or are constrained by significantly different laws. It is often adopted in fast-moving consumer markets in which large transaction data sets that require sophisticated analytics are the norm. The expert resource role is also common in business markets ranging from chemicals to manufacturing in which the capability to estimate customer value is important. In these instances, the

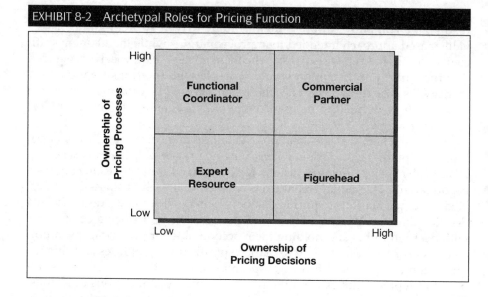

EXHIBIT 8-2   Archetypal Roles for Pricing Function

pricing function often serves merely as an internal consulting resource supporting the divisions with specialized skills such as data analysis, project management, and building a business case for change.

The role of the pricing function begins to shift when it is asked to take control of the pricing processes and play a role that is more of a *functional coordinator*. Pricing in this environment may be viewed more *tactically* with greater emphasis placed on how the decisions are made than on what the decisions are. We have found that sales-driven organizations in areas such as technology and medical devices often ask pricing to take on this type of functional coordinator role while leaving decision rights with the senior marketing and sales executives.

The pricing function assumes a *commercial partner* role when it is given authority over both pricing decisions and processes. This role is relatively common in capital goods markets where price levels are highly visible and the products have complex value propositions, as well as heavily regulated markets such as pharmaceuticals. Even in these markets, it is rare that the pricing function owns all of the pricing decision rights, however. Instead, it usually works in partnership with other commercial leaders to establish and enforce price points.

The final role for the pricing function, the *figurehead*, occurs when the pricing organization owns the right to make key decisions, but does not have the power to enforce those decisions in the market place. Few companies would intentionally design their pricing organization in this way because it virtually ensures that pricing policies will have little credibility and be weakly enforced, if at all. Nevertheless, this type of role for pricing is all too common because it enables other functional areas to control pricing without having formal authority. This type of role for pricing often leads to the increased politicization of pricing and is not a construct that we would advocate.

Exhibit 8-3   Pricing Structure Archetypes

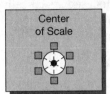

Center
of Scale

• Pricing owned and
managed at
corporate level

Center
of Expertise

• Pricing decisions
and strategy
supported by
corporate pricing

Dedicated
Support Unit

• Independent pricing
organizations exist
in each business unit

Another important factor to consider when designing a pricing function is the degree of centralization. More centralized pricing can be effective when a company operates within a single market or has business units operating in similar market contexts. Centralized pricing in these contexts enables the company to invest in developing a core of expertise that can be leveraged across markets. The benefits of a centralized pricing function diminish, however, when business units are operating in different markets. In those instances, it may be more productive to push decision-making out to the business units while maintaining coordination and support mechanisms more centrally.

These two dimensions of a pricing function, the role and degree of centralization, provide the underpinnings for three archetypal organizational structures for the pricing function (Exhibit 8-3). The actual choice of an organizational design may involve some combination of these archetypes because each potential choice involves trade-offs that can enhance or detract from the ability to execute the pricing strategy. Nevertheless, we have found these archetypal structures prevalent across markets.

The first archetype is the "Center of Scale" in which pricing decisions are made and managed at the corporate level. In these organizations, the role of the business unit is to collect data and enforce process compliance in support of the pricing decisions made at the corporate office. Centers of Scale-type pricing functions often assume the role of commercial partner or expert resource and are more prevalent in mature consumer markets such as automobiles and packaged goods, where maintaining consistent market prices is crucial. It only takes one adventurous product or sales manager to start a price war! One approach to preventing such an unfortunate event is to maintain pricing decisions more centrally.

The second functional archetype is the "Center of Expertise," which is characterized by the business units maintaining control of the pricing decisions and pricing processes. In this structure, the pricing function provides a vehicle for sharing best practices and supports the development of more effective pricing strategies. The central group will often have specialized skills such as the ability to perform advanced analytics or manage projects that would not be cost effective to distribute to individual business units. Often the group assumes the role of functional coordinator. As noted previously, this team will often serve as an internal consulting function focused specifically on pricing that improves pricing outcomes through knowledge transfer. Markets with unique local conditions such as retail and telecommunications will often have functional coordinators that assist local area managers in decision-making.

The final functional archetype is the "Dedicated Support Unit" in which each business unit has a dedicated pricing group that is only loosely aligned with corporate pricing (if that function even exists). The role is typically either a functional coordinator or commercial partner. This type of structure is appropriate for diversified businesses with little overlap in market type and can be found in an array of industries, including basic materials and information technology.

There are other factors beyond centralization and mission that contribute to the choice of organizational structure for the pricing function. For example, culture is often an important consideration as illustrated by a large bank we worked with in South America. The bank, like many South American businesses, had a relationship-oriented culture that held discussion and consensus in decision-making as a core value. The company operated in similar markets across the continent, which would have suggested a more centralized structure to the pricing function. But a centralized pricing organization would not have worked for this company because it would have inhibited consensus building at the level of the business units and branches. In contrast, the decision-making culture at a company such as Microsoft is very data driven and benefits from a more centralized organization with the people and skills to perform sophisticated analyses to support strategy recommendations. The key in organizational design, then, is to understand potential trade-offs and make a thoughtful choice for an organizational structure.

Decision Rights

Formal structure is not the only consideration when organizing for a pricing; it is also necessary to allocate decision rights to managers both within and outside of the pricing function that will participate in the pricing process. Allocating decision rights ensures that each participant understands their role and the constraints on what they can and cannot do with respect to pricing. Failure to formally allocate pricing decision rights leads to more inconsistent pricing and greater conflict as managers attempt to influence pricing decisions. A business services company unwittingly ran into this problem when they created a Key Account team and gave them the right to make "strategic" discount decisions directly with the company's largest customers. Unfortunately, the traditional sales force never had their own decision rights for pricing adjustments reduced and continued to provide their own price quotes to these same customers. Large accounts started to receive multiple prices for purchase and began to actively solicit additional quotes in hopes of getting a better deal. Although large accounts grew considerably under the

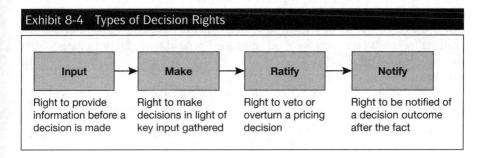

Exhibit 8-4   Types of Decision Rights

Input	Make	Ratify	Notify
Right to provide information before a decision is made	Right to make decisions in light of key input gathered	Right to veto or overturn a pricing decision	Right to be notified of a decision outcome after the fact

key account program, average selling prices declined rapidly, along with profitability.

Decision rights, as the name implies, define the scope and role of each person's participation in the decision-making process as illustrated in Exhibit 8-4. There are four types of decision rights. Given the large amount of data required to make pricing decisions, many managers are given "input" rights to pricing decisions. As the name implies, input rights enable an individual to provide information before the decision is made. Typically, input rights are granted to individuals from finance, forecasting, and research that provide critical data but are not responsible for commercial outcomes. In contrast to "input" rights, which can be allocated to many individuals, the "make" decision rights should belong to only one person or committee. This ensures clear accountability for pricing decisions and creates an incentive to follow up on pricing choices to ensure that they are implemented correctly.

Ratification rights provide a mechanism for senior managers to overturn pricing decisions when they conflict with broader organizational priorities. It is essential to separate "make" and "ratify" rights to ensure that senior managers can make a productive contribution to the decision-making process. Granting ratification rights to a senior manager balances the need to incorporate her strategic perspective into the decision-making process against protecting her time and ensuring that she does not get bogged down in day-to-day pricing operations. Finally, "notification" rights should be allocated to individuals that will use or be affected by the pricing decisions in other decision-making processes. For example, it is quite common to grant notification rights for pricing decisions to members of the product development team so that they can build more robust business cases for new products and services.

Pricing Processes

Once the organization structure has been established and decision rights have been defined, the final step for organizing the pricing function involves the creation of a clearly defined set of pricing processes. In many organizations, pricing processes are defined quite narrowly, including only price-setting and discount approval activities. But strategic pricing spans all of the activities that contribute to more profitable commercial outcomes. For example, the negotiation process might not be considered part of the "pricing" function, but it is one of the most critical determinants of transaction profitability. Excluding negotiations from the pricing process would leave an unmanaged gap or profit leak. Therefore, it is essential to think broadly when defining pricing processes.

How does one know when current pricing processes are not working effectively? There are a number of indicators of ineffective pricing processes:

- Frequent deviations from agreed price schedules and unclear pricing authority
- Frequent non-standard customer requests
- A large number of uncollected charges and an increased number of write-offs
- Excessive unearned discounts and waived up-charges
- Increased pricing errors
- Increased order processing and fulfillment errors

Correcting these problems can improve profits substantially, making the investment to define new pricing processes a good one. Thankfully, the steps to address these issues are fairly straightforward:

Step 1 Define Major Pricing Activities This step involves the definition of the major process activities such as opportunity assessment, price setting, negotiation, and contracting. The objective is to put boundaries around the commercial system so that all relevant activities affecting profitability are included.

Step 2 Map Current Processes This step creates a visual depiction of the processes by which pricing decisions are currently made, as illustrated in Exhibit 8-5. Even if there are no formally defined processes currently in place, this is a critical step for finding the source of undesirable pricing outcomes.

Step 3 Identify Profit Leaks This step uses a variety of pricing analytics (discussed in the next section) to identify where profit leaks are occurring in the current pricing process.

Step 4 Redesign Process This final step creates a series of redesigned pricing processes for each of the major pricing activities identified in step one. In order to implement the new processes, it is frequently necessary to revise decision rights to account for new individuals included in the revised process and to account for current decision-makers from whom decision rights have been taken away.

MOTIVATION

Establishing clearly defined processes and decision rights ensures that pricing strategy choices will be made in a consistent and repeatable manner. But to ensure that those decisions will also maximize profits, they must be based on accurate, useful information and individuals must be motivated to act

Exhibit 8-5 Map of Decision-Making Process for a Manufacturing Company

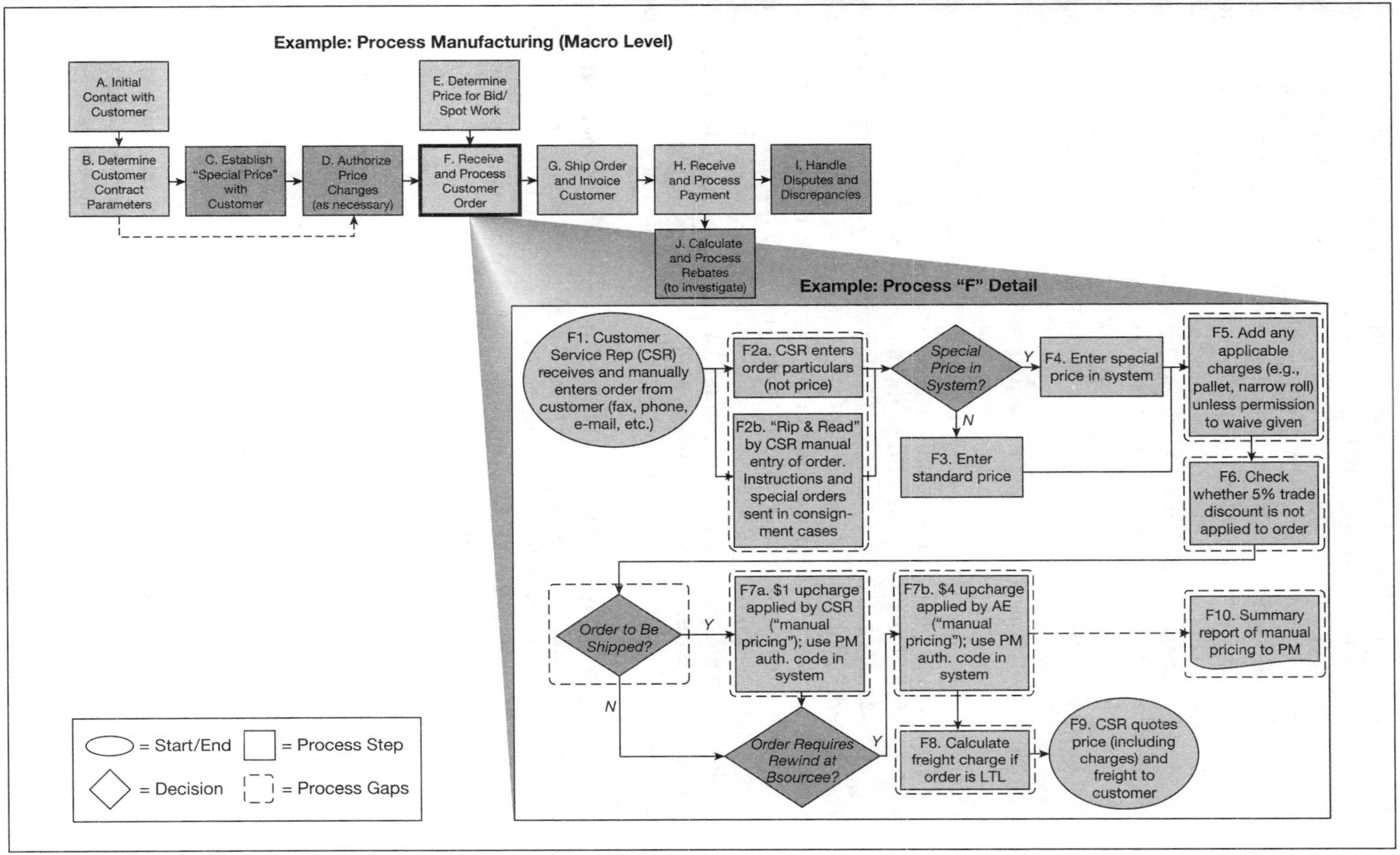

Example: Process Manufacturing (Macro Level)

A. Initial Contact with Customer

B. Determine Customer Contract Parameters

C. Establish "Special Price" with Customer

D. Authorize Price Changes (as necessary)

E. Determine Price for Bid/ Spot Work

F. Receive and Process Customer Order

G. Ship Order and Invoice Customer

H. Receive and Process Payment

I. Handle Disputes and Discrepancies

J. Calculate and Process Rebates (to investigate)

Example: Process "F" Detail

F1. Customer Service Rep (CSR) receives and manually enters order from customer (fax, phone, e-mail, etc.)

F2a. CSR enters order particulars (not price)

F2b. "Rip & Read" by CSR manual entry of order. Instructions and special orders sent in consignment cases

Special Price in System?

Y — F4. Enter special price in system

N — F3. Enter standard price

F5. Add any applicable charges (e.g., pallet, narrow roll) unless permission to waive given

F6. Check whether 5% trade discount is not applied to order

Order to Be Shipped?

Y — F7a. $1 upcharge applied by CSR ("manual pricing"); use PM auth. code in system

N

Order Requires Rewind at Bsourcee?

Y — F7b. $4 upcharge applied by AE ("manual pricing"); use PM auth. code in system

F8. Calculate freight charge if order is LTL

F10. Summary report of manual pricing to PM

F9. CSR quotes price (including charges) and freight to customer

Legend:

⬭ = Start/End

☐ = Process Step

◇ = Decision

⌐ ¬ = Process Gaps

appropriately based on it. All too often, critical pricing choices are based on anecdotal data that provide a limited, and often incorrect, understanding of market conditions. Or the reverse, when even the best analysis and decisions are undermined by poorly constructed organization and incentives.

The need for effective information became apparent to a consumer packaged goods company we know that gave increasing authority to its divisions while incenting them to improve average selling price. Through a combination of price increases and bundled offerings, the regional managers were able to increase margin percentages and hit their targets. In the process, however, they also lost sufficient volume that total profits began to fall. Unfortunately, the management team failed to recognize the profit impact of their decisions because they lacked an effective measurement system to track prices and total contribution. It wasn't until the company missed its income targets for several quarters, causing the stock price to drop, that the management team became motivated to collect data necessary to identify the problem. It then took a significant promotional campaign and targeted rebating to get the company back to their original levels of price and profit performance.

The array of analytics that can inform pricing decisions is practically endless, covering data about product costs, cost-to-serve, purchase trends, customer value, transaction prices, and more. It is beyond the scope of this text to detail all of these analytics and demonstrate how they can best be used to improve strategy choices. Therefore, we focus on two categories that have historically proved most useful to pricing strategists: customer analytics and process analytics. In addition, we will review analytics that gage the efficacy of the pricing decision processes we described in the discussion of the pricing function earlier in this chapter.

Customer analytics focus on understanding customer motivations and behaviors that are relevant to pricing choices. We have already examined one of these analyses with the discussion of value assessment in Chapter 2. We will now focus on two additional analytics that have proven helpful in pricing strategy development: purchase trend analysis and customer profitability.

Customer Analytics

One of the biggest challenges facing pricing strategists is to spot changes in customer or competitor behaviors in time to develop an effective response. For example, it can be quite difficult to know when a competitor has cut prices in an attempt to gain market share, because those cuts are not always announced or otherwise made visible. Typically, information regarding a competitor's price changes trickles in from customers, salespeople, and distribution partners over a period of months. By the time the noise has been filtered from the data, the damage has been done and the competitor has gained an advantage.

PERFORMANCE TREND ANALYSIS   It is essential to monitor trends in market data in order to spot threats to profitability and opportunities for improved pricing. But which data should be collected? Competitive pricing data can be

Exhibit 8-6   Performance Trend Analysis

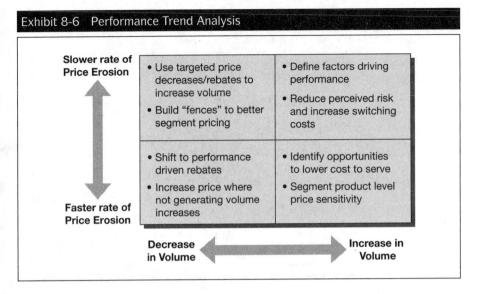

difficult to obtain and does not necessarily provide the most comprehensive view of market dynamics. An alternative is to track customer price and purchase volumes over time, as illustrated in Exhibit 8-6. This simple customer performance trend analysis is done at the customer level for either specific products or across product portfolios. The power of the analysis is that it suggests specific recommendations for addressing the potential problems and opportunities revealed in the purchase trends. For example, customers in the upper left-hand quadrant have seen their prices erode at a slower rate or increase, while volumes decreased. Customers with the biggest decrease in sales volume are thus demonstrating that they are price sensitive and might respond favorably to targeted discounts.

In contrast, customers in the lower left-hand quadrant have received lower prices while also decreasing their volumes. There could be several reasons for this purchase pattern such as the entrant of a low-price competitor, a change in the customers' own markets, or that these customers have especially aggressive procurement groups that have managed to cut better deals than other customers. Regardless of the root cause, the purchase trend analysis helps pinpoint problematic customers so that the specific problem can be identified and effective remedies can be devised.

CUSTOMER PROFITABILITY   Historically, marketers have long tracked product profitability as a key metric for managing the product portfolio and allocating marketing resources. In recent years, however, customer profitability has emerged as another metric that is instrumental to marketers seeking to improve profitability. Customer profitability measures are created by assessing average prices paid by specific customers and combining them with cost-to-serve measures allocated at the customer level. Creating customer profitability

EXHIBIT 8-7   Customer Profitability Map

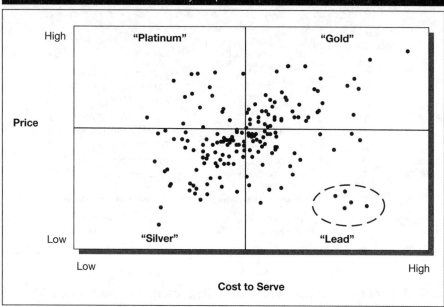

measures often requires some effort, because most accounting systems do not allocate costs at the customer level. But the benefits are generally worth the effort because customer profitability analysis provides actionable guidance to improve the profitability of the customer portfolio.

The data in Exhibit 8-7, drawn from a financial services firm, shows one approach for analyzing customer profitability that charts each customer based on average selling price and cost-to-serve. There are opportunities for profit improvement in each quadrant, and the fact that customers are charted individually allows for highly targeted actions. The "Platinum" customers located in the upper left-hand quadrant new to be protected. They are sometimes taken for granted because pay high prices and do not incur a lot of costs. However, it is essential to understand why these customers are paying a premium and to ensure they are getting good value for that price. Otherwise, they may be lost when competitors discover them and offer a better deal. In contrast, the "Lead" customers in the lower right quadrant merit a different course of action. The most egregious of these "outlaws" (circled in Exhibit 8-7, in the lower right quadrant) must be made profitable by either reducing cost-to-serve or raising prices. Raising prices on the unprofitable customers in this quadrant can result in two outcomes; the customer pays the higher price because of the value delivered, or they defect and move to a competitor. This is a low-risk move for the company because it will increase average profitability, and, often, total profitability, regardless of the outcome.

Assessing customer profitability provides high-level guidance for pricing or cost-reduction moves that can improve company profits. Additional

EXHIBIT 8-8   Individual Customer Profitability

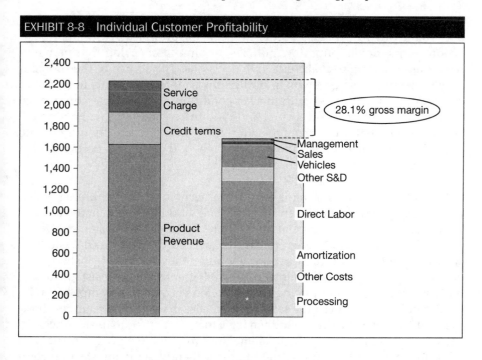

profit improvement opportunities can be uncovered by a more detailed individual customer profitability assessment, as illustrated in Exhibit 8-8. This analysis, which details the specific sources of revenue and cost, allows for the comparison of individual customers to segment averages to identify outliers that are consuming too many resources or not generating sufficient revenues. This individual customer profitability analysis, from the same financial services firm, was instrumental in helping management take corrective actions such as increased use of automation and the bulking of claims that helped reduce direct labor costs and processing costs and drove a 37 percent improvement in profitability.

Process Management Analytics

The renowned physicist, Lord Kelvin, once noted that "if you can not measure it, you can not improve it." This quote captures the intent behind process management analytics: to measure unsatisfactory pricing outcomes (such as profit leaks) and trace them back to the pricing process, where they can be "sealed." Whereas customer analytics focus on strategy development, analytics reviewing the process efficacy can identify "profit leaks" in the pricing process caused by unwarranted or unmanaged discounts. Process analytics are generally performed on transaction data containing individual records of each transaction's products, volume, prices, and discounts. The goal is to identify types of customers or transactions that are getting excessive discounts and then to trace the source of those discounts back to the pricing process in order to "seal" the profit leak by changing decision rights, developing new policies, or simply ensuring that mangers have the right data to make effective decisions. The source of the problem may range from a salesperson granting unwarranted discounts to a pricing policy that is not aligned with market conditions. The process compliance analytics we discuss below, price bands and price waterfalls, will not necessarily reveal what the corrective action for a bad outcome should be. The analytics will, however, help to pinpoint where the problem occurs, which is a useful first step toward correcting it.

PRICE BANDS Price banding is a statistical technique for identifying which customers are paying significantly more or significantly less than the band of "peer" prices for a given type of transaction. This identifies customers whose aggressive tactics enable them to earn unmerited discounts and customers who are paying more than average because they have not pushed hard enough for appropriate discounts. Exhibit 8-9 graphs the inconsistent, apparently random pattern of pricing that we often encounter at companies with flawed policies. However, the sales force or sales management team responsible might argue that there is a hidden logic to it—a method to the madness. To the extent that they are right, and sometimes they are, the pricing manager's job is to make that logic transparent to himself and the pricing steering committee. To the extent that the variation is truly random, and therefore, damaging the firm's profit and price integrity, the pricing committee's job is to create policies to eliminate it.

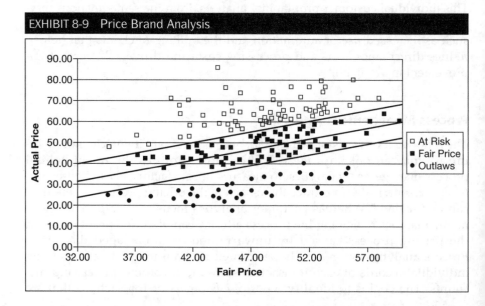

EXHIBIT 8-9 Price Brand Analysis

There are five steps to a price band analysis:

1. Identify the legitimate factors (service levels, size of orders, geographic region, customer's business type, and so forth) that justify price variations across accounts based on value.
2. Perform a regression of price levels or discount percentages against measures of those legitimate variations:

$$\text{Percent discount} = f(\text{volume, services, region, etc.}) + \epsilon$$

3. For each observation (an actual customer account or order), use the regression equation to estimate the price or discount that this customer would have gotten if given the average discount offered by all sales reps for each of the legitimate discount factors relevant to that customer. This is the "fitted value" of the regression. Label these the "peer prices," which are defined as the average price for transactions or customers with the same characteristics.
4. Plot the actual prices customers pay and compare them to the peer prices along the regression line; examine the positive and negative differences, as illustrated in Exhibit 8-9. Plot a line one standard deviation above and one standard deviation below the "peer price" line to reveal the outliers. To the extent that price variation is caused by legitimate factors, the variables in the regression will "explain" the actual price distribution well, the R^2 (called the *coefficient of determination*) will be high (between .8 and 1.0) and the band will be narrow. To the extent that discounting is random, or occurs for reasons that no one is willing to propose as legitimate, the R^2 will be low (below .4) and the band around the fair price line will be wide.

Once the analysis is completed, the next step is to brainstorm possible causes of the random variation and identify correlations to test those hypotheses. For example, do a minority of sales reps account for most of the negative variation while a different group accounts for the positive? Is the negative-variation minority composed of the newest reps while the group accounting for the positive differences is more experienced? If so, the solution may be to document what the savvy reps know about selling value and sharing that information with the low performing group. Other explanations for the random variation could relate to the customer's buying process (is it centralized?), indicating a need for different policies. In one case, the analysis revealed a pattern that was ultimately traced to one sales rep in a particularly corrupt market who was taking bribes for price concessions.

PRICE WATERFALLS   In some companies, the possible sources of lost revenue and profit are many and poorly tracked. In a classic and oft-quoted article, two McKinsey consultants used waterfall analysis to show how simply managing the plethora of discounts can improve company profitability.[1] Exhibit 8-10 illustrates this *price waterfall* analysis. Although the company might estimate account profitability by the invoice price, there are often many other sources

EXHIBIT 8-10 Price Waterfall Analysis

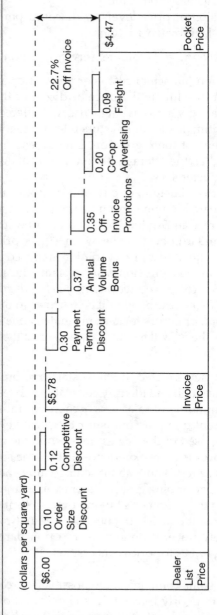

(dollars per square yard)

$6.00 — Dealer List Price

0.10 Order Size Discount

0.12 Competitive Discount

$5.78 — Invoice Price

0.30 Payment Terms Discount

0.37 Annual Volume Bonus

0.35 Off-Invoice Promotions

0.20 Co-op Advertising

0.09 Freight

22.7% Off Invoice

$4.47 — Pocket Price

of profit leakage along the way. The "pocket price," revenue that is actually earned after all the discounts are netted out, is often much less. More important, the amount of leakage could range from very small to absurdly high. In one case, a company that analyzed its pocket prices discovered that sales to some of its customers resulted in more leakages than the gross margin at list price! In addition to the salesperson's commission, there was a volume incentive for the retailer, a commission for the buying group to which the retailer belonged, a co-op advertising incentive, an incentive discount for the distributor to hold inventories, an early payment discount for the distributor, a coupon for the end customer, and various fees for processing the coupons.

Agreements to let the customer pay later, to let the customer place smaller orders, to give the customer an extra service at no cost, and so on all add up. The result can become a much wider variance in pocket prices than in invoice prices. Because companies often monitor such concessions less closely than explicit price discounts, these giveaways tend to grow. This does not mean that such discounts should be stopped; they often provide valuable incentives and can be effective in hiding discounts while still maintaining the important appearance of price integrity. The danger is simply in letting them go unmanaged, without applying rigid policies on their use. For example, after discovering that sales reps waived shipping charges for customers much more often than necessary, a large distributor imposed policies to require more documentation before such orders were processed. That simple policy change resulted in tens of millions more dollars to the bottom line.

Performance Measures and Incentives

Few things have the ability to motivate individual behaviors more than performance measures tied to compensation and incentives. Yet, many companies struggle to obtain the desired results from their compensation programs as evidenced by the more than 58 percent of managers in our research who indicated that their incentive plans encourage choices that reduce company profits. This data raises the question of why it is so difficult to design effective incentive programs. The first, and often most challenging barrier, involves ensuring that performance measures motivate the right behaviors. Employees enagage in complex activities every day, and companies often get caught in the trap of trying to design metrics and incentives to guide all of them. But the inclusion of too many metrics becomes confusing for the employee and leads to a loss of focus and an increase in frustration as well-intentioned employees struggle to figure out the right thing to do.

Instead of trying to create an overly complicated set of performance metrics, companies should settle on a limited set of metrics that are tied closely to *profitability* and then hold people accountable for their performance against those measures. Consider the dilemma facing sales representatives, independent dealers, and manufacturers' representatives who are compensated based on a percentage of *sales*. Say that the company's margin is 10 percent on high-volume deals. A sales rep who invests twice as much time with the account, selling value and/or getting the customer to change behaviors that drive up costs, might at best be able to increase the profit earned on the deal by an additional 10 percent of sales—doubling the profitability. Even if all that increase is in price, however, the sales rep's revenue-based commission increases by only 10 percent at most. In contrast, instead of trying to sell value, one of her colleagues spends the same amount of time selling a second deal of equal size with only a 10 percent margin. As a result, the colleague's effort increases the company's profit contribution by the same amount, but he earns twice as much commission for doing so. Even if the colleague has to cut the price by 5 percent to win the deal, reducing the profit by half, he still gets a bigger commission while the sales rep who spent time selling value rather than volume hears about her failure to keep pace.

Until you fix these perverse incentives associated with revenue-based measurement and compensation—driving revenue at the expense of profit—it will be difficult to get sales reps to do the right thing. The key to aligning sales incentives with those of the company is to link compensation with profitability. Exhibit 8-11 explains how to do that using a contribution margin-based formula. More than just theory, paying for profitability provides mutually beneficial sales incentives. And it encourages salespeople to pay more attention to value drivers linked to innovative product features, quality improvements, and delivery speed. Once the company aligns sales incentives, salespeople will begin clamoring for the other things they need to succeed. At one company, for example, sales reps traded in their company sedans for vehicles in which they could transport product to new customers with an urgent need, because that would contribute to follow-on sales and higher commissions.

Another challenge to the design of an effective incentive plan is the lack of alignment among performance measures across the organization. Paying salespeople based on profitability will have little impact on company profits if others with pricing decision rights are measured on market share. For example, a high-tech manufacturer we worked with had given the finance group ratification rights for price-setting to ensure that prices were set with sufficient financial prudence. One financial policy that was strictly enforced was that all products must maintain a minimum 64 percent gross margin or be eliminated from the product portfolio. The financial staff, which was evaluated on the ability to maintain gross margins, routinely vetoed requests for any prices that fell below the 64 percent threshold regardless of the market conditions or the volume. Not surprisingly, the sales organization, whose commission was based on sales volume, had a very low regard for the business acumen of the financial staff that "just didn't get it." Moreover, the salespeople would spend hours each week devising creative ways to work around the financial staff to get approval for high-volume, lower-margin deals.

The first step toward gaining alignment of metrics and incentives across the organization is to document current objectives and incentives for all of those that have been granted decision rights in the pricing process. That documentation enables you to highlight potential conflicts that can detract from the effective decision making. Ideally, the next step will be to change the

EXHIBIT 8-11 Creating a Sales Incentive to Drive Profit

The key to inducing the sales force to sell value is to measure their performance and compensate them not just for sales volume, but also for profit contribution. Although some companies have achieved this by adding Rube Goldberg—like complexity to their compensation scheme, there is a fairly simple, intuitive way to accomplish the same objective. Give sales people sales goals as before, but tell them that the sales goals are set at "target" prices. If they sell at prices below or above the "target," the sales credit they earn will be adjusted by the profitability of the sale.

The key to determining the sales credit that someone would earn for making a sale is calculating the *profitability factor* for each class of product. To induce sales-people to maximize their contribution to the firm, actual sales revenue should be adjusted by that profitability factor (called the sales "kicker") to determine the sales credit. Here is the formula:

Sales Credit = [Target Price − k(Target Price − Actual Price)] × Units Sold

where k is the profitability factor (or "kicker").

The profitability factor should equal 1 divided by the product's percentage contribution margin at the target price, in order to calculate sales credits varying proportionally to the product's profitability. For example, when the contribution margin is 20 percent, the profitability factor equals 5 (1.0/0.20). When a salesperson grants a 15 percent price discount, the discount is multiplied by the profitability factor of 5, reducing the sales credit by 75 percent rather than by 15 percent had there been no profitability adjustment. Consequently, when $1,000 worth of product is sold for $850, it produces only $250 of sales credit. But when $500 worth of product is sold for $550 (a 10 percent price premium), the salesperson earns $750 of sales credit ($500 + 5 × $50).

Because salespeople are more likely to take a short-term view of profitability and can always move on to another company, the most motivating profitability factor for the firm is usually *higher* than the minimum kicker value based solely on the contribution margin. Obviously, the importance of this adjustment is directly related to the variable contribution margin. The larger the margin and, presumably, the greater the product's importance to the firm, the greater the profitability factor's ability to align what's good for the salesperson with what's good for the company.

This is not merely theory. As companies have moved toward more negotiated pricing, many have adopted this scheme in markets as diverse as office equipment, market research services, and door-to-door sales. Although a small percentage of salespeople cannot make the transition to value selling and profit-based compensation, most embrace it with enthusiasm. Managers should be prepared for the consequences, however, because salespeople's complaints about the company's competitiveness do not subside. Instead, salespeople who previously fretted about the company's high prices begin complaining about slow deliveries, quality defects, lack of innovative product features, the need for better sales support to demonstrate value, and so on. In short, sales force attention moves from reflexive gripes about price to legitimate concerns about value drivers the company does or does not provide to customers. This is a good thing.

incentive plan so that decision-makers will share common objectives as they make pricing choices. But changing incentives can be time consuming and can involve considerable upheaval in the organization and, thus, may not always be a desirable option. In those instances, it is necessary to create policies for how pricing decisions will be made and ensure that the policy compliance is tracked with various price management analytics.

MANAGING THE CHANGE PROCESS

Organizational structure, decision rights, processes, and incentives are important levers that provide managers with the opportunity to make pricing choices in different and more profitable ways. Transforming an organization into one that ascribes to and executes on the principles of strategic pricing requires that managers act in ways that may run counter to their past experience and training. Some individuals may be resistant to change because they legitimately believe that the new approach is less effective, while others may be resistant because their compensation would be adversely affected under the new approach. Regardless of the reason, individuals must to be motivated to go through a potentially uncomfortable transition process before accepting a new pricing strategy.

There are a number of levers that can be used to facilitate adoption of the new approach including clear leadership from senior management and demonstrating successes through trial projects. Successful change efforts require an integrated and consistent use of these change levers to overcome organizational inertia and effect change.

Senior Management Leadership

One of the most important actions that leaders can take to encourage adoption of strategic pricing is to truly "talk the talk and walk the walk." All too often, senior managers indicate strong support for a new pricing strategy and then revert to ad hoc discounts the first time a customer asks for a lower price. Not only must senior leaders avoid falling back on old pricing practices, they must actively seek high-profile opportunities to demonstrate support for the new strategy. A telecommunications company we worked with had invested heavily to develop a more strategic approach to pricing in its consumer markets. The implementation plan included extensive training for the sales team and conducting a couple of high-profile negotiations with the new approach to demonstrate its effectiveness. The company seemed to be on its way to making a successful transition when the COO, who had been a tireless advocate for the strategy, began to respond to pressure from the board to meet sales targets by offering "one-time" discounts to win business. As soon as the regional sales managers learned about these discounts, they demanded the right to negotiate similar discounts. It was not long before these pricing "exceptions" became the norm across the organization and the pricing strategy was abandoned. In this example, the COO missed a critical opportunity to send a clear message about the organization's commitment to the new strategy and, instead, began the process that left the organization stuck in its old pricing habits.

Senior managers have many opportunities to signal their support of a new pricing strategy. Specific actions they should consider include:

1. Mandate a comprehensive training program to a) introduce the strategic pricing concepts and b) demonstrate what "good looks like" based on company specific examples of recent "wins" with the new approach.
2. Build in regular progress review sessions with business leaders to discuss challenges and to hold individuals accountable for progress.
3. Seize opportunities to communicate support for the new approach such as internal blogs, newsletters, and speeches.
4. Ensure that other senior leaders are actively involved in the decision-making process so that they can understand the challenges and model desirable behaviors.

Demonstration Projects

Perhaps the most important method for helping managers understand and adopt strategic pricing is the use of demonstration projects that test the new approach and provide an example of "what good looks like." Successful demonstration projects can be pivotal in building momentum for the new approach and should be given as much exposure as possible. They should be designed to demonstrate the strategy and provide feedback and real outcomes from the commercial teams. They should be focused and of limited duration, or they risk losing the attention of the organization and undermining interest in the new strategy. A good example is when an entertainment company tested a new pricing strategy and price points by selecting a very specific post-holiday period and one focused metric to track growth in total gross profit. By focusing on a discrete period and clearly defining success, the organization built not only interest in the new strategy, but also credibility when it quickly declared the strategy a success and began a full rollout.

A challenge that must be overcome when designing a demonstration project is how to define a baseline for measurement. Skeptical managers across the organization will ask, "How do I know if it was the pricing strategy that drove the outcomes when there are so many moving parts in the market and with our own commercial activities?" The best and quickest way to address this concern is to treat the demonstration project as a price experiment in which two similar groups of customers are selected. One group receives the new strategy and new prices while the other maintains current prices and policies. This provides an objective measure of the effect of the new strategy and builds credibility within the organization. The consumer entertainment company did a thoughtful job of defining a control sample of similar products that were used to establish a baseline against which the new strategy could be tested. The results of the test were then distributed to everyone in the sales organization through webcasts and sales meetings. The test contributed significantly to the organization's acceptance of the new prices.

One of the major benefits of demonstration projects is that the leaders of the project often become internal champions for the change effort. There is no better spokesperson for strategic pricing than someone who has experienced the outcomes first-hand. This is especially true for pricing, where even small barriers are seen as reason for abandoning an effort and sticking with the tried and true. Having more managers express confidence in the new pricing approach legitimizes the effort and provides confidence that it can lead to success. While having the most senior leader supporting an effort can be extremely important to success, there is also great value in having junior managers' support, as they face challenges similar to their peers, giving them strong credibility.

Summary

Implementing new strategic pricing is one of the most challenging activities facing commercial leaders today because there are so many pieces to the puzzle. In this chapter, we have outlined the major elements required to structure the pricing function and ensure that pricing decisions are made consistently across the organization. Success requires a combination of structural changes (such as process redesign and decision rights allocation) and individual motivation levers (such as incentives and metrics) that enable managers to make more profitable decisions. The degree of change is substantial, and we would be negligent if we did not acknowledge that the change process can often take years to complete. However, the data from our research clearly show that the financial results justify the effort—firms adopting the principles of strategic pricing and implementing those principles throughout the organization earn on average 24 percent higher operating incomes then their industry peers.[2]

Notes

1. Michael Marn and Robert Rosiello, "Managing Price, Gaining Profit," *Harvard Business Review* 70 (September–October 1992): 84–93.

2. Monitor Pricing Benchmarking Study, 2007.

CHAPTER 9

Costs

How Should They Affect Pricing Decisions?

In most companies, there is ongoing conflict between managers in charge of covering costs (finance and accounting) and managers in charge of satisfying customers (marketing and sales). Accounting texts warn against prices that fail to cover full costs, while marketing texts argue that customer willingness-to-pay must be the sole driver of prices. The conflict between these views wastes company resources and leads to pricing decisions that are imperfect compromises. Profitable pricing involves an integration of costs and customer value. To achieve that integration, however, requires letting go of misleading ideas and forming a common vision of what drives profitability.[1] In this chapter and in Chapter 10 on financial analysis, we explain when costs are relevant for pricing, how marketers should use costs in pricing decisions, and the role that finance should play in defining the price-volume trade-offs that marketers should use in evaluating pricing decisions.

THE ROLE OF COSTS IN PRICING

Costs should never determine price, but costs do play a critical role in formulating a pricing strategy. Pricing decisions are inexorably tied to decisions about sales levels, and sales involve costs of production, marketing, and administration. It is true that how much buyers will pay is unrelated to the seller's cost, but it is also true that a seller's decisions about which products to produce and in what quantities depend critically on their cost of production.

The mistake that cost-plus pricers make is not that they consider costs in their pricing, but that they select the quantities they will sell and the buyers they will serve before identifying the prices they can charge. They then try to impose cost-based prices that may be either more or less than what buyers will pay. In contrast, effective pricers make their decisions in exactly the opposite order. They first evaluate what buyers can be convinced to pay and only then choose quantities to produce and markets to serve.

Firms that price effectively decide what to produce and to whom to sell it by comparing the prices they can charge with the costs they must incur. Consequently, costs do affect the prices they charge. A low-cost producer can charge lower prices and sell more because it can profitably use low prices to attract more price-sensitive buyers. A higher-cost producer, on the other hand, cannot afford to underbid low-cost producers for the patronage of more price-sensitive buyers; it must target those buyers willing to pay a premium price. Similarly, changes in costs should cause producers to change their prices, not because that changes what buyers will pay, but because it changes the quantities that the firm can profitably supply and the buyers it can profitably serve. When the cost of jet fuel rises, most airlines are not naive enough to try passing on the fuel cost through a cost-plus formula while maintaining their previous schedules. But some airlines do raise their average revenue per mile. They do so by reducing the number of flights they offer in order to fill the remaining planes with more full-fare passengers. To make room for those passengers, they eliminate or reduce discount fares. Thus the cost increase for jet fuel affects the mix of prices offered, increasing the average price charged. However, that is the result of a strategic decision to reduce the number of flights and change the mix of passengers served, not the result of an attempt to charge higher prices for the same service to the same people.

Such decisions about quantities to sell and buyers to serve are an important part of pricing strategy for all firms and the most important part for many. In this chapter, we discuss how a proper understanding of costs enables one to make those decisions correctly. First, however, a word of encouragement: understanding costs is probably the most challenging aspect of pricing. You will probably not master these concepts on first reading this chapter. Your goal should be simply to understand the issues involved and the techniques for dealing with them. Mastery of the techniques will come with practice.

DETERMINING RELEVANT COSTS

One cannot price effectively without understanding costs. To understand one's costs is not simply to know their amounts. Even the least effective pricers, those who mechanically apply cost-plus formulas, know how much they spend on labor, raw materials, and overhead. Managers who really understand their costs know more than cost levels; they know how their costs will change with the changes in sales that result from pricing decisions.

Not all costs are relevant for every pricing decision. A first step in pricing is to identify the relevant costs: those that actually determine the profit impact of the pricing decision. Our purpose in this section is to set forth the guidelines for identifying the relevant costs once they are measured. In principle, identifying the relevant costs for pricing decisions is actually fairly straightforward. They are the costs that are incremental (not average) and avoidable (not sunk). In practice, identifying costs that meet these criteria can be difficult. Consequently, we will explain each distinction in detail and illustrate it in the context of a practical pricing problem.

WHY INCREMENTAL COSTS?

Pricing decisions affect whether a company will sell less of the product at a higher price or more of the product at a lower price. In either scenario, some costs remain the same (in total). Consequently, those costs do not affect the relative profitability of one price versus another. Only costs that rise or fall (in total) when prices change affect the relative profitability of different pricing strategies. We call these costs incremental because they represent the increment to costs (positive or negative) that results from the pricing decision.

Incremental costs are the costs associated with changes in pricing and sales. The distinction between incremental and nonincremental costs parallels closely, but not exactly, the more familiar distinction between variable and fixed costs. Variable costs, such as the costs of raw materials in a manufacturing process, are costs of doing business. Because pricing decisions affect the amount of business that a company does, variable costs are always incremental for pricing. In contrast, fixed costs, such as those for product design, advertising, and overhead, are costs of being in business.[2] They are incremental when deciding whether a price will generate enough revenue to justify being in the business of selling a particular type of product or serving a particular type of customer. Because fixed costs are not affected by how much a company actually sells, most are not incremental when management must decide what price level to set for maximum profit.

Some fixed costs, however, are incremental for pricing decisions, and they must be appropriately identified. Incremental fixed costs are those that directly result from implementing a price change or from offering a version of the product at a different price level. For example, the fixed cost for a restaurant to print menus with new prices or for a public utility to gain regulatory approval of a rate increase would be incremental when deciding whether to make those changes. The fixed cost for an airline to advertise a new discount service or to upgrade its planes' interiors to offer a premium-priced service would be incremental when deciding whether to offer products at those price levels.

To further complicate matters, many costs are neither purely fixed nor purely variable. They are fixed over a range of sales but vary when sales go outside that range. The determination of whether such semifixed costs are incremental for a particular pricing decision is necessary to make that decision correctly. Consider, for example, the role of capital equipment costs when deciding whether to expand output. A manufacturer may be able to fill orders for up to 100 additional units each month without purchasing any new equipment simply by using the available equipment more extensively. Consequently, equipment costs are nonincremental when figuring the cost of producing up to 100 additional units. If the quantity of additional orders increased by 150 units each month, though, the factory would have to purchase

quipment. The added cost of new equipment would then become
and relevant in deciding whether the company can profitably
price low enough to attract that additional business.

To understand the importance of properly identifying incremental costs
when making a pricing decision, consider the problem faced by the business
manager of a symphony orchestra. The orchestra usually performs two Saturday evenings each month during the season with a new program for each performance. It incurs the following costs for each performance:

Fixed overhead costs	$1,500
Rehearsal costs	$4,500
Performance costs	$2,000
Variable costs (e.g., programs, tickets)	$1 per patron

The orchestra's business manager is concerned about her very thin
profit margin. She has currently set ticket prices at $10. If she could sell out
the entire 1,100-seat hall, total revenues would be $11,000 and total costs
$9,100, leaving a healthy $1,900 profit per performance.[3] Unfortunately, the
usual attendance is only 900 patrons, resulting in an average cost per ticket
sold of $9.89, which is precariously close to the $10 admission price. With
revenues of just $9,000 per performance and costs of $8,900, total profit per
performance is a dismal $100.

The orchestra's business manager does not believe that a simple price increase would solve the problem. A higher price would simply reduce attendance more, leaving less revenue per performance than the orchestra earns
now. Consequently, she is considering three proposals designed to increase
profits by reaching out to new markets. Two of the proposals involve selling
seats at discount prices. The three options are:

1. A "student rush" ticket priced at $4 and sold to college students one-half
hour before the performance on a first-come, first-served basis. The manager
estimates she could sell 200 such tickets to people who otherwise would not
attend. Clearly, however, the price of these tickets would not cover even half
the average cost per ticket.

2. A Sunday matinee repeat of the Saturday evening performance with tickets
priced at $6. The manager expects she could sell 700 matinee tickets, but 150 of
those would be to people who would otherwise have attended the higher-
priced Saturday performance. Thus net patronage would increase by 550, but
again the price of these tickets would not cover average cost per ticket.

3. A new series of concerts to be performed on the alternate Saturdays. The
tickets would be priced at $10, and the manager expects that she would sell
800 tickets but that 100 tickets would be sold to people who would attend the
new series instead of the old one. Thus net patronage would increase by 700.

Which, if any, of these proposals should the orchestra adopt? An analysis of the alternatives is shown in Exhibit 9-1. The revenue gain is clearly
smallest for the student rush, the lowest-priced alternative designed to attract

EXHIBIT 9-1	Analysis of Three Proposals for the Symphony Orchestra		

	I **Student Rush**	II **Sunday Matinee**	III **New Series**
Price	$4	$6	$10
× Unit sales	$200	$700	$800
= Revenue	$800	$4,200	$8,000
− Other sales forgone	(0)	($1,500)	($1,000)
Revenue gain	$800	$2,700	$7,000
Incremental rehearsal cost	0	0	$4,500
Incremental performance cost	0	$2,000	$2,000
Variable costs	$200	$550	$700
Incremental costs	$200	$2,550	$7,200
Net profit contribution	$600	$150	($200)

a fringe market, while the revenue gain is greatest for the new series, which attracts many more full-price patrons. Still, profitability depends on the incremental costs as well as the revenues of each proposal. For the student rush, neither rehearsal costs nor performance costs are incremental. They are irrelevant to the profitability of that proposal since they do not change regardless of whether this proposal is implemented. Only the variable per-patron costs are incremental, and therefore relevant, for the student-rush proposal. For the Sunday matinee, however, the performance cost and the per-patron cost are incremental and affect the profitability of that option. For the totally new series, all costs except overhead are incremental.

To evaluate the profitability of each option, we subtract from revenues only those costs incremental to it. For the student rush, that means subtracting only the $200 of per-patron costs from the revenues, yielding a contribution to profit of $600. For the Sunday matinee, it means subtracting the performance cost and the variable per-patron costs for those additional patrons (550) who would not otherwise have attended any performance, yielding a profit contribution of $150. For the new series, it means subtracting the incremental rehearsal, performance, and per-patron costs, yielding a net loss of $200. Thus, the lowest priced option, which also happens to yield the least amount of additional revenue, is in fact the most profitable.

The setting out of alternatives, as in Exhibit 9-1, clearly highlights the best option. In practice, opportunities are often missed because managers do not look at incremental costs, focusing instead on the average costs that are more readily available from accounting data. Note again that the orchestra's current average cost (total cost divided by the number of tickets sold) is $9.89 per patron and would drop to $8.27 per patron if the student-rush proposal were adopted. The student rush tickets, priced at $4 each, cover less than half the average cost per ticket. The manager who focuses on average cost would be misled into rejecting a profitable proposal in the mistaken belief that the price would be inadequate. Average cost includes costs that are not incremental and are therefore irrelevant to evaluating the proposed opportunity. The adequacy of any price can be ascertained only by looking at the incremental cost of sales and ignoring those costs that would be incurred anyway.

Although the orchestra example is hypothetical, the problem it illustrates is realistic. Scores of companies profit from products that they price below average cost when average cost includes fixed costs that are not true costs of sales.

- Packaged goods manufacturers often supply generic versions of their branded products at prices below average cost. They can do so profitably because they can produce them with little or no incremental costs of capital, shipping, and selling beyond those already incurred to produce their branded versions.
- A leading manufacturer of industrial cranes also does milling work for other companies whenever the firm's vertical turret lathes would not otherwise be used. The price for such work does not cover a proportionate share of the equipment cost. It is, however, profitable work since the equipment must be available to produce the firm's primary product. The equipment cost is, therefore, not incremental to the additional milling work.
- Airlines fly weekend flights that do not cover a proportionate share of capital costs for the plane and ground facilities. Those costs must be incurred to provide weekday service and so are irrelevant when judging whether weekend fares are adequate to justify this service. In fact, weekend fares often add incrementally more to profits precisely because they require no additional capital.

In each of these cases, the key to getting the business is having a low price. Yet one should never be deceived into thinking that low-price sales are necessarily low-profit sales. In some cases, they make a disproportionately large contribution to profit because they make a small incremental addition to costs.

WHY AVOIDABLE COSTS?

The hardest principle for many business decision makers to accept is that only avoidable costs are relevant for pricing. Avoidable costs are those that either have not yet been incurred or can be reversed. The costs of selling a product, delivering it to the customer, and replacing the sold item in inventory are avoidable, as is the rental cost of buildings and equipment that are not covered by a long-term lease. The opposite of avoidable costs is sunk costs—those costs that a company is irreversibly committed to bear. For example, a company's past expenditures on research and development are sunk costs since they cannot be changed regardless of any decisions made in the present. The rent on buildings and equipment within the term of a current lease is sunk, except to the extent that the firm can avoid the expense by subletting the property.[4]

The cost of assets that a firm owns may or may not be sunk. If an asset can be sold for an amount equal to its purchase price times the percentage of its remaining useful life, then none of its cost is sunk since the cost of the unused life can be entirely recovered through resale. Popular models of airplanes often retain their value in this way, making avoidable the entire cost of their depreciation from continued use. If an asset has no resale value, then its cost is entirely sunk even though it may have much useful life remaining. A neon sign depicting a company's corporate logo may have much useful life remaining, but its cost is entirely sunk since no other company would care to buy it. Frequently, the cost of assets is partially avoidable and partially sunk. For example, a new truck could be resold for a substantial portion of its purchase price but would lose some market value immediately after purchase. The portion of the new price that could not be recaptured is sunk and should not be considered in pricing decisions. Only the decline in the resale value of the truck is an avoidable cost of using it.

From a practical standpoint, the easiest way to identify the avoidable cost is to recognize that the cost of making a sale is always the current cost resulting from the sale, not costs that occurred in the past. What, for example, is the cost for an oil company to sell a gallon of gasoline at one of its company-owned stations? One might be inclined to say that it is the cost of the oil used to make the gasoline plus the cost of refining and distribution. Unfortunately, that view could lead refiners to make some costly pricing mistakes. Most oil company managers realize that the relevant cost for pricing gasoline is not the historical cost of buying oil and producing a gallon of gasoline, but rather the future cost of replacing the inventory when sales are made. Even LIFO (last-in, first-out) accounting can be misleading for companies that are drawing down large inventories. To account accurately for the effect of a sale on profitability, managers should adopt NIFO (next-in, first-out) accounting for managerial decision making.[5]

The distinction between the historical cost of acquisition and the future cost of replacement is merely academic when supply costs are stable. It becomes very practical when costs rise or fall.[6] When the price of crude oil rises, companies quickly raise prices, long before any gasoline made from the more expensive crude reaches the pump. Politicians and consumer advocates label this practice "price gouging," since companies with large inventories of gasoline increase their reported profits by selling their gasoline at much higher prices than they paid to produce it. So what is the real incremental cost to the company of selling a gallon of gasoline?

Each gallon of gasoline sold requires the purchase of crude oil at the new, higher price for the company to maintain its gasoline inventory. If that price is not covered by revenue from sales of gasoline, the company suffers reduced cash flow from every sale. Even though the sales appear profitable from a historical cost standpoint, the company must adding to its working capital (by borrowing money or by retaining a larger portion of its earnings) to pay the new, higher cost of crude oil. Consequently the real "cash" cost of making a sale rises immediately by an amount equal to the increase in the replacement cost of crude oil.

What happens when crude oil prices decline? If a company with large inventories held its prices high until all inventories were sold, it would be undercut by any company with smaller inventories that could profitably take advantage of the lower cost of crude oil to gain market share. The company would see its sales, profits, and cash flow decline. Again, the intelligent company bases its prices on the replacement cost, not the historical cost, of its inventory. In historical terms, it reports a loss. However, that loss corresponds to an equal reduction in the cost of replacing its inventories with cheaper crude oil. Since the company simply reduces its operating capital by the amount of the reported loss, its cash flow remains unaffected by that "loss."

Unfortunately, even levelheaded businesspeople often let sunk costs sneak into their decision making, resulting in pricing mistakes that squander profits. The case of a small midwestern publisher of esoteric books illustrates this risk. The publisher customarily priced a book at $20 per copy, which included a $4 contribution to overhead and profit. The firm printed 2,000 copies of each book on the first run and normally sold less than half in the first year. The remaining copies were added to inventory. The company was moderately profitable until the year when, due to a substantial increase in interest rates, the $4 contribution per book could no longer fully cover the interest cost of its working capital.

Recognizing a problem, the managers called in a pricing consultant to show them how to improve the profitability of their prices in order to cover their increased costs. They did not expect the consultant's recommendation that they instead run a half-price sale on all their slow-moving titles. The publisher's business manager pointed out that half price would not even cover the cost of goods sold. He explained to the consultant, "Our problem is that our prices are not currently adequate to cover our overhead. I fail to see how cutting our prices even lower—eliminating the gross margin we now have so that we cannot even cover the cost of production—is a solution to our problem."

The business manager's logic was quite compelling, but his argument was based on the fallacy of looking at sunk costs of production as a guide to pricing rather than looking at the avoidable cost of holding inventory. No doubt, the firm regretted having printed many of the books in its warehouse, but since the production cost of those books was no longer avoidable regardless of the pricing strategy adopted, and since the firm did not plan to replace them, historical production costs were irrelevant to any pricing decision.[7] What was relevant was the avoidable cost of working capital required to hold the books in inventory.

If, by cutting prices and selling the books sooner instead of later, the publisher could save more in interest than it lost from a price cut, then price-cutting clearly would increase profit even while reducing revenue

EXHIBIT 9-2	The Cumulative Interest Cost of Holding a Book in Inventory							

Years Inventory Held	1	2	3	4	5	6	7	8
Interest cost to hold inventory*	$1.80	$3.90	$6.43	$9.39	$12.88	$16.99	$21.85	$27.59

*Interest cost to year $n = \$10(1.18n - 1)$.

below the cost of goods sold. In this case, the publisher could ultimately sell all books for $20 if it held them long enough. By selling some books immediately for $10, however, the company could avoid the interest cost of holding them until it could get the higher price. Exhibit 9-2 shows the cumulative interest cost of holding a book in inventory, given that it could be sold immediately for $10 and that the cost of capital at the time was 18 percent. Since the interest cost of holding a book longer than four years exceeds the proposed $10 price cut, any book for which the firm held more than four years of inventory could be sold more profitably now at half price than later at full price.[8]

The error made by the business manager was understandable. It is a common mistake among people who think about pricing problems in terms of a traditional income statement.

AVOIDING MISLEADING ACCOUNTING

Unfortunately, accounting statements can often be misleading. One must approach them with care when making pricing decisions. Let us further examine the publisher's error presented above, and others, to better understand the pitfalls of accounting data and how to deal with them. By accounting convention, an income statement follows this form:

Sales revenue

− Cost of goods sold

= GROSS PROFIT

− Selling expenses

− Depreciation

− Administrative overhead

= OPERATING PROFIT

− Interest expense

= PRETAX PROFIT

− Taxes

= NET PROFIT

This can lead managers to think about pricing sequentially, as a set of hurdles to be overcome in order. First managers try to get over the gross profit hurdle by maximizing their sales revenue and minimizing the cost of goods sold. Then they navigate the second hurdle by minimizing selling expenses, depreciation, and overhead to maximize the operating profit. Similarly, they minimize their interest expense to clear the pretax profit hurdle and minimize their taxes to reach their ultimate goal of a large, positive net profit. They imagine that by doing their best to maximize income at each step, they will surely then reach their goal of a maximum bottom line.

Unfortunately, the road to a profitable bottom line is not so straight. Profitable pricing often calls for sacrificing gross profit in order to reduce expenses further down the line. The publisher in our last example could report a much healthier gross profit by refusing to sell any book for less than $20, but only by bearing interest expenses that would exceed the extra gross profit, leaving an even smaller pretax profit. Moreover, interest is not the only cost that can be reduced profitably by trading off sales revenue. Discount sales through direct mail often save selling expenses that substantially exceed a reduction in sales revenue. While such discounts depress gross profit, the greater savings in selling expenses produce a net increase in operating profit. Discounting for a sale prior to the date of an inventory tax may also save more on tax payments than the revenue loss.

Effective pricing cannot be done in steps. It requires that one approach the problem holistically, looking for each trade-off between higher prices and higher costs, and cutting gross profit whenever necessary to cut expenses by even more. The best way to avoid being misled by a traditional income statement is to develop a managerial costing system independent of the system used for financial reporting,[9] as follows:

> Sales revenue
> − Incremental, avoidable variable costs
> _____
> = TOTAL CONTRIBUTION
> − Incremental, avoidable fixed costs
> _____
> = NET CONTRIBUTION
> − Other fixed or sunk costs
> _____
> = PRETAX PROFIT
> − Income taxes
> _____
> = NET PROFIT

The value of this reorganization is that it first focuses attention on costs that are incremental and avoidable and only later looks at costs that are nonincremental and sunk for the pricing decision. In this analysis, maximizing the profit contribution of a pricing decision is the same as maximizing the net profit, since the fixed or sunk costs subtracted from the profit contribution are not influenced by the pricing decisions and since income taxes are determined by the pretax profit rather than by unit sales.

One could not do such a cost analysis simply by reorgani.
bers on a traditional income statement. The traditional income
ports quarterly or annual totals. For pricing, we are not concei
cost of all units produced in a period; we are concerned only wi ⎯ ⎯⎯ ⎯⎯⎯ ⎯⎯
the units that will be affected by the decision to be made. Thus, the relevant
cost to consider when evaluating a price reduction is the cost of the additional
units that the firm expects to sell because of the price cut. The relevant cost to
consider when evaluating a price increase is the avoided cost of units that the
firm will not produce because sales will be reduced by the price rise. For any
managerial decision, including pricing decisions, it is important to isolate and
consider only the costs that affect the profitability of that decision.

ESTIMATING RELEVANT COSTS

The essence of incremental costing is to measure the cost incurred because a
product is sold, or not incurred because it is not sold. We cannot delve into all the
details of setting up a useful managerial accounting system here. For our purposes, it will suffice to caution that there are four common errors that managers
frequently make when attempting to develop useful estimates of true costs.

1. *Beware of averaging total variable costs to estimate the cost of a single
unit.* The average of variable costs is often an adequate indicator of the incremental cost per unit, but it can be dangerously misleading in those cases
where the incremental cost per unit is not constant. The relevant incremental
cost for pricing is the actual incremental cost of the particular units affected by
a pricing decision, which is not necessarily equal to average variable cost.
Consider the following example:

A company is currently producing 1,100 units per day, incurring a total materials cost of $4,400 per day and labor costs of $9,200 per day. The labor costs
consist of $8,000 in regular pay and $1,200 in overtime pay per day. Labor and
materials are the only two costs that change when the firm makes small changes
in output. What then is the relevant cost for pricing? One might be tempted to
answer that the relevant cost is the sum of the labor and materials costs
($13,600) divided by total output (1,100 units), or approximately $12.36 per unit.
Such a calculation would lead to serious underpricing when demand is strong,
since the real incremental cost of producing the last units is much higher than
the average cost. A price increase, for example, could eliminate only sales that
are now produced on overtime at a cost substantially above the average.

What is the cost of producing the last units, those that might not be sold
if the product's price was raised? It may be reasonable to assume that materials costs are approximately the same for all units, so that average materials
cost is a good measure of the incremental materials cost for the last units. Thus
a good estimate of the relevant materials cost is $4 per unit ($4,400/1,100). We
know, however, that labor costs are not the same for all units. The company
must pay time-and-a-half for overtime, which are the labor hours that could
be eliminated if price is increased and if less of the product is sold. Even if
workers are equally productive during overtime and regular hours, producing

approximately 100 units per day during overtime hours, the labor cost is $12 per unit ($1,200/100), resulting in a labor and materials cost for the last 100 units of $16 each, substantially above the $12.36 average cost.[10]

2. *Beware of accounting depreciation formulas.* The relevant depreciation expense that should be used for all managerial decision making is the change in the current value of assets. Depreciation of assets is usually calculated in a number of different ways depending on the intended use of the data. For reporting to the Internal Revenue Service, depreciation is accelerated to minimize tax liability. For standard financial reporting, rates of depreciation are estimated as accurately as possible but are applied to historical costs.[11] For pricing and any other managerial decision-making, however, depreciation expenses should be based on forecasts of the actual decline in the current market value of assets as a result of their use.

Failure to accurately measure depreciation expenses can severely distort an analysis of pricing options. For example, the author of one marketing textbook wrote that a particular airline could price low on routes where its older planes were fully depreciated, but had to price high on routes where new planes were generating large depreciation charges. Such pricing would be quite senseless. Old planes obviously have a market value regardless of their book value. The decline in that market value should either be paid for by passengers who fly on those planes, or the planes should be sold. Similarly, if the market value of new planes does not really depreciate as quickly as the financial statements indicate, excessive depreciation expenses could make revenues appear inadequate to justify what are actually profitable new investments. The relevant depreciation expense for pricing is the true decline in an asset's resale value.

3. *Beware of treating a single cost as either all relevant or all irrelevant for pricing.* A single cost on the firm's books may have two separate components—one incremental and the other not, or one avoidable and the other sunk—that must be distinguished. Such a cost must be divided into the portion that is relevant for pricing and the portion that is not. Even incremental labor costs are often not entirely unavoidable (see "Peak Pricing: An Application of Incremental Costing" on next page).

In past recessions, some steel producers found when they considered laying off high-seniority employees that the avoidable portion of their labor costs was only a small part of their total labor costs. Their union contracts committed them to pay senior employees much of their wages even when these employees were laid off. Consequently, those companies found that the prices they needed to cover their incremental, avoidable costs were actually quite low, justifying continued operations at some mills even though those operations produced substantial losses when all costs were considered.

4. *Beware of overlooking opportunity costs.* *Opportunity cost* is the contribution that a firm forgoes when it uses assets for one purpose rather than another. Opportunity costs are relevant costs for pricing even though they do not appear on financial statements. They should be assigned hard numbers in any managerial accounting system, and pricers should incorporate them into their analyses as

Peak Pricing: An Application of Incremental Costing

The adverse financial impact of average costing is greatest for those companies, such as service providers, whose products are not storable. Such companies face the problem of having to build capacity to serve temporary but predictable "peaks" in demand. This creates the interesting situation where the cost of capacity goes from being incremental to sunk, and back to incremental again, over the period of a year, a month, a week, or even a day. Airlines face peaks at the beginning and ends of weeks but have excess capacity midweek and on weekends. Telecom companies face peaks in the middle of each weekday but have excess capacity in the evenings and on weekends. Restaurants, car rental companies, marketers of advertising space, commercial printers, health clubs, resorts, electric utilities, and landscape maintenance companies all face substantial peaks and valleys in demand for nonstorable products or services. One way to manage capacity in those cases, and to thus maximize profitability, is with price.

The key to using price to manage capacity profitably is to understand how to allocate the capacity costs over time. Most companies make the mistake of averaging the capacity cost over all of the units produced. If an electric utility sells 40 percent of its kilowatts during a few peak hours, and 60 percent during the other 21 hours in the day, then 40 percent of the capacity cost (the depreciation and maintenance cost for the power plants) would be allocated to the peak hours. This results in each kilowatt being assigned the same capacity charge. Although this is the usual approach (utilities have even been required to cost and price this way by regulation), it makes no sense in principle and undermines profitability in practice. Why? Because the need for the capacity is created entirely by the peak period demand. Off-peak demand can be satisfied without the additional capacity, so capacity costs are not incremental to decisions that affect the volume of off-peak sales. Consequently, the cost of capacity above what is necessary to meet off-peak demand should be allocated entirely to the peak period sales.

One effect of allocating those costs only to sales in the peak period is to raise the hurdle required to justify peak-period investment. The way to ensure that capacity costs are covered is to make no capacity investments that cannot be entirely justified by the revenue from peak demand. If additional capacity really is required only for a few hours a day, a few days a week, or a few months a year, then prices in those periods should be covering all the cost of the capacity, or the capacity should not be built. The other effect is to reveal the surprisingly high profitability of the lower-price, lower-margin sales in off-peak periods. Because the contribution from off-peak sales is not required to cover the cost of capacity, which will be there whether or not the capacity is used, that contribution falls directly to the bottom line. Companies that fail to realize this overinvest for peak demand and then are forced either to cut their prices to fill their off-peak capacity or to suffer even greater losses during off-peak periods. On net, they invest themselves into unprofitability.

As a company moves toward pricing differently for the peaks and valleys, its average price decreases, but its profit and return on capital invested will increase. For companies with a peak capacity problem, it is usually far more important that they earn a high return per unit of capacity than it is for them to earn a high contribution margin per sale. For many years, hotels mismeasured their success by their ability to command and increase their "average daily rate." Of course, one way to increase average daily rate is simply to rent no rooms except at times of peak demand when the hotel can ask for and get its highest rates. That is unlikely, however, to yield a good return on assets. When hotels began being managed more rationally, the industry adopted a new measure, "revenue per available room," that changed the incentive to manage capacity. The bottom line became "Get all you can get at peak, but make sure you fill the room and earn something at off peak."

they would any other cost. In the earlier example of the book publisher, the cost of capital required to maintain the firm's inventory was the cost of borrowed funds (18 percent). It, therefore, generated an explicit interest expense on the firm's income statement. A proper analysis of the publisher's problem would have been no different had we assumed that the inventory was financed entirely with internally generated funds. Those internally generated funds do not create an interest expense on the publisher's income statement, but they do have alternative uses. Internally generated funds that are used to finance inventories could have been used to purchase an interest-bearing note or could have been invested in some profitable sideline business such as printing stationery. The interest income that could have been earned from the best of these alternatives is an incremental, avoidable cost of using internally generated funds, just as the interest paid explicitly is an incremental, avoidable cost of using borrowed funds.

The same argument would apply when costing the use of a manufacturing facility, a railroad right-of-way, or the seat capacity of an airline. The historical cost of those assets is entirely irrelevant and potentially a very misleading guide to pricing. There is often, however, a current cost of using those assets that is very relevant. That cost occurs whenever capacity used either could be used to make and sell some other product, or could be rented or sold to some other company. Even though the historical cost is sunk, the relevant cost of using those assets is positive whenever there are competing profitable uses. That opportunity cost is the contribution that must be forgone if the assets are not sold or used to produce the alternative product or service. It can easily exceed not only the historical cost but also even the replacement cost of the capacity.

Even if a company has current excess capacity but there is some probability that future business might have to be turned away, the capacity should be assigned an opportunity cost for pricing. Airlines, for example, stop selling discounted seats for a particular flight long before the flight is full. The opportunity cost of selling a discounted seat is near zero only if that seat would otherwise certainly be empty at flight time. As a plane's capacity fills, however, the probability increases that selling a discounted seat will require turning away a passenger who would have paid full fare on the day of the flight. The probability of such a passenger wanting the seat, times the contribution that would be earned at full price, is the opportunity cost of selling a discounted seat in advance.

Obviously, moving beyond these costing principles to estimating the true cost of a sale is not easy. Too often, however, managers shrink from the task

Opportunity Costs: A Practical Illustration

An airline's most important cost for pricing is the "opportunity cost" of its capacity. Incremental costs other than capacity costs (for example, food, ticketing) are literally trivial in comparison. An airline that took the historical cost or even the replacement cost of buying planes would miss many opportunities for profitable pricing and, in a competitive market, would soon go bankrupt because most of the profitability of an airline comes from the "incremental" revenue that it generates selling some seats at prices below the average cost per seat. The key to making such a strategy profitable is to understand on an ongoing basis the expected opportunity cost of selling a seat at any particular time on any particular flight.

What is the opportunity cost of a seat? On Saturday afternoon to nonresort locations, it is probably zero since there is no way that the plane will ever be filled. At most times, however, a plane could easily be filled by offering a low discount price during the month before the flight. The opportunity cost of selling such a seat is the contribution that could be earned from a full-fare passenger, usually a business traveler, times the probability that such a price-insensitive passenger will in fact buy the seat before the plane departs. For example, if a plane currently has empty seats one month before the flight, the airline uses historical booking patterns to estimate that it has a 70 percent probability that the plane will depart with at least one empty seat. That means that there is a 30 percent probability that a seat would not be available to a last-minute passenger willing to pay full fare. If the contribution from a full-fare ticket for the flight is $500, then the "opportunity cost" to sell a discount ticket in advance is $0.3 \times \$500 = \$150$, to which we add the cost of ticketing and incremental fuel, to estimate the total cost of offering the ticket. This costing system explains why the price of a discount ticket on the same flight might go up or down many weeks before a flight departs, while there are still many seats available. Airlines have sophisticated "yield management" systems that use historical booking patterns to estimate the probability of an empty seat at departure. If a plane is not filling up as rapidly as historically expected, the probability of an empty seat goes up, the opportunity cost of selling more discounted seats goes down, so the airline's management system may offer some tickets at an exceptionally low price. If, however, a group of seven businesspeople suddenly books the flight, the probability of filling the flight jumps substantially, the opportunity cost goes up, and the airline's yield management system automatically blocks additional sales of the cheapest tickets.

because of the cost and complexity of measuring true costs on an ongoing basis. Usually, in our experience, it is possible to get much closer to true costs by doing even a simple point-in-time study of cost drivers. We have, for example, worked with a company that charged every item produced the same amount for paint, even though some items were produced in large lots and others in small lots. By doing a simple statistical regression, using prior year data, paint purchases by color as a function of production of that color product, and average lot size, we rationally reallocated paint costs to reflect the higher costs of small batches. In other cases, we have relied on cost drivers as subjective as a plant foreman's judgment about the relative difficulty of making different types of products. Are such judgments highly accurate? Probably not. That is not a reason to avoid making them if that is the best you can do with the time and money available. It is better to make pricing decisions based on rough approximations of the true costs of products or services than on precise accounting of costs that are sure to be, at best, irrelevant and, at worst, highly misleading.

ACTIVITY-BASED COSTING

Activity-based costing (ABC) provides more realistic estimates of how support costs change with increments in sales volume.[12] For example, traditional cost accounting systems use bases like direct labor and machine hours to allocate to products the expenses of support activities. Instead, ABC segregates support expenditures by activities, and then assigns those expenditures based on the drivers of the activities and how they are linked to product sales volume. Some applications of ABC have allowed firms to estimate not just manufacturing costs, but also costs to serve different customers. ABC enables managers to identify the characteristics or drivers that cause some customers to be more expensive or less expensive to serve. Robert Kaplan[13] identified the following differences in characteristics of high cost-to-serve versus low cost-to-serve customers:

High Cost-to-Serve Customers	Low Cost-to-Serve Customers
Order custom products	Order standard products
Small order quantities	High order quantities
Unpredictable order quantities	Predictable order quantities
Customized delivery	Standard delivery
Change delivery requirements	No changes in delivery requirements
Manual processing	Electronic processing (EDI)
Large amounts of presales support (marketing, technical, sales resources)	Little to no presales support (standard pricing and ordering)
Large amounts of postsales support (installation, training, warranty, field service)	No postsales support
Require company to hold inventory	Replenish inventory as produced
Pay slowly (high accounts receivable)	Pay on time

ABC extends incremental costing to cost categories that are neither fixed nor variable, but are semifixed costs. For example, these may be costs associated with order entry personnel, or shipping personnel, that are incurred in less frequent outlays or lumps, but nonetheless change with larger changes in volume. ABC allocates these semifixed costs according to activity drivers, usually related to transactions associated with the function—for example, the number of orders received by the order entry department, or the number of shipments shipped by the shipping department. ABC is especially valuable in refining the manager's estimate of the true cost-to-serve an incoming customer order.

PERCENT CONTRIBUTION MARGIN AND PRICING STRATEGY

There are three benefits to determining the true unit cost of a product or service for pricing. First, it is a necessary first step toward controlling costs. The best way to control variable costs is not necessarily appropriate for controlling fixed costs. Second, it enables management to determine the minimum price at which the firm can profitably accept incremental business that will not affect the pricing of its other sales. Third, and most important for our purposes, it enables management to determine the contribution margin for each product sold, which, as will be seen in Chapter 10 on financial analysis, is essential for making informed, profitable pricing decisions.

The percent contribution margin is the share of price that adds to profit or reduces losses. It is not the return on sales, which is used by financial analysts to compare the performance of different companies in the same industry. The return on sales indicates the average profit as a percentage of the price after accounting for all costs. Our concern, however, is not with the average, but with the added profit resulting from an additional sale. Even when variable costs are constant, the added profit from a sale exceeds the average profit because some costs are fixed or sunk. The share of the price that adds to profit, the contribution margin, is everything above the share required to cover the incremental variable cost of the sale.

When variable cost is constant for all units affected by a particular pricing decision, it is proper to calculate the percent contribution margin from aggregate sales data. After calculating the sales revenue and total contribution margin resulting from a change in sales, one can calculate the percent contribution margin, or %CM, as follows:

$$\%CM = \frac{\text{Total contribution margin}}{\text{Sales revenue}} \times 100$$

When variable costs are not constant for all units (for example, when the units affected by a price change are produced on overtime), it is important to calculate a dollar contribution margin per unit for just the units affected by the price change. The dollar contribution margin per unit, $CM, is simply

$$\$CM = \text{Price} - \text{Variable cost}$$

where variable cost is the cost per unit of only those units affected by the price change and includes only those costs that are avoidable. With the dollar contribution margin, one can calculate the percent contribution margin without being misled when variable costs are not constant. The formula for this calculation of the percent contribution margin is

$$\%CM = \frac{\$CM}{Price}$$

which gives the percent contribution margin in decimal form.

The size of the contribution as a percentage of the price has important strategic implications. First, the percent contribution margin is a measure of the leverage between a firm's sales volume and its profit. It indicates the importance of sales volume as a marketing objective. To illustrate, look at Exhibit 9-3. A company sells two products, each with the same net profit on sales, but with substantially different contribution margins. A company using full-cost pricing would, therefore, treat them the same. However, the actual effect of a price change for these two products would be radically different because of their varying cost structures (see Exhibit 9-3).

Product A has high variable costs equal to 80 percent of its price. Its percent contribution margin is, therefore, 20 percent. Product B has low variable costs equal to 20 percent of its product's price. Its percent contribution margin is therefore 80 percent. Although at current sales volumes each product earns the same net profit, the effect on each of a change in sales volume is dramatically different. For product A, only $0.20 of every additional sales dollar increases profit or reduces losses. For product B, that figure is $0.80.

EXHIBIT 9-3 Effect of Contribution Margin on Break-Even Sales Changes

	Product A	Product B
Percentage of selling price accounted for by:		
Variable costs	80.0	20.0
Fixed or sunk costs	10.0	70.0
Net profit margin	10.0	10.0
Contribution margin	20.0	80.0
Break-even sales change (%) for a:		
5% Price reduction/advantage	+33.3	+6.7
10% Price reduction/advantage	+100.0	+14.3
20% Price reduction/advantage	∞	+33.3
5% Price increase/premium	−20.0	−5.9
10% Price increase/premium	−33.3	−11.1
20% Price increase/premium	−50.0	−20.0

The lower part of Exhibit 9-3 illustrates the impact of this difference on pricing decisions. In order for product A, with its relatively small percent contribution margin, to profit from a 5 percent price cut, its sales must increase by more than 33 percent, compared with only 6.7 percent for product B with its larger percent contribution margin. To profit from a 10 percent price cut, product A's sales must increase by more than 100 percent, compared with only 14.3 percent for product B. Clearly, this company cannot justify a strategy of low pricing to build volume for product A nearly as easily as it can for product B. The opposite conclusion follows for price increases. Product A can afford to lose many more sales than product B and still profit from higher prices. Consequently, it is much easier to justify a premium price strategy for product A than for product B.

Second, the percent contribution margin is an indicator of the firm's ability to compete against competitors. If a competitor believes it has a substantially higher percent contribution margin than you do, then it is likely that the competitor will engage in price discounting to drive sales volume because of the leverage between sales volume and profit. On the other hand, knowing that you have comparable or higher percent contribution margins than your competitor provides some assurance that you have the ability to retaliate and counterattack opportunistic moves by competitors who attempt to lure customers with price discounting.

Third, the percent contribution margin is a measure of the extent to which you can use segmentation pricing to serve and penetrate multiple market segments. *Segmentation pricing* means setting different prices for different market segments, each of which has a different cost to serve and different level of price sensitivity. For a given product, the greater your percent contribution margin, the more flexibility you have to set higher prices for some customer segments and lower prices for other segments. This enables you to serve not only customers who are willing to pay premium prices but also customers that are price sensitive and only willing to pay lower prices. Many companies strategically design their cost structure to ensure that their variable costs remain low so they can maintain a high percent contribution margin, which enables them to penetrate many market segments of varying price sensitivities. They support these penetration strategies with high fixed costs that enable them to drive product volume through investments in advertising, sales promotions, price discounting, and intensive distribution systems.

MANAGING COSTS IN TRANSFER PRICING

A frequently overlooked opportunity to use costs as a source of advantage in pricing occurs when the company can manage the structure of the prices of its upstream suppliers. These upstream suppliers might be independent companies or independent divisions of the same company that set the prices of products that pass between them. This situation, known as *transfer pricing*, represents one of the most common reasons why independent companies and

EXHIBIT 9-4 Inefficiencies in Transfer Pricing		

	Current Price, Costs, Sales	10% Price Cut, 30% Sales Increase	Change
Independent Manufacturing, Inc.			
Current unit sales	1,000,000	1,300,00	
Price	$2.00	$1.80	
Variable materials cost	$1.20	$1.20	
Variable labor cost	$0.20	$0.20	
Fixed cost	$0.40	$0.31	
Contribution margin	$0.60	$0.40	
%CM	30%	22%	
Annual pretax profit	$200,000	$120,000	($80,000)
Alpha Parts Inc.			
Current unit sales	1,000,000	1,300,000	
Price	$0.30	$0.30	
Variable cost	$0.05	$0.05	
Fixed cost	$0.20	$0.15	
Contribution margin	$0.25	$0.25	
Annual pretax profit	$50,000	$125,000	$75,000
Beta Parts Inc.			
Current unit sales	1,000,000	1,300,000	
Price	$0.90	$0.90	
Variable cost	$0.35	$0.35	
Fixed cost	$0.40	$0.31	
Contribution margin	$0.55	$0.55	
Annual pretax profit	$150,000	$315,000	$165,000

divisions are sometimes less price competitive and profitable than their vertically integrated competitors.

Exhibit 9-4 illustrates this often-overlooked opportunity. Independent Manufacturing, Inc. sells its product for $2 per unit in a highly competitive market. To manufacture the product, it buys different parts from two suppliers, Alpha and Beta, at a total cost per unit of $1.20. The parts purchased from Alpha cost $0.30 and those from Beta cost $0.90.

Independent Manufacturing conducts a pricing analysis to determine whether any changes in its pricing might be justified. It determines that its contribution margin (price minus variable cost) is $0.60, or 30 percent of its price.[14]

It then calculates the effect of a 10 percent price change in either direction. For a 10 percent price cut to be profitable, Independent must gain at least 50 percent more sales (Chapter 10 presents the formulas for performing these calculations). For a 10 percent price increase to be profitable, Independent can afford to forgo no more than 25 percent of its sales.

Independent's managers conclude that there is no way that they can possibly gain from a price cut, since their sales will surely not increase by more than 50 percent. On the other hand, they are intrigued by the possibility of a price increase. They feel sure that the inevitable decline would be far less than 25 percent if they could get their major competitors to follow them in the increase.

As Independent's management considers how to communicate to the industry the desirability of a general price increase, one of its major competitors, Integrated Manufacturing, Inc. announces its own 10 percent price cut. Independent's management is stunned. How could Integrated possibly justify such a move? Integrated's product is technically identical to Independent's, involving all the same parts and production processes, and Integrated is a company with a market share equal to Independent's. The only difference between the two companies is that Integrated recently began manufacturing its own parts.

That difference, however, is crucial to this story (see Exhibit 9-5). Assume that Integrated currently has all the same costs of producing parts as Independent's suppliers, Alpha and Beta, and expects to earn a profit from those operations. It also has the same costs of assembling those parts

---

EXHIBIT 9-5   Efficiency from Cost Integration

	Current Price, Costs, Sales	10% Price Cut, 30% Sales Increase	Change
Integrated Manufacturing, Inc.			
Current unit sales	1,000,000	1,300,000	
Price	$2.00	$1.80	
Variable materials cost	None	None	
Variable labor cost ($0.20 + $0.05 + $0.35)	$0.60	$0.60	
Fixed cost ($0.40 + $0.20 + $0.40)	$1.00	$0.77	
Contribution margin	$1.40	$1.20	
%	70%	67%	
Annual pretax profit	$400,000	$560,000	$160,000

($0.20 incremental labor plus $0.40 fixed per unit). Moreover, Integrated enjoys no additional economies of logistical integration. Despite these similarities, the two companies have radically different cost structures, which respond quite differently to changes in volume and which cause the two companies to experience price changes differently. Integrated has no variable materials cost corresponding to Independent's variable materials cost of $1.20 per unit. Instead, it incurs additional fixed costs of $0.60 per unit ($0.20 plus $0.40) and incremental variable costs of only $0.40 per unit ($0.05 plus $0.35).

This difference in cost structure between Integrated (high fixed and low variable) and Independent (low fixed and high variable) gives Integrated a much higher contribution margin per unit than Independent's margin. For Integrated, $1.40, or 70 percent of each additional sale, contributes to bottom-line profits. For Independent, only $0.60, or 30 percent of each additional sale, falls to the bottom line. Integrated's break-even calculations for a 10 percent price change are, therefore, quite different. For a 10 percent price cut to be profitable, Integrated has to gain only 16.7 percent more sales. But for a 10 percent price increase to pay off, Integrated could afford to forgo no more than 12.5 percent of its sales.

It is easy to see why Integrated is more attracted to price cuts and more averse to price increases than is Independent. For Integrated, sales must grow by only 16.7 percent to make a price cut profitable, compared with 50 percent for Independent. Similarly, Integrated could afford to lose no more than 12.5 percent of sales (compared with as much as 25 percent for Independent) and still profit from a price increase. How can it be that two identical sets of costs result in such extremely different calculations? The answer is that Independent, like most manufacturers, pays its suppliers on a price-per-unit basis. That price must include enough revenue to cover the suppliers' fixed costs and a reasonable profit if Independent expects those suppliers to remain viable in the long run. Consequently, fixed costs and profit of both Alpha and Beta become variable costs of sales for Independent. Such incrementalizing of nonincremental costs makes Independent much less cost competitive than Integrated, which earns more than twice as much additional profit on each unit it sells.

Independent's cost disadvantage is a disadvantage to its suppliers as well. Independent calculates that it requires a 50 percent sales increase to make a 10 percent price cut profitable. Independent, therefore, correctly rejects a 10 percent price cut that would increase sales by 30 percent. With current sales of 1 million units, such a price cut would cause Independent's profit to decline by $80,000. Note, however, that the additional sales volume would add $240,000 ($75,000 plus $165,000) to the profits of Independent's suppliers, provided that they produce the increased output with no more fixed costs. They would earn much more than Independent would lose by cutting price. It is clear why Integrated sees a 10 percent price cut as profitable when Independent does not. As its own supplier, Integrated captures the additional profits that accrue within the entire value chain (Alpha, $75,000; Beta, $165,000) as a result of increases in volume.[15]

Once Independent recognizes the problem, what alternatives does it have, short of taking the radical step of merging with its suppliers? One alternative is for Independent to pay its suppliers' fixed costs in a lump-sum payment, perhaps even retaining ownership of the assets while negotiating low supply prices that cover only incremental costs and a reasonable return. The lump-sum payment is then a fixed cost for Independent, and its contribution margin on added sales rises by the reduction in its incremental supply cost. Boeing and Airbus sometimes do this with parts suppliers, agreeing to bear the fixed cost of a part's design and paying the supplier for the fixed costs of tooling and setup. They then expect a price per unit that covers only the supplier's variable costs and a small profit. As a result, the airplane manufacturers bear the risk and retain the rewards from variations in volume. That gives the airplane manufactures a larger incremental margin on each additional sale and so a greater incentive to make marketing decisions, including pricing decisions, which build volume.

An alternative approach is to negotiate a high price for initial purchases that cover the fixed costs, with a lower price for all additional quantities that cover only incremental costs and profit. Auto companies use this system; allowing a supplier to be a sole source with high margins up to a certain volume, presumably enough to recover design and development costs. Beyond that volume, they make the design public and usually expect all suppliers to match the lowest price on offer. Since the lower supply price is the incremental cost of additional sales, Sears can profitably price its products lower to generate more volume. In Independent Manufacturing's case, it might negotiate an agreement with Alpha and Beta that guarantees enough purchases at $0.30 and $0.90, respectively, to cover their fixed costs, after which the price would fall to $0.10 and $0.50, respectively.

Both of these systems for paying suppliers avoid incrementalizing fixed costs, but they do not avoid the problem of incrementalizing the suppliers' profits. They work well only when the suppliers' profits account for a small portion of the total price suppliers receive. Lump-sum payments could be paid to suppliers to cover negotiated profit as well as fixed costs. This is risky, however, since profit per unit remains the suppliers' incentive to maintain on-time delivery of acceptable quality merchandise. Consequently, when a supplier has low fixed costs but can still demand a high profit because of little competition, a third alternative is often used. The purchaser may agree to pay the supplier a small fee to cover incremental expenses and an additional negotiated percentage of whatever profit contribution is earned from final sales.

It is noteworthy that most companies do not use these methods to compensate suppliers or to establish prices for sales between independent divisions. Instead, they negotiate arm's-length contracts at fixed prices or let prevailing market prices determine transfer prices.[16] One reason is that it is unusual to find a significant portion of costs that remain truly fixed for large changes in sales. In most cases, the bulk of costs that accountants label fixed are actually semifixed; additional costs would have to be incurred for suppliers to substantially increase their sales, making those costs incremental. One notable case where costs are substantially fixed is in the semiconductor industry. The overwhelming cost of semiconductors is the fixed cost of product development, not the variable or semifixed costs of production. Consequently, integrated manufacturers of products using semiconductors have often had a significant cost advantage. Bowmar, the company that pioneered the handheld calculator, was ultimately driven from the market precisely because it was not cost competitive with more integrated suppliers and failed to negotiate contracts that avoided the incrementalization of their fixed costs of product development.

Companies that buy computer software to sell as part of their products should note that software, too, is a high-fixed-cost product that often represents a substantial portion of the cost of software-aided products. Manufacturers of everything from smart phones to robots used in manufacturing can acquire software from independent software development houses. If they agree to pay for that software on a per-unit basis, however, they may ultimately find that they are not cost competitive with companies that either write their own software or that have an up-front pricing arrangement with their suppliers.

Summary

Costs are central considerations in pricing. Without understanding which costs are incremental and avoidable, a firm cannot accurately determine at what price, if any, a market can profitably be served. By erroneously looking at historical costs, a firm could sell its inventory too cheaply. By mistakenly looking at nonincremental fixed costs, a firm could overlook highly profitable opportunities where price is adequate to more than cover the incremental costs. By overlooking opportunity costs, successful companies frequently underprice their products. In short, when managers do not understand the true cost of a sale, their companies unnecessarily forgo significant profit opportunities. They tend to overprice when they have excess capacity, while underpricing and overinvesting when sales are strong relative to capacity.

Having identified the right costs, one must also understand how to use them. The most important reason to identify costs correctly is to be able to calculate an accurate contribution margin. The contribution margin is a measure of the leverage between a product's profitability and its sales volume. An accurate contribution margin enables management to determine the amount by which sales must increase following a price cut or by how little they must decline following a price increase to make the price change profitable. Understanding how changes in sales will affect a product's profitability is the first step in pricing the product effectively. It is, however, just the first step. Next, one must learn how to judge the likely impact of a price change on sales. That requires understanding how buyers are likely to perceive a price change and how competitors are likely to react to it.

The coordination of pricing with suppliers, although not actually economizing resources, can improve the efficiency of pricing by avoiding the incrementalization of a supplier's nonincremental fixed costs and profit. Any of these strategies can generate cost advantages that are, at least in the short run, sustainable. Even cost advantages that are not sustainable, however, can generate temporary savings that are often the key to building more sustainable cost or product advantages later.

Notes

1. Gerald Smith and Thomas Nagle, "Financial Analysis for Profit-Driven Pricing," *Sloan Management Review* 35, no. 3 (Spring 1994).

2. Beware of costs classified as "overhead." Often costs end up in that classification, even though they are clearly variable, simply because "overhead" is a convenient dumping ground for costs that one has not associated with the products that caused them to be incurred. A clue to the existence of such a misclassification is the incongruous term "variable overhead."

3. Revenue = 1,100 × $10. Cost = $1,500 + $4,500 + $2,000 + ($1 × 1,100).

4. Most economics and accounting texts equate avoidable costs with variable costs, and sunk costs with fixed costs, for theoretical convenience. Unfortunately, those texts usually fail to explain adequately that this is an assumption rather than a necessarily true statement. Consequently, many students come away from related courses with the idea that a firm should always continue producing if price at least covers variable costs. That rule is correct only when the variable costs are entirely avoidable and the fixed costs are entirely sunk. In many industries (for example, airlines) the fixed costs are often avoidable since the assets can be readily resold. Whenever the fixed costs are avoidable if a decision is not made to produce a product, or to produce it in as large a quantity, they should be considered when deciding whether a price is adequate to serve a market.

5. LIFO and NIFO costs are the same in any accounting period when a firm makes a net addition to its inventory. In periods during which a firm draws down its inventory, LIFO will understate costs after the firm uses up the portion of its inventory values at current prices and begins "dipping into old layers" of inventory valued at unrealistic past prices.

6. Neil Churchill, "Don't Let Inflation Get the Best of You," *Harvard Business Review* (March–April 1982).

7. The forward-looking production cost of replacing the book in inventory would have been relevant if the firm intended to maintain its current inventory levels.

8. We are assuming here that the half-price sale will not reduce the rate of sales after the sale is over. When it will, then one must add the discounted value of those lost sales to the price discount and compare that figure with the interest cost of holding the inventory. In other industries (for example, hotels and theaters), the cost of capacity is variable (you can build a hotel with any number of rooms or a theater with any number of seats), but this cost becomes sunk after capacity is built.

9. Robert S. Kaplan, "One Cost System Isn't Enough," *Harvard Business Review* 66 (January–February 1988): 61–66.

10. The calculation of the portion of output produced on overtime (assuming equal productivity) is as follows: $1,200 overtime is the equivalent in hours of $800 regular time ($1,200/1.5) and is 9.1 percent of the total hours worked ($800/[$8,000 + $800]). Multiplying 9.1 percent by 1,100 units shows that 100 units are produced on overtime if production is at a constant rate.

11. Since 1979, however, the Financial Accounting Standards Board (FASB) has required that large, publicly held corporations also report supplemental information on increases

or decreases in current costs of inventory, property, plant, and equipment, net of inflation. See FASB Statement of Financial Standards No. 33, "Financial Reporting and Changing Prices" (1979).

12. See Robert S. Kaplan, "Introduction to Activity-Based Costing," Harvard Business School Note 9-197-076 (1997; revised July 5, 2001); Robert S. Kaplan, "Using Activity-Based Costing with Budgeted Expenses and Practical Capacity," Harvard Business School Note 9-197-083 (1999); Robin Cooper and Robert S. Kaplan, "The Promise— And Peril—of Integrated Cost Systems," *Harvard Business Review* (July–August 1998): 109–119; Robert Kaplan and Robin Cooper, *Cost and Effect* (Cambridge, MA: Harvard Business School Press, 1997); Robert S. Kaplan, "Cost System Analysis," Harvard Business School Note 9-195-181 (1994); Robin Cooper and Robert S. Kaplan, "Profit Priorities from Activity-Based Costing," *Harvard Business Review* (May–June 1991): 2–7; Robin Cooper and Robert S. Kaplan, "Activity-Based Systems: Measuring the Costs of Resource Usage," *Accounting Horizons* (September 1992): 1–13; James P. Borden, "Review of Literature on Activity-Based Costing," *Cost Man-*

agement 4 (Spring 1990): 5–12; Peter B. B. Turney, "Ten Myths About Implementing an Activity-Based Cost System," *Cost Management* 4 (Spring 1990): 24–32; George J. Beaujon and Vinod R. Singhal, "Understanding the Activity Costs in an Activity-Based Cost System," *Cost Management* 4 (Spring 1990): 51–72.

13. Robert S. Kaplan, "Using ABC To Manage Customer Mix and Relationships," Harvard Business School Note 9-197-094 (1997).

14. $CM = $2.00 - $1.20 - $0.20 = $0.60
    %CM = $0.60/$2.00 \times 100 = 30\%$

15. An integrated company does not automatically gain this advantage. If separate divisions of a company operate as independent profit centers setting transfer prices equal to market prices, they will also price too high to maximize their joint profits. To overcome the problem while remaining independent, they need to adopt one of the solutions suggested for independent companies.

16. For a related recent perspective see Thomas W. Malone, "Bringing the Market Inside," *Harvard Business Review* 82, no. 4 (April 2004): 106–115. For a succinct summary of tax-relevant transfer pricing methods, see "Transfer Pricing Clarified," *Finance Week* (May 24, 2004): 66.

CHAPTER 10

Financial Analysis
Pricing for Profit

Internal financial considerations and external market considerations are, at most companies, antagonistic forces in pricing decisions. Financial managers allocate costs to determine how high prices must be to achieve profit objectives. Marketing and sales staff analyze buyers to determine how low prices must be to achieve sales objectives. The pricing decisions that result are politically charged compromises, not thoughtful implementations of a coherent strategy. Although common, such pricing policies are neither necessary nor desirable. An effective pricing decision should involve an optimal blending of, not a compromise between, internal financial constraints and external market conditions.

Unfortunately, few managers have any idea how to facilitate such a cross-functional blending of these two legitimate concerns. From traditional cost accounting, they learn to take sales goals as "given" before allocating costs, thus precluding the ability to incorporate market forces into pricing decisions. From marketing, they are told that effective pricing should be entirely "customer driven," which ignores costs except as a minimum constraint below which the sale would become unprofitable. Perhaps along the way, these managers study economics and learn that, in theory, optimal pricing is a blending of cost and demand considerations. In practice, however, they find the economist's assumption of a known demand curve hopelessly unrealistic.

Consequently, pricing at most companies remains trapped between cost- and customer-driven procedures that are inherently incompatible. This chapter suggests how managers can break this tactical pricing deadlock and infuse strategic balance into pricing decisions. Many marketers argue that costs should play no role in market-based pricing. This is clearly wrong. Without perfect segmentation (the ability to negotiate independently a unique price for every customer), pricers must make trade-offs between charging higher margins to fewer customers and lower margins to more customers.

Once the true cost and contribution of a sale are understood, managers can appropriately integrate costs into what is otherwise a market-driven approach to pricing strategy.

This chapter describes a simple, logically intuitive procedure for quantitatively evaluating the potential profitability of a price change. First, managers develop a baseline, or standard of comparison, to measure the effects of a price change. For example, they might compare the effects of a pending price change with the product's current level of profitability, or with a budgeted level of profitability, or perhaps with a hypothetical scenario that management is particularly interested in exploring. Second, they calculate an incremental "break-even" for the price change to determine under what market conditions the change will prove profitable. Marketing managers must then determine whether they can actually meet those conditions.

The key to integrating costs and quantitatively assessing the consequences of a price change is the incremental break-even analysis. Although similar in form to the common break-evens that managers use to evaluate investments, incremental break-even analysis for pricing is quite different in practice. Rather than evaluating the product's overall profitability, which depends on many factors other than price, incremental break-even analysis focuses on the incremental profitability of price changes. Consequently, managers start from a baseline reflecting current or projected sales and profitability at the current price. Then they ask whether a change in price could improve the situation. More precisely, they ask:

- How much would the sales volume have to increase to profit from a price reduction?
- How much could the sales volume decline before a price increase becomes unprofitable? Answers to these questions depend on the product's contribution margin.

The sample problems in this chapter introduce the four equations involved in performing such an analysis and illustrate how to use them. They are based on the experience of Westside Manufacturing, a small company manufacturing pillows for sale through specialty bedding and dry cleaning stores. Although the examples are, for simplicity, based on a small manufacturing business, the equations are equally applicable for analyzing any size or type of business that cannot negotiate a unique price for each customer.[1] If customers can be somewhat segmented for pricing, the formulas apply to pricing within a segment.

Following are Westside Manufacturing's income and costs for a typical month:

Sales	4,000 units
Wholesale price	$10.00 per unit
Revenue	$40,000
Variable costs	$5.50 per unit
Fixed costs	$15,000

Westside is considering a 5 percent price cut, which, it believes, would make it more competitive with alternative suppliers, enabling it to further increase its sales. Management believes that the company would need to incur no additional fixed costs as a result of this pricing decision. How much would sales have to increase for this company to profit from a 5 percent cut in price?

BREAK-EVEN SALES ANALYSIS: THE BASIC CASE

To answer Westside's question, we calculate the break-even sales change. This, for a price cut, is the minimum increase in sales volume necessary for the price cut to produce an increase in contribution relative to the baseline. Fortunately, making this calculation is simple, as will be shown shortly. First, however, it may be more intuitive to illustrate the analysis graphically (see Exhibit 10-1).

In this exhibit, it is easy to visualize the financial trade-offs involved in the proposed price change. Before the price change, Westside receives a price of $10 per unit and sells 4,000 units, resulting in total revenues of $40,000 (the total area of boxes a and b). From this Westside pays variable costs of $5.50 per unit, for a total of $22,000 (box b). Therefore, before the price change, total contribution is $40,000 minus $22,000, or $18,000 (box a). In order for the proposed price cut to be profitable, contribution after the price cut must exceed $18,000.

After the 5 percent price reduction, Westside receives a price of only $9.50 per unit, or $0.50 less contribution per unit. Since it normally sells 4,000 units, Westside would expect to lose $2,000 in total contribution (box c) on

EXHIBIT 10-1 Finding the Break-Even Sales Change

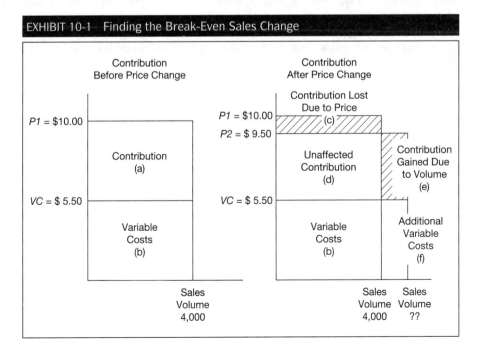

sales that it could have made at a higher price. This is called the price effect. Fortunately, the price cut can be expected to increase sales volume.

The contribution earned from that increased volume, the volume effect (box e), is unknown. The price reduction will be profitable, however, when the volume effect (the area of box e) exceeds the price effect (the area of box c). That is, in order for the price change to be profitable, the gain in contribution resulting from the change in sales volume must be greater than the loss in contribution resulting from the change in price. The purpose of break-even analysis is to calculate the minimum sales volume necessary for the volume effect (box e) to balance the price effect (box c). When sales exceed that amount, the price cut is profitable.

So, how do we determine the break-even sales change? We know that the lost contribution due to the price effect (box c) is $2,000, which means that the gain in contribution due to the volume effect (box e) must be at least $2,000 for the price cut to be profitable. Since each new unit sold following the price cut results in $4 in contribution ($9.50 − $5.50 = $4), Westside must sell at least an additional 500 units ($2,000 divided by $4 per unit) to make the price cut profitable.

The minimum percent change in sales volume necessary to maintain at least the same contribution following a price change can be directly calculated by using the following simple formula (see Appendix 9A for derivation):

$$\frac{-\Delta P}{CM + \Delta P}$$

In this equation, the price change and contribution margin may be stated in dollars, percents, or decimals (as long as their use is consistent). The result of this equation is a decimal ratio that, when multiplied by 100, is the percent change in unit sales necessary to maintain the same level of contribution after the price change. The minus sign in the numerator indicates a trade-off between price and volume: Price cuts increase the volume and price increases reduce the volume necessary to achieve any particular level of profitability. The larger the price change—or the smaller the contribution margin—the greater the volume change necessary to generate at least as much contribution as before.

Assume for the moment that there are no incremental fixed costs in implementing Westside's proposed 5 percent price cut. For convenience, we make our calculations in dollars (rather than in percents or decimals). Using the contribution margin equation (see Chapter 8), we derive the following:

$$\$CM = \$10 - \$5.50 = \$4.50$$

Given this, we can easily calculate the break-even sales change as follows:

$$\% \text{ Break-even sales change } = \frac{-(-\$0.50)}{\$4.50 + (-\$0.50)} = 0.125 \text{ or } 12.5\%$$

Thus, the price cut is profitable only if sales volume increases more than 12.5 percent. Relative to its current level of sales volume, Westside would have to sell at least 500 units more to maintain the same level of profitability it had prior to the price cut, as shown below:

$$\text{Unit break-even sales change } = 0.125 \times 4,000 = 500 \text{ units}$$

If the actual increase in sales volume exceeds the break-even sales change, the price cut will be profitable. If the actual increase in sales volume falls short of the break-even sales change, the price change will be unprofitable. Assuming that Westside's goal is to increase its current profits, management should initiate the price reduction only if it believes that sales will increase by more than 12.5 percent, or 500 units, as a result.

If Westside's sales increase as a result of the price change by more than the break-even amount—say, by an additional 550 units—Westside will realize a gain in profit contribution. If, however, Westside sells only an additional 450 units as a result of the price cut, it will suffer a loss in contribution. Once we have the break-even sales change and the profit contribution, calculating the precise change in contribution associated with any change in volume is quite simple: It is simply the difference between the actual sales volume and the break-even sales volume, times the new contribution margin (calculated after the price change). For Westside's 550-unit and 450-unit volume changes, the change in contribution equals the following:

$$(550 - 500) \times \$4 = \$200$$
$$(450 - 500) \times \$4 = -\$200$$

The $4 in these equations is the new contribution margin ($9.50 − $5.50). Alternatively, you might have noticed that the denominator of the percent break-even formula is also the new contribution margin.

We have illustrated break-even analysis using Westside's proposed 5 percent price cut. The logic is exactly the same for a price increase. Since a price increase results in a gain in unit contribution, Westside can "absorb" some reduction in sales volume and still increase its profitability. How much of a reduction in sales volume can Westside tolerate before the price increase becomes unprofitable? The answer is this: until the loss in contribution due to reduced sales volume is exactly offset by the gain in contribution due to the price increase. As an exercise, calculate how much sales Westside could afford to lose before a 5 percent price increase becomes unprofitable.

It is important to note that the calculation resulting from the break-even sales change formula is expressed as the percent change in *unit volume* required to break even, not the percent change in monetary sales (for example, the percent change in dollar sales) required to break even. In the case of a price cut, the percent break-even sales change in units necessary to justify the price cut is larger than the percent break-even sales change in sales dollars because the price is now lower.

To convert from the percent break-even sales change in units to the percent break-even sales change in dollars, you can apply the following simple conversion formula:

$$\% \text{ BE}(\$) = \% \text{ BE(units)} + \% \text{ Price change} \left[1 + \% \text{ BE(units)}\right]$$

For example, for Westside's proposed 5 percent price cut above, the percent break-even sales change in unit volume terms was 12.5 percent. What is the corresponding percent break-even sales change in *dollar sales* terms? The answer is calculated as follows:

$$\% \ BE(\$) = 0.125 + (-0.05)(1 + 0.125)$$
$$= 6.88\%$$

Thus, to break even on the proposed 5 percent price cut, Westside would have to increase its total dollar sales by 6.88 percent, which is exactly equivalent to a 12.5 percent increase in unit volume.

BREAK-EVEN SALES INCORPORATING A CHANGE IN VARIABLE COSTS

Thus far, we have dealt only with price changes that involve no changes in unit variable costs or in fixed costs. Often, however, price changes are made as part of a marketing plan involving cost changes as well. A price increase may be made along with product improvements that increase variable costs, or a price cut might be made to push the product with lower variable selling costs. Expenditures that represent fixed costs might also change along with a price change. We need to consider these two types of incremental costs when calculating the price–volume trade-off necessary for making pricing decisions profitable. We begin this section by integrating changes in variable cost into the financial analysis. In the next section, we do the same with changes in fixed costs.

Fortunately, dealing with a change in variable cost involves only a simple generalization of the break-even sales change formula already introduced. To illustrate, we return to Westside Manufacturing's proposed 5 percent price cut. Suppose that Westside's price cut is accompanied by a reduction in variable cost of $0.22 per pillow, resulting from Westside's decision to use a new synthetic filler to replace the goose feathers it currently uses. Variable costs are $5.50 before the price change and $5.28 after the price change. By how much would sales volume have to increase to ensure that the proposed price cut is profitable?

When variable costs change along with the price change, managers simply need to subtract the cost change from the price change before doing the break-even sales change calculation. Unlike the case of a simple price change, managers must state the terms on the right-hand side of the equation in currency units (dollars, euros, yen, and so forth) rather than in percentage changes:

$$\% \ \text{Break-even sales change} = \frac{-(\$\Delta P - \$\Delta C)}{\$CM + (\$\Delta P - \$\Delta C)}$$

where Δ indicates "change in," P = price, and C = cost. Note that when the change in variable cost ($\$\Delta C$) is zero, this equation is identical to the break-even formula previously presented. Note also that the term ($\$\Delta P - \$\Delta C$) is the change in the contribution margin and that the denominator (the original contribution margin plus the change) is the new contribution margin. Thus, the general form of the break-even pricing equation is simply written as follows:

$$\% \text{ Break-even sales change } = \frac{-\$\Delta CM}{\text{New } \$CM}$$

For Westside, the next step in using this equation to evaluate the proposed price change is to calculate the change in contribution margin. Recall that the change in price is $9.50 − $10 or −$0.50. The change in variable costs is −$0.22. Thus, the change in contribution can be calculated as follows:

$$\$\Delta CM = (\$\Delta P - \$\Delta C) = -\$0.50 - (-\$0.22) = -\$0.28$$

Previous calculations illustrated that the contribution margin before the price change is $4.50. We can, therefore, calculate the break-even sales change as follows:

$$\% \text{ Break-even sales change } = \frac{-(-\$0.28)}{\$4.50 + (\$0.28)} = 0.066, \text{ or } +6.6\%$$

In units, the break-even sales change is 0.066 × 4,000 units, or 265 units.

Given management's projection of a $0.22 reduction in variable costs, the price cut can be profitable only if management believes that sales volume will increase by more than 6.6 percent, or 265 units. Note that this increase is substantially less than the required sales increase (12.5 percent) calculated before assuming a reduction in variable cost. Why does a variable cost reduction lower the necessary break-even sales change? Because it increases the contribution margin earned on each sale, making it possible to recover the contribution lost due to the price effect with less additional volume. This relationship is illustrated graphically for Westside Manufacturing in Exhibit 10-2. Westside can realize a gain in contribution due to the change in variable costs (box f), in addition to a gain in contribution due to any increase in sales volume.

BREAK-EVEN SALES WITH INCREMENTAL FIXED COSTS

Although most fixed costs do not impact the incremental profitability of a pricing decision (because they do not change), some pricing decisions necessarily involve changes in fixed costs, even though these costs do not otherwise change with small changes in volume. The management of a discount airline considering whether to reposition as a higher-priced business travelers' airline would probably choose to refurbish its lounges and planes. A regulated utility would need to cover the fixed cost of regulatory hearings to gain approval for a higher price. A fast-food restaurant would need to advertise its promotionally priced "special-value" meals to potential customers. These are incremental fixed costs, necessary for the success of a new pricing strategy but unrelated to the sales volume actually gained at those prices. Recall also that semifixed costs remain fixed only within certain ranges of sales. If a price

EXHIBIT 10-2   Finding the Break-Even Sales Change Given a Change in Variable Costs

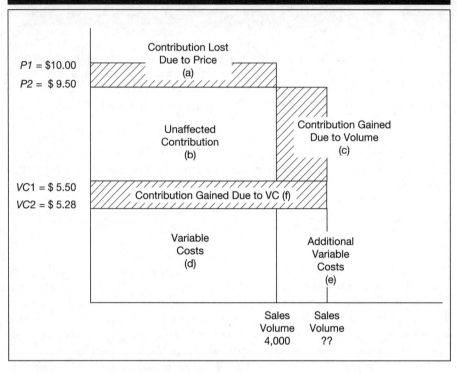

change causes sales to move outside that range, the level of semifixed costs increases or decreases. Such changes in fixed and semifixed costs need to be covered for a price change to be justified, since without the price change these incremental costs can be avoided.

Fortunately, calculating the sales volume necessary to cover an incremental fixed cost is already a familiar exercise for many managers evaluating investments independent of price changes. For example, suppose a product manager is evaluating a $150,000 fixed expenditure to redesign a product's packaging. The product's unit price is $10, and unit variable costs total $5. How many units must be sold for the firm to recover the $150,000 incremental investment? The answer, as found in most managerial economics texts, is given by the following equation:

$$\text{Break-even sales volume} = \frac{\$ \text{ Change in fixed costs}}{\$CM}$$

Remembering that the $CM equals price − variable cost, the break-even sales volume for this example is:

$$\text{Break-even sales volume} = \frac{\$150,000}{\$10 - \$5} = 30,000 \text{ units}$$

How can the manager do break-even analysis for a change in pricing strategy that involves both a price change and a change in fixed cost? She simply adds the calculations for (a) the break-even sales change for a price change and (b) the break-even sales volume for the related fixed investment.

The break-even sales change for a price change with incremental fixed costs is the basic break-even sales change plus the sales change necessary to cover the incremental fixed costs. Since we normally analyze the break-even for a price change as a percent and the break-even for an investment in units, we need to multiply or divide by initial unit sales to make them consistent. Consequently, the unit break-even sales change with a change in fixed costs is as follows:

$$\text{Unit break-even sales change} = \frac{-\$\Delta CM}{\text{New }\$CM} \times \text{Initial unit sales} + \frac{\$\text{ Change in fixed costs}}{\text{New }\$CM}$$

The calculation for the percent break-even sales change is as follows:

$$\text{\% Break-even sales change} = \frac{-\$\Delta CM}{\text{New }\$CM} + \frac{\$\text{ Change in fixed costs}}{\text{New }\$CM \times \text{Initial unit sales}}$$

In both cases, if the "$ change in fixed costs" is zero, we have the break-even sales change equation for a simple price change.

To illustrate the equations for a price cut, return again to the pricing decision faced by Westside Manufacturing. Westside is considering a 5 percent price cut. We already calculated that it could profit if sales increase by more than 12.5 percent. Now suppose that Westside cannot increase its output without incurring additional semifixed costs. At the company's current rate of sales—4,000 units per month—it is fully utilizing the capacity of the equipment at its four workstations. To increase capacity enough to handle 12.5 percent more sales, the company must install equipment for another workstation, at a monthly cost of $800. The new station raises plant capacity by 1,000 units beyond the current capacity of 4,000 units. What is the minimum sales increase required to justify a 5 percent price reduction, given that it involves an $800 increase in monthly fixed costs? The answer is determined as follows:

$$\text{Unit break-even sales change} = 0.125 \times 4{,}000 \text{ units} + \frac{\$800}{\$4} = 700 \text{ units}$$

$$\text{\% Break-even sales change} = 0.125 \times \frac{\$800}{\$4 \times 4{,}000 \text{ units}} = 0.175, \text{ or } 17.5\%$$

The company could profit from a 5 percent price reduction if sales increased by more than 700 units (17.5 percent), which is less than the 1,000 units of added capacity provided by the new workstation. Whether a prudent manager should actually implement such a price decrease depends on other factors as well: How likely is it that sales will increase substantially more than the break-even minimum, thus adding to profit? How likely is it that sales will increase by less, thus reducing profit? How soon could the decision be reversed, if at all, if sales do not increase adequately?

Even if management considers it likely that orders will increase by more than the break-even quantity, it should hesitate before making the decision. If orders increase by significantly less than the break-even minimum, this company could lose substantially, especially if the cost of the new workstation is largely sunk once the expenditure has been made. On the other hand, if orders increase by significantly more, the most the company could increase its sales without bearing the semifixed cost for further expansion is 25 percent, or 1,000 units. Consequently, management must be quite confident of a large sales increase before implementing the 5 percent price reduction.

Consider, however, if the company has already invested in the additional capacity and if the semifixed costs are already sunk. The monthly cost of the fifth workstation is then entirely irrelevant to pricing, since that cost would have to be borne whether or not the capacity is used. Thus, the decision to cut price rests entirely on management's judgment of whether the price cut will stimulate unit sales by more than 12.5 percent. If the actual sales increase is more than 12.5 percent but less than 17.5 percent, management will regret having invested in the fifth workstation. Given that this cost can no longer be avoided, however, the most profitable course of action is to price low enough to use the station, even though that price will not fully cover its cost.

BREAK-EVEN SALES ANALYSIS FOR REACTIVE PRICING

So far we have restricted our discussion to proactive price changes, where the firm contemplates initiating a price change ahead of its competitors. The goal of such a change is to enhance profitability. Often, however, a company initiates reactive price changes when it is confronted with a competitor's price change that will impact the former's sales unless it responds. The key uncertainty involved in analyzing a reactive price change is the sales loss the company will suffer if it fails to meet a competitor's price cut, or the sales gain the company will achieve if it fails to follow a competitor's price increase. Is the potential sales loss sufficient to justify cutting price to protect sales volume? Or is the potential sales gain enough to justify forgoing the opportunity for a cooperative price increase? A slightly different form of the break-even sales formula is used to analyze such situations.

To calculate the break-even sales changes for a reactive price change, we need to address the following key questions: (1) What is the minimum potential sales loss that justifies meeting a lower competitive price? (2) What is the minimum potential sales gain that justifies not following a competitive price increase? The basic formula for these calculations is this:

$$\frac{\% \text{ Break-even sales change}}{\text{for reactive price change}} = \frac{\text{Change in price}}{\text{Contribution margin}} = \frac{\Delta P}{CM}$$

To illustrate, suppose that Westside's principal competitor, Eastside, has just reduced its prices by 15 percent. If Westside's customers are highly loyal, it probably would not pay for Westside to match this cut. If, on the other hand, customers are quite price sensitive, Westside may have to match this price cut to minimize the damage. What is the minimum potential loss in sales volume that justifies meeting Eastside's price cut? The answer (calculated in percentage terms) is as follows:[2]

$$\frac{\text{\% Break-even sales change}}{\text{for reactive price change}} = \frac{-15\%}{45\%} = -0.333, \text{ or } 33.3\%$$

Thus, if Westside expects sales volume to fall by more than 33 percent as a result of Eastside's new price, it would be less damaging to Westside's profitability to match the price cut than to lose sales. On the other hand, if Westside expects that sales volume will fall by less than 33 percent, it would be less damaging to Westside's profitability to let Eastside take the sales than it would be to cut price to meet this challenge.

This analysis has focused on minimizing losses in the face of a competitor's proactive price reduction. However, the procedure for analysis is the same when a competitor suddenly raises its prices. Suppose, for example, that Eastside raises its price by 15 percent. Westside might be tempted to match Eastside's price increase. If, however, Westside does not respond to Eastside's new price, Westside will likely gain additional sales volume as Eastside's customers switch to Westside. How much of a gain in sales volume must be realized in order for no price reaction to be more profitable than a reactive price increase? The answer is similarly found using the break-even sales change formula with a reactive price change. If Westside is confident that sales volume will increase by more than 33.3 percent if it does not react, a nonreactive price policy would be more profitable. If Westside's management does not expect sales volume to increase by 33.3 percent, a reactive price increase would be more profitable.

Of course, the competitive analysis we have done is, by itself, overly simplistic. Eastside might be tempted to attack Westside's other markets if Westside does not respond to Eastside's price cut. And Westside's not matching Eastside's price increase might force Eastside to roll back its prices. These long-run strategic concerns might outweigh the short-term profit implications of a decision to react. In order to make such a judgment, however, the company must first determine the short-term profit implications. Sometimes long-term competitive strategies are not worth the short-term cost.

CALCULATING POTENTIAL FINANCIAL IMPLICATIONS

To grasp fully the potential impact of a price change, especially when the decision involves incremental changes in fixed costs, it is useful to calculate the profit impact for a range of potential sales changes and to summarize them with a break-even table and chart. Doing so is relatively simple after having calculated the basic break-even sales change. Using this calculation, one can then simulate what-if scenarios that include different levels of actual sales volume following the price change.

The top half of Exhibit 10-3 is a summary of the basic break-even sales change analysis for Westside's 5 percent price cut, with one column summarizing the level of contribution before the price change (the column labeled

EXHIBIT 10-3   Break-Even Sales Analysis and Break-Even Sales Simulated Scenarios: Westside Manufacturing Proposed 5% Price Reduction

Break-Even Sales Change Summary	Baseline	Proposed Price Change
Price/unit	$10.00	$9.50
% Price change		−5%
$ Contribution/unit	$4.50	$4.00
% Contribution	45%	42%
Break-even sales change (%)		12.5%
Break-even sales change (units)		500
Total sales volume (units)	4,000	4,500
Total contribution	$18,000	$18,000

Break-Even Sales Change Simulated Scenarios

		% Change in Actual Sales Volume	Unit Change in Actual Sales Volume	Change in Contribution After Price Change	Incremental Fixed Costs	Total Change in Profit After Price Change
Simulated Scenarios	1	0.0	0	−2,000	800	−2,800
	2	5.0	200	−1,200	800	−2,000
	3	10.0	400	−400	800	−1,200
	4	12.5	500	0	800	−800
	5	17.5	700	800	800	0
	6	20.0	800	1,200	800	400
	7	25.0	1,000	2,000	800	1,200
	8	30.0	1,200	2,800	1,600	1,200
	9	40.0	1,600	4,400	1,600	2,800

"Baseline") and one column summarizing the contribution after the price change (the column labeled "Proposed Price Change"). The bottom half of Exhibit 10-3 summarizes nine what-if scenarios showing the profitability associated with changes in sales volume ranging from 0 to 40 percent given incremental semifixed costs of $800 per 1,000 units. Columns 1 and 2 show the actual change in volume for each scenario. Columns 3 through 5 calculate the change in profit that results from each change in sales.

To illustrate how these break-even sales-change scenarios are calculated, let us focus for a moment on scenario 6, where actual sales volume is projected to increase 20 percent. A 20 percent change in actual sales volume is equivalent to an 800-unit change in actual sales volume, since 800 units is 20 percent of the baseline sales volume of 4,000 units. How does this increase in sales translate into changes in profitability? Column 3 shows that a 20 percent (or an 800-unit) increase in sales volume results in a change in contribution after the price change of $1,200. This is calculated by taking the difference between the actual unit sales change (800 units) and the break-even sales change shown in the top half of Exhibit 10-3 (500 units) and multiplying by the new contribution margin after the price change ($4). However, the calculations made in column 3 do not take into account the incremental fixed costs required to implement the price change (shown in column 4). Column 5 shows the change in profit after subtracting the change in fixed costs from the incremental contribution generated. Where there is inadequate incremental contribution to cover the incremental fixed costs, as in scenarios 1 through 4, the change in profit is negative. Scenario 5 illustrates the break-even sales change. Scenarios 6 through 9 are all profitable scenarios since they result in greater profit after the price change than before.

The interrelationships among contribution, incremental fixed costs, and the sales change that results from a price change are often easier to comprehend with a graph. Exhibit 10-4 illustrates the relationships among the data in Exhibit 10-3. Appendix 10B (at the end of this chapter) explains how to produce break-even graphs, which are especially useful in comprehending the implications of price changes when many fixed costs become incremental at different sales volumes.

EXHIBIT 10-4   Break-Even Analysis of a Price Change

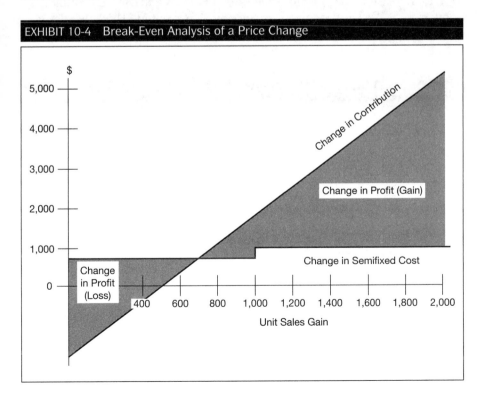

BREAK-EVEN SALES CURVES

So far we have discussed break-even sales analysis in terms of a single change in price and its resultant break-even sales change. In the example above, Westside Manufacturing considered a 5 percent price reduction, which we calculated would require a 17.5 percent increase in sales volume to achieve enough incremental contribution to cover the incremental fixed cost. However, what if the company wants to consider a range of potential price changes? How can we use break-even sales analysis to consider alternative price changes simultaneously? The answer is by charting a break-even sales curve, which summarizes the results of a series of break-even sales analyses for different price changes.

Constructing break-even sales curves requires doing a series of what-if analyses, similar to the simulated scenarios discussed in the last section. Exhibits 10-5 and 10-6 show numerically and graphically a break-even sales curve for Westside Manufacturing, with simulated scenarios of price changes ranging from 125 percent to 220 percent. Note in Exhibit 10-6 that the vertical axis shows different price levels for the product, and the horizontal axis shows a volume level associated with each price level. Each point on the curve represents the sales volume necessary to achieve as much profit after the price change as would be earned at the baseline price. For example, Westside's baseline price is $10 per unit, and baseline sales volume is 4,000 units. If, however, Westside cuts the price by 15 percent to $8.50, its sales volume would have to increase 70 percent to 6,800 units to achieve the same profitability. Conversely, if Westside increases its price by 15 percent to $11.50, its sales volume could decrease 25 percent to 3,000 units and still allow equal profitability.

EXHIBIT 10-5 Break-Even Sales Curve Calculations (with Incremental Fixed Costs)

Price Change	Price	Break-Even Sales Change	Unit Break-Even Sales Change	Unit Break-Even Sales Volume	Incremental Fixed Costs	Break-Even Sales Change with IFC
25%	$12.50	−35.7%	−1,429	2,571	0	−35.7%
20%	$12.00	−30.8%	−1,231	2,769	0	−30.8%
15%	$11.50	−25.0%	−1,000	3,000	0	−25.0%
10%	$11.00	−18.2%	−727	3,273	0	−18.2%
5%	$10.50	−10.0%	−400	3,600	0	−10.0%
0%	$10.00	0.0%	0	4,000	0	0.0%
−5%	$9.50	12.5%	500	4,500	$800	17.5%
−10%	$9.00	28.6%	1,143	5,143	$1,600	40.0%
−15%	$8.50	50.0%	2,000	6,000	$2,400	70.0%
−20%	$8.00	80.0%	3,200	7,200	$4,000	120.0%

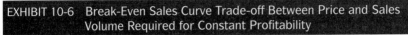
EXHIBIT 10-6   Break-Even Sales Curve Trade-off Between Price and Sales
Volume Required for Constant Profitability

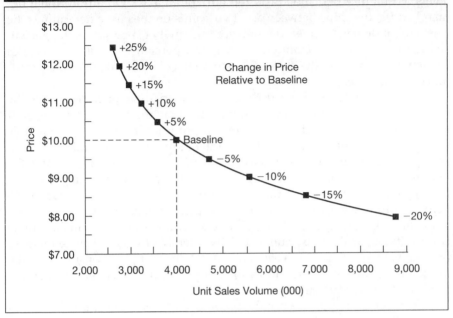

The break-even sales curve is a simple, yet powerful tool for synthesiz-
ing and evaluating the dynamics behind the profitability of potential price
changes. It presents succinctly and visually the dividing line that separates
profitable price decisions from unprofitable ones. Profitable price decisions
are those that result in sales volumes in the area to the right of the curve. Unprofitable price decisions are those that result in sales volumes in the area to
the left of the curve. What is the logic behind this? Recall the previous discussion of what happens before and after a price change. The break-even sales
curve represents those sales volume levels associated with their respective
levels of price, where the company will make just as much net contribution after the price change as it made before the price change. If the company's sales
volume after the price change is greater than the break-even sales volume
(that is, actual sales volume is to the right of the curve), the price change will
add to profitability. If the company's sales volume after the price change is
less than the break-even sales volume (that is, the area to the left of the curve),
the price change will be unprofitable. For example, for Westside a price of
$8.50 requires a sales volume of at least 6,800 units to achieve a net gain in
profitability. If, after reducing its price to $8.50, management believes it will
sell more than 6,800 units (a point to the right of the curve), then a decision to
implement a price of $8.50 per unit would be profitable.

The break-even sales curve also clearly illustrates the relationship between the break-even approach to pricing and the economic concept of price
elasticity. Note that the break-even sales curve looks suspiciously like the

traditional downward-sloping demand curve in economic theory, in which different levels of price (on the vertical axis) are associated with different levels of quantity demanded (on the horizontal axis). On a traditional demand curve, the slope between any two points on the curve determines the elasticity of demand, a measure of price sensitivity expressed as the percent change in quantity demanded for a given percent change in price. An economist who knew the shape of such a curve could calculate the profit-maximizing price.

Unfortunately, few firms use economic theory to set price because of the unrealistic expectation that they first have to know their demand curve, or at least the demand elasticity around the current price level. To overcome this shortcoming, we have addressed the problem in reverse order. Rather than asking, "What is the firm's demand elasticity?" we ask, instead, "What is the minimum demand elasticity required?" to justify a particular pricing decision. Break-even sales analysis calculates the minimum or maximum demand elasticity required to profit from a particular pricing decision. The break-even sales curve illustrates a set of minimum elasticities necessary to make a price cut profitable, or the maximum elasticity tolerable to make a price increase profitable. One is then led to ask whether the level of price sensitivity in the market is greater or less than the level of price sensitivity required by the firm's cost and margin structure.

This relationship between the break-even sales curve and the demand curve is illustrated in Exhibits 10-7 and 10-8, where hypothetical demand

EXHIBIT 10-7   Break-Even Sales Curve Relationship between Price Elasticity of Demand and Profitability

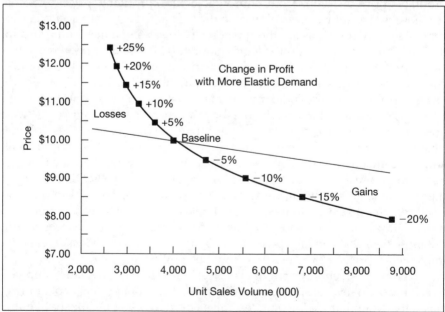

EXHIBIT 10-8   Break-Even Sales Curve Relationship Between Price Elasticity of Demand and Profitability: Changes in Profit with More Inelastic Demand

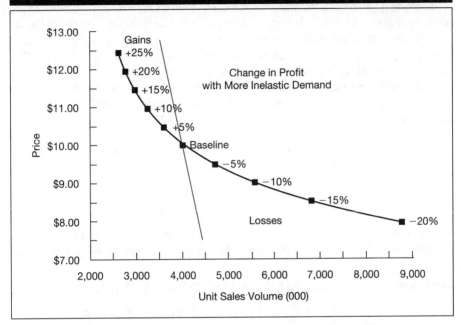

curves are shown with Westside's break-even sales curve. If demand is more elastic, as in Exhibit 10-7, price reductions relative to the baseline price result in gains in profitability, and price increases result in losses in profitability. If demand is less elastic, as in Exhibit 10-8, price increases relative to the baseline price result in gains in profitability, and price reductions result in losses in profitability. Although few, if any, managers actually know the demand curve for their product, we have encountered many who can comfortably make judgments about whether it is more or less elastic than is required by the break-even sales curve. Moreover, although we have not found any market research technique that can estimate a demand curve with great precision, we have seen many (described in Chapter 12 on price and value measurement) that could enable management to confidently accept or reject a particular break-even sales level as achievable.

WATCHING YOUR BASELINE

In the preceding examples, the level of baseline sales from which we calculated break-even sales changes was assumed to be the current level. For simplicity, we assume a static market. In many cases, however, sales grow or decline even if price remains constant. As a result, the baseline for calculating break-even sales changes is not necessarily the current level of sales. Rather, it is the level that would occur if no price change were made.

Consider, for example, a company in a high-growth industry with current sales of 2,000 units on which it earns a contribution margin of 55 percent. If the company does not change its price, management expects that sales will increase by 20 percent (the projected growth of total industry sales) to 2,400 units. However, management is considering a 5 percent price cut in an attempt to increase the company's market share. The price cut would be accompanied by an advertising campaign intended to heighten consumer awareness of the change. The campaign would take time to design, delaying implementation of the price change until next year. The initial sales level for the constant contribution analysis, therefore, would be the projected sales in the future, or 2,400 units. Consequently, the break-even sales change would be calculated as follows:

$$\% \text{ Break-even sales change } = \frac{-(-5\%)}{55\% + (-5\%)} = 0.10, \text{ or } 10\%$$

or

$$0.10 \times 2,400 = 240 \text{ units}$$

If the current sales level is used in the calculation, the unit break-even sales change is calculated as 200 units, understating the change required by 40 units.

COVERING NONINCREMENTAL FIXED AND SUNK COSTS

By this point, one might be wondering about the nonincremental fixed and sunk costs that have been ignored when analyzing pricing decisions. A company's goal must surely be to cover all of its costs, including all fixed and sunk costs, or it will soon go bankrupt. This concern is justified and is central to pricing for profit, but it is misguided when applied to justify higher prices.

Note that the goal in calculating a contribution margin and in using it to evaluate price changes and differentials is to set prices to maximize a product's profit contribution. Profit contribution, you will recall, is the income remaining after all incremental, avoidable costs have been covered. It is money available to cover nonincremental fixed and sunk costs and to contribute to profit. When managers consider only the incremental, avoidable costs in making pricing decisions, they are not saying that other costs are unimportant. They simply realize that the level of those costs is irrelevant to decisions about which price will generate the most money to cover them. Since nonincremental fixed and sunk costs do not change with a pricing decision, they do not affect the relative profitability of one price versus an alternative. Consequently, consideration of them simply clouds the issue of which price level will generate the most profit to cover them.

All costs are important to profitability since they all, regardless of how they are classified, have to be covered before profits are earned. At some point, all costs must be considered. What distinguishes value-based pricing from cost-driven pricing is when they are considered. A major reason that this approach to pricing is more profitable than cost-driven pricing is that it encourages managers to think about costs when they can still do something about them. Every cost is incremental and avoidable at some time. For example, even the cost of product development and design, although it is fixed and sunk by the time the first unit is sold, is incremental and avoidable before the design process begins. The same is true for other costs. The key to profitable pricing is to recognize that customers in the marketplace, not costs, determine what a product can sell for. Consequently, before incurring any costs, managers need to estimate what customers can be convinced to pay for an intended product. Then they decide what costs they can profitably incur, given the expected revenue.

Of course, no one has perfect foresight. Managers must make decisions to incur costs without knowing for certain how the market will respond. When their expectations are accurate, the market rewards them with sales at the prices they expected, enabling them to cover all costs and to earn a profit. When they overestimate a product's value, profit contribution may prove inadequate to cover all the costs incurred. In that case, a good manager seeks to minimize the loss. This can be done only by maximizing profit contribution (revenue minus incremental, avoidable costs). Shortsighted efforts to build nonincremental fixed and sunk costs into a price that will justify past mistakes will only reduce volume further, making the losses worse.

CASE STUDY: Ritter & Sons

The Westside Manufacturing example illustrates the principles of costing and financial analysis in the context of one product with easily defined costs. Applying these analysis tools in a more typical corporate setting is usually much more complex. The following case study illustrates how one company dealt with more complex incremental costing issues, and then used the financial analysis tools presented in this chapter to develop well-reasoned proposals for more profitable pricing. Note how, even in the absence of complete information, these tools enable managers to fully integrate the information they have, cross-functionally, to make better decisions.

Ritter & Sons is a wholesale producer of potted plants and cut flowers. Ritter's most popular product is potted chrysanthemums (mums), which are particularly in demand around certain holidays, especially Mother's Day, Easter, and Memorial Day, but they maintain a high level of sales throughout the year. Exhibit 10-9 shows Ritter's revenues, costs, and sales from mums for a recent fiscal year. After attending a seminar on pricing, the company's chief financial officer, Don Ritter, began to wonder whether this product might somehow be priced more profitably. A serious examination of the effect of raising and lowering the wholesale price of mums from the current price of $3.85 per unit was then begun.

Ritter's first step was to identify the relevant cost and contribution margin for mums. Looking only at the data in Exhibit 10-9, Don was somewhat uncertain how to proceed. He reasoned that the costs of the cuttings, shipping, packaging, and pottery were clearly incremental and avoidable and that the cost of administrative overhead was fixed. He was far less certain about labor and the capital cost of the greenhouses. Some of Ritter's work force consisted of long-time employees whose knowledge of planting techniques was highly valuable. It would not be practical to lay them off, even if they were not needed during certain seasons. Most production employees, however, were transient laborers who were hired during peak seasons and who found work elsewhere when less labor was required.

EXHIBIT 10-9	Cost Projection for Proposed Crop of Mums	
Crop Preparer: DR	**6" Mums Total**	**Per Unit**
Unit sales	86,250	1
Revenue	*$332,063*	*$3.85*
Cost of cuttings	34,500	0.40
Gross margin	*297,563*	*3.45*
Labor	51,850	0.60
Shipping	26,563	0.31
Package foil	9,056	0.10
Package sleeve	4,312	0.05
Package carton	4,399	0.05
Pottery	14,663	0.17
Capital cost allocation	66,686	0.77
Overhead allocation	73,320	0.85
Operating profit	$46,714	$0.54

After consulting with the production manager for potted plants, Don concluded that about $7,000 of the labor cost of mums was fixed. The remaining $44,850 (or $0.52 per unit) was variable and thus relevant to the pricing decision.

Don also wondered how he should treat the capital cost of the greenhouses. He was sure that the company policy of allocating capital cost (interest and depreciation) equally to every plant sold was not correct. However, when Don suggested to his brother Paul, the company's president, that since these costs were sunk, they should be entirely ignored in pricing, Paul found the suggestion unsettling. He pointed out that Ritter used all of its greenhouse capacity in the peak season, that it had expanded its capacity in recent years, and that it planned further expansions in the coming year. Unless the price of mums reflected the capital cost of building additional greenhouses, how could Ritter justify such investments?

That argument made sense to Don. Surely the cost of greenhouses is incremental if they are all in use, since additional capacity would have to be built if

Ritter were to sell more mums. But that same cost is clearly not incremental during seasons when there is excess capacity. Ritter's policy of making all mums grown in a year bear a $0.77 capital cost was simply misleading since additional mums could be grown without bearing any additional capital cost during seasons with excess capacity. Mums grown in peak seasons, however, actually cost much more than Ritter had been assuming, since those mums require capital additions. Thus, if the annual cost of an additional greenhouse (depreciation, interest, maintenance, heating) is $9,000, and if the greenhouse will hold 5,000 mums for three crops each year, the capital cost per mum would be $0.60 [$9,000/(3 × 5,000)] only if all greenhouses are fully utilized throughout the year. Since the greenhouses are filled to capacity for only one crop per year, the relevant capital cost for pricing that crop is $1.80 per mum ($9,000/5,000), while it is zero for pricing crops at other times.[3]

As a result of his discussions, Don calculated two costs for mums: one to apply when there is excess capacity in the

	With Excess Capacity	At Full Capacity
EXHIBIT 10-10 Relevant Cost of Mums		
Price	$3.85	$3.85
− Cost of cuttings	0.40	0.40
− Incremental labor	0.52	0.52
− Other direct costs	0.68	0.68
= Dollar contribution margin	$2.25	$2.25
− Incremental capital cost	0	1.80
= Profit contribution	$2.25	$0.45

greenhouses and one to apply when greenhouse capacity is fully utilized. His calculations are shown in Exhibit 10-10. These two alternatives do not exhaust the possibilities. For any product, different combinations of costs can be fixed or incremental in different situations. For example, if Ritter found itself with excess mums after they were grown, potted, and ready to sell, the only incremental cost would be the cost of shipping. If Ritter found itself with too little capacity and too little time to make additions before the next peak season, the only way to grow more mums would be to grow fewer types of other flowers. In that case, the cost of greenhouse space for mums would be the opportunity cost (measured by the lost contribution) from not growing and selling those other flowers. The relevant cost for a pricing decision depends on the circumstances. Therefore, one must begin each pricing problem by first determining the relevant cost for that particular decision.

For Ritter, the decision at hand involved planning production quantities and prices for the forthcoming year. There would be three crops of mums during the year, two during seasons when Ritter would have excess growing capacity and one during the peak season, when capacity would be a constraint. The relevant contribution margin would be $2.25, or 58.5 percent ($2.25/3.85), for all plants. In the peak season, however, the net profit contribution would be consider-

ably less because of the incremental capital cost of the greenhouses.

Don recognized immediately that there was a problem with Ritter's pricing of mums. Since the company had traditionally used cost-plus pricing based on fully allocated average cost, fixed costs were allocated equally to all plants. Consequently, Ritter charged the same price ($3.85) for mums throughout the year. Although mums grown in the off-peak season used the same amount of greenhouse space as those grown during the peak season, the relevant incremental cost of that space was not always the same. Consequently, the profit contribution for mums sold in an off-peak season was much greater than for those sold in the peak season. This difference was not reflected in Ritter's pricing.

Don suspected that Ritter should be charging lower prices during seasons when the contribution margin was large and higher prices when it was small. Using his new understanding of the relevant cost, Don calculated the break-even sales quantities for a 5 percent price cut during the off-peak season, when excess capacity makes capital costs irrelevant, and for a 10 percent increase during the peak season, when capital costs are incremental to the pricing decision. These calculations are shown in Exhibit 10-11.

Don first calculated the percent break-even quantity for the off-peak season, indicating that Ritter would need at least a 9.3 percent sales increase to justify a

EXHIBIT 10-11   Break-Even Sales Changes for Proposed Price Changes

5% Off-Peak Season Price Cut

$$\text{Break-even sales change} = \frac{-(-5.0)}{58.5 - 5.0} = +9.3\%$$

10% Peak Season Price Increase

$$\text{Break-even sales change} = \frac{-10.0}{58.5 + 10.0} = -14.6\%$$

$$\text{Break-even sales with incremental fixed costs*} = -14.6\% + \frac{-\$9,000}{\$2.635 \times 45,000}$$

$$= -22.2\%$$

*The new dollar contribution margin is $2.635 after the 10% price increase.

5 percent price cut in the off-peak season. Then he calculated the basic break-even percentage for a 10 percent price increase during the peak season. If sales declined by less than 14.6 percent as a result of the price increase (equal to 6,570 units, given Ritter's expected peak season sales of 45,000 mums), the price increase would be profitable. Don also recognized, however, that if sales declined that much, Ritter could avoid constructing at least one new greenhouse. That capital cost savings could make the price increase profitable even if sales declined by more than the basic break-even quantity. Assuming that one greenhouse involving a cost of $9,000 per year could be avoided, the break-even decline rises to 22.2 percent (equal to 9,990 units). If a 10 percent price increase caused Ritter to lose less than 22.2 percent of its projected sales for the next peak season, the increase would be profitable.

Judging whether actual sales changes were likely to be greater or smaller than those quantities was beyond Don's expertise. He calculated a series of "what if" scenarios, called break-even sales change simulated scenarios, and then presented his findings to Sue James, Ritter's sales manager (see Exhibit 10-12).

Sue felt certain that sales during the peak season would not decline by 22.2 percent following a 10 percent price increase. She pointed out that the ultimate purchasers in the peak season usually bought mums as gifts. Consequently, they were much more sensitive to quality than to price. Fortunately, most of Ritter's major competitors could not match Ritter's quality since they had to ship their plants from more distant greenhouses. Ritter's local competition, like Ritter, would not have the capacity to serve more customers during the peak season. The high-quality florists who comprised most of Ritter's customers were, therefore, unlikely to switch suppliers in response to a 10 percent peak-period price increase. If peak season sales remained steady, profit contribution would increase significantly, by about $50,000. If peak season sales declined modestly, the change in profit contribution would still be positive.

Sue also felt that retailers who currently bought mums from Ritter in the off-peak season could probably not sell in excess of 9.3 percent more, even if they cut their retail prices by the same 5 percent that Ritter contemplated cutting the wholesale price. Thus, the price cut would be profitable only if some retailers who normally bought mums from competitors were to switch and buy from Ritter. This possibility would depend on whether competitors chose to defend their market shares by matching Ritter's

EXHIBIT 10-12   Break-Even Sales Change Simulated Scenarios

Scenario	With Excess Capacity 5% Off-Peak Season Price Cut		
	% Change in Actual Sales Volume	Unit Change in Actual Sales Volume	Change in Contribution After Price Change
1	0%	—	$(16,504)
2	5%	4,313	$ (7,631)
3	10%	8,625	$ 1,242
4	15%	12,938	$ 10,115
5	20%	17,250	$ 18,988
6	25%	21,563	$ 27,861
7	30%	25,875	$ 36,734
Baseline price			$ 3.85
Baseline contribution margin			$ 2.25
New price			$ 3.66
New contribution margin			$ 2.06

Scenario	At Full Capacity 10% Peak Season Price Increase		
	% Change in Actual Sales Volume	Unit Change in Actual Sales Volume	Change in Contribution After Price Change
1	0%	0	$ 50,454
2	−5%	−4,313	$ 39,090
3	−10%	−8,625	$ 27,727
4	−15%	−12,938	$ 16,363
5	−20%	−17,250	$ 5,000
6	−25%	−21,563	$ (6,364)
7	−30%	−25,875	$(17,727)
Baseline price			$ 3.85
Baseline contribution margin			$ 2.25
New price			$ 4.24
= −12.5% New contribution margin			$ 2.64

price cut. If they did, Ritter would probably gain no more retail accounts. If they did not, Ritter might capture sales to one or more grocery chains whose price-sensitive customers and whose large expenditures on flowers make them diligent in their search for the best price.

Don and Sue needed to identify their competitors and ask, "How does their pricing influence our sales, and how are they likely to respond to any price changes we initiate?" They spent the next two weeks talking with customers and with Ritter employees who had worked for competitors, trying to formulate answers. They learned that they faced two essentially different types of competition. First, they competed with one other large local grower, Mathews Nursery, whose costs are similar to Ritter's. Because Mathews's sales area generally overlapped Ritter's, Mathews would probably be forced to meet any Ritter price cuts. Most of the competition for the largest accounts, however, came from high-volume suppliers that shipped plants into Ritter's sales area as well as into other areas. It would be difficult for them to cut their prices only where they competed with Ritter. Moreover, they already operated on smaller margins because of their higher shipping costs. Consequently, they probably would not match a 5 percent price cut.

Still, Sue thought that even the business of one or two large buyers might not be enough to increase Ritter's total sales in the off-peak season by more than the break-even quantity. Don recognized that the greater price sensitivity of large buyers might represent an opportunity for segmented pricing. If Ritter could cut prices to the large buyers only, the price cut would be profitable if the percentage increase in sales to that market segment alone exceeded the break-even increase. Perhaps Ritter could offer a 5 percent quantity discount for which only the large, price-sensitive buyers could qualify.[4] Alternatively, Ritter might sort its mums into "florist quality" and "standard quality," if it could assume that its

florists would generally be willing to pay a 5 percent premium to offer the best product to their clientele.

Don decided to make a presentation to the other members of Ritter's management committee, setting out the case for increasing price by 10 percent for the peak season and for reducing price to large buyers by 5 percent for the two off-peak seasons. To illustrate the potential effects of the proposed changes, he calculated the change in Ritter's profits for various possible changes in sales. To illustrate the profit impact for a wide range of sales changes, he presented the results of his calculations graphically. The graph he used to illustrate the effect of a 10 percent price increase at various changes in sales volume is reproduced in Exhibit 10-13. After Don's presentation, Sue James explained why she believed that sales would decline by less than the break-even quantity if price were raised in the peak season. She also felt sales might increase more than the break-even percent if price were lowered in the off-peak seasons, especially if the cut could be limited to large buyers.

Since Ritter has traditionally set prices based on a full allocation of costs, some managers were initially skeptical of this new approach. They asked probing questions, which Don and Sue's analysis of the market enabled them to answer. The management committee recognized that the decision was not clear-cut. It would ultimately rest on uncertain judgments about sales changes that the proposed price changes would precipitate. If Ritter's regular customers proved to be more price-sensitive than Don and Sue now believed, the proposed 10 percent price increase for the peak season could cause sales to decline by more than the break-even quantity. If competitors all matched Ritter's 5 percent price cut for large buyers in the off-peak season, sales might not increase by as much as the break-even quantity.

The committee accepted the proposed price changes. In related decisions, they postponed construction of one new greenhouse and established a two-quality

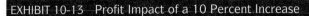

EXHIBIT 10-13   Profit Impact of a 10 Percent Increase

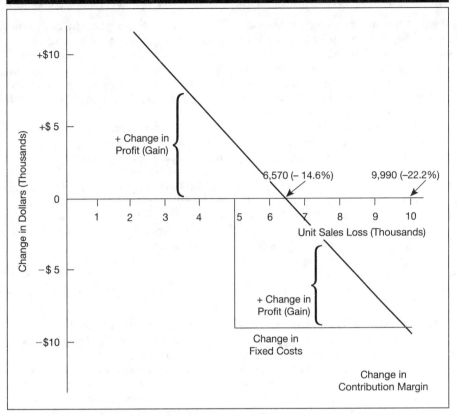

approach to pricing mums based on selecting the best for "florist quality" and selling the lower-priced "standard quality" mums only in lots of 1,000. Finally, they agreed that Don should give a speech at an industry trade show on how this pricing approach could improve capital utilization and efficiency. In the speech, he would reveal Ritter's decision to raise its price in the peak season. (Perhaps Mathews's management might decide to take such information into account in independently formulating its own pricing decisions.) He would also let it be known that if Ritter were unable to sell more mums to large local buyers in the off-peak season, it would consider offering the mums at discount prices to florists outside of its local market. This plan, it was hoped, would discourage nonlocal competitors from fighting for local market share, lest the price-cutting spread to markets they found more lucrative.

At this point, there was no way to know if these decisions would prove profitable. Management could have requested more formal research into customer motivations or a more detailed analysis of nonlocal competitors' past responses to price-cutting. Since past behavior is never a perfect guide to the future, the decision would still have required weighing the risks involved with the benefits promised. Still, Don's analysis ensured that management identified the relevant information for this decision and weighed it appropriately.

Summary

The profitability of pricing decisions depends largely on the product's cost structure and contribution margin and on market sensitivity to changes in price. In Chapter 9, we discuss the importance of identifying the costs that are most relevant to the profitability of a pricing decision, namely, incremental and avoidable costs. Having identified the right costs, one must also understand how to use them. The most important reason to identify costs correctly is to be able to calculate an accurate contribution margin. An accurate contribution margin enables management to determine the amount by which sales must increase following a price cut, or by how little they may decline following a price increase, to make the price change profitable. Understanding how changes in sales will affect a product's profitability is the first step in pricing the product effectively.

It is, however, just the first step. Next, one must learn how to judge the likely impact of a price change on sales, which requires understanding how buyers are likely to perceive a price change and how competitors are likely to react to it. We consider these subjects in the next two chapters on competition and value measurement.

Notes

1. The rule for analyzing the profitability of independently negotiated prices is simple: A price is profitable as long as it covers incremental costs. Unfortunately, many managers make the mistake of applying that rule when prices are not independent across customers. They assume, mistakenly, that because they negotiate prices individually, they are negotiating them independently. In fact, because customers talk to one another and learn the prices that others pay, prices are rarely independent. The low price you charge to one customer will eventually depress the prices that you can charge to others.

2. This equation can also accommodate a change in variable cost by simply replacing the "change in price" with the "change in price minus the change in variable cost."

One can also add to it the breakeven necessary to cover a change in fixed costs.

3. We are assuming that a greenhouse depreciates no more rapidly when in use than when idle. If it did depreciate faster when used, the extra depreciation would be an incremental cost even for crops grown during seasons with excess capacity.

4. This option could expose Ritter to the risk of a legal challenge if Ritter's large buyers compete directly with its small buyers in the retailing of mums. Ritter could rebut the challenge if it could justify the 5 percent discount as a cost saving in preparing and shipping larger orders. If not, then Ritter may want to try more complicated methods to segment the market, such as offering somewhat different products to the two segments.

Appendix 10A

DERIVATION OF THE BREAK-EVEN FORMULA

A price change can either increase or reduce a company's profits, depending on how it affects sales. The break-even formula is a simple way to discover at what point the change in sales becomes large enough to make a price reduction profitable, or a price increase unprofitable.

Exhibit 10A-1 illustrates the break-even problem. At the initial price P, a company can sell the quantity Q. Its total revenue is P times Q, which graphically is the area of the rectangle bordered by the lines 0P and 0Q. If C is the product's variable cost, then the total profit contribution earned at price P is (P − C)Q. Total profit contribution is shown graphically

as the rectangle left after subtracting the variable cost rectangle (OC, OQ) from the revenue rectangle (OP, OQ).

If this company reduces its price from P to P′, its profits will change. First, it will lose an amount equal to the change in price, ΔP, times the amount that it could sell without the price change, Q. Graphically, that loss is the rectangle labeled A. Somewhat offsetting that loss, however, the company will enjoy a gain from the additional sales it can make because of the lower price. The amount of the gain is the profit that the company will earn from each additional sale, P′ − C, times the change in sales, ΔQ. Graphically, that gain

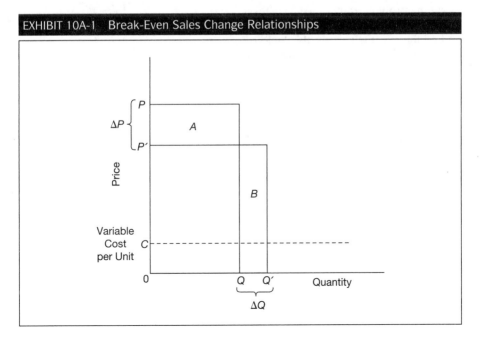

EXHIBIT 10A-1   Break-Even Sales Change Relationships

is the rectangle labeled B. Whether or not the price reduction is profitable depends on whether or not rectangle B is greater than rectangle A, and that depends on the size of ΔQ.

The logic of a price increase is similar. If P' were the initial price and Q' the initial quantity, then the profitability of a price increase to P would again depend on the size of ΔQ. If ΔQ were small, rectangle A, the gain on sales made at the higher price, would exceed rectangle B, the loss on sales that would not be made because of the higher price. However, ΔQ might be large enough to make B larger than A, in which case the price increase would be unprofitable.

To calculate the formula for the break-even ΔQ (at which the gain from a price reduction just outweighs the loss or the loss from a price increase just outweighs the gain), we need to state the problem algebraically. Before the price change, the profit earned was $(P - C)Q$. After the change, the profit was $(P' - C)Q'$. Noting, however, that $P' = P + \Delta P$ (we write, "+ ΔP" since ΔP is a negative number) and that $Q' = Q + \Delta Q$, we can write the profit after the price change as $(P + \Delta P - C)(Q + \Delta Q)$. Since our goal is to find the ΔQ at which profits would be just equal before and after the price change, we can begin by setting those profits equal algebraically:

$$(P - C)Q = (P + \Delta P - C)(Q + \Delta Q)$$

Multiplying this equation through yields

$$PQ - CQ = PQ + \Delta PQ - CQ$$
$$+ P\Delta Q + \Delta P\Delta Q - C\Delta Q$$

We can simplify this equation by subtracting PQ and adding CQ to both sides to obtain

$$0 = \Delta PQ + P\Delta Q + \Delta P\Delta Q - C\Delta Q$$

Note that all the remaining terms in the equation contain the "change sign" Δ. This is because only the changes are relevant for evaluating a price change. If we solve this equation for ΔQ, we obtain the new equation

$$\frac{\Delta Q}{Q} = \frac{-\Delta P}{P + \Delta P - C}$$

which, in words, is

% Break-even sales change

$$= \frac{-\text{Price Change}}{\text{CM} + \text{Price change}}$$

To express the right side in percentages, multiply the right side by

$$\frac{\left(\dfrac{1}{P}\right)}{\left(\dfrac{1}{P}\right)}$$

Appendix 10B

BREAK-EVEN ANALYSIS OF PRICE CHANGES

Break-even analysis is a common tool in managerial accounting, particularly useful for evaluating potential investments. Unfortunately, the traditional forms of break-even analysis appropriate for evaluating investment decisions are often misleading when applied to pricing decisions. Individual investments (Should the company buy a new computer? Should it develop a new product? Should it field a sales force to enter a new market?) can often be evaluated apart from other investments. Consequently, it is appropriate to use traditional break-even analysis, which compares the total revenue from the investment with its total cost.

Usually, however, one cannot set a price for each individual sale independent of other sales. To gain an additional sale by charging one customer a lower price normally requires charging other customers, at least others in that same market segment, the lower price as well. Consequently, it is usually misleading to evaluate the profitability of an additional sale by comparing only the price earned from that sale to the cost of that sale. To comprehend the profit implications of a price change, one must compare the change in revenue from all sales with the change in costs.

The need to focus attention on the changes in revenues and costs rather than on their totals requires a different kind of break-even analysis for pricing decisions. Where traditional break-even analysis of investments deals with total revenue and all costs, break-even analysis of pricing decisions deals with the change in revenue

in excess of variable cost (the dollar contribution margin) and with the change in incremental fixed costs. In the body of this chapter, you learned a number of formulas for break-even analysis of pricing decisions and saw how to use them in the Westside Manufacturing example. In this appendix, you will learn how to use those equations to develop break-even graphs and to analyze more complex pricing problems involving multiple sources of fixed costs that become incremental at different quantities.

DEVELOPING A BREAK-EVEN CHART

A break-even chart, such as Exhibit 10-4 is useful in determining the possible effects of a price change. It plots both the change in the dollar contribution margin and the changes in relevant costs, enabling the pricing analyst to see the change in net profit that a change in sales volume would generate. To develop such a chart, it is useful to begin by preparing a table, such as Exhibit 10-5, organizing all relevant data in a concise form.

As an illustration, let us examine the case of PQR Industries. PQR manufactures and markets home video equipment. One of the most popular items in the company's product line is a digital video recorder with current sales of 4,000 units at $250 each. Sales have been growing rapidly and are expected to reach 4,800 units in the next year if the price remains unchanged. Variable costs are

$112.50 per unit, resulting in the following percent contribution margin:

$$\% \, CM = \frac{\$250.00 - \$112.50}{\$250.00}$$

$$= 0.55 = 55\%$$

Despite its projected growth in sales at the current price, PQR is considering a 5 percent price cut to remain competitive and retain its share in this rapidly growing market. Since the cut would be implemented in the next year, the initial sales level, or baseline, is next year's projected sales (4,800 units). Calculation of the break-even sales change is as follows:

% Break-even sales change

$$= \frac{-(-5.0)}{55.0 + (-5.0)} = \frac{5}{50}$$

$$= 0.10 = 10\%$$

Unit break-even sales change

$$= 0.10 \times 4,800 \text{ units} = 480 \text{ units}$$

Production capacity is currently limited to 5,000 units but can be increased by purchasing equipment that costs $15,000 for each additional 1,000 units of capacity. The break-even sales change, considering this change in fixed costs, is:

% Break-even sales change (with incremental fixed costs)

$$= 10 + \frac{\$15,000}{\$125.00 \times 4,800} = 12.5\%$$

Unit break-even sales

$$= 0.125 \times 4,800 \text{ units} = 600 \text{ units}$$

Note that the price cut brings the price down to $237.50, resulting in a new dollar contribution margin of $125 per unit.

Since the actual sales change that would result from the price cut is unknown, a break-even table and chart should be prepared to show the profitability of the price change at various possible sales changes.

Exhibit 10B-1 shows a break-even table for PQR's proposed 5 percent price cut. The first two columns show the

EXHIBIT 10B-1   Break-Even Table for PQR Industries' Proposed 5% Price Cut

(1)	(2)	Change in (3)	(4)	(5)
Sales				
(%)	(Units)	Contribution Margin	Fixed Costs	Profit Contribution
0.0	0	−$60,000	0	−$60,000
5.0	240	−$30,000	$15,000	−$45,000
10.0	480	0	$15,000	−$15,000
12.5	600	$15,000	$15,000	0
15.0	720	$30,000	$15,000	$15,000
20.0	960	$60,000 ·	$15,000	$45,000
25.0	1200	$90,000	$15,000	$75,000
30.0	1440	$120,000	$30,000	$90,000
40.0	1920	$180,000	$30,000	$150,000

Note: Proposed change; −5% or $12.50/unit; initial price = $250; % CM = 45%; semifixed cost = $15,000 per 1,000 units capacity over 5,000 units.

potential levels of sales changes. Column 3 shows the change in total contribution margin that would result at each level using the change in profit formula. In the case of a 5 percent change in sales, the result would be:

$$\text{Change in profit} = (240 \text{ units} - 480 \text{ units}) \times \$125/\text{unit} = -\$30,000$$

Subtracting the change in fixed costs shown in column 4 from column 3 results in column 5, the change in profit contribution. Alternatively, we could have generated column 5 more directly by

calculating the break-even sales change including the change in fixed costs and substituting that number in the change in profit equation (see Exhibit 10B-1 and Exhibit 10B-2).

When plotted on a graph, the data from this table form a break-even chart (Exhibit 10B-2). The horizontal axis represents the change in unit sales and the vertical axis represents dollars of change. The line labeled "change in fixed costs" shows the increase in costs due to added capacity, as taken from column 4 of the table. The data in column 3 were used to

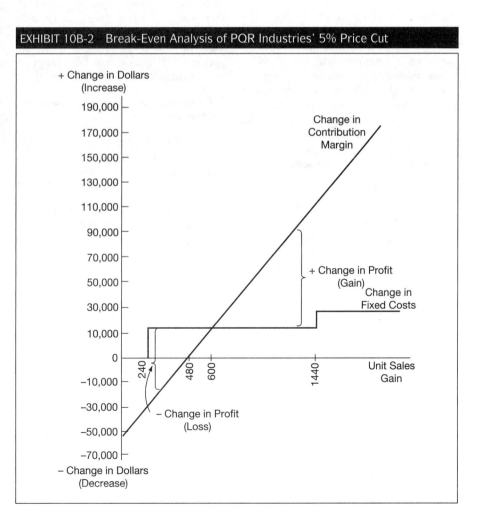

EXHIBIT 10B-2 Break-Even Analysis of PQR Industries' 5% Price Cut

plot the "change in contribution margin" line. The distance between the two lines represents the change in profit contribution (column 5). At the points where the "change in contribution margin" line is above the "change in fixed costs" line, the change in profit contribution (and net profit) is positive. The price cut would be profitable if sales changed by those amounts.

BREAK-EVEN ANALYSIS WITH MORE THAN ONE INCREMENTAL FIXED COST

To this point, we have always assumed that a company has only one fixed cost that changes with a price change. Frequently, however, a company will have several semifixed costs that change at different levels of volume. This makes analysis of a price change more complicated and the use of break-even analysis more essential to the management of that complexity.

Let us return to PQR Industries. Because of the cost of adding new equipment, management investigated alternative methods of increasing production. It was determined that the addition of one machine operator could delay purchase of new equipment until sales exceeded 5,400 units (or 600 units more than the baseline initial sales). Although labor costs are normally variable with production, machine operators are skilled laborers who, according to union rules, can only be hired as full-time employees working only at their specialties. The result is that a machine operator's salary is a semifixed cost. It was also discovered that the union contract required one skilled worker to be added for each 1,000 units of increased production. Finally, the plant engineer informed management that there was space for only one additional piece of equipment. If more equipment were purchased, more space would have to be rented, at a cost of $105,000 per year. The situation is summarized as follows:

Sales	4,800 units
Wholesale price	$250/unit
Variable cost	$112.50/unit

Semifixed costs:

Machine operators	$7,500 per 1,000 units of added production
Equipment	$15,000 per 1,000 units of added production beyond a 600-unit gain
Space	$105,000 per year for rental if more than one machine is added

Due to the complexity of these costs, there is more than one break-even sales change and a single calculation is not sufficient. For example, any increase in sales will require the hiring of a machine operator. The break-even sales change for a 5 percent price cut becomes:

% Break-even sales change (with cost of machine operator)

$$= 10\% + \frac{\$7,500}{\$125 \times 4,800} = 11.25\%$$

Unit break-even sales change
$$= 0.1125 \times 4,800 \text{ units} = 540 \text{ units}$$

If, however, the total sales exceed 5,400 units and equipment must be purchased, a new calculation is required as follows:

% Break-even sales change (with cost of equipment)

$$= 11.25\% + \frac{\$15,000}{\$125 \times 4,800} = 13.75\%$$

Unit break-even sales change
$$= 0.1375 \times 4,800 \text{ units} = 660 \text{ units}$$

If more space would have to be rented, still another break-even calculation would be required.

It seems obvious that when there are multiple sources of incremental fixed costs, analysis via calculation of break-even sales changes could become both tedious and confusing. A break-even table and chart are usually essential to the clear sorting out of these problems. Organizing the data into a table (Exhibit 10B-3) and

EXHIBIT 10B-3 Revised Break-Even Table for PQR Industries' Proposed 5% Price Cut

Sales			Changes in				
(%)	(Units)	Contribution Margin ($)	Cost of Operators ($)	Cost of Equipment ($)	Cost of Space ($)	Total Fixed Costs ($)	Profit Contribution ($)
0.00	0	−60,000	0	0	0	0	−60,000
5.00	240	−30,000	7,500	0	0	7,500	−37,500
10.00	480	0	7,500	0	0	7,500	−7,500
11.25	540	7,500	7,500	0	0	7,500	0
12.50	600	15,000	7,500	0	0	7,500	7,500
13.75	660	22,500	7,500	15,000	0	22,500	0
15.00	720	30,000	7,500	15,000	0	22,500	7,500
20.00	960	60,000	7,500	15,000	0	22,500	37,500
25.00	1,200	90,000	15,000	15,000	0	30,000	60,000
30.00	1,440	120,000	15,000	15,000	0	30,000	90,000
35.00	1,680	150,000	15,000	30,000	105,000	150,000	0
40.00	1,920	180,000	15,000	30,000	105,000	150,000	30,000

Note: Proposed change: −5%, or $12.50/unit; initial price = $250; % CM = 45%; semifixed costs = $7,500/1,000 units for machine operators $15,000/1,000 units over 5,400 units for equipment $90,000/year for space rental if more than one piece of equipment is added.

EXHIBIT 10B-4   Revised Break-Even Analysis of PQR Industries' 5% Cut

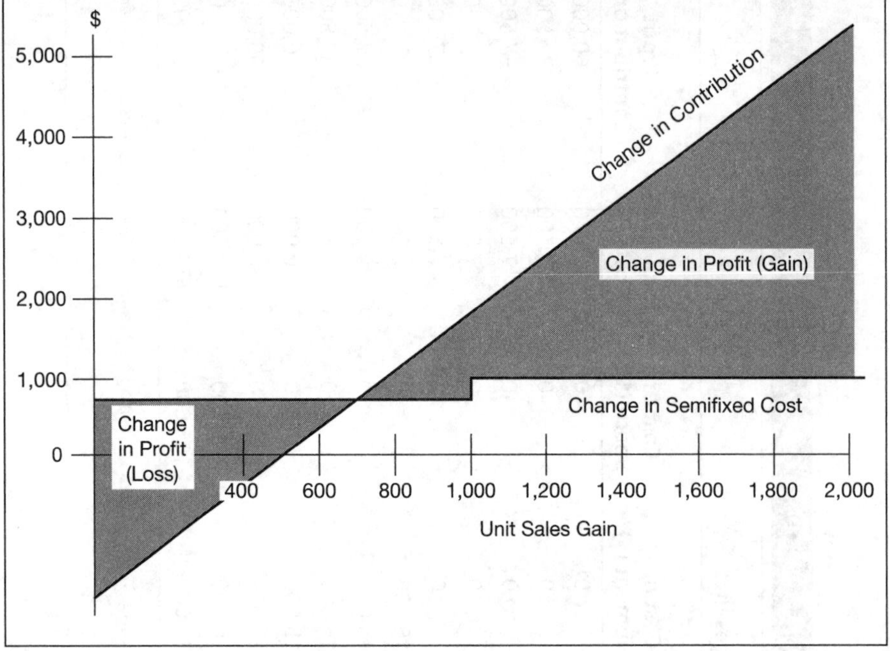

plotting it on a graph (Exhibit 10B-4) make the options much clearer. At changes in sales of between 540 and 600 units, the price change is slightly profitable. Once the change in sales exceeds 600 units, however, fixed costs must rise again due to the need for more equipment, and profits will become negative and will not return to positive again until the change in sales exceeds 660 units, causing the change in contribution to rise above the change in fixed costs.

Note that 12.5 percent, or 600 units, is the maximum sales change possible before additional costs must be incurred. To determine whether the investment in additional equipment is worthwhile, management must decide whether the possibility that sales will grow enough to achieve a profit contribution of more than $7,500 (that is, by more than 15 percent) after the equipment is purchased would be enough to justify forgoing the more certain profit to be gained from reaching only a 12.5 percent increase in sales.

This type of situation arises whenever there is a change in fixed costs, most dramatically when the second machine is bought and space must be rented. It seems unlikely that sales growth due to the price change would be sufficient to justify renting more space. In fact, sales would have to increase by more than 53 percent before such an increase in fixed costs would produce a positive net profit. Moreover, the investment would not be justified if the profit that could be earned by not meeting the entire sales gain were higher.

BREAK-EVEN GRAPHS

The calculations for determining break-even sales changes for a price increase are the same as those for a price cut. For price increases, however, sales volumes decline rather than increase. Consequently, the direction of the horizontal axis measures declines in sales volumes rather than increases.

To illustrate, let us consider again the case of PQR Industries. In addition to digital video recorders, PQR sells flat panel TVs for $3,000. Variable costs of $1,650 per unit leave the company with a contribution margin of $1,350 per unit, or 45 percent. The company is considering a price increase next year on this item. The initial sales level for evaluating the increase (next year's projected sales) is 4,000 units, which exceeds the company's current capacity of 3,600 units.

Concern about capacity constraints and the slowing growth of the market for this product have caused management to consider instituting a price increase in order to maximize profits. The break-even sales change for the proposed 5 percent price increase is:

$$\frac{-(5)}{45 + 5} = -10\%$$

Unit break-even sales change
$$= -0.10 \times 4{,}000 \text{ units} = -400 \text{ units}$$

As long as the price increase causes sales to decline by less than 10 percent or 400 units, the price increase will cause the total dollar contribution from this product to increase.

To increase production beyond the current 3,600-unit capacity, additional equipment must be bought at a cost of $150,000. If, however, as a result of the price increase, sales decrease to the point that current capacity is sufficient, purchase of new equipment would not be necessary. The expenditure avoided is a negative change in fixed costs from the level required to achieve the 4,000-unit baseline sales level. A new break-even sales change is calculated as follows:

% Break-even sales change (including change in fixed costs)

$$= -10\% + \frac{-\$150{,}000}{\$1{,}500 \times 4{,}000} = -12.5\%$$

On the basis of the data in Exhibit 10B-5, we can produce a break-even

		Change in		
(1)	(2)	(3)	(4)	(5)
Sales (%)	Sales (Units)	Contribution Margin ($)	Fixed Costs ($)	Profit Contribution ($)
0.0	0	600,000	0	600,000
5.0	200	800,000	0	300,000
10.0	400	0	−150,000	150,000
12.5	500	−150,000	−150,000	0
15.0	600	−300,000	−150,000	−150,000
20.0	800	−600,000	−150,000	−450,000
25.0	1000	−900,000	−150,000	−750,000
30.0	1200	−1,200,000	−150,000	−1,050,000

Note: Proposed change −5% or $150/unit initial price = $3,000; % CM = 45%; semifixed cost = $150,000 for capacity over 3,600 units.

EXHIBIT 10B-6 Break-Even Analysis for PQR Industries' 5% Price Increase

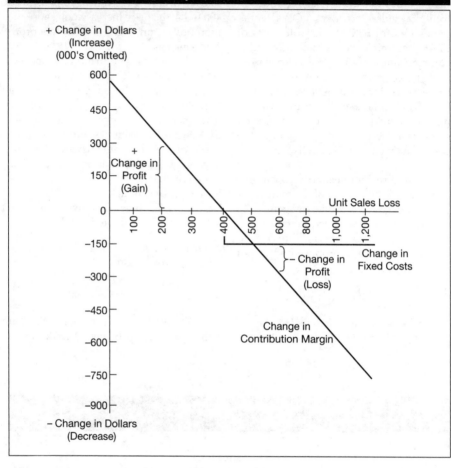

graph for this price change (Exhibit 10B-6). The lines representing changes in contribution margin and fixed costs run opposite to the directions we are accustomed to seeing for price cuts, but the change in profit contribution, as indicated by the relative positions of these lines, is still interpreted as in earlier examples.

To verify this, let us refer to the graph and examine the results of a 5 percent, or 200-unit, sales decrease. At this point, there has been no change in fixed costs. Therefore, the change in profitability should equal a positive $300,000, the distance between the line indicating change in contribution margin and the horizontal axis. Reference to the related table will show that this is indeed true.

Summary

Predicting the outcome of a price change is not an exact science, as later chapters will show. A manager should, therefore, consider all possible outcomes of such a change in order to choose the wisest course of action. Tables and graphs of break-even analyses are useful, easily produced tools for this purpose.

Acknowledgment

This chapter was coauthored by Professor Gerald E. Smith of Boston College.

CHAPTER **11**

■ ■ ■ ■ ■

Competition
Managing Conflict Thoughtfully

Pricing against competition is more challenging and hazardous than pricing a unique product.[1] In the absence of competition, managers can anticipate the effect of a price change entirely by analyzing buyers' price sensitivity. When a product is just one among many, however, competitors can wreak havoc with such predictions. Price discounting in competitive markets—whether explicit or disguised with rebates, coupons, or generous payment terms—is almost a sure bet to enhance immediate sales and profits. It is easy to become seduced by these quick highs and fail to recognize the long-term consequences. The price cut that boosts your sales today will invariably change the industry you compete in tomorrow. Frequently, that change is for the worse.

In the early 1990s, Alamo was the most profitable (as a percentage of sales) and fastest growing rental car company in America, despite being only the fifth largest. Its low-cost operating model enabled it to dominate leisure rental markets such as Florida and Hawaii. But Alamo's management was impatient for growth and had the cash to pursue it. Within the United States, the largest and most lucrative rental car segment was business travel that originated at airports. Alamo figured that even if it could win only a small share of that market by undercutting the rates offered by Hertz and Avis, it could generate a lot of profit given its low overhead costs per car.

That was not to be, for reasons that in retrospect were entirely predictable. Alamo succeeded in pursuing individual, budget-conscious business travelers, but not the large corporate accounts that comprised the most volume. Alamo had neither the facilities nor the experience to woo and satisfy business travelers who wanted first and foremost a quick getaway. Alamo's success was built on its capacity and expertise at handling large crowds that arrived on charter flights and in tour groups. Its high profits reflected its low overhead costs to serve that segment.

Still, in 1992, Alamo slashed rates and began moving to on-airport locations in cities beyond its core markets. In doing so, Alamo underestimated its own vulnerability. Hertz and Avis had apparently realized that they knew nothing about serving large tour groups efficiently, nor did they want them creating backlogs that would frustrate their valuable business clientele. But once Alamo began using its profit to attack their market, it was bound to prompt a response. The response was swift. Within two years, Hertz opened the largest car rental facility in the world in Alamo's biggest market, Orlando, Florida, with 66 counters and luggage-transfer stations that made life easier for tourists with lots of stuff in tow. To fill this facility, Hertz began undercutting Alamo's deals with European tour operators, who proved much more willing to switch suppliers to save a few dollars per car than were Hertz's corporate business customers that Alamo was trying to woo. That year, Alamo's profits fell into the red. The company was sold the next year.[2]

The lesson here is not that a profitable company should not attempt to grow share. The lesson is that a company needs to make competitive decisions that leverage its competitive advantages and minimize its vulnerabilities. This is not to argue that underpricing the competition is never a successful strategy in the long run, but the conditions necessary to make it successful depend critically upon how customers and competitors react to it. The goal of this chapter is to provide guidelines for anticipating those reactions, influencing them, and integrating them into a long-term strategic plan.

UNDERSTANDING THE PRICING GAME

Pricing is like playing chess; those who make moves one at a time based upon what they see in front of them will invariably be beaten by those who envision the game several moves ahead. Like chess, pricing is a "game," as defined by game theorists, because outcomes depend not only on a company's own pricing decisions but also on how customers and competitors respond to them. Unfortunately, pricing strategically for sustainable profitability is a type of game requiring skills foreign to many marketing and sales managers. What most of us know about competition we learned from sports, academics, and perhaps from intracompany sales contests. The rules for success in these types of competition are quite different from those for success in pricing. The reason, in technical jargon, is that the former are all examples of "positive-sum" games, whereas pricing is a "negative-sum" game. Understanding the difference is crucial to playing the pricing game successfully.[3]

Positive-sum games are those in which the very process of competition creates benefits. Consequently, the more prolonged and intense the game—in sports, academics, or sales—the greater the rewards to the players. The winner always finds playing such games worthwhile and even the loser may gain enough from the experience so as not to regret having played. In fact, people with a healthy attitude toward these activities often seek opportunities to challenge themselves. Such a strong competitive spirit is a criterion commonly used to identify job candidates with potential for success in sales.

Unfortunately, that same gung-ho attraction to competition is quite un-healthy when applied to negative-sum games: those in which the process of competition imposes costs on players. Warfare, labor actions, and dueling are negative-sum games because the loser never benefits from participation and even the winner may end the confrontation wounded. The longer the conflict drags on, the more likely it is that even the winner will find that playing was not worth the cost. Price competition is usually a negative-sum game since the more intense price competition is, the more it undermines the value of the market over which one is competing.[4] Price competitors do well, therefore, to forget what they learned about competing from sports and other positive-sum games, and to try instead to draw lessons from less familiar competitions such as warfare or dueling.

Students of actual warfare, who are cognizant of its cost, do not make the mistake of equating success with winning battles. Lidell Hart, author of more than 30 books on military strategy, offers advice to political and military leaders that marketers would do well to note:

> Fighting power is but one of the instruments of grand strategy—which should [also] take account of and apply . . . financial pressure, diplomatic pressure, commercial pressure, and . . . ethical pressure, to weaken the opponent's will. . . . It should not only combine the various instruments, but also regulate their use as to avoid damage to the future state of peace.[5]

In short, winning battles is not an end in itself, and warfare is certainly not the only means to an end.

For marketers, as for diplomats, warfare should be a last resort, and even then the potential benefits of using it must be weighed against the cost. Fortunately, there are many positive-sum ways for marketers to compete. Creating new products, creating new ways to deliver service, communicating more effectively with customers about benefits, and reducing the costs of operation are all positive-sum forms of competition. Precisely because they create profits, rather than dissipate them, building capabilities for positive-sum forms of competition is the basis of a sustainable strategy. Competing on price alone is at best a short-term strategy until competitors find it threatening enough to react.

COMPETITIVE ADVANTAGE: THE ONLY SUSTAINABLE SOURCE OF PROFITABILITY

How can companies become strong competitors? Unfortunately, many managers erroneously believe that the measure of competitive success is market share (see Box 11-1). That may be a successful strategy if only one firm attempts to pursue it. When many competitors pursue this same strategy, they engage in negative-sum competition, which does little more than destroy profitability for everyone. Fortunately, there are strategies that promote positive-sum competition. Rather than attracting customers by taking less in profit,

BOX 11-1

Market-Share Myth

A common myth among marketers is that market share is the key to profitability. If that were true, of course, recent history would have shown General Motors to be the world's most profitable automobile company; United, the most profitable airline; and Philips, the most profitable manufacturer of electrical products ranging from light bulbs to color televisions. In fact, these companies, while sales leaders, have been financial also-rans. The source of this myth—these examples notwithstanding—is a demonstrable correlation between market share and profitability. As any student of statistics should know, however, correlation does not necessarily imply a causal relationship.

A far more plausible explanation for the correlation is that both profitability and market share are caused by the same underlying source of business success: a sustainable competitive advantage in meeting customer needs more effectively or in doing so more efficiently.* When a company has a competitive advantage, it can earn higher margins due to either a price premium or a lower cost of production. That advantage, if sustainable, also discourages competitors from targeting the company's customers or from effectively resisting its attempts to expand. Consequently, although a less fortunate company would face equally efficient competitors who could take market shares with margin-destroying price competition, a company with a competitive advantage can sustain higher market share even as it earns higher profits. Market share, rather than being the key to profitability, is, like profitability, simply another outcome of a fundamentally well-run company.

Unfortunately, when management misperceives the symptom of a poor strategy (insufficient or declining market share) as a cause and seeks it by some inappropriate means, such as price-cutting, the expected increase in profitability doesn't materialize. On the contrary, a grab for market share unjustified by an underlying competitive advantage will usually reduce the company's own and its industry's profitability. The ultimate objective of any strategic plan should not be to achieve or even sustain sales volume, but to build and sustain competitive advantage. Profitability and, in many cases, market share growth will follow. In fact, contrary to the myth that a

---

*Robert Jacobson and David Aaker, "Is Market Share All That It's Cracked Up to Be?," *Journal of Marketing* 49 (Fall 1985): 11–22; Richard Schmalensee, "Do Markets Differ Much?" *The American Economic Review* 75, no. 3 (June 1985): 341–351; William W. Alberts, "The Experience Curve Doctrine Reconsidered," *Journal of Marketing* 53 (July 1989): 36–49; Cathy Anterasiun, John L. Graham, and R. Bruce Money, "Are U.S. Managers Superstitious about Market Share?" *Sloan Management Review* (Summer 1996): 67–77; Linda L. Hellofs and Robert Jacobson, "Market Share and Customers' Perceptions of Quality: When Can Firms Grow Their Way to Higher Versus Lower Quality?" *Journal of Marketing* 63 (January 1999): 16–25.

higher market share causes higher profitability, changes in profitability usually precede changes in market share, not the other way around. For example, Wal-Mart's competitive advantages made it the most profitable retailer in the United States long before it became the largest, whereas Sears's poor profitability preceded by many years its loss of the dominant market share. This pattern of changes in profitability leading, not following, changes in market share is equally visible in the automobile, steel, and banking industries.

A strategic plan based on building volume, rather than on creating a competitive advantage, is essentially a beggar-thy-neighbor strategy—a negative-sum game that ultimately can only undermine industry profitability. Every point of market share won by reducing margins (either by offering a lower price or by incurring higher costs) invariably reduces the value of the sales gained. Since competitors can effectively retaliate, they probably will, at least partially eliminating any gain in sales while reducing the value of a sale even further. The only sustainable way to increase relative profitability is by achieving a competitive advantage that will enable you to increase sales and margins. In short, the goal of a strategic plan should not be to become bigger than the competition (although that may happen) but to become better. Such positive-sum competition, rather than undermining the profitability of an industry, constantly renews it.*

---

*For evidence that there are profit leaders in the bottom and middle ranges of market share almost as frequently as in the top range, see William L. Shanklin, "Market Share Is Not Destiny," *Journal of Business & Industrial Marketing* 4 (Winter–Spring 1989): 5–16.

these strategies attract customers by creating more value or more operating efficiency. They involve either adding to the value of what is offered without adding as much to cost or reducing costs without equally reducing the value offered.

We call these sources of profitable growth competitive advantages because competitors cannot immediately duplicate them, except at a higher cost. Many managers completely misunderstand the concept of competitive advantage and its importance for long-term profitability. We hear them report that they have a "competitive advantage" in having more stores than the competition, more knowledgeable salespeople, or higher quality. None of these are competitive advantages unless they also enable the firm to deliver value more cost-effectively than one's competitors can. Offering customers a more attractive offer by accepting a lower margin than the competition may be a sales advantage, but it is not a sustainable competitive advantage.

How can a firm achieve competitive advantage? Sometimes it's by luck. Aramco, the Saudi oil company, enjoys oil fields from which oil can be more cheaply extracted than from those in Alaska, the North Sea, or Kazakhstan.

Often, advantage comes from moving first on a new idea. By winning a patent, by gaining economies of scale, or by preempting the best locations, a firm may achieve an advantage that would be more costly for a later entrant to match. Zipcar built a 10-year lead in the hourly car rental segment, branding itself as a green alternative to car ownership. It invested heavily in technology that automated the car rental process and created both user and community goodwill that has facilitated placement of its products as well as a strategy for placing cars in high traffic areas that increase member utilization. While the traditional rental car companies have their sights on this growing market, Zipcar's loyal base and experience will not be easily overcome, even by well-funded competitors.[6]

More often, competitive advantages are carved out of the efficient management of a firm's value chain. Michael Porter, the Harvard competition guru, cites three ways that companies can proactively manage operations to achieve competitive advantage.[7]

- *Needs-Based Positioning*—based on serving the needs of only a particular customer segment or niche, which enables the firm to tailor its operations to meet the unique needs of that segment more cost-effectively.
- *Access-Based Positioning*—based on the company's ability to gain access to customers in unique ways. Access can be a function of geography or customer scale. For example, serving a uniquely wide or narrow geographic market, based on the firm's cost structure, can create a unique cost and service advantage.
- *Variety-Based Positioning*—competing in industries by choosing selected activities as part of strategically designed value chains, including coalitions with strategic partners that coordinate or share value chains to give a company a shared cost or differentiation advantage.

The Flip Video digital video recorder, now owned by Cisco Systems, is a recent example of a simple product effectively using needs-based positioning to outmaneuver much larger and experienced rivals. Flip Video is based on the simple premise that in this age of YouTube and information sharing, the most important attributes a video recorder must have for many consumers are portability and simplicity. The Flip Video is the size of a mobile phone, has a very simple user interface (with five buttons including on/off), and easily attaches to computers through a built-in USB arm. Introduced in 2007, the Flip Video has surpassed more than two million unit sales based largely on word of mouth and favorable media reviews, while the market leaders have seen video recorder sales flatten in 2008 and into 2009.[8]

The U.S. beer industry offers a classic case of "access-based positioning," both widening and narrowing of geographic reach to achieve competitive advantage. Companies with a national presence, such as Anheuser-Busch InBev and MillerCoors, enjoy a huge competitive advantage in purchasing television advertising space at low national rates. They have leveraged that advantage to eliminate smaller, national competitors. Even while smaller national competitors have struggled to survive, microbrewers have multiplied and prospered by pursuing a different geographic strategy. Companies such as Smuttynose Brewing in Portsmouth, New Hampshire, and Old Dominion in northern Virginia, rely on a local caché and word-of-mouth promotion to operate small but profitable businesses.

Microsoft's operating software strategy offers a good example of "variety-based positioning." As the desktop computer market emerged, Microsoft famously chose to focus not on producing complete desktop computer systems, like Apple or IBM, but only on producing the operating system—the strategic gateway to the proper functioning of computer hardware. As traditional public utilities have come under competitive pressure, they have looked for opportunities to gain cost or product advantages by coordinating activities into combined value chains. The local electric company has become a consolidator of direct mail, which it mails along with the monthly bill. Its incremental mailing costs are lower than for traditional mailers (since a bill has to be sent anyway), and it can promise that a higher percentage of recipients will actually open the envelope rather than file it in the wastebasket.

As these examples illustrate, the key to achieving sustainable profitability is to manage the business for competitive advantage. Unfortunately, most companies in competitive markets are driven by a focus on revenue growth, which they pursue by trying to be all things to all people, rather than by a focus on creating value more cost-effectively. Porter calls the failure to achieve either a value or a cost advantage "getting stuck in the middle." When such companies are exposed to competitors, some of whom offer higher quality or service while others offer lower prices, the firm's profitability gets squeezed despite its size.[9]

In the absence of a competitive advantage, it is suicidal to drive growth with price. During the Internet technology "bubble" of the late 1990s, thousands of Internet retailers and willing investors were hoping to prove this statement wrong. They accepted lower, even negative, margins simply to build share in the belief that ultimately the high value of the Internet would make them profitable. They ignored a simple economic principle: Competition drives out profitability except for those with a source of advantage that prevents competitors from fully matching their costs or their value proposition. As it turns out, the companies with the competitive advantages for competing on the Web (name recognition, low cost of customer acquisition, economies of scale) are exactly those who have the advantages in bricks and mortar space.

There are a few exceptions, namely, those Internet newcomers who could create advantages that competitors could not duplicate. eBay, for example, enjoys margins and profitability that exceed those of both online and bricks-and-mortar competitors, not just because of the high value of trading online, but because of the difficulty, those price-cutting competitors would face in trying to duplicate its online offerings. The value of an auction is directly related to the size of the base of participants in it (like the value of a telephone network). Once eBay gained a large user base advantage, it became impossible for any competitor to duplicate the value it offers traders. Similarly, Amazon has carefully created profiles of buyer preferences along with their credit and mailing information that for many people makes shopping on Amazon a more efficient and pleasant experience than shopping with either an online or traditional competitor.

REACTING TO COMPETITION: THINK BEFORE YOU ACT

Many managers are so fully aware of the risks of price wars and the importance of competing from a position of strength that they think coolly and logically before initiating price competition. It is much harder for most of us to think logically about whether or how to respond when we are already under attack. Consequently, we will discuss in step-by-step detail how to analyze a competitive situation and formulate responses in price-competitive markets that are not of your making.

When is it financially more prudent to accommodate a competitive threat, at least in the near term until you can improve your capabilities, than to retaliate? Thinking through this question does much more than prepare you, intellectually and psychologically, to make the best competitive response. It also reveals weakness in your competitive position. If you do not like how often you must accommodate a competitor because your company cannot fight the threat successfully, you will begin searching for a competitive strategy that either increases your advantage or moves you further from harm's way.

Exhibit 11-1 illustrates the complex flow of thinking required to make thoughtful decisions about reacting to price competition. The exhibit begins with the assumption that one or more competitors have cut their prices or have introduced new products that offer at least some of your customers more value for their money. How should you respond? Some theorists argue that one should never respond since there are better, positive-sum ways to compete on product or service attributes. While that is often true, the time to have explored and implemented those ways was usually long before a competitive price threat. At the time of the threat, a firm's strategic capabilities are fixed in the short run. The question at hand is whether to respond with price when threatened with a loss of sales by a lower-priced competitor. To determine whether a price response is better than no response, one must answer the following questions and explore the interrelationships illustrated in Exhibit 11-1.

1. *Is there a response that would cost less than the preventable sales loss?* Although the need to ask this question might seem obvious, many managers simply stop thinking rationally when threatened. They match any price cut without asking whether the cost is justified by the benefit, or whether the same benefit could be achieved by structuring a more thoughtful response. In Chapter 10, we introduced formulas for financial analysis of a reactive price change. If we conclude that reacting to a price change is cheaper than

EXHIBIT 11-1 Thoughtfully Reacting to Price Competition

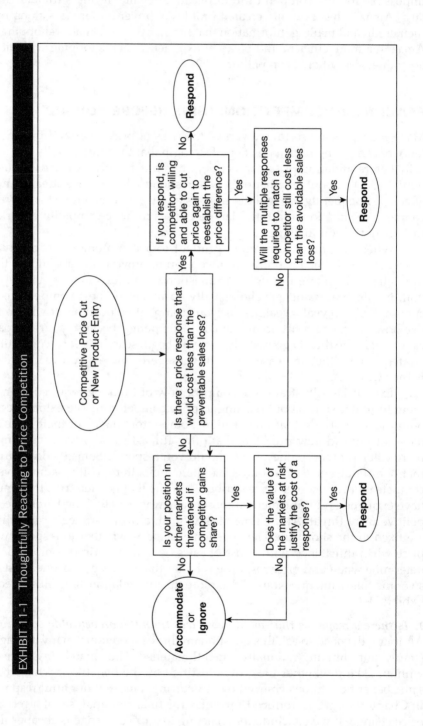

losing the sales, then it may be a good business decision. On the other hand, if a competitor threatens only a small portion of your expected sales, the sales loss associated with ignoring the threat may be much less than the cost associated with retaliation. Since the threat is small, the cost of cutting the price on all of your sales in order to prevent the small loss is likely to be prohibitive. Sometimes the cost of retaliation exceeds the benefits even when the competitor is larger.

It is also important to be realistic about how much of the projected sales loss is really preventable. When a new grocery chain opens with lower prices, the established competitors can surely reduce the sales loss by matching its prices. Still, even if they match, some people will shift to the new store simply because it is newer or more convenient to where they live. They will not return even if the competitor's price advantage is eliminated. Similarly, companies in business markets sometimes unadvisedly delay lowering prices to their most loyal customers even as market conditions are forcing them to lower prices to others. Once those customers learn, often from a competitor's sales rep, that their loyalty has been taken advantage of, matching price is unlikely to win them back. On the contrary, it may simply confirm that they have been gouged.

By constraining an organization's competitive reactions to only those that are cost-effective, managers also force their organizations to think about how to make their price reactions more cost-effective. Following are some principles that can substantially reduce the cost of reacting to a price threat.

- Focus your reactive price cut on only those customers likely to be attracted by the competitor's offer. This requires developing a "flanking" offer that is attractive or available only to the more price-sensitive buyer. Often, such an offer can be developed in a short period of time since it involves merely eliminating some element of the product or service not highly valued by the price-sensitive segments. During the recession in 2009, consumers began migrating to cheaper house brand grocery and cleaning products while supermarkets began promoting them more aggressively, resulting in an 18 percent decline in revenues for Procter & Gamble. In response, the company introduced flanking brands, like Tide Basic detergent at prices 20 percent lower than the original brands.[10] Many analysts have questioned the wisdom of this move, but there is an obvious benefit: it prevents some of the defection to house brands and gives P&G the ability to kill this new competitor when consumers again feel able to pay for its more value-added brands.

- Focus your reactive price cut on only the incremental volume at risk. A cheaper competitor will often be unable to entirely replace an incumbent's business, but will be able to gain a share of its competitor's business. For example, if a smaller independent television network, such as the CW Network in North America cuts its ad rates, advertisers are not going to abandon ABC, NBC, CBS, or Fox. They are, however, going to be more likely to divert some dollars to CW from the big networks. A big network could neutralize that threat by offering to discount its ad rates to the level of the independent network's rates just for the amount of advertising likely to be diverted. One way this could be structured is as a discount for all purchases in excess of, say, 80 percent of the prior year's purchases or expected purchases. These types of contracts are common not just for advertising, but also for drugs and medical supplies sold to health maintenance organizations (HMOs). Retaliatory discounts applicable only to the incremental volume at risk are also common when pricing to retailers and distributors.

• Focus your reactive price cut on a particular geographic area or product line where the competitor has the most to lose, relative to you, from cutting the price. For example, Taiwan Cement Corporation (TCC) began a drive to grow its share in the Philippines by building its own unloading facility there and acquiring new mixing capacity, after which it began undercutting Philippine prices. What TCC failed to think through was the fact that its high prices and high share (38 percent) in Taiwan left it vulnerable to retaliation. Cemex, the share leader in the Philippines but with only small share (5 percent) in Taiwan, reacted the next year by exporting more cement to Taiwan than TCC was exporting to the Philippines, driving the price from $58 per ton to $43 per ton in just one year.

• Raise the cost to the competitor of its discounting. If the competitor's price move is limited only to new customers and the competitor has a market of existing customers, it may be possible to retaliate without cutting your own price at all. Retaliate by educating the competitor's existing customers that they are being treated unfairly. A client of ours did this simply by making sales calls to its competitor's most profitable accounts. In the process of the call, the salesperson casually suggested, "You are probably paying about $X for this product now." When the customer questioned this, the salesperson confessed that he really did not know what they were paying but had surmised the figure based on the prices that his competitor offered recently to some other accounts, which he named. In short order, the customer was on the phone demanding similar discounts, and the competitor quickly backtracked on its aggressive offers. Even in consumer markets, it is sometimes possible to appeal to customers' sense of fairness or civic pride to convince them to reject a discounter. Small, local retailers have successfully done this to prevent Wal-Mart from opening stores in Vermont that would no doubt destroy the less efficient, but traditional, local retailers.

Retailers frequently use a related tactic of widely promoting a policy that promises to match the price of low-priced competitors. If a competitor advertises a lower price, then the retailer offers to refund the difference to any of its customers paying a higher price within a reasonable time period, say 30 days following the sale. Only a few very price-sensitive buyers will take the time to gather evidence of the lower advertised competitor prices, and then ensure that the sales receipt for their purchased model matches precisely the competitor's advertised model—all for merely the value of the price differential, often relatively small. However, the price-matching policy is not targeted at all buyers, or even just price-sensitive buyers; instead, it is a signal to other retail competitors of the futility of aggressive price discounting strategies. After the substantial reduction in margins they incur by heavy discounting, their competitors simply neutralize the advantage by rebating to customers the difference; these deep-discount competitors are better off playing by the rules of established nonprice competition in the category. In North Carolina, the Big Star and Winn-Dixie supermarket chains both announced price-matching policies to "meet or beat" the prices of aggressive rival Food Lion. Two years later, the number of products with essentially the same prices across these three competitors increased significantly, and the prices for these products increased as well.[11]

• Leverage any competitive advantages to increase the value of your offer as an alternative to matching the price. The key to doing this without simply replacing a price war with a quality or service war is to make offers that are less costly for you to offer than for your competitor to match. If, for example, you have much better quality, offer a better warranty. If you have more service centers in more locations, offer faster service. Major airlines respond to price competition from smaller upstarts by offering increased frequent flyer miles on newly competitive routes. Because of their large route systems, frequent flyers accumulate miles faster and enjoy more choices of destinations than anything the small competitors could offer other than price. Moreover, the more sophisticated yield management systems of the large airlines minimized the cost of such programs more effectively than smaller carriers could.

If any of these options is less costly than simply allowing the competitor to take some sales, it is worth continuing to pursue the idea of a response, using the question on the right side of Exhibit 11-1. If, on the other hand, it would cost more to respond than to accept the sales loss, one should continue to examine the option of not responding, using the questions on the left-hand side.

2. If you respond, is your competitor willing and able to cut price again to reestablish the price difference? Matching a price cut will do you no good if the competitor will simply reestablish the advantage. Ask yourself why the competitor chose to compete on price in the first place. If that competitor currently has little market share relative to the share that could be gained with a price advantage, and has no other way to attract customers, then it has little to lose from bringing price down as low as necessary to gain sales. This is especially the case where large sunk costs create substantial "exit barriers."

At one point, we had a pharmaceuticals company ask us to recommend a pricing strategy to defend against a new entrant. Management was initially surprised when we told them that defending their sales with price was unwise. Only after thinking about the problem from the competitor's standpoint did they fully understand the competitive dynamics they faced. Customers had no reason to try the competitor's new drug without a price advantage since it offered no clinical advantages. The new entrant had absolutely nothing to lose by taking the price down, since it had no sales anyway. Given that the huge investment to develop and test the drug was entirely sunk but that the manufacturing cost was small, winning sales even at a low price would be a gain. The conclusion was obvious that the competitor would cut price as often as necessary to establish a price advantage. It our client insisted upon preventing the new competitor from gaining significant market share, they would destroy the value of the market.

3. Will the multiple responses required to match a competitor still cost less than the avoidable sales loss? Think about the total cost of a price war, not just the cost of the first shot, before concluding that the cost is worth bearing to defend the sales at risk. If our pharmaceuticals' client had retaliated and closed the price gap enough to keep the competitor from winning sales, the competitor would simply have to cut its price further. The process would have continued until one or the other stopped it, which was likely to be our client, who had much more to lose from a downward price spiral. If our client was ultimately going to let the competitor have a price advantage, it was better to let them have it at a high price than at a low one. Once the competitor gained some sales, it too would have something to lose from a downward price spiral. At that time, an effort to stop the discount and redirect competition to more positive-sum activities, such as sales calls, product improvement, and patient education, would be more likely to succeed.

4. Is your position in other (geographic or product) markets threatened if a competitor is successful in gaining share? Does the value of the markets at risk justify the cost of a response? Some sales have a value that far exceed the contribution directly associated with them. Following Dell's introduction of a new line of computer printers, Hewlett-Packard (HP) immediately severed its relationship to supply HP printers to Dell, signaling the strategic importance to HP of its printer business. HP also retaliated by cutting its PC prices to match Dell's, where Dell had much more to lose. Finally, HP realized that Dell's printer strategy had its own limitations. Dell sources its printers and cartridges from a third-party supplier, Lexmark, limiting Dell's typical cost advantage. So HP defended its lucrative printer business, not with price, but with aggressive product innovations. It introduced new printer models, including digital printing with greater savings for corporate customers, that led to higher revenues and overall printer market share gains.[12]

Retaliatory price cuts are all too often justified by vague "strategic" reasons unrelated to profitability. Before approving any retaliatory price cut for strategic reasons, two things should be required. The first is a clear statement of the long-term strategic benefit and risks. The benefit can be additional sales in this market in the future. It can be additional immediate sales of complementary products, such as sales of software and peripherals if one wins the sale of a computer. It can be a lower cost of future sales because of a competitive cost advantage resulting from the added volume. The risks are that a targeted price cut will spread to other customers and other markets, and that competitors will react, again creating a downward price spiral that undermines profits and any possibility of long-term gain.

The second requirement to justify a strategic price cut is a quantitative estimate of the value of the strategic benefit. This need to quantify often encounters resistance because managers feel that the task is too onerous and will require unnecessary delay. Usually, however, rough estimates are all that is necessary to achieve enough precision to make a decision. A company told us that they always defended price in the institutional segment of their market because sales in that segment drove retail sales. While the relationship was no doubt true, the magnitude of the effect was important given that pricing to the institutional segment had fallen to less than manufacturing cost. A simple survey of retail customers about how they began using the product revealed that only about 16 percent of retail sales were driven by institutional sales. We then estimated the cost of maintaining those sales by retaining all of the client's current institutional sales and compared that with the cost of replacing those sales through expenditures on alternative forms of promotion. That simple analysis drove a complete change in the institutional pricing strategy. Moreover, as institutional prices rose, "leakage" of cheap institutional product into the retail chain market declined, producing an additional return that had not been anticipated.

HOW SHOULD YOU REACT?

Competitive pricing strategy involves more than just deciding whether or not to react with price. It also involves deciding how to adapt your company's competitive strategy to the new situation. Exhibit 11-2 summarizes the strategic options and when to use them. In addition to the costs and benefits of retaliation that are weighed using the process described in Exhibit 11-1, this exhibit introduces the concept of strategic "weakness" and "strength." These concepts refer to a competitor's relative competitive advantage. Competitive "weakness" and "strength" have little to do with market share, despite the common tendency to equate them. Before its bankruptcy filing in 2009, the high cost structure of General Motors made the company a relatively weak competitor in the automobile market, despite a high market share, because (at least in the North American automobile market) it had higher incremental costs per dollar revenue than its major rivals. In contrast, the low-cost structure of Southwest Airlines makes it a stronger competitor, even when competing against larger airlines, because its low cost per seat mile generates higher profits despite its lower prices.

When you decide that retaliation is not cost-effective, one option is simply to ignore the threat. This is the appropriate response when facing a "weak" competitor, with no competitive product or cost advantages. In that case, the amount of your sales at risk is small and is likely to remain so. In these same circumstances, some authors and consultants recommend a more aggressive option—commonly known as the "deep pockets" strategy—and

EXHIBIT 11-2   Options for Reacting to Price Competition

		Competitor Is Strategically	
		Weaker	Neutral or Stronger
Price Reaction Is	Too Costly	IGNORE	ACCOMMODATE
	Cost-Justified	ATTACK	DEFEND

pursue it to their own detriment. Their logic is that even if retaliation is too costly relative to the immediate sales gained, a large company can win a price war because it can afford to subsidize losses in a market longer than its weak competitor can. Two misconceptions lead people down this dead-end path. One is the meaning of "winning." This is no doubt a strategy to successfully defend market share, but the goal, at least for a publicly owned company, is not market share but profit. The second misconception is that by destroying a weak competitor one can actually destroy competition. Often the assets of the bankrupt competitor are bought cheaply by a new competitor now able to compete from a lower cost base. Even if the assets are not bought, elimination of a weak competitor serving the price-sensitive segment of the market creates the opportunity for a stronger competitor to enter and use that as a basis from which to grow. Consequently, a costly strategy to kill weak competitors makes sense only in an already unprofitable industry where a new entrant is unlikely to replace the one eliminated.

When a price-cutting competitor is relatively "strong" and the cost of re-taliation is greater than the value of the sales loss prevented, one cannot afford simply to ignore the threat and proceed as if nothing had changed. A strong competitor who is gaining share is a threat to survival. To maintain a prof-itable future, one must actively accommodate the threat with changes in strat-egy. This is what Sears faced as Wal-Mart's network of stores grew to include Sears's traditional suburban markets. There was simply no way that Sears could match Wal-Mart's prices, given Wal-Mart's famously efficient distribu-tion system and Sears's more costly locations.

Sears's only logical response was to accommodate Wal-Mart as a com-petitor in its markets. Accommodating a threat is not the same as ignoring or confronting it. Accommodating means actively adjusting your own competitive strategy to minimize the adverse impact of the threat while reconciling yourself to live with it. Sears opted to eliminate its lower-margin product lines, remaking its image as a high-fashion retailer that competed less with Wal-Mart and more with traditional department stores.

A European industrial manufacturer took this same rack when it learned that an American company that previously exported product to Europe was about to build production capacity in the United Kingdom, with a generous government subsidy. Realizing that defending its market directly would produce nothing but a bloody price battle, the company refocused its marketing strategy away from the more price-sensitive segments, while creating incentives for less price-sensitive segments to sign longer-term contracts. As a result, the American firm's sales were focused in the least desirable segment where price-sensitive customers made it more vulnerable to a price war than were the traditional European competitors. Accommodating the competitor's entry was costly, but much less so than a futile attempt to prevent the entry with price competition.

The only situation in which it makes sense to use an attack response is when the competitor is weaker and the attack is cost justified. One reason this is rare is that it usually requires a misjudgment on the part of the competitor, who attempts to use price as a weapon from a position of weakness. That is exactly what Linens 'n Things tried to do, with flashy "sales" and "closeouts" designed to build same-store traffic after its 2006 leveraged buyout. Bed Bath & Beyond, its stronger competitor, matched the discounts and increased its 20-percent-off mail coupons. Lacking the capital to fight a sustained price war, Linens 'n Things filed for bankruptcy in 2008.[13]

More common is the case where the price-cutting competitor is strong, or at least as strong as the defending companies whose sales are under attack. Often because of the attacker's strategic strength, the amount of sales at risk is so great that a vigorous defense is cost justified. The purpose of a "defend" response is not to eliminate the competitor, but rather simply to convince the competitor to back off. The goal is to get the competitor to recognize that aggressive pricing is not really in its financial interest and to refrain from it in the future. This is often the position taken by established airlines in competition with new entrants on a route, many of which have lower cost structures. The defender is careful to limit the time period and the depth of its price responses, signaling a willingness to return prices to prior levels as soon as the competitor withdraws the threat. Sometimes these battles last no more than a few days or weeks, as competitors watch to see if the defender can fashion a cost-effective defense.

Partisans of pricing for market share would no doubt disagree with the restrained approach that we have prescribed. Large market-share companies, they would argue, are often better capitalized and, thus, better able to finance a price war than are smaller competitors. Although price-cutting might be more costly for the larger firm in the short run, it can bankrupt smaller competitors and, in the long run, reestablish the leader's market share and its freedom to control market prices. Although such a "predatory" response to competition sounds good in theory, there are two reasons why it rarely works in practice. First, predatory pricing is a violation of U.S. and European antitrust laws if the predatory price is below the predator's variable cost. Such a pricing tactic may in some cases be a violation when the price is below the average of all costs.[14] Consequently, even if a large competitor can afford to price low enough to bankrupt its smaller competitors, it often cannot do so legally. Second, and more important, predation is cost effective only if the predator gains some competitive advantage as a result of winning the war. This occurs in only two cases: when eliminating a competitor destroys an important differentiating asset (for example, its accumulated goodwill with customers) or when it enables the predator to gain such a cost advantage (such as economies of experience or scale) that it can profitably keep its prices low enough to discourage new entrants. In the absence of this, new entrants can purchase the assets of the bankrupt competitor, operating at a lower cost base and competing against a large firm now itself financially weakened by the cost of the price war.

An example of the long-term futility of price competition occurred in the club warehouse segment of retailing. As market growth slowed in the mid 1990s, club retailers all tried to grow by gaining market share, although none had the competitive advantage to justify such growth. For example, Sam's Club (operated by Wal-Mart), Pace (operated by Kmart), and Costco each opened large warehouse locations within months of each other in El Centro, California, a small city of only 75,000. Costco invaded one of Pace's strongholds in Anchorage, Alaska, by building not one, but two club warehouses. Pace retaliated by building a second club warehouse in Anchorage— leading to significant overcapacity in a minor market. Pace invaded Sam's Club's home turf in Dallas, Texas, with plans for a new club warehouse; Sam's Club retaliated immediately by building three more Dallas club warehouses (in addition to six existing locations), locating one next to the Pace store under construction. To attract customers to these new stores, each cut margins precipitously, as charges were filed alleging predatory pricing below cost. By the end of the decade, of eight original club warehouse competitors two to three emerged "victorious"—Sam's (which acquired most of the Pace locations) and Costco (which merged with Price Club); BJ's remained a smaller regional survivor. The exit of the failed club warehouses left behind many huge empty warehouses. It also left a lot of disappointment among the "winners." Even five years later, Sam's Club stores have never recovered their profitability, and have fallen far short of the performance of the traditional Wal-Mart stores.[15]

The key to surviving a negative-sum pricing game is to avoid confrontation unless you can structure it in a way that you can win and the likely benefit from winning exceeds the likely cost. Do not initiate price discounts unless the short-term gain is worth it after taking into account competitors' long-term reactions. Do not react to a competitor's price discounts except with price and nonprice tactics that cost less than accommodating the competitor's behavior would cost. If managers in general were to follow these two simple rules, far fewer industries would be ravaged by destructive price competition.

MANAGING COMPETITIVE INFORMATION

The key to managing competition profitably is diplomacy, not generalship. This does not necessarily mean being "Mr. Nice Guy." Diplomats are not always nice, but they manage information and expectations to achieve their goals without unnecessary confrontation. If they find it necessary to use force, they seek to limit its use to the amount necessary to make their point. In the diplomacy of price competition, the meaning that competitors ascribe to a move is often far more important than the move itself.

The decision to cut price to gain a customer may have radically different long-term effects, depending upon how the competitor interprets the move. Without any other information, the competitor would probably interpret the move as an opportunistic grab for market share and respond with defensive cuts of its own. If, however, the discount is structured to mimic exactly an offer that the same competitor made recently to one of your loyal customers, the competitor may interpret the cut as reflecting your resolve to defend that segment of the market. As such, the cut may actually reduce future opportunism and help stabilize industry prices.

Consider how the competitor might interpret one more alternative: your price cut is totally unprovoked but is exceptionally large, more than you have ever offered before and probably more than is necessary to take the business. Moreover, it is preceded by an announcement that your company's new, patented manufacturing process not only added to capacity but also substantially reduced incremental manufacturing costs. In this case, an intelligent competitor might well interpret the price cut as fair warning that resistance against your grab for market share will be futile.

Managing information to influence a competitor's expectations, and to accurately form your own expectations, is the key to achieving goals without unnecessary negative-sum confrontation. Managing information requires collecting and evaluating information about the competition, as well as communicating information to the market that may influence competitors' moves in ways desirable to your own objectives.

Collect and Evaluate Information

Many companies operate with little knowledge of their competitors' prices and pricing strategies. Consequently, they cannot respond quickly to changes. In highly competitive markets, such ignorance creates conditions that invite price warfare. Why would an opportunist ever cut price if it believed that other companies were willing to retaliate? The answer is that the opportunist's management believes that, by quietly negotiating or concealing its price cuts, it can gain sufficient sales volume to justify the move before the competitors find out. This is especially likely in industries with high fixed costs (high percentage contribution margins) and during peak seasons when disproportionate amounts of business are at stake.

To minimize such opportunistic behavior, competitors must identify and react to it as quickly as possible.[16] If competitors can react in one week rather than three, the opportunist's potential benefit from price-cutting is reduced by two thirds. At the extreme, if competitors could somehow react instantly, nearly all benefit from being the first to cut price could be eliminated. In highly competitive markets, managers "shop" the competitors' stores and monitor their advertising on a daily basis to adjust their pricing[17] and the large chains maintain communication systems enabling them to make price changes quickly in response to a competitive threat. As a consequence, by the time most customers even learn what the competition is promoting in a given week, the major competitors have already matched the price.

Knowledge of competitors' prices also helps minimize a purchasing agent's ability to promulgate misinformation. Frequently in business-to-business markets, price wars begin without the intention of any competitor involved. They are caused by a purchasing agent's manipulation of information. A purchasing agent, frustrated by the inability to get a better price from a favored supplier, may falsely claim that he or she has been offered a better deal from a competitor. If the salesperson doesn't respond, a smart purchasing agent may give the threat more credibility by giving the next order to a competitor even without a price concession. Now the first company believes that its competitor is out "buying business" and will, perhaps, match the claimed "lower price" on future orders to this customer, rewarding this customer's duplicitous behavior. If the first company is more skilled in price competition, it will not match the "lower price," but rather will retaliate by offering the same discount to other good customers of the competitor. The competitor will now see this company as a threat and begin its own cuts to defend its share. Without either competitor intending to undermine the industry price level, each has unwittingly been led to do so. The only way to minimize such manipulation is to monitor competitors' prices closely enough so that you can confidently predict when a customer is lying.[18]

Even when purchasers do not lie openly, their selective communication of information often leaves salespeople with a biased perspective. Most salespeople think that their company's prices are too high for market conditions. Think about how a salesperson is informed about price. Whenever the salesperson loses a piece of business, the purchaser informs the salesperson that the price was "too high." When he or she wins the business, however, the purchaser never tells the salesperson that the price was unnecessarily low. The purchaser says the job was won with "the right price." Salespeople get little or no information about how much margin they may have left on the table.

There are many potential sources of data about competitors' prices, but collecting those data and converting the data into useful information usually requires a formalized process. Many companies require that the sales force regularly include information on competitors' pricing in their call reports. Having such current information can substantially reduce the time necessary to respond to opportunism since someone collecting information from multiple salespeople and regions can spot a trend much more quickly than can an individual salesperson or sales manager. Favored customers can also be a good source of information. Those that are loyal to the company, perhaps because of its quality or good service, do not want their competitors to get lower prices from another source. Consequently, they will warn the favored company when competitors issue new price sheets or when they hear that someone is discounting to someone else. A partnership with such a customer is very valuable and should be treated as such by the seller.

In highly competitive markets, the information collected should not be limited to prices. Understanding plans and intentions is equally important. We recently worked with a client frustrated by the low profitability in its service industry, despite record revenue growth. In the process, we learned that the industry had suffered from overcapacity but recently had experienced multiple mergers. What was the purpose of those mergers? Was it to gain cost efficiencies in manufacturing or sales that would enable the new company to offer low prices more profitably? Or was it to eliminate some inefficient capacity, enabling the merged company to consolidate its most profitable customers in fewer plants, eliminating the need to win "incremental business." We found answers to those questions in the competitor's briefings to securities analysts, causing our client to rethink its own strategy.

Trade associations, independent industry monitoring organizations, securities analysts, distributors, and technical consultants that advise customers on large purchases are all good sources of information about competitors' current pricing moves and future intentions. Sometimes trade associations will collect information on prices charged in the prior week and disseminate it to members who have submitted their own prices. The airlines' computerized reservations systems give the owners of those systems an advance look at all price changes, enabling them to respond even before travel agents see changes. Monitoring price discussions at trade shows can also be another early tip-off. In retail businesses, one can simply "shop" the competitive retailers on a regular basis. In the hotel industry, nearby competitors regularly check their competitors' prices and room availability on particular nights by calling to make an unguaranteed reservation. If price competition is important enough as a determinant of profit in an industry, managers can easily justify the cost to monitor it.[19]

Selectively Communicate Information

It is usually much easier for managers to see the value of collecting competitive information than it is for them to see the value in knowingly revealing similar information to the competition. After all, information is power. Why should anyone want to reveal a competitive advantage? The answer: so that you can avoid having to use your advantage in a negative-sum confrontation.

The value of sharing information was obvious, after the fact, to a company supplying the construction industry. Unlike most of its competitors as well as most economists, the company accurately predicted a recession and construction slowdown looming on the horizon. To prepare, the company wisely pared back its inventories and shelved expansion plans just as its competitors were continuing to expand. The company's only mistake was to keep its insight a secret. Management correctly felt that by retrenching more quickly than its competitors, it could weather the hard times more successfully, but when competitors desperately cut prices to clear bloated inventories, the entire industry suffered. Had the company shared its insight and discouraged everyone from overexpansion, its own financial performance, while perhaps relatively less outstanding, would have been absolutely more profitable. It is usually better to earn just an average return in a profitable industry than to earn an exceptional return in an unprofitable one.

Even company-specific information—about intentions, capabilities, and future plans—can be useful to reveal unless doing so would preclude achieving a first-mover advantage into a new market. Such information, and the information contained in competitors' responses, enables a company to establish plans "on paper" that are consistent with competitors' intentions, rather than having to reach consistency through the painful process of confrontation.

• *Preannounce price increases.*   One of the most important times to communicate intentions is when planning a price increase. Even when a price increase is in the independent interest of all suppliers, an attempt to raise prices will often fail. All may not immediately recognize that an increase is in their interest, and some may hope to gain sales at the expense of the price leaders by lagging in meeting the increase. Other times, an increase may not be in the competitor's interest (perhaps because its costs are lower), meaning that any attempt to raise prices will ultimately fail. Consequently, before initiating a price increase that it expects competitors to follow, a firm's management should publicly explain the industry's need for higher prices and, if possible, announce its own increase far in advance of the effective date. As we discussed in Chapter 4, this "toe in the water" approach enables management to pull back from the price increase if competitors do not join in. This approach can be repeated multiple times until competitors understand that a price increase won't go through without them.

• *Show willingness and ability to defend.*   When threatened by the potential opportunism of others, a firm may deter the threat by clearly signaling its commitment and ability to defend its market. When major carriers realized that Southwest Airlines' model for serving mid-size airports directly might in fact be a more profitable one than their "hub and spoke" models, many announced that they would duplicate Southwest's strategy with services such as "Continental Lite" and United's "Ted." Soon after the announcement, Herb Kelleher, the founder and then CEO of Southwest, announced after a visit to Boeing that he had taken options to buy three Boeing 767 jets. When asked why he was taking those options, given that Southwest had always flown Boeing 737s exclusively, Kelleher replied, "In case I need 'em." He followed by indicating that the 767s would be the most efficient jets for flying between the hub cities of bigger carriers who might be tempted to challenge Southwest.

• *Back up opportunism with information.* While an opportunistic price cut to buy market share is usually shortsighted, it is sometimes an element of a thoughtful strategy. This is most often the case when a company uses pricing to leverage or to enhance a durable cost advantage. Even companies with competitive advantages, however, often win only pyrrhic victories in battles for market share. Although they ultimately can force competitors to cede market share, the costs of battle frequently exceed the ultimate value of the reward. This is especially true when the war reduces customer price expectations and undermines loyal buyer–seller relationships.

The key to profitably using price as a weapon is to convince competitors to capitulate. A Japanese company invited the two top operations managers of its American competitor to the opening of its new plant. After attending the opening ceremony, the company took all guests through the highly automated facility. The American managers were surprised to see the process so highly automated, all the way to final packing, since quality control usually required human intervention at many points in the process. When asked about this, the Japanese hosts informed the guests that this plant was the first to use a new, proprietary process that essentially eliminated the major source of defects. They also indicated that development of the process had taken them more than a decade.

On the way home, realizing now what could be done, the American engineers were eagerly speculating about how this improvement might be achieved and how much they should ask for in a budget to pursue research. They also wondered why their Japanese counterparts would reveal the existence of such an important trade secret. Within a few months they got their answer. The Japanese competitor announced a 20 percent price cut for exports of this product to the American market. If you were the American competitor with a large market share, how would knowledge of this trade secret change your likely response? In this case, the American company wisely chose to "adapt" rather than "defend."

Although the information disclosures discussed here are the most common, they are hardly comprehensive. Almost every public decision a company makes will be gleaned for information by astute competitors.[20] Consequently, companies in price-competitive industries should take steps to manage how their moves are seen by competitors, just as they manage the perceptions of stockholders and securities analysts. For example, will competitors in a highly price-competitive industry interpret closure of a plant as a sign of financial weakness or as a sign that the company is taking steps to end an industrywide overcapacity problem? How they interpret such a move will probably affect how they react to it. Consequently, it is in the company's interest to supply information that helps them make a favorable interpretation. Think twice, however, before disseminating misleading information that competitors will ultimately discover is incorrect. You may gain in the short run, but you will undermine your ability to influence competitors' decisions and, therefore, to manage price competition in the long run.

WHEN SHOULD YOU COMPETE ON PRICE?

We have been discussing the benefits of avoiding negative-sum competitive confrontation, but some companies clearly benefit from underpricing their competitors. Did not the Japanese automakers in the 1970s, Wal-Mart in the 1980s, and Dell Computer in the 1990s build their strategies around gaining share with lower prices? Yes, and understanding the special circumstances that enabled them to grow using price is necessary for anyone trying to replicate such success. For each of those companies at the times and places they used price to grow, price competition was not a negative-sum game. Every one of these successful price competitors first created business models that enabled them to cut incremental costs below those of their competitors. So long as each could attract customers with a price difference smaller than its cost advantage, it could win customers without reducing industry profitability. In fact, by serving customers more cost-effectively, these companies actually earned profits from each customer in excess of those earned by the competition—making their competitive efforts a positive-sum game.

However, a competitive cost advantage was not by itself enough to succeed. All of these companies also orchestrated a campaign of information to convince their competitors that their cost advantages were decisive. Their competitors wisely allowed them to maintain attractive price differentials, at least temporarily, until the competitors could figure out how to replicate those costs. Eventually, even these companies recognize that unless they can continue to cut costs faster than competitors, price-cutting cannot be a profitable growth strategy indefinitely. Consequently, they ultimately must shift their strategies toward adding more value in ways that enable them to sustain their large market shares without having to sustain a price advantage indefinitely.

Under what conditions are the rewards of aggressive pricing large enough to justify such a move? There are only four:

1. If a company enjoys a substantial incremental cost advantage or can achieve one with a low-price strategy, its competitors may be unable to match its price cuts. Wal-Mart, Dell, and Southwest Airlines created low-cost business models that enabled them to grow profitably using price. In some markets, there may be an "experience effect" that justifies aggressive pricing based on the promise of lower costs. By pricing low and accumulating volume faster than competitors, a firm reduces its costs below those of competitors, thus creating a competitive advantage through low pricing.

2. If a company's product offering is attractive to only a small share of the market served by competitors, it may rightly assume that competitors will be unwilling to respond to the threat. The key to such a strategy, however, is to remain focused. Enterprise Rental Car managed to grow quite large before any major competitor responded because Enterprise stuck to serving off-airport customers.

3. If a company can effectively subsidize losses in one market because of the profits it can generate selling complementary products, it may be able to establish a price differential that competitors will be unable to close. Microsoft, for example, priced its Windows software very low relative to value in order to increase sales of other Microsoft software that runs on it. Amazon.com's rationale for its low pricing on books was to build up a body of loyal customers to which it could sell a broad range of other products.

4. Sometimes price competition expands a market sufficiently that, despite lower margins and competitors' refusals to allow another company to undercut them, industry profitability can still increase. Managers who take this course are assuming that they have insight that their competitors lack and are, in effect, leading the industry toward pricing that is, in fact, in everyone's best interest. Before embarking on a price-based strategy, ask which of these your rationale is and recognize that the strategy can rarely be built on price alone or sustained indefinitely.

Summary

No other weapon in a marketer's arsenal can boost sales more quickly or effectively than price. Price discounting—whether explicit or disguised with rebates, coupons, or generous terms—is usually a sure way to enhance immediate profitability. However, gaining sales with price is consistent with long-term profitability only when managed as part of a marketing strategy for achieving, exploiting, or sustaining a longer-term competitive advantage. No price cut should ever be initiated simply to make the next sale or to meet some short-term sales objective without being balanced against the likely reactions of competitors and customers. The key to profitable pricing is building and sustaining competitive advantage. There are times when price-cutting is consistent with building advantage, but it is never an appropriate substitute for it.

Notes

1. Sections of this chapter were first published as an article entitled "Managing Price Competition," *Marketing Management* 2, vol. 1 (Spring 1993): 36–45.
2. "Rocky Road—Alamo Maps a Turnaround," *Wall Street Journal*, August 14, 1995, B1; and "Chip Burgess Plots Holiday Coup to Make Hertz No. 1 in Florida", *Wall Street Journal*, December 22, 1995, B1.
3. For more on the practical applications of game theory, see Adam Brandenburger and Barry Nalebuff, *Competition* (New York: Doubleday, 1996); Rita Koselka, "Evolutionary Economics: Nice Guys Don't Finish Last," *Fortune* October 11, 1993, 110–114; and Kenichi Ohmae, "Getting Back to Strategy," *Harvard Business Review* (November–December 1988): 149–156.
4. Price competition is a positive-sum game only when total industry contribution rises as a result. This can happen when market demand is sufficiently stimulated by the price cuts, when a low-cost competitor can win share with a price advantage less than its cost advantage, or when a firm's costs are sufficiently reduced by a gain in market share

that total industry profits can increase even as prices fall.

5. B. H. Liddell Hart, *Strategy* (New York: Meridian, 1967, 322).

6. Keegan, Paul, "The Best New Idea in Business," Fortune, September 14, 2009.

7. Michael E. Porter, "What Is Strategy," *Harvard Business Review* (November–December 1996): 60–78. See also Michael E. Porter, *Competitive Strategy* (New York: The Free Press, 1980, 34).

8. "Cisco Buys Flip Video Maker for $590 million," *CNET News*, March 19, 2009. Sony Corp. investor relations release Q1 2009, July 30, 2009.

9. Porter, *op. cit.*, pp. 41–43. A firm can become large without getting "stuck in the middle" simply by taking on multiple segments. The segments must be managed, however, as a conglomerate of focused businesses rather than as a one-size-fits-all marketing organization. Procter & Gamble is an excellent example of a large company that nevertheless carefully targets each product to meet the needs of a particular focused segment.

10. Ellen Byron, "Tide Turns 'Basic' for P&G in Slump," *Wall Street Journal*, August 6, 2009.

11. Akshay R. Rao, Mark E. Bergen, and Scott Davis, "How to Fight a Price War," *Harvard Business Review* (March–April 2000): 11, 107–116.

12. "As Alliances Fade, Computer Firms Toss Out Playbook," *Wall Street Journal*, October 15, 2002, A1; "Dude, You're Getting A Printer; Dell's Printer Business Is Puny Next to HP's, But It's Quickly Gaining Ground," *Business Week Online*, April 19, 2004, 12.

13. "Slump Spurs Grab for Markets," *The Wall Street Journal*, August 24, 2009.

14. See the discussion on predatory pricing in Chapter 13.

15. "Store Wars," *Fortune Small Business* (November 2003); "Warehouse Club-War Leaves Few Standing, And They Are Bruised," *Wall Street Journal*, November 18, 1993, A1, 16.

16. Note that this principle applies in the other direction as well. If competitors quickly follow price increases, the cost of leading such increases is vastly reduced. Consequently, companies that wish to encourage responsible leadership by other firms would do well to follow their moves quickly, whether up or down.

17. See Francine Schwadel, "Ferocious Competition Tests the Pricing Skills of a Retail Manager," *Wall Street Journal*, December 11, 1989, 1.

18. Another useful tactic that can control such duplicitous behavior in U.S. markets is to require the customer, in order to get the lower price, to initial a clause on the order form that states the customer understands this is "a discriminatorily low price offered solely to meet the price offered by a competitor." Since falsely soliciting a discriminatorily low price is a Robinson-Patman Act violation, the purchasing agent is discouraged from using leverage unless he or she actually has it.

19. For more guidance on collecting competitive information, see "These Guys Aren't Spooks, They're Competitive Analysts," *Business Week*, October 14, 1991, 97; and Leonard M. Fuld, *Competitor Intelligence: How to Get It—How to Use It* (New York: Wiley & Sons, 1985).

20. For a comprehensive and insightful survey of the research on communicating competitive information, see Oliver P. Heil and Arlen W. Langvardt, "The Interface Between Competitive Market Signaling and Antitrust Law," *Journal of Marketing* 58, no. 3 (July 1994): 81–96.

CHAPTER 12

Measurement of Price Sensitivity
Research Techniques to Supplement Judgment

Quantitative estimates of customer price sensitivity and willingness-to-pay can substantially improve both price setting and price segmentation. Indeed, some estimate of price sensitivity, whether it be quantitative or qualitative, is required for the price setting process described in Chapter 6. Sometimes research can provide very specific estimates of the impact of prices on sales volume. Other times estimates provide only a rough indication of a customer's willingness-to-pay given a set of circumstances. At their worst, estimates of price sensitivity fail to reflect the real nature of the buying decision, misleading management into making ineffective pricing decisions. This is often the case when a research design causes respondents to pay much more attention to price than real customers would. In almost all cases, it is possible to develop an estimate of price sensitivity somehow. The key to using the estimate to make a better decision is to recognize that even a very precise estimate is not necessary very accurate or unbiased. It is only an approximation of the actual value or price sensitivity. We always need to consider how differences between a real purchase situation in the future and an experiment in the present or past can change the impact of price on choice.

There are numerous procedures for measuring and estimating price sensitivity. Each procedure offers particular advantages over the others in terms of accuracy, cost, and applicability, so the choice is not arbitrary. One must think carefully about the appropriate procedure for any particular product before beginning research. In no case should a manager use a particular technique just because it is cheap, convenient, or fast. Instead, managers need to carefully assess their needs and adopt techniques that are most appropriate for the given situation. Even if the cost for those techniques is high, the benefit is often sufficiently large to justify the expense.

TYPES OF MEASUREMENT PROCEDURES

Procedures for estimating price sensitivity differ on two major dimensions: the conditions of measurement and the variable being measured. Exhibit 12-1 classifies the various procedures according to these two dimensions. The conditions of measurement range from a completely uncontrolled to a highly controlled research environment. When making uncontrolled measurements, researchers are only observers. They measure what people actually do, or say they would do, in a situation not of the researcher's making. For example, marketing researchers might collect data on consumer purchases of laundry detergent in a grocery store, but the prices and other variables that influence those purchases are beyond their control. This is often the case when analyzing historical sale data.

In contrast, when making controlled measurements, researchers manipulate the important variables that influence consumer behavior to more precisely observe their effect. Researchers conducting an experimentally controlled study of price sensitivity for a laundry detergent could select the prices as well as the advertising and shelf placement of various brands in order to make the data more useful. They might attempt to gain even more control by conducting a laboratory experiment in a simulated store, carefully selecting the individuals whose purchases would be recorded. Participants for the experiment could be chosen to represent various demographic variables (such as race, gender, income, and family size) in proportions equal to those of the product's actual market or to represent a particular group (such as mothers with children) to whom the product was intended to appeal. Generally, controlled research produces more accurate estimates of the effects of the controlled variables on price sensitivity, but depending on the level of realism, it is often costly to implement in a "real-world" setting. A laboratory setting is often used

EXHIBIT 12-1 Techniques for Measuring Price Sensitivity		
	Conditions of Measurement	
Variable Measured	**Uncontrolled**	**Experimentally Controlled**
Actual purchases	• Historical sales data • Panel data • Store scanner data	• In-store experiments • Laboratory purchase experiments
Preferences and intentions	• Direct questioning • Buy-response survey • In-depth interview	• Simulated purchase experiments • Trade-off (conjoint) analysis

to better control other factors that may affect price sensitivity as well as to reduce costs, but these improvements come at the expense of realism.

The dependent variable for estimating price sensitivity is either actual purchases or purchase preferences and intentions. Actual-purchase studies measure behavior, whereas preference-intention studies measure the intended choices that people claim they would make in a hypothetical purchase situation. Since the ultimate goal of the research is to estimate how people respond to price changes in actual-purchase situations, research that measures actual behavior is generally more desirable, but it is also more costly, time-consuming, and sometimes impractical, given the need to move products to market quickly. The following discussion summarizes these research techniques and some of the trade-offs of choosing one method over another.

Uncontrolled Studies of Actual Purchases

One way to estimate price sensitivity is to analyze past sales data. Naturally, one would expect this to work well in assessing the price sensitivity of customers for existing products in which consumers have prior-use experience. Given the increased use of scanners in supermarkets and mass merchandisers, and the databases maintained on their most frequent customers by hotels, airlines, and websites, analysis of historical data is becoming an increasingly important source of information to model customer sensitivity to prices and price deals. Still, changes in (1) the number of brands on the market, (2) how recently competitors offered price promotions, (3) the amount and effectiveness of advertising by each brand, (4) increased price sensitivity of more-educated consumers, and (5) general economic conditions can undermine the ability of historical data analysis to diagnose the true effects of a price change.

There are three types of past sales data from which a marketing researcher might attempt to estimate price sensitivity: (1) historical sales data—sales reports from a company's own records or from a sales-monitoring service, (2) panel data—individual purchase reports from members of a consumer panel, and (3) store scanner data—sales data for an individual retail outlet.

HISTORICAL SALES DATA Sales data collected as part of a company's regular operation are cheap and available for all products that have prior sales histories. Given the ability to actually track data on a daily or even real-time basis, marketers are able to analyze trends and project future movement of product sales. One needs to be careful in recognizing that sales data only allow for the estimation of price elasticity of the next level in the channel. For example, in a retail environment, unless a manufacturer sells directly to the end-user, its sales data reflect shipments to retailers, not actual retail sales during the period. Retailers may stockpile products purchased at promotional prices with no intention of passing the savings on to the consumer, or in anticipation of increases in demand on the part of consumer in a later period. Understanding this, some marketers have direct links with the inventory movement of their retail outlets, combined with up-to-date retail price data. While this is generally part of the inventory-management system to facilitate timely replacement of stock, it also provides the marketer with instant data that can be analyzed for important trends in demand.

In the past, using historical data for any product not sold directly to the end consumer was problematic. Sales data was usually available only at an aggregated level for a long period of time—say a week. In any given week, some stores will charge higher prices than others. Over time, the same store will put the product on sale for a week and then return its price to the regular level. These price variations influenced sales but were masked by the aggregation. Now, however, nearly all retailers use scanners to track sales and most sell their data to manufacturers. Since sales can be observed within short time frames, and loyalty cards can even enable tracking changes in an individual shopper's behavior over time, researchers can now readily track the impact of regular and promotional price differences. Unfortunately, data that aggregate sales for all stores over a number of weeks conceal these individual price differences. Given the aggregation in the data, the researcher is forced to explain sales variations by looking at only the average retail price across stores and throughout the time period. Since average prices have less variation and fewer observations than actual prices at individual stores in particular weeks, the data have less statistical power than data on individual purchase prices. In addition, some stores serve segments that are substantially more price responsive than others; aggregated sales data will mask these differences and will lead to price elasticity estimates that may, on average, be correct, but do not really apply to any single store setting.

PANEL DATA   A number of marketing research companies collect individual purchase data from panels of a few thousand households. Each household keeps a daily record of all brands purchased and price paid or uses a special credit card that tracks purchases. Since products are purchased daily, the data for each household must be aggregated to produce a series on weekly or biweekly purchases. Such data have a number of advantages:

1. One can accumulate observations more quickly with weekly panel data than with bimonthly or quarterly sales data, reducing the problem that other factors may change and reduce the comparability of the data.
2. One can observe the actual price paid, rather than an average of the retail prices that different stores charge, and one can identify sales that were made with coupons or promotions that alter the price actually paid.[1] This captures more price variation in the data, making the effects of price changes easier to detect.
3. One can get data on the sales and prices of competing products (provided someone in the panel bought them), as well as on sales of one's own product.
4. One can correlate price sensitivity with various demographic classifications of consumers and possibly identify opportunities for segmentation.[2]

One potential drawback is that panel data may not be adequately representative of the market as a whole. Of all households invited to join a panel, fewer than 5 percent accept the offer and accurately record their purchases. There is reason to suspect, therefore, that panel members are a biased sample of the population. Moreover, the fact that panel members must record their purchases tends to make them more price aware, and thus more price sensitive. This problem increases the longer a household participates in a panel. Fortunately, technological advances have enabled research companies to develop panels that do not require consumers to record most their purchases.[3] Instead, in-store scanners record purchases automatically whenever panel members identify themselves in the store's checkout line. This vastly simplifies panel membership, increasing the panel participation rate to more than 70 percent and attenuating the problem of heightened price awareness. Further, the data tend to be more representative of real purchasing behavior of consumers without the bias that has been problematic in the past.

A second potential drawback to panel data is that typically only one member of the household agrees to participate in the panel, yet in most households multiple people perform shopping duties. As a result, it is easy to miss purchase data from the nonparticipating member(s) of the household who often have very different criteria for making purchase decisions. For example, if the nonparticipating family member joins Costco and purchases cereal by the bushel, the family is essentially out of the cereal market for a while, no matter how substantial a discount is offered to the participating panel member. Given the ever-widening use of scanners and the ability to link scanner data with panel data, increasing numbers of consumer products can be analyzed using this type of analysis. The superiority of panel data estimates over those from aggregate sales data is due to the availability of more observations from a shorter and more comparable time period. With the availability of advertising and other promotional data, researchers are able to estimate price sensitivities for different customer groups with a reasonable degree of reliability (Box 12-1). Since multiple companies share the cost of the same ongoing research, estimates based on panel data are also less expensive than estimates based on an equal number of observations from proprietary research.

STORE SCANNER DATA An alternate source of actual sales comes from auditing price transactions and sales at individual retail stores. Modern technologies have made accurate daily sales and price data available at reasonable cost. Retailers generate such data as part of their normal operations. The high frequency of scanner data makes it vastly superior to aggregate sales data, providing marketers with almost immediate information on the movement of their product. And although scanner data lacks the balanced and complete demographics of consumer panel data, loyalty programs have made it possible to infer demographics and to track purchases over time. Scanner data also costs a lot less than panel data. When store

BOX 12-1

Using Panel Data to Measure the Impact of Promotion on Choice

The authors of a recent study asked two important questions: whether consumers are getting more price sensitive and whether the group of price-sensitive consumers is growing. To evaluate these and other questions, they examined more than eight years of usage data from a panel of consumers and were able to compare those data with quarterly advertising data from producers within a household nonfood product category. They were able to evaluate three different types of price promotions: temporary price reduction, price feature of the product, or the offering of a coupon. For their analysis, they used a multinomial logit model to evaluate the impact of the promotional (price and nonprice) activities on the consumer's choice of a product. Further, they were able to segment users into loyal and non-loyal segments and compare the price sensitivities of the two groups. The summarized results indicated the following:

Consumer's Sensitivities to:	Average Price Sensitivities	Sensitivity Changes Over Time
1. Loyal segment		
Price	$-.28$	Increase
Price promotion	.02	Increase
Nonprice promotion	.03	Decrease*
2. Non-loyal segment		
Price	-1.70	Increase
Price promotion	.04	Increase
Nonprice promotion	.09	Decrease*
Non-loyal segment size		Increase*

*Indicates significant at $p < .05$, all else $p < .001$.

The price sensitivities are shown across all of the periods analyzed. Based on the elasticities, the loyal segment showed little price sensitivity, but it did increase over time. The non-loyal, price-oriented segment showed higher price sensitivities that increased over time as well. The study authors did note that the size of the non-loyal segment increased over time, indicating that "an increasing proportion of consumers have become more price and promotion sensitive over time."

Source: Carl F. Mela, Sunil Gupta, and Donald R. Lehmann, "The Long-Term Impact of Promotion and Advertising on Consumer Brand Choice," *Journal of Marketing Research* (May 1997): 248–261.

scanner data can be combined with panel data that track the demographic and broader behavioral characteristics of consumers, researchers often get huge insights into shoppers' price sensitivity and purchasing behaviors. Scanner data have become a major source of information on the price sensitivity of consumer-packaged goods.[4]

While sales data—in the form of panels and scanner data—are quite prevalent in the consumer packaged goods industry, in many business-to-business markets there are simply too few transactions and market over-sight to develop similar data sets. However, not all is lost. We recently spoke with a firm that created a competitive sales database. Specifically, the firm (a tractor manufacturer) created an internal database in which its sales force would register any competitive bid information. Over time the company built a database of competitive price information, which, combined with the record of its own bid outcome history, allows the firm to estimate the price sensitivity of customers, by segment if necessary, as well as to estimate the incremental value its tractors offered over the competition. For this project, the total investment for this multi-billion-dollar firm was on the order of $50,000.

There is some level of bias in the data that one needs to be aware of—the competitive quotes are being obtained from customers who have an incentive to provide low prices. One thus needs to adjust the distribution to reflect the bias; the level of bias can be estimated if one can confirm actual quotes for a sample of transactions and measure the actual level of bias. One also needs to be careful to "normalize" competitive quotes so that equivalent comparisons are being made. Are after-sale services, special financing terms, or training included, for example?

Further, when the quote history is overlaid with actual sales success data, it is possible to estimate the probability at which a sale is imminently likely, as well as the decline in the probability in a sale as price increases—a form of estimating price sensitivity as well as a way to estimate the amount of "money left on the table" in successful bids.

Finally, as firms update their pricing capabilities, many are discovering new opportunities to study responses to pricing actions. For example, as companies invest in technologies that allow for rapid and frequent price changes, they can look to yield management techniques that allow for the study of demand changes in response to pricing actions. Motel 6 for example, has the ability to post prices electronically on its billboards and can change these prices—at nearly no cost—by the hour. In only a short span of time, this company can study the price responsiveness of its customers by location, by day of week, and indeed even by time of day. As companies add to their ability to set and manage prices, new opportunities will become available to create "natural experiments" to allow for the study of price reactions at relatively low cost.

ANALYZING HISTORICAL DATA Analysis of historical sales data often involves application of linear regression analysis. This statistical technique attempts to show how much of the historical variation in a product's sales can be explained by each of the explanatory variables, including price, that the researcher includes in the analysis. One should not expect, however, that the researcher will necessarily succeed in identifying the effect of price with such an analysis. If there has been little historical variation in a product's price, then no statistical technique applied to its sales data can reveal the effect of price changes. Moreover, if every time price was changed and some other variable—such as advertising—was also changed, the best one can do is discover the joint effect of such a simultaneous change on sales. Fortunately, the use of more sophisticated multivariate techniques such as time series analysis or structural equations modeling can often provide estimates of their cross-impacts on demand.

In any case, one must be careful to recognize the limits of a successful analysis of historical data. To estimate any equation, the researcher must develop a mathematical form for the relationship between price and sales. To the extent that the assumed form incorrectly specifies the relationship, estimates of price sensitivity may be misleading. Moreover, the researcher's estimate of price sensitivity is valid only over the range of price and advertising levels used to estimate it. There is no reason to believe that the same relationship would necessarily apply to price changes outside that range. One also needs to be careful to recognize that it is not enough to consider just a point estimate of price sensitivity; one needs to also look at the size of the corresponding error terms to understand the quality and accuracy of the estimate. Finally, regardless of how well an estimated equation fits past data, its value in predicting the effect of future price changes rests on the assumption that the future is like the past. The more other factors change, the less the past can predict the future. Despite these limitations, if a researcher has a lot of historical data with enough price variation in it, useful estimates of price sensitivity are possible.[5] For multiproduct companies, an understanding of price responsiveness can be used to help optimize demand flow across a product line. Specifically, prices can be adjusted to direct demand to specific products to better manage inventories, obtain better leverage with suppliers, and yet at the same time allow a wide product selection for customers who require specific items.

Exhibit 12-2 shows the results of research that utilized regression analysis to evaluate the importance of various product attributes to two groups of credit card holders: those who are loyal (more than one year of ownership) and those who are new (less than one year). The categorization of customers as new or loyal was based on input from the managers of the credit-card company who found that people who used their card for at least one year tended to stay users for an extended period of time. Of interest is the marginal increase in price sensitivity as measured by sensitivity to interest rates, for non-loyal customers (attribute importance of 0.16 compared to 0.14 for loyal customers) and the very large difference in needs for service. The researchers were also able to run regression equations for different time periods and determine how attribute importance was changing over time.

Experimentally Controlled Studies of Actual Purchases

A researcher might attempt to estimate price sensitivity by generating experimental purchase data. Such data may come from pricing experiments

EXHIBIT 12-2 Use of Regression Analysis

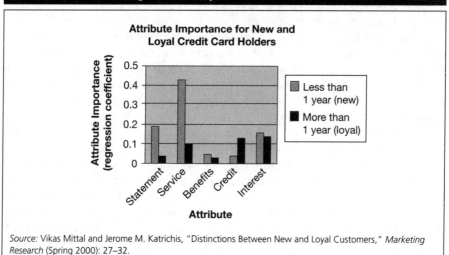

Source: Vikas Mittal and Jerome M. Katrichis, "Distinctions Between New and Loyal Customers," *Marketing Research* (Spring 2000): 27–32.

conducted in a store without the buyers' knowledge or from pricing experiments conducted in a laboratory. Since the researcher controls the experiment, price variations can be created as desired to generate results while holding constant other marketing variables, such as advertising levels and in-store displays, which often change with price variations in uncontrolled sales data. The researcher can examine the effect of a number of different prices quickly and either (1) exclude many unwanted external effects in the laboratory experiment or (2) establish a control for the in-store experiment that will take account of them. Moreover, all this can be done while still providing buyers with purchase decisions that are comparable to those they make under normal conditions. As a result, to the degree that the experimental setting reflects the actual purchase environment, experimental research provides fairly reliable estimates of price sensitivity.

IN-STORE PURCHASE EXPERIMENTS   An in-store purchase experiment relies on actual purchase data collected when buyers are unaware that they are participating in an experiment. Although the term "in-store" reflects the fact that most such experiments are conducted in stores, the principles of in-store experimentation are equally applicable to any natural purchase environment. Such experiments are often easier to conduct for products sold through more controlled direct-retail methods, such as mail-order catalogs, than for those sold in traditional retail stores. For example, the researcher can select a subset of the mailing list to receive catalogs with experimental prices that differ from those in the regular catalog. Even in direct sales to business, one can sometimes select a representative sample of customers from one sales area, offer them an experimental price, and monitor the difference between sales to those buyers and to those in other regions where sales are made at the regular price.

The simplest design for an in-store pricing experiment involves monitoring sales at the historical price to obtain a base level of sales and then initiating a price change to see how sales change from that base level. In practice, this is a very common experimental design that can yield useful information; however, it fails to exploit one of the major advantages of experimentation: the ability to control for external factors. Without such control, the researcher is forced to make the tenuous assumption that any sales change from the base level resulted from the price change alone, not from changes in other factors. Fortunately, the addition of an experimental control store (or mail sample or sales territory) can reduce this problem substantially. To establish such a control, the researcher finds a second store in which sales tend to vary over the base period in the same way that they vary in the first store, indicating that factors other than price influence both stores' sales in the same way. The researcher then changes price only in the first store, but continues to monitor sales in both stores. Any change in sales in the control store indicates to the researcher that some factor other than price is also causing a change in sales. To adjust the results, the researcher subtracts from the sales in the experimental store an amount equal to the change in sales in the control store before determining the effect of the price change alone.[6]

One of the greatest benefits of in-store experimentation is the ability to test for interactions between price and other marketing variables that, in historical data, tend to change together. Unfortunately, the cost of such experimentation is very high because each additional factor studied requires the inclusion of more stores. The experimental design with the greatest amount of information, called a full factorial design, would require enough stores to match every level tested for each marketing variable with every level of the other variables. Usually, the researcher is forced to use a less-than-perfect experiment, called a fractional factorial design, that sacrifices some precision (generally by assuming away interaction effects) in order to reduce the number of stores required.[7]

Although many articles illustrate the successful application of in-store experimentation to estimate price sensitivity, the greatest impediment to using in-store experiments is the high cost of monitoring sales, analyzing the data, and securing the cooperation of retailers.[8] Although in theory this is an inexpensive experiment because as few as two stores for one week could constitute a test, accurate tests require many stores and last for months. A large number of stores are necessary to reduce the problem of an external factor influencing just one store and to obtain a representative sample of consumers whose behavior can reasonably be generalized to the market as a whole. It is often necessary to set a long time period for an in-store test in order to get past the short-run inventory effect on price sensitivity that initially masks the long-term effect. Consequently, a good in-store experiment is very expensive. When, for example, Quaker Oats conducted an in-store experiment that focused on the effect of price alone, the study required 120 stores and ran for three months. Such a study can easily cost several million dollars.[9]

In addition to the financial and time cost of in-store experiments, there are other drawbacks. There is the potential loss of consumer goodwill when some buyers are charged higher prices than others. On the other hand, charging prices below normal can become too costly when the product is a large-expenditure durable good such as a car or a piece of industrial equipment. An in-store test also involves the very real risk of being discovered by a competitor. If the product is new, a company may not wish to give its competitors an advance look. Moreover, when competitors find out about a test market, they often take steps, such as special promotions or advertising in selected areas, to contaminate the results.[10] Thus, although in-store experiments have the potential for yielding very high-quality estimates, market researchers are more often forced to use alternatives. The closest of those alternatives is a laboratory purchase experiment.

LABORATORY PURCHASE EXPERIMENTS Laboratory purchase experiments attempt to duplicate the realism of in-store experimentation without the high cost or the possible exposure to competitors. A typical laboratory experiment takes place in a research facility at a shopping mall. Interviewers intercept potential participants who are walking by and screen them to select only those who are users of the product category being researched. Based on information from a short pretest questionnaire, the researchers can control the proportion of participants in each demographic classification (for example, gender, age, race, income, or family size) to ensure that the experimental population is representative of the actual population of buyers, a technique known as proportionate sampling. If members of some demographic categories cannot be found in adequate numbers in the mall, telephone interviews may be used to contact such people and offer them an incentive to come and participate in the experiment.

The laboratory researcher can control who participates and can quickly manipulate prices and other elements in the purchase environment (such as shelf location and point-of-purchase displays), all at a single location. Moreover, the researcher can almost entirely eliminate external factors such as changes in competitors' prices, stock-outs of competing products, or differences among stores that may contaminate the results of an in-store test. Participants exposed to different prices see exactly the same display at the same location in the laboratory experiment. Even effects associated with the time of day can be controlled by constantly changing prices for each new participant in the experiment. Thus, if testing three different price levels, approximately one third of the consumers who take the test at any hour can be exposed to each price level. This ability to control the experiment so closely enables the researcher to draw inferences from far fewer purchases in much less time than would be possible with an in-store experiment.

Laboratory research facilities vary greatly depending on the sophistication of the research organization and the budget of the client company. The simplest facilities may consist of an interviewing room with a display of products from a single product category. The price for each brand is clearly marked, and the participant is invited to make a purchase. In theory, since the consumer is actually making a purchase, or can choose not to buy at all, the purchase decision in a simple laboratory experiment is the same one that the consumer would make shopping in an actual retail store. In practice, however, that conclusion may not be true. The problem lies in the artificiality of a simple laboratory environment. First, a single display in a laboratory encourages the consumer to give the purchase decision much more attention than would be typical in an actual shopping situation. Research indicates that most grocery shoppers do not even look at most prices when actually shopping in a supermarket. In a laboratory, however, consumers do not want to appear careless. They are, therefore, much more likely to note and respond to price differences. Second, when consumers know they are being watched from behind one-way mirrors, they may act as they think they should rather than as they would in real life. Thus some consumers may buy the low-priced brand just to appear to be smart shoppers, or the high-priced brand so as not to appear stingy. They may also buy something from the category out of a feeling of obligation to the researcher who gave them the money, even though they would not buy from that category in a store.

To overcome these limitations, a few research companies offer highly sophisticated laboratory research facilities. The most elaborate facilities attempt to duplicate as closely as possible the actual conditions under which consumers buy the product. These facilities contain complete simulated stores the size of small convenience stores. Before entering the simulated store, consumers may view reruns of television programs within which are embedded television commercials for the research product, or they may read magazines within which are print advertisements for the product. When consumers finally enter the store, they are invited to do all their shopping, purchasing whatever they want, just as they would on a regular shopping trip.

The cost of even the most sophisticated laboratory experiment is only a small fraction of the cost of in-store testing. As a result, the leading marketers of consumer packaged goods and small appliances rely extensively on this research technique when making pricing decisions.[11] In the past decade, the number and frequency of laboratory purchase experiments for products sold via Internet web sites has boomed. The cost to design a realistic purchase environment, to control the promotional message, and to recruit respondents on the Internet is so low that it is possible to test more frequently, to get answers faster, and to employ much larger samples than marketers would usually have considered. Companies that design this type of research can solicit participants via pop-up ads on targeted websites. To reach buyers in very "thin" markets, such as purchasers of industrial equipment or adventure vacations, marketers can buy e-mail lists to solicit participants. Consequently, a realistic Internet purchase experiment can take as little as a week and cost one-tenth what similar research would cost in another purchase environment. Box 12-2 describes a laboratory experiment for a company considering entry into an existing Internet marketplace.

BOX 12-2

Measuring Price Sensitivity for e-Books

An online retailer wanted to test its ability to price some popular electronic book titles above the established level of $9.99 or less per download. The reason is that publishers were resisting e-book publishing for their latest and best publicized titles, fearing that e-books would cannibalize more profitable sales of newly released hardbacks. The retailer hoped to understand whether its customers would accept a segmented pricing model with higher prices for new, best-seller titles—particularly since bookstores generally price hard copies of newly released titles as loss leaders to draw store traffic. Such a model might use a lower e-book price for older tiles that had migrated to paperback while continuing to price e-book titles that are still in hard back at higher prices.

The company engaged Grail Research to design an online laboratory experiment, recruit 2,000 respondents, and analyze the results. To protect its reputation, the online laboratory store was given a name not associated with the retailer. The goal of the experiment was to understand the extent to which higher prices would affect consumers' e-book purchase behavior. The market research company spent one and a half weeks designing the experiment with the retailer and recruiting respondents from e-mail lists of electronic book purchasers. Respondents participating in the experiment were first asked their genre preferences, following which they were presented with several e-book options in each of their preferred genres. The e-books varied in price and time since publication. Some e-books were given prices above the standard $9.99 and some were priced at or below $9.99. The experiment was designed to replicate the actual experience a consumer would have purchasing a book online. Respondents were asked to add e-books to their shopping basket as if they were actually shopping on a website and they could monitor how much they had in their shopping cart. At the end of the experiment, respondents were presented with their total order and cost and given the opportunity to remove items from their shopping basket before confirming their order.

Only one and a half weeks after the launch online, more than 2,000 respondents had completed the experiment through confirming a purchase. After another week, the research company had completed its analysis of price sensitivity by demographic, type of book, and various other segmentations. The chart below shows the answer to the retailer's main research question. The online experiment demonstrated that e-book demand is relatively price inelastic for prices below $9.99 but very elastic for prices above $9.99 for titles generally available anywhere. However, respondents did show a willingness to purchase new titles, not generally available in paperback or in e-book format, at prices above $9.99. The experiment proved very insightful for the online book retailer. They learned that there was some upward flexibility in their prices for newer books, but a downward adjustment for older books would

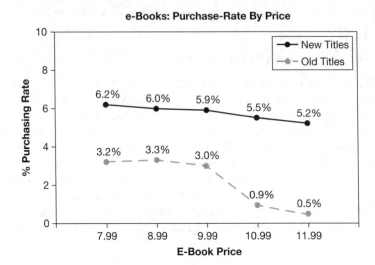

not generate sufficient additional purchases to justify the drop in price. As a result of the experiment, the retailer decided to launch a segmented pricing model, offering publishers the chance to earn higher profits on e-book sales if they authorized them along with the hardback edition.

Source: Grail Research. Although this description is based on an actual study, some details have been changed to maintain client confidentiality.

Uncontrolled Studies of Preferences and Intentions

The most common research technique for directly estimating price sensitivity is the survey of brand preferences or purchase intentions. Companies prefer to measure preferences or intentions, rather than actual purchases, for a number of reasons:

1. Survey data costs much less to collect than purchase data.
2. Survey data can be measured for large durable goods, such as automobiles or photocopiers, for which in-store or laboratory experiments at various prices are impractical.
3. Survey data can be collected even before a product is designed, when the information is most valuable in directing product development.
4. The results can be collected quickly.

Unfortunately, the problem with survey research is that many consumers do not provide answers that are a reliable guide to their actual purchase behavior. The reasons are varied, but one of the main issues is that surveys require a level of abstraction that the respondent may or may not be able to perform. This is especially true of new products that are wholly unfamiliar or whose application is not readily apparent. As a result, determination of value delivered, or willingness-to-pay, is difficult to arrive at even for a committed respondent. In order to solve this problem, some research companies cross-validate the results of one survey with the results of another, often using slightly different methods of data collection and questioning. For example, a firm might collect data using personal interviews and validate the results by telephoning a different group of respondents and asking the same set of questions. The closer the results are from the two samples and methods, the more valid and accurate the final results.

DIRECT QUESTIONING   Very early in the development of survey techniques for marketing, researchers learned that it was futile to ask consumers outright, "What is the most you would be willing to pay for this product?" Direct questioning sometimes elicits bargaining behavior, with consumers stating a lower price than they would actually pay. Other times, it elicits a desire to please the researcher or to not appear stingy, prompting consumers to state a higher price than they would actually pay. Frequently, it simply elicits a cursory answer that consumers would change were they to give the question the same thought as an actual purchase decision. Consequently, uncontrolled direct questioning as a research technique to estimate price sensitivity should never be accepted as a valid methodology. The results of such studies are at best useless and are potentially highly misleading.

BUY-RESPONSE SURVEYS   A slight variant of the direct-question survey involves showing consumers a product at a preselected price and asking if they would purchase at that price. Surprisingly, although directly asking consumers what they would pay usually yields meaningless answers, asking them if they would buy at a preselected price yields answers that are at least plausible. When the answers given by different consumers for different price levels are aggregated, they produce what looks like a demand curve for market share, sometimes called a purchase probability curve (Box 12-3). Presumably, questioning willingness-to-buy generates better responses simply because it is structured more like an actual purchase decision than as an open-ended question about what the consumer would pay. Also, the consumer has no opportunity to bargain with the researcher.[12] Interestingly, there are a number of studies that have documented cultural differences that lead to large amounts of substantial and systematic variation in the accuracy of buy-response surveys across countries such as the United States, Germany, and Japan, among others.

ATTRIBUTE RATING   Another method for evaluating price sensitivity is to include price as one of the attributes describing a product or a purchase situation. Consumers rate the importance of each attribute using a variety of scaling techniques. Those scales can be a one to five or a one to 10 importance rating or simply an evaluation of the percent of respondents mentioning the attribute as being important.[13] This approach is problematic because responses tend to be offhand and overly positive, due to halo effects, where respondents tend to not carefully discriminate among listed attributes and give similar ratings or responses to many attributes, especially those adjacent to each other.

BOX 12-3

Purchase Probability Curves: A Simple Buy-Response Study— Opportunity for a Higher Price

A software firm developed a product for law firms that would easily produce high-quality legal documents and would manage document storage and billing of time for both small and large offices. The original estimates of price were $500 per unit. Chadwick Martin Bailey, Inc. conducted a national study to measure price sensitivity for the product. It began the process by conducting extensive exploratory research, including focus groups and semistructured interviews. This phase of the research initially indicated that prices in the range of $6,000 might be perfectly acceptable to a large segment of attorneys. A random sample of 603 attorneys was contacted by telephone and asked the likelihood of purchase at $2,000, $4,000, $6,000, or $8,000, yielding about 150 responses per price point. Probability of purchase was measured using a 0–10 likelihood of purchase scale, and all responses in the 8–10 range were used as a basis for assessing price sensitivity. At $2,000, 49 percent of the firms would have bought the package. Demand was found to be very inelastic for higher prices, as shown in Figure A. Movement from $4,000 to $8,000 in price made little difference in the proportion of law firms willing to buy the product, but it produced large differences in revenue from sales, as shown in Figure B.

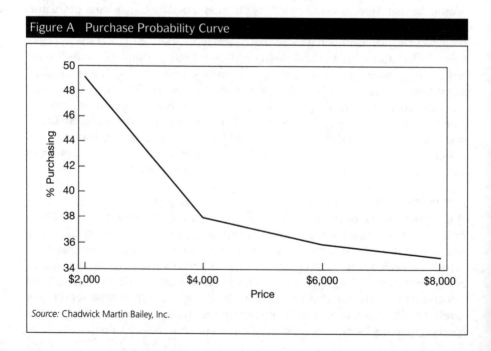

Figure A Purchase Probability Curve

Source: Chadwick Martin Bailey, Inc.

Figure B   Total Revenue Estimates

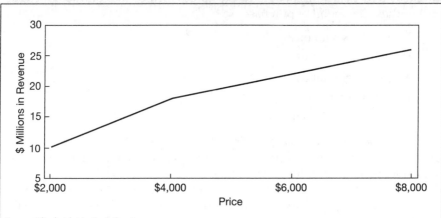

Source: Chadwick Martin Bailey, Inc.

This study was provided by Chadwick Martin Bailey, Inc., a planning and market research firm located in Boston, Massachusetts.

One cannot, however, treat buy-response data as directly comparable to or directly predictive of the sales that would actually occur at the corresponding prices in a store. Most problematic is the fact that consumers' answers depend on their recollection of the actual prices of competing products. To the extent that they overestimate or underestimate competing prices, they will misjudge their willingness-to-buy. Even with this form of the question, some consumers will still want to please the researcher, or will fear appearing stingy, and so will falsely claim a willingness to buy the brand over competing brands regardless of the price.

Nevertheless, such research is useful (1) as a preliminary study to identify a range of acceptable prices for a new product and (2) to identify changes in price sensitivity at different points in time or place, assuming that the biases that affect these studies remain the same and so do not affect the observed change. For example, buy-response surveys for low-involvement consumer packaged goods often reveal little difference in consumers' willingness-to-buy at different prices before they try a new product, but a significant difference at different price points after they have tried it. In interpreting the study, one would not want to take the absolute percentage of consumers who claimed they would buy as an accurate prediction of the percentage of consumers who would actually buy at different prices. However, differences in the stated probability of purchase before and after trial may reliably predict the change in price sensitivity caused by the product trial.

Intention measurement is also sometimes used successfully to predict actual purchases when researchers have past experience that allows them to adjust for the bias in subjects' stated intentions. Typically, purchase intentions are measured by asking people to indicate which of the following best describes their likelihood of purchase:

Definitely would buy

Probably would buy

Might/might not buy

Probably would not buy

Definitely would not buy

The leading survey research firms have asked such questions of millions of buyers for thousands of products. Consequently, they are able to develop adjustments that reflect the average bias in these answers for various product classes. Thus, an experienced researcher might expect that only 80 percent of people answering "definitely would buy," 50 percent answering "probably would buy," 25 percent answering "might/might not buy," and 10 percent answering "probably would not buy" will actually purchase.

IN-DEPTH INTERVIEWS   An in-depth interview is a "semistructured" method that is used to elicit responses from customers on how they use products and services, from which the research infers value rather than asking about value directly. The interview is often conducted one-on-one with a respondent and lasts for one to two hours. In a consumer environment, it is used to understand how individuals and families use products and how they might value different features or positioning approaches. In a business-to-business environment, the interviewers attempt to understand how businesses gain revenues or reduce costs by using a specific product or service; to do this successfully, one needs to have a deep understanding of the respondent's business. In-depth interviews in pricing research are useful in (1) understanding which product or service features and benefits are important to a customer, (2) assessing the monetary or psychological value of these features and benefits that a customer receives as a result of using the product or service, and (3) assessing roughly what a customer might be willing to pay to obtain these features and benefits. In-depth interviews are also used to develop economic-value models of how much a customer could gain in monetary terms from purchase of the product. The model then becomes part of a promotional campaign to increase customers' willingness-to-pay. Such models work well for business customers, where most benefits can be translated into additional revenues or costs saved. It also works well in consumer markets where the benefit is a cost saving (for example, the value of buying a more efficient refrigerator).

Like a focus group, an in-depth interview is relatively unstructured and is usually conducted by an experienced interviewer who has a specific interview guide and objective, such as to quantify the value of differentiating features. In-depth interviews are used less frequently in market research due to the need for highly specialized interviewers, the expense per interview, and the small sample size.[14] This is especially true for consumer pricing research for mass-market products and services. However, for more complex business-to-business pricing research, the interviews—in terms of the quality of information obtained with regard to customer value and willingness-to-pay—often yield much more fruitful insights and analysis. For example, in business markets, in-depth interviews enable the interviewer to probe customer needs, customer experiences, how they attempt to deal with problems, how the supplier's products or services could solve these problems, and the value to the customer of the consequent savings or gains they would realize from using the firm's products or services.

In-depth interviews do not ask customers directly how much they would be willing to pay. Instead, the interview focuses on the financial benefits to the customer that a product or service could influence. It is also possible to get a sense of perceived value by identifying other items that the customer buys to achieve the same benefit. For example, *evoked anchoring,* one method used successfully in business-to-business markets, asks respondents to identify items in their budget that they might consider a trade-off in order to obtain the value and benefits promised by a supplier's proposed product or service solution. For example, when helping a software client to price relationship–management software, we identified that one benefit was reduced customer turnover. By asking potential buyers of the software to identify the costs to acquire new customers, we could infer the value to retain them.

In-depth interviews enable marketers to understand not only what someone might perceive their product or service to be worth, but also why it is worth that much. The in-depth interview attempts to understand the needs that the product addresses and how the product or service addresses them. The process often uncovers ways that suppliers can enhance their current product or service offerings and, in doing so, provide the basis for creating more differentiated products that can be sold at higher prices. It also exposes who in the buying organization has goals that are likely to benefit from purchase of the product.[15]

The interview must be conducted outside the context of a selling opportunity or a negotiation, since customers are unlikely to reveal value at such times. However, the data garnered often form the basis of a value-based selling approach in which salespeople, armed with an understanding of how their products differ from those of competitors and how those differences create value for customers, can justify their pricing to the customer and to themselves. Companies often can use the information gained from in-depth interviews to develop "value case histories." These case histories describe the experience of a particular customer in using a firm's products and the specific value that the customer received. These case histories eventually become a sales support tool.[16]

The in-depth interview is an excellent method for developing a better understanding of how different product and service features create value for customers, especially customers in a business-to-business environment. It is especially useful in moving beyond the core product and understanding how different service and support elements can create incremental value for a user and provide insights into how a product might be priced to capture that value. It often identifies similar service and support characteristics that can successfully differentiate what are often thought of as commodity products.[17] A common concern is that customers won't provide the data. However, our experience is that most customers are quite willing to share insights and data that will help suppliers serve them better.

Experimentally Controlled Studies of Preferences and Intentions

To solve some of the problems of bias and extraneous factors when measuring preferences and intentions, researchers try to exercise some control over the purchase situation presented to respondents.

The questions must be designed to make the survey respondents consider the questions in the same way they would consider an actual purchase decision. The extent to which that can ever be fully accomplished is still an open question, but marketing researchers, recognizing the potential value of accurate survey information, are certainly trying.

SIMULATED PURCHASE EXPERIMENTS Many researchers believe that the best way to get consumers to think about a survey question and to respond as they would in a purchase situation is to simulate the purchase environment as closely as possible when asking the survey questions. With this type of research, the researcher asks the consumers to imagine that they are on a shopping trip and desire to make a purchase from a particular product class. Then the researcher shows the consumers pictorial representations, descriptions, or sometimes actual samples of brands along with prices and asks the consumers to choose among them, given various prices. Since actual products need not be used, this technique enables one to test pricing for new product concepts, as part of a general concept test, before the concepts are actually developed into products.

The primary difference between such a simulated purchase experiment and a laboratory purchase experiment is that participants only simulate the choice decision to purchase a product and so do not get to keep their choices.[18] The simulated purchase experiment is a widely used tool in pricing research that overcomes two important drawbacks of other types of surveys. If it is structured as a choice task among alternative brands, a consumer's thought process should more closely approximate the process actually used when making a purchase. Also, since consumers have no way of knowing which brand is the one of interest to the researcher, they cannot easily think of the choice as a bargaining position or as a way to please the researcher. Thus, simulated purchase experiments can sometimes predict price sensitivity reasonably well.[19]

While any type of research is prone to bias, the simulated purchase experiments can often be an acceptable method for gaining quick and low-cost information on the buying behavior of consumers. If, for example, a company wants to estimate the price sensitivity of a product sold nationally, the cost of hundreds of in-store experiments throughout the country would be prohibitive. If the company conducted both an in-store experiment and a simulated purchase experiment in a few locations and found them reasonably consistent, it could confidently use the latter to cover the remaining locations and to conduct future research on that product class. Even if the experiment showed a consistent tendency to be biased, simulated purchase experiments could still be used successfully after the results had been adjusted by the amount of that previously identified bias.

TRADE-OFF (CONJOINT) ANALYSIS   An experimental technique, called trade-off (or conjoint) analysis, has become popular for measuring price sensitivity as well as sensitivity to other product attributes.[20] The particular strength of trade-off analysis is its ability to disaggregate a product's price into the values consumers attach to each attribute. Consequently, trade-off analysis can help a company identify the differentiation value of unique product attributes and, more important, design new products that include only those attributes that consumers are willing to pay for as well as how much they are likely to pay for the entire product and service package. Currently, trade-off analysis aids in the design of a range of products, from automobiles and office equipment to household cleaners and vacation packages.

The basic data for trade-off analysis are consumers' answers to questions that reveal not their directly stated purchase intentions, but rather the preferences that underlie those intentions. The researcher collects such data by asking respondents to make choices between pairs of fully described products or between different levels of just two product attributes. The product descriptions are designed to vary systematically in the levels of certain attributes that define the product as well as the price. When multiple levels of price are included in the study design, it is possible to assess not only the value assigned to certain product attributes but also to arrive at an estimate of price elasticity. The data are collected with a questionnaire or online.

After obtaining a consumer's preferences for a number of product or attribute pairs, the researcher then manipulates the data to impute the value (called utility) that each consumer attaches to each product attribute and the relative importance that each attribute plays in the consumer's purchase decision.[21] With these data, the researcher can predict at what prices the consumer would purchase products containing various combinations of attributes, including combinations that do not currently exist in the marketplace. The researcher can also estimate how much of one attribute the consumer is willing to trade off in order to obtain more of another attribute—for example, how much more price a consumer is willing to trade off in order to obtain more fuel efficiency in a new automobile.

With similar data from a number of consumers who are representative of a market, the researcher can develop a model to predict the share of a market segment that would prefer any particular brand to others at any particular price. Since the researcher has collected data that reveal underlying preferences, consumers' preferences can be predicted, or interpolated, even for levels of price and other attributes not specifically asked about in the questionnaire, provided the attributes are continuously measurable and bounded by the levels that were asked about in the survey. When the researcher knows independently the size of the market and market segments, it is possible to create a simulation model for testing different price-offer combinations. Box 12-4 provides an example of such a process. Readers should note how the basic features were varied along with price in order to develop a relationship between features and value, here termed "feature utility."

It is useful to contrast trade-off analysis with direct questioning methods. By having respondents evaluate a product in its entirety rather than in the more abstract form of individual attributes, responses are more likely to mimic actual choices. For example, in a study of recent MBA graduates, when asked about individual job attributes, the most important was the people and culture of the company. Salaries were rated low on the list of attributes under consideration. However, when the same students we asked to choose the job they would prefer among various job descriptions, analysis revealed that salary was the most important job attribute, followed by the region and location of job; people and workplace culture ranked only fourth.

Of all methods used to estimate price sensitivity from preferences or intentions, trade-off analysis promises the most useful information for strategy formulation. The researchers can do more than simply identify the price sensitivity of the market as a whole; they can identify customer segments with different price sensitivities and, to the extent that those differences result from differences in the economic value of product attributes, can also identify the specific product attributes that evoke the differences. Consequently, researchers can describe the combination of attributes that can most profitably skim or penetrate a market. The economic value of a product can also be identified even when the product is not yet developed by presenting consumers with different experimental product combinations in the form of pictorial and descriptive product concepts, or new product prototypes.

As a result of these promised advantages, the use of trade-off analysis by both market research firms and internal research departments has grown rapidly, but the performance of trade-off analysis is only as good as its ability to predict actual purchase behavior. There are, however, a number of reasons why a prudent manager might suspect the reliability of this technique for some markets. Trade-off analysis is an experimental procedure that introduces bias to the extent that it does not simulate the actual purchase environment. The respondent taking a conjoint test is encouraged to focus much more attention on price and price differences than may occur in a natural purchase environment. Thus, while trade-off analysis is still useful for studying non-price trade-offs, it should not be trusted to predict choice for "low involvement" products for which there is little evidence that the purchasers carefully compare price and other attributes across brands when making a decision. It also is of little value where purchasers have much more difficulty obtaining and comparing price and product attributes in a real purchase situation. For

BOX 12-4
A Conjoint Study: Power Powder Ski

Conjoint Example: Power Powder Ski

A small sporting goods manufacturer designed a downhill ski that incorporated electronic vibration control, promising downhill skiers easier turning, reduced "chatter" on rough surfaces, and a general reduction in the physical effort of skiing. To commercialize the most financially lucrative offer, the company commissioned a market research study to address several questions that would inform the marketing strategy. Three of the research questions involved pricing:

(i) What is the demand for the product, including the price-volume trade-off?
(ii) For what segment(s) of skiers could the offer be targeted most profitably?
(iii) Given the innovative technology, would it be financially worthwhile to offer a longer warranty than the standard 90 days?

To address these questions, a market survey was developed that collected information on skier demographics, ability levels, and willingness-to-pay for different types of benefits. The survey was administered to 1,200 skiers across North America. The survey revealed four major segments:

- **Budget shoppers** are generally beginner and intermediate skiers who make purchases only when old equipment is worn out or outgrown.
- **Value-seekers**, who range in ability from intermediate to expert, consider new purchases frequently, but they make careful price-value trade-offs before actually spending any money.
- **Innovators** are intermediate to expert skiers who readily buy new technology.
- **Elite skiers**, who actively participate in ski clubs and race competitively, test new equipment to find out what works best for them before purchasing it.

In addition to questions about personal demographics and past purchases, the survey included a conjoint-based simulated purchase exercise that asked respondents to evaluate several scenarios for their next potential ski purchase and indicate their most likely choice. Respondents were informed about the benefits of the new technology and then presented with several buying scenarios that included buying new skis with the electronic damping technology, buying well-known conventional skis, or keeping the skis they have and making no new purchase.

The early analysis of the survey generated disappointing findings: Overall the market was quite sensitive to price. Revenues were maximized at the $450 price point, but the Power Powder Ski captured a disappointingly small share with a rapid drop-off at still higher prices. Complicating matters, the company would incur a high variable cost due to cost of the additional technology and the royalty arrangement with the patent holder. Even at a profit-maximizing price for the overall market, the potential return was not worth the risk. Fortunately, one of the benefits of conjoint data is the ability to slice samples in various different ways. Analysis of just the "innovators" revealed that they did indeed have a higher "take rate" for the product and, importantly, the rate fell off much less rapidly at higher prices. Although only a small subset of the market, innovators could profitably support a price of $800. Furthermore, it turns out that it is much cheaper to sell to innovators because they actively seek out new products—as a result, advertising costs are significantly lower, and the manufacturer would not require an extensive distribution network. Apparently the higher take rate among the innovators reflected a demographic subset: 35- to 50-year-old men who had, in their youth, been very good skiers but were now feeling the effects of age in their knees. The promise of lower effort, reduced chatter, and easier turning were benefits for which this group was willing and able to pay a significant premium. This finding opened the possibility that there was also an opportunity to sequentially "skim" the market with a high initial price at launch.

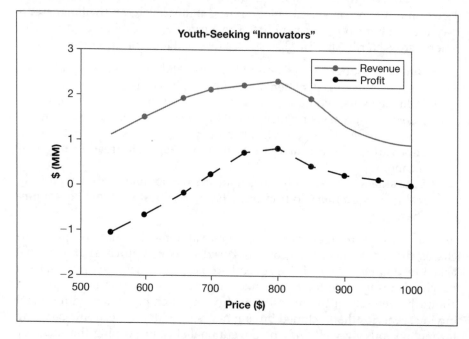

Finally, conjoint analysis enabled the company to isolate and measure the impact of individual features on willingness-to-pay and overall purchase rates. The research revealed that moving form a 90-day to a one-year warranty more than doubled the take rate of the product by respondents in the target segment.

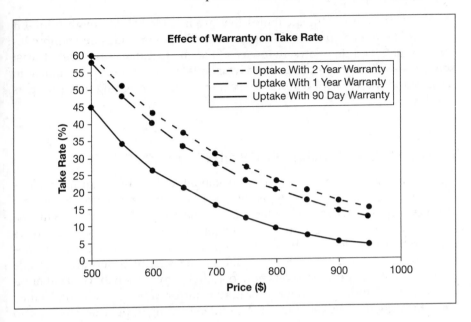

Effect of Warranty on Take Rate

Source: Georg Muller, Monitor Company Group study. The product category and price levels have been changed to protect client confidentiality. Otherwise, the data outputs shown above are actual outputs from the research.

example, research companies have compared the predicted effects of price on physicians prescribing decisions with data on the actual price of the pharmaceuticals they prescribed. Conjoint tests invariably predict much higher price sensitivity among physicians than, in fact, is revealed by prescribing behavior. Also, if respondents have little experience with the product category, as is usually the case with innovative product categories, the technique poorly predicts the trade-offs that customers will make because of their inability to map differences in features into likely benefits.

Because trade-off analysis measures underlying preferences, researchers do have the ability to check if an individual consumer's responses are at least consistent. Consumers who are not taking the survey seriously, or who are basically irrational in their choice processes, are then easily identified and excluded from the sample. Even more comforting are three separate studies that show a high degree of consistency, or reliability, when subjects are asked to repeat a trade-off questionnaire a few days after having taken it initially.[22] Since the subjects are unlikely to remember exactly how they answered the questions in the earlier session, the consistency of the answers over time strongly suggests that they do accurately reflect true underlying preferences. More comforting still is the result of a study showing that the exclusion from the questionnaire of some product attributes a subject might consider important does not bias the subject's responses concerning the trade-offs among the attributes that are included.[23] Although trade-off analysis is more costly than a simple survey, it also provides much more information. Given its relatively low cost and the fact that it has met at least some tests of reliability, it certainly warrants consideration particularly to understand the value of features by segment when designing new products and offers.

USING MEASUREMENT TECHNIQUES APPROPRIATELY

Numerical estimates of price sensitivity can either benefit or harm the effectiveness of a pricing strategy, depending on how management uses them. This is especially true when respondents have considerable experience with the use and purchase of a product. If managers better understand their buyers and use that knowledge to formulate judgments about buyers' price sensitivity, as discussed in Chapter 6, an attempt to measure price sensitivity can be very useful. It can give managers new, objective information that can either increase their confidence in their prior judgments or indicate that perhaps they need to study their buyers further. An understanding of price sensitivity also provides a reference by which to judge proposed price changes—how will sales respond as we increase or decrease prices? Combined with variable cost data, it is possible to judge whether proposed changes in price will have a positive effect on profits.

Integrating soft managerial judgments about buyers and purchase behavior with numerical estimates based on hard data is fundamental to successful pricing. Managerial judgments of price sensitivity are necessarily imprecise while empirical estimates are precise numbers that management can use for profit projections and planning. However, precision doesn't necessarily mean accuracy. Numerical estimates of price sensitivity may be far off the mark of true price sensitivity. Accuracy is a virtue in formulating pricing strategy; precision is only a convenience.

No estimation technique can capture the full richness of the factors that enter a purchase decision. In fact, measurements of price sensitivity are precise specifically because they exclude all the factors that are not conveniently measurable. Some estimation techniques enable the researcher to calculate a confidence interval around a precise estimate, indicating a range within which we may have some degree of statistical certainty that the true estimate of price sensitivity lies. That range is frequently wider than the interval that a well-informed manager could specify with equal confidence simply from managerial judgment. Unfortunately, researchers often do not (or cannot) articulate such a range to indicate just how tenuous their estimates are. When they do, managers often ignore it. Consequently, managers deceive themselves into thinking that an estimate of price sensitivity based on hard data is accurate when in fact it is only a point estimate of something we can never predict with 100 percent accuracy. Fortunately, a manager does not have to make the choice between judgment and empirical estimation.

Used effectively, they are complementary, with the information from each improving the information that the other provides.

Using Judgment for Better Measurement

Any study of price sensitivity should begin with the collection of information about buyers—who they are, why they buy, and how they make their purchase decisions—since those are the essential inputs in the formulation of judgment. At the outset, this information should come from open-ended, qualitative, or exploratory research that enables managers to discover facts and formulate impressions other than those for which they may have been specifically looking.[24] In industrial markets, such research may consist of accompanying salespeople to observe the purchase process. After a sale, managers might follow up to ask how and why the purchase decision was made. One can also look at past bid histories to see the correlation between various price levels and the likelihood of winning the bid. In many cases, managers can interview important customers and intermediaries by telephone to gain their impressions about a variety of price and marketing issues.[25] In consumer markets, such research may consist of observing consumers discussing their purchase decisions in focus groups or in-depth interviews as previously discussed. Insights generated from such informal observation could then be confirmed with more formal research in the form of a survey administered to a larger number of buyers.

Having formed judgments about buyers based on qualitative impressions developed from observing them, a manager will often find it practical and cost-effective to expand this understanding through original primary research that attempts to measure certain aspects of buyer behavior, such as price sensitivity. That attempt is far more likely to produce useful results, to the extent that management already understands the way buyers make their purchase decisions and uses that information to help structure the attempt at measurement. There are a number of ways that managerial judgment can, and should, guide the measurement effort.

1. For experimentally controlled data estimation, managerial judgment should determine the focus of the research on certain target demographic groups and provide guidance for generalizing from those groups to the population as a whole.
   - Management may know that 80 percent of its product's buyers are women who are employed full-time. That information is important if the researcher plans to measure price sensitivity with an in-home survey or an experiment in a shopping center. On a typical day between 9:00 a.m. and 5:00 p.m., few of the experimental subjects at home or in the shopping center would be representative of that product's buyers. To get a representative sample, the researcher might need to conduct the in-home survey in the evenings or the experiment only during the lunch hour at locations near where many women work. He or she might also ask a prescreening question (Are you employed full-time?).

- If management also knows that different demographic groups buy the product in different quantities, that information can be used to scale the survey results differently for different subjects in the sample to reflect their relative impact on the product's actual sales.

2. For historical data estimations, the intervention of informed managerial judgment into the analysis is even more essential, since the lack of any experimental control invariably results in data that are full of potential statistical problems. Managerial judgment should be used to reduce random error and solve statistical problems.

   - The effect of price changes tends to get overwhelmed in historical purchase data by the amount of sales variation caused by other factors, which may not be obvious to the researcher but may be to managers who know their buyers. For example, a researcher analyzing many years' worth of data on the sales of a frozen seafood product could substantially improve the estimation of price sensitivity if management pointed out that many buyers purchase the product as part of their religious observance of Lent, a Christian holiday that shows up at a different time every year. That one bit of information about why consumers buy would enable the researcher to eliminate a substantial amount of random variation in the data that would otherwise yield a biased estimate of price sensitivity if it were not included.

   - The researcher using historical data is also often confounded by the problem called colinearity, where different explanatory variables change together. Perhaps, at the same time that a firm offers a promotional price deal, it always offers retailers a trade deal in return for a special product display. Without additional input from management, the researcher cannot sort out the effect of the price deal from that of the display. If, however, management knows that buyers of the product are like those of another product that is sometimes sold on special displays without a price deal, the researcher could use sales data from that other product to solve the colinearity problem with this one. Alternatively, if managers are confident in making a judgment about the effectiveness of special displays (for example, that they account for between one-third and one-half of the total sales change), that information can likewise help the researcher to narrow an estimate of the effect of price on sales.[26]

3. Managerial judgment should also be used to select the appropriate structure for an experiment or survey, and the appropriate specification of a statistical equation for analysis of historical data.

   - A manager who has studied buyers should know the length of the purchase cycle (time between purchases) and the extent of inventory holding, both of which will govern the necessary length of an experiment or the number of lagged variables to include when analyzing historical data. Failure to appropriately specify the purchase cycle could cause a researcher to grossly miscalculate price sensitivity by ignoring the longer-term effects of a price change.

- Management may have much experience indicating that an advertisement affects buyers differently when the advertisement focuses on price rather than on other product attributes. If so, the researcher should separate those types of advertising in an experiment or in historical data analysis. The researcher might also treat price advertising as having an effect that interacts with the level of price, and nonprice advertising as having an independent effect.

4. For survey research, managerial judgment should guide the preparation of product descriptions, to ensure that they include the variables relevant to buyers and that they describe them with the appropriate connotations.

  - For an automobile survey, management can point out that the amount of time required to accelerate to 65 mph is an important attribute to include when describing a sports car, but not when describing a family car.
  - For a survey on radios, managers can point out that the word "knob" in a description will carry a connotation much different from the word "control," which may influence buyers' perceptions about other attributes such as reliability and state-of-the-art technology.

The common failure to use this type of managerial input (or the failure of management to know buyers well enough to provide it) is no doubt one reason why research to measure price sensitivity is often disappointing.

When measurement embodies managerial judgment, it is much more likely to provide useful information, but even then the results should never be taken uncritically. The first question to ask after any marketing research is, "Why do the results look the way they do?" The measurement of price sensitivity is not an end result but a catalyst to learn more about one's buyers. If the results are inconsistent with prior expectations, one should consider how prior judgment might have been wrong. What factors may have been overlooked, or have been given too little weight, leading to the formulation of incorrect expectations about price sensitivity? One should also consider how bias might have been introduced into the measurement process. Perhaps the measurement technique heightened buyers' attention to price or the sample subjects were unrepresentative of the product's actual buyers. Regardless of the outcome of such an evaluation, one can learn more about the product's buyers and the factors that determine their price sensitivity. Even when one concludes that the measurement technique biased the results, the bias reveals information (for example, that the low level of price sensitivity that management expected is substantially due to buyers' low attention to price in the natural purchase environment, or that a segment of people who do not regularly buy the firm's product has a different sensitivity to price).

Using Internet-Based Techniques

Since the advent of the Internet, market researchers and their clients are increasingly using on-line surveys for gathering customer and market data.

Online research is often far less expensive and much faster than traditional research methods—for example, you avoid the costs of mailing or telephone staff. It tends to obtain better response rates because it is less intrusive and more convenient to simply click a "respond" button in an e-mail. However, online research may not be generalizable to an entire market because of sampling bias—online respondents are not necessarily representative of the broader target population. Minorities, lower-income households, rural residents, and older people, for example, are less likely to be represented among online samples. Nonetheless, online research can be particularly effective for identifying very specific or specialized subgroups to target for research. Esearch.com, for example, sends out qualifying questionnaires to many online respondents to find those with specific product or service needs, and then follows up with that smaller pool of respondents with more in-depth research. Eli Lilly, an Esearch.com client, used this online qualifying process to identify people with obscure ailments for which the company is developing treatments.[27]

Outside Sources of Data

In addition to performing experiments and evaluating available sales data, one should be aware of the many external sources of data that are available to shed light on price sensitivity. Public records such as those found at government institutions or industry trade groups contain vast sources of data and information on historical sales trends, industry actions, as well as a record of other factors that may affect the market of interest. Market research firms specialize in performing the types of experiments and analyses described in this chapter. The journals published by various academic and industry institutions offer lessons from the past that may apply to new products. The Society of Competitive Intelligence Professionals (SCIP) is an industry trade group that is devoted to the quest of finding competitive intelligence.[28]

Other secondary sources of data for industrial markets, including the Census of Manufacturers, the Survey of Industrial Buying Power, and numerous other governmental and private sources[29] can tell sellers the types of businesses their buyers engage in and the share of the total market each accounts for, the average size of their purchases in major product classes, and their growth rates. In consumer markets, consumer panel surveys are widely available to tell managers the demographics of their buyers (income, family size, education, use of coupons) as well as those of their closest competitors. Other companies develop complete psychographic profiles of buyers that go beyond just demographics to delve into the innermost psychological motivations for purchase. These are relatively inexpensive sources of data from which management can form judgments about price sensitivity.

Regardless of the method of intelligence gathering, recognize that the key aim of the marketer is to listen to the voice of the customer, understand how product attributes get translated into benefits, and how benefits are converted into a willingness to pay money to obtain a good.

Selecting the Appropriate Measurement Technique

The choice among measurement techniques is not arbitrary. Each is more appropriate than another under certain circumstances. Information about trade-offs between price and attributes is most valuable when a company is developing new products or improving old ones. Since one cannot use historical data or a purchase experiment to test undeveloped products, one must turn to research on preferences and intentions that require only product descriptions or experimental prototypes. Trade-off (Conjoint) analysis is a great choice at this point. But surveys of preferences, like conjoint analysis, often yield poor predictions of actual price sensitivity in real-world purchase situations because they create an artificial purchase environment in which price awareness and knowledge of substitutes is made easy. At the time of product development, however, those are not factors about which management need be concerned. Product development focuses on efforts to enhance the attractiveness of the product when customers are aware of differences. Even when survey research accurately measures only the effect of product attributes on price sensitivity, it is a useful tool for product development, although it may be inadequate for actually setting prices later on.

Once a product is developed, management would like to have measurements that capture as many of the different determinants of price sensitivity as possible. In-store or sophisticated laboratory purchase experiments are definitely the first choice for frequently purchased, low-cost products. With few exceptions, such products are bought by consumers who have low price awareness and give the purchase decision little attention. Consequently, surveys to estimate price sensitivity for such products focus much more attention on price in the purchase decision than would occur naturally, thus distorting the estimates. The cost of in-store experiments, however, may make them impractical for testing on a large scale. In that case, management might best do a few in-store experiments with matched simulated purchase surveys. If the amount of bias in the latter is stable, the survey could be used for further research and adjusted by the amount of the bias between the survey and the in-store experiments.

When the fully developed product is a high-cost durable good such as a TV set or a photocopier, an in-store experiment is impractical. A laboratory purchase experiment may be practical since experimental control permits inferences from fewer purchases but will be too costly for many products. Fortunately, high-value products are also products for which consumers naturally pay great attention to price. In fact, they may give all aspects of the purchase careful thought because it involves a large expenditure. Consequently, a simple laboratory experiment or a simulated purchase survey may be reasonably accurate in predicting price sensitivity for these types of products. Even a buy-response survey may be useful to identify the range of prices that potential customers might find acceptable for such products, although the exact estimates of sales at various prices should not be treated with much confidence.

Once a product has been on the market for a while, historical data become available. Such data are most useful when managers are willing to implement marketing decisions in ways that can increase the research value of the data. For example, sales data become more useful if price changes are sometimes accompanied by a change in advertising and other times not, enabling marketing researchers to isolate their separate effects. A log of unusual events that cause distortions in the actual sales data (for instance, a strike by a competitor's truckers may be causing stock-outs of the competitor's product and increased sales of yours) is also extremely useful when the time comes to adjust the historical data. Moreover, as managers talk with and observe buyers, they should keep questions in mind that would aid the researcher using historical data: What is the length of the purchase cycle? To what extent do buyers purchase extra for inventories when price is expected to rise in the future? Even if historical data are so filled with random variations that no conclusions can be drawn from them with confidence, they may still point toward possible relationships between price and sales or other marketing variables that would be worth examining with another research technique.

Summary

Numerical estimation of price sensitivity is no shortcut to knowing a product's buyers—who they are, how they buy, and why they make their purchase decisions. Numerical estimates are an important source of objective information that can supplement the more subjective observations that usually dominate managerial judgments about price sensitivity. As a supplement, they can substantially improve the accuracy of such judgments and the effectiveness of a firm's pricing.

Measurement techniques differ in the variables they measure and in the conditions of measurement. The variable measured may be either actual purchases or preferences and intentions. Since the ultimate goal of research is to predict customers' actual purchases, research based on actual purchase data is generally more reliable than research based on preferences and intentions. Unfortunately, collecting and analyzing actual-purchase data costs more, requires much more time, and is entirely impossible for products that are not yet fully developed and ready for sale. Consequently, most research on price sensitivity infers purchase behavior from questions potential customers answer about their preferences and intentions.

Pricing research studies range from those that are completely uncontrolled to those in which the experimenter controls almost completely the alternative products, their prices, and the information that customers receive. Although research techniques that permit a high degree of experimental control are more costly than uncontrolled research, the added cost is usually worth it. Uncontrolled data on actual purchases are plagued by too little variation in prices and too many variables changing at once. Uncontrolled data on preferences and intentions are biased by people's untruthful responses and by their inability to recall competitive prices. In contrast, controlled in-store experiments and sophisticated laboratory purchase experiments often predict actual price sensitivity well. Even experiments using preferences and intentions seem to warrant confidence when they are highly controlled. In particular, trade-off analysis is proving highly useful in predicting at least that portion of price sensitivity determined by the unique-value effect.

The appropriate technique for numerically estimating price sensitivity depends on the product's stage of development. When a product is still in the concept or prototype stage, research measuring preferences or intentions is the only option. Trade-off analysis is especially useful at this stage because it can identify the value of individual product attributes, thus helping to decide which combination of attributes will enable the firm to price the product most profitably. When a product is ready for the market, in-store or laboratory purchase experiments are more appropriate because they more realistically simulate the actual purchase environment. After a product has been on the market for a while, actual purchase data can be an inexpensive source of estimates, provided that management monitors sales frequently and makes some price changes independently of changes in other marketing variables. Even when actual purchase data cannot provide conclusive answers, they can suggest relationships that can then be measured more reliably with other techniques.

Regardless of the technique used to measure price sensitivity, it is important that managers not allow the estimate to become a substitute for managerial judgment. The low accuracy of many numerical estimates makes blind reliance on them very risky. One always needs to be aware of the range of values an elasticity estimate can take, the factors that can influence price sensitivity, and one must generally get an understanding of the range of values one can expect. They always should be compared with a manager's own expectations, based on his or her more general knowledge of buyers and their purchase motivations. When inconsistencies occur, the manager should reexamine both the measurement technique and the adequacy of his or her understanding of buyers. The quality of numerical estimates depends in large part on the quality of managerial judgment that guides the estimation process. Managers who know their buyers can get substantially better estimates of price sensitivity when they use that knowledge (1) to select a sample of consumers that accurately represents the product's market, (2) to identify and explain extraneous changes in sales that might camouflage an effect, (3) to provide information to sort out the effects of price from other variables that tend to change with it, (4) to identify an appropriate equation or experimental structure, and (5) to properly describe the product for survey research.

Notes

1. Actually, the researcher observes only the price that the consumer reports having paid. There is some risk of erroneous reporting, which weakens the data but does not bias it. Fortunately, this problem is being solved by technologies that enable consumers to avoid the task of reporting.
2. See Ronald E. Frank and William Massy, "Market Segmentation and the Effectiveness of a Brand's Dealing Policies," *Journal of Business* 38 (April 1965): 186–200; Terry Elrod and Russell S. Winer, "An Empirical Evaluation of Aggregation Approaches for Developing Market Segments," *Journal of Marketing* 46 (Fall 1982): 65–74.
3. The companies are Information Resources Inc. (headquarters in Chicago) and Burke Marketing Research (headquarters in Cincinnati, Ohio).

4. See, for example, David R. Bell, Joengwen Chiang, and V. Padmanabhan, "The Decomposition of Promotional Response: An Empirical Generalization," *Marketing Science* 18, no. 4 (1999): 504–526; Shuba Srinivasan, Peter T. L. Popkowki Leszczyc, and Frank M. Bass, "Market Share Response and Competitive Interaction: The Impact of Temporary, Evolving, and Structural Changes in Prices," *International Journal of Research in Marketing* 17 (2000): 281–305; and Koen Pauwels, Shuba Srinivasan, and Philip Hans Franses, "When Do Price Thresholds Matter in Retail Categories?" *Marketing Science* 26, no. 1 (January–February 2007): 83–100.

5. For a brief introduction to regression analysis, see Thomas C. Kinnear and James R. Taylor, *Marketing Research: An Applied Approach*, 4th ed. (New York: McGraw-Hill, 1991, 626–628); or Mark L. Bereson and David M. Levine, *Basic Business Statistics: Concepts and Application* (Upper Saddle River, NJ: Prentice Hall, 1992, Chapter 16).

6. In practice, of course, there are always some external factors that will affect only one store's sales, undermining the effectiveness of the control. For example, the control store may run out of a competing brand. One can reduce the distorting effect of such factors by increasing the number of both experimental and control stores, but at a corresponding increase in cost.

7. For guidance in the proper design of either a field or laboratory experiment, see Thomas Cook and Donald T. Campbell, "The Design and Conduct of Quasi-Experimental and True Experiments in Field Settings," in *Handbook of Industrial and Organizational Psychology*, ed. Marvin Dunnette (Chicago: Rand McNally, 1976, 223–235).

8. William Applebaum and Richard Spears, "Controlled Experimentation in Marketing Research," *Journal of Marketing* 14 (January 1950): 505–517; Edward Hawkins, "Methods of Estimating Demand," *Journal of Marketing* 21 (April 1957): 430–534; William D. Barclay, "Factorial Design in a Pricing Experiment," *Journal of Marketing Research* 6 (November 1969): 427–429; Sidney Bennet and I. B. Wilkinson, "Price-Quantity Relationship and Price Elasticity Under In-Store Experimentation," *Journal of Business Research* 2 (January 1974): 27–38; Gerald Eskin, "A Case for Test Marketing Experiments," *Journal of Advertising Research* 15 (April 1975): 27–33; Gerald Eskin and Penny Baron, "Effect of Price and Advertising in Test Market Experiments," *Journal of Marketing Research* 14 (November 1977): 499–508.

9. Barclay, "Factorial Design in a Pricing Experiment," p. 428.

10. Paul Solman and Thomas Friedman, *Life and Death in the Corporate Battlefield* (New York: Simon and Schuster, 1982, Chapter 24).

11. Several good discussions of the increased use and application of laboratory test markets (called Simulated Test Marketing by the authors) can be found in Kevin J. Clancy and Robert S. Shulman, "Simulated Test Marketing: A New Technology for Solving an Old Problem," in *A.N.A./The Advertiser* (Fall 1995): 28–33; and also in Kevin J. Clancy and Robert S. Shulman, "Test for Success: How Simulated Test Marketing Can Dramatically Improve the Forecasting of a New Product's Sales," *Sales and Marketing Management* (October 1995): 111–114.

12. One might well argue that buy-response surveys should be included with the experimentally controlled studies since the researcher does

exercise control over the price asked. That observation is correct. The reason that buy-response questioning is better than direct questioning is precisely because the researcher introduces a bit of control. Still, the amount of control that the researcher can exercise in these studies is slight. No attempt is made to control the respondents' perception of competitive prices, exposure to promotion, or demographics.

13. Henry Assael, *Consumer Behavior and Marketing Action,* 2nd ed. (Boston: Kent Publishing, 1983).

14. For a good discussion on the application of and difference between focus group and depth interviews as unstructured/uncontrolled data-collection techniques, see Thomas C. Kinnear and James R. Taylor, *Marketing Research: An Applied Approach,* 4th ed., (New York: McGraw-Hill, 1991).

15. Abbie Griffin and John R. Hauser, "The Voice of the Customer," *Marketing Science* 12, no. 1 (Winter 1993): 1–27.

16. F. James C. Anderson and James A. Narus, "Business Marketing: Understand What Customers Value," *Harvard Business Review* (November–December 1998): 53–65.

17. For an excellent discussion on the types of value drivers and how to uncover those value drivers in both consumer and business-to-business research, read Ian C. MacMillan and Rita Gunther McGrath, "Discovering New Points of Differentiation," *Harvard Business Review* (July–August 1997): 133–145.

18. D. Frank Jones, "A Survey Technique to Measure Demand Under Various Pricing Strategies," *Journal of Marketing,* 39 (July 1975), pp. 75–77.

19. John R. Nevin, "Laboratory Experiments for Estimating Consumer Demand," *Journal of Marketing Research* 11 (August 1974): 261–268.

20. The first article on trade-off analysis to appear in the marketing literature was Paul E. Green and Vithala R. Rao, "Conjoint Measurement for Quantifying Judgemental Data," *Journal of Marketing Research* 8 (August 1971): 355–363. For a nontechnical discussion of applications specifically to pricing, see Patrick J. Robinson, "Applications of Conjoint Analysis to Pricing Problems," in *Market Measurement and Analysis,* ed. David B. Montgomery and Dick R. Wittink (Cambridge, MA: Marketing Science Institute, 1980, 183–205).

21. The following articles describe data manipulation procedures for conjoint analysis: J. B. Kruskal, "Analysis of Factorial Experiments by Estimating Monotone Transformations of the Data," *Journal of the Royal Statistical Society,* Series B (1965): 251–263; Dove Peckelman and Subrata Sen, "Regression Versus Interpolation in Additive Conjoint Measurement," *Association for Consumer Research* (1976): 29–34; Philip Cattin and Dick Wittink, "Further Beyond Conjoint Measurement: Toward Comparison of Methods," *1976 Association for Consumer Research Proceedings* (1976): 41–45.

22. Franklin Acito, "An Investigation of Some Data Collection Issues in Conjoint Measurement," in *1977 Proceedings American Marketing Association,* ed. B. A. Greenberg and D. N. Bellenger (Chicago: American Marketing Association, 1977, 82–85); James McCullough and Roger Best, "Conjoint Measurement: Temporal Stability and Structural Reliability," *Journal of Marketing Research* 16 (February 1979): 26–31; Madhav N. Segal, "Reliability of Conjoint Analysis: Contrasting Data Collection Procedure," *Journal of Marketing Research* 19 (February 1982): 139–143.

23. McCullough and Best, "Conjoint Measurement," pp. 26–31.

24. Bobby J. Calder, "Focus Groups and the Nature of Qualitative Marketing Research," *Journal of Marketing Research* 14 (August 1977): 353–364.

25. Johnny K. Johansson and Ikujiro Nonaka, "Marketing Research the Japanese Way," *Harvard Business Review* (May/June 1987).

26. For the reader trained in classical statistics, these suggestions for adjusting the data with managerial judgment may seem unscientific. But it is important to keep in mind that the purpose of numerical measurement of price sensitivity is to derive useful estimates, not to objectively test a theory. If managers have strongly held beliefs, in light of which the historical record of sales could yield much better estimates, it is simply wasteful to ignore those beliefs simply because they may not be objective. See Edward E. Leamer, "Let's Take the Con Out of Econometrics," *American Economic Review* 73 (March 1983): 31–43.

27. "Survey Your Customers—Electronically," *Harvard Management Update* (April 2000): 3–4.

28. See, for example, http://www.scip.org.

29. The Census of Manufacturers is a publication of the U.S. Department of Commerce. For other federal sources, see the Commerce Department publication titled *A Guide to Federal Data Sources on Manufacturing*. The "Survey of Industrial Buying Power" is published annually as an issue of *Sales and Marketing Management* magazine. Other useful sources of information about the demographics and motivations of buying firms can be obtained from the buying firms' trade associations (such as the Rubber Manufacturers Association and the National Machine Tool Builders Association) and from privately operated industrial directory and research companies (for example, Predicasts, Inc., Dun & Bradstreet, Standard & Poor's).

CHAPTER 13

■ ■ ■ ■ ■

Ethics and the Law
Understanding the Constraints on Pricing

When making pricing decisions, the successful strategist must consider not only what is profitable, but also what will be perceived as ethical and legal. Unfortunately, good advice on both of these issues is all too often unavailable or misleading. Attorneys who do not specialize in antitrust law tend to be overly conservative—advising against activities that are only sometimes illegal or that could trigger an investigation. In fact, benign changes in questionable pricing policies are often all that is necessary to make them both profitable and defensible. On the other hand, product and sales managers eager to achieve quarterly objectives will sometimes fail to consider these constraints at all, resulting in costly condemnations of their companies in courts of law or public opinion. This chapter is intended to raise awareness of the issues and educate you enough to question the advice you receive.

ETHICAL CONSTRAINTS ON PRICING

"Perhaps no other area of managerial activity is more difficult to depict accurately, assess fairly, and prescribe realistically in terms of morality than the domain of price."[1] This oft-quoted assessment reflects the exceptional divergence of ethical opinions with respect to pricing. Even among writers sympathetic to the need for profit, some consider it unethical to charge different prices unless they reflect differences in costs, while others consider pricing unethical unless prices are set "equal or proportional to the benefit received."[2] Consequently, there is less written on ethics in pricing than on other marketing issues, and what is written tends to focus on the easy issues, like deception and price-fixing.[3] The tougher issues involve strategies and tactics for gaining profit.

EXHIBIT 13-1 When Is a Price Ethical? Ethical Constraints

Level	The Exchange Is Ethical When	Implication/Proscription
1	The price is paid voluntarily.	"Let the buyer beware."
2	". . . and is based on equal information."	No sales without full disclosure (used-car defects, risks of smoking).
3	". . . and does not exploit buyers' 'essential needs'."	No "excessive" profits on essentials such as life-saving pharmaceuticals.
4	". . . and is justified by costs."	No segmented pricing based on value. No excessive profits based on shortages, even for nonessential products.
5	". . . and provides equal access to goods regardless of one's ability to cover the cost."	No exchange for personal gain. Give as able and receive as needed.

This book is intended to help managers capture more of the value created by the products and services they sell. In many cultures, and among many who promulgate ethical principles, such a goal is morally reprehensible. Although this opinion was once held by the majority, its popularity has generally declined over the past three centuries due to the success of capitalism and the failure of collectivism to deliver an improvement in material well-being. Still, many people, including many in business practice and education, believe that there are legitimate ethical constraints on maximizing profit through pricing.

It is important to clarify your own and your customers' understanding of those standards before ambiguous situations arise. The topology of ethical constraints in pricing illustrated in Exhibit 13-1 is a good place to start. Readers should determine where to draw the line concerning ethical constraints—for themselves and their industry—and determine as well how other people (family, neighbors, social groups) might view such decisions.

Most people would reject the idea of zero ethical constraints, in which the seller can dictate the price and terms and force them on an unwilling buyer. Sale of "protection" by organized crime is universally condemned. The practice of forcing employees in a one-company town to buy from the "company store" is subject to only marginally less condemnation. Even when the government itself is the seller that is forcing people to purchase goods and services at a price (tax rate) it sets, people generally condemn the transaction unless they feel empowered to influence the terms. This level of ethical constraint was also used to condemn the "trusts" that, before the antitrust laws, sometimes used reprehensible tactics to drive lower-priced competitors out of business. By denying customers alternative products, trusts arguably forced them to buy theirs.

Ethical level one, embodied in all well-functioning, competitive market economies, requires that all transactions be voluntary. Early capitalist economies, and some of the most dynamic today (for instance, that of Hong Kong), condone any transaction that meets this criterion. The legal principle of *caveat emptor*, "Let the buyer beware," characterized nearly all economic transactions in the United States prior to the twentieth century. In such a market, people often make regrettable purchases (for example, expensive brand-name watches that turn out to be cheap substitutes and stocks in overvalued companies). On the other hand, without the high legal costs associated with meeting licensing, branding, and disclosure requirements, new business opportunities abound even for the poor—making unemployment negligible.

Ethical level two imposes a more restrictive standard, condemning even voluntary transactions by those who would profit from unequal information about the exchange. Selling a used car without disclosing a known defect, concealing a known risk of using a product, or misrepresenting the benefits achievable from a product are prime examples of transactions that would be condemned by this ethical criterion. Thus, many would condemn selling land in Florida at inflated prices to unwary out-of-state buyers, or selling lottery tickets to the poor, since the seller could reasonably expect these potential buyers to be ignorant of, or unable to process, information needed to make an informed decision. Since sellers naturally know more about the features and benefits of products than most consumers do, they may have an ethical duty to disclose what they know completely and accurately.[4]

Ethical level three imposes a still more stringent criterion: that sellers earn no more than a "fair" profit from sales of "necessities" for which buyers have only limited alternatives. This principle is often stated as follows: "No one should profit from other people's adversity." Thus, even nominally capitalist societies sometimes impose rent controls on housing and price controls on pharmaceutical costs and physicians' fees. Even when this level of ethical constraint is not codified into law, people who espouse it condemn those who raise the price of ice during a power failure or the price of lumber following a hurricane, when the demand for these products soars.

Ethical level four extends the criteria of ethical level three to all products, even those with many substitutes and not usually thought of as necessities. Profit is morally justifiable only when it is the minimum necessary to induce companies and individuals to make decisions for the good of less-advantaged members of society.[5] Profit is ethically justifiable only as the price society must pay to induce suppliers of capital and skills to improve the well-being of those less fortunate. Profits from exploiting unique skills, great ideas, or exceptional efficiency (called "economic rents") are morally suspect in this scenario unless it can be shown that everyone, or at least the most needy, benefits from allowing such profits to be earned, such as when a high-profit company nevertheless offers lower prices and better working conditions than its competitors. Profits from speculation (buying low and selling high) are clearly condemned, as is segmented pricing (charging customers different prices to capture different levels of value), unless those prices actually reflect differences in cost.

Ethical level five, the most extreme constraint, is inconsistent with markets. In some "primitive" societies, everyone is obliged to share good fortune with those in the tribe who are less fortunate. "From each according to his ability, to each according to his need" is the espoused ethical premise of Marxist societies and even some respected moral philosophers. Those that have actually tried to put it into practice, however, have eventually recoiled at the brutality necessary to force essentially self-interested humans "to give according to their abilities" without reward. Within families and small, self-selected societies, however, this ethical principle can thrive. Within social and religious organizations, members often work together for their common good and share the results. Even within businesses, partnerships are established to share, within defined bounds, each other's good and bad fortune.

For each level of ethical constraint on economic exchange, one must determine the losses and gains, for both individuals and societies, that will result from the restriction. What effect does each level have on the material and social well-being of those who hold it as a standard? Should the same standards be applied in different contexts? For example, is your standard different for business markets than it is for consumer markets? Would your ethical standards change when selling in a foreign country where local competitors generally hold a higher or lower ethical standard than yours? In assessing the standards that friends, business associates, and political representatives apply, managers must ask themselves if their personal standards are the same for their business as well as for their personal conduct. For example, would they condemn an oil company for earning excess profits as a result of higher crude prices, yet themselves take excess profits on a house that had appreciated substantially in a hot real estate market? If so, are they hypocrites or is there some justification for holding individuals and firms to different standards?

Although we certainly have our own beliefs about which of these ethical levels is practical and desirable in dealing with others, and would apply different standards in different contexts, we feel that neither we nor the people who claim to be experts on business ethics are qualified to make these decisions for someone else. Each individual must make his or her own decisions and live with the personal and social consequences.

Regardless of one's personal ethical beliefs about pricing, it would be foolish to ignore the legal constraints on pricing. Antitrust law in the United States has developed over the years to reflect both citizens' moral evaluations of companies' actions and companies' attempts to get laws passed that protect them from more efficient or aggressive competitors. As the summary below illustrates, the meaning of these laws changes over time as courts respond to changing social attitudes and the placement of judges with differing political views.

THE LEGAL FRAMEWORK FOR PRICING

When making pricing decisions, the strategist must consider not only what is profitable, but also what is lawful. Since the late nineteenth century, the United States has been committed to maintaining price competition through establishing and enforcing antitrust policy. Statutes, regulations, and guidelines, as well as countless judicial decisions, have defined what constitutes anticompetitive pricing behavior and the rules under which the government and private parties may pursue those who engage in it.

For more than 120 years, U.S. antitrust law has responded to a complex and dynamic marketplace by being both of these things, resulting in policies that are always being scrutinized and questioned and sometimes stretched and revised. The overall trend in the United States for the last several decades has been to move away from judging behavior based on economic assumptions toward focusing on demonstrable economic effect, something that has fostered a great deal of contemporary pricing freedom. Of course, a necessary companion to evolving policies, as well as the lag time sometimes necessary for the law to catch up with the marketplace, is ambiguity. In return for some uncertainty, there is more latitude for businesses to cope creatively with both new and old challenges.

This section discusses key aspects of the law of pricing, focusing primarily on that of general applicability in the United States at the federal level.[6] Due to the long history of U.S. law in the pricing area, it has served as a model for other parts of the world, including the European Union (EU) and Japan. For example, EU antitrust law historically prohibited such things as territorial restrictions on intermediaries that interfered with cross-border trade, but a safe harbor became effective in 2000.[7] That, much like the change in the U.S. view that occurred more than 20 years earlier, recognizes a supplier's legitimate interest in controlling how its products are resold under certain circumstances.

In the United States, the antitrust laws are enforced by both government and private parties. The Department of Justice is empowered to bring criminal and civil actions, although the former are reserved primarily for price-fixing and hardcore cartel activity.[8] At the same time, the Federal Trade Commission (FTC) may bring civil actions,[9] as can private parties. Often, civil plaintiffs pursue injunctions to stop certain conduct and, in the case of private parties, they may also or alternatively seek three times their actual economic damages (something known as "treble damages"), as well as their legal fees and court costs.[10] While the volume of private antitrust litigation dwarfs that brought by the government, private suits often follow significant government cases.

The Effect of Sarbanes-Oxley on Pricing Practices

In direct response to the high-visibility corporate finance scandals involving such companies as Enron and WorldCom, the Sarbanes-Oxley Act—a significant and sweeping piece of securities reform legislation—became law in 2002.[11] Because one of the main purposes of the act is to facilitate more accurate public disclosure of financial information and provide accountability measures in reporting and monitoring of corporate conduct, its impact on pricing practices and antitrust compliance in general is to cause more rigor than had been present in many companies before the law was passed. While most of the requirements of Sarbanes-Oxley apply only to an "issuer," or a publicly-traded or listed company,[12] some commentators have recommended that even private companies should strive to comply with the full demands of this law.[13]

Among other things, Sarbanes-Oxley specifically provides for stricter financial and auditing procedures and reporting. For example, the act requires that an issuer's chief financial officer (CFO) and chief executive officer (CEO) certify financial reporting documents (such as the company's quarterly and annual reports) and make the knowing certification of non-compliant financials a criminal offense.[14] The act also outlines disclosure procedures and internal accounting control mechanisms, as well as whistle-blowing provisions, including language that makes retaliation against truthful informants subject to criminal penalties of a fine or up to 10 years' imprisonment, or both.[15]

While Sarbanes-Oxley was not created with the express intent of policing antitrust compliance in pricing matters, the broad scope of the act clearly affects this area. Some of the most obvious examples in the context of pricing policies and related issues include tighter controls on the accounting and disclosure procedures relating to the treatment and use of discounts, allowances and promotional funds in general, regardless of whether a company is giving or getting them. As a result, companies are well advised, among other things, to address in their internal control policies requirements and guidelines for pricing and pricing actions, process documentation for such actions, and a procedure for investigating and responding to employee reports of internal violations.

PRICE-FIXING OR PRICE ENCOURAGEMENT

In an effort to reduce or avoid market risks, business people have long been interested in setting prices with their competitors or dictating or influencing the prices charged by their downstream intermediaries, such as distributors, dealers, and retailers. Over the years, U.S. law has taken a rather dim view of this behavior. At the same time, it is now clear that there is some flexibility in what competitors—which collectively affect market prices—can do, but the biggest changes are in the area of distribution channels, where price setting is lawful if done properly.

There are two types of price-fixing: horizontal and vertical. In the former, competitors agree on the prices they will charge or key terms of sale affecting price. In the latter, a supplier and a reseller agree on the prices the reseller will charge or the price-related terms of resale for the supplier's products. However, where an intermediary, such as an independent sales representative, does not take ownership of the supplier's products and acts only as the supplier's agent, there cannot be any vertical price-fixing because the law views the sale as taking place directly between the supplier and the end user, with the intermediary serving as a conduit. Consequently, the supplier is only setting its own prices and terms of sale.[16]

The primary law in this area is Section 1 of the Sherman Act, an 1890 statute that prohibits "[e]very contract, combination . . . or conspiracy in restraint of trade."[17] The contract, combination, or conspiracy requirement necessarily means that there must be an agreement between two or more individuals or entities. As a result, the law does not reach unilateral behavior.[18] Moreover, in the horizontal context, the Sherman Act does not ban merely imitating a competitor's pricing behavior (something called "conscious parallelism").[19]

Sometimes, there are written contracts or other direct evidence of price-fixing conspiracies. Far more often, evidence of agreement must be inferred from the actions of the parties involved. Although conscious parallelism by itself is not enough to establish an agreement, when uniform or similar behavior is coupled with one or more "plus factors," courts have found concerted activity. Perhaps the most powerful of these factors exists when the conduct in question would be against the self-interest of each party if it acted alone, but consistent with their self-interest if they all behaved the same way, such as the uniform imposition of unpopular restrictions or price increases in the face of surplus.[20] Another factor exists when the opportunity to collude (often shown by communications between or among the parties) is followed by identical or similar actions, although the probative effect of such opportunity or communications can be undercut by legitimate business explanations.[21]

Once concerted action has been found, the next step is to evaluate it. Case law has further refined Section 1 of the Sherman Act to require two levels of proof, depending on the nature of the alleged offense. Some offenses are considered to be "per se" illegal, while others are analyzed under the "rule of reason." Per se offenses require that the presence of the objectionable practice be proven and that there be antitrust injury and damages, while offenses subject to the rule of reason add a third element—that the practice at issue be unreasonably anticompetitive. In general, it is easier to prove a violation under the per se test and more difficult to do so under the rule of reason, because the latter requires detailed economic analysis and a balancing of procompetitive and anticompetitive effects. Of course, the rule of reason also provides defendants with the opportunity to justify their behavior, something denied under the per se rule.

Historically, all arrangements affecting price were presumed to be unreasonably anticompetitive on their face and, therefore, per se illegal. However, during the past 30 years or so, the U.S. Supreme Court has placed more emphasis on showing demonstrable economic effect rather than relying on assumptions, so there has been an erosion of per se application to both horizontal and vertical pricing issues.

Horizontal Price-Fixing

In the horizontal arena, direct price-fixing—competitors in the stereotypical smoke-filled room agreeing to set prices or rig bids—remains per se illegal.

The same treatment is accorded to indirect price-fixing, where there is an ambiguous arrangement between competitors that a court has determined constitutes illegal price-fixing after conducting a detailed factual review or market analysis.[22]

However, when a restriction on price is merely the incidental effect of a desirable procompetitive activity (sometimes referred to as "incidental price-fixing"), it is now clear that the more forgiving rule of reason applies. This point is illustrated by *National Collegiate Athletic Association v. Board of Regents*, where the U.S. Supreme Court applied the rule of reason and noted that rules covering athletic equipment and schedules were appropriate, but those that limited the television exposure of member football teams were an unreasonable restriction on output that unlawfully increased prices.[23]

RESALE PRICE-FIXING OR ENCOURAGEMENT

Vertical Price-Fixing

Vertical price-fixing by agreement was considered per se illegal in the U.S. until a pair of modern-day Supreme Court cases spaced ten years apart established the current rule that all forms of resale price setting—maximum, minimum, or exact—are judged under federal law by the rule of reason. The 1997 decision in *Khan* overturned a 29-year old case to declare that the rule of reason applies to maximum price agreements, while the far more controversial *Leegin* decision in 2007 jettisoned a 96-year old precedent by extending *Khan* to minimum prices (and the analytically equivalent exact prices).[24] Likely because maximum prices have the effect of holding down costs, while minimum or exact prices prop them up, bills have been introduced both in Congress and at the state level to legislatively overturn *Leegin* by restoring the per se rule to minimum resale price agreements, but, so far, only Maryland's efforts have been enacted into law.[25] While application of the rule of reason in this context is too new to assess its effect and the empirical evidence supporting the consumer welfare arguments in favor of going back to the per se rule is lacking, the emotion is not, increasing the odds that Congress will turn back the clock, other states will join Maryland, or both.[26]

However, regardless whether *Leegin* survives, none of the legislative efforts aimed at minimum resale price *agreements* affect the Supreme Court's 1919 ruling in *Colgate* that setting maximum, minimum or exact resale prices without an agreement (that is, unilaterally) is not illegal price-fixing prohibited under the Sherman Act.[27] As a result, a supplier may announce a price at which its product must be resold (that is, establish a ceiling, floor, or exact price policy) and refuse to sell to any reseller that does not comply, as long as there is no agreement between the supplier and its reseller on resale price levels. Even when resellers follow the supplier's resale price policy, there is no unlawful agreement. With this latitude, many manufacturers of desirable branded products have successfully discouraged the discounting of their products in such diverse industries as consumer electronics, furniture, appliances, sporting goods, tires, luggage, handbags, videos, agricultural supplies, electronic test equipment, and automotive accessories and replacement parts.

A frequent justification given for minimum or exact resale price policies is to permit resellers sufficient margin to provide a selling environment that is consistent with the supplier's objectives for its products, including brand image. For example, the supplier may want knowledgeable salespeople, showrooms, substantial inventory, and superior service. Of course, such policies also may help support higher supplier margins. Sometimes, the imposition of such policies is sought by resellers to insulate them from price competition. As long as there is no agreement on price levels, such requests, even if acted upon by the supplier, are not unlawful.[28]

Pricing policies may be used broadly or selectively to cover everything from a single product to all of those in a supplier's line. Similarly, they can be used in certain geographic areas and with specific channels of distribution in which price erosion is a problem, or they can be used throughout the country. In any event, a policy violation typically requires that the supplier stop selling the offending reseller the products involved, although it also is permissible to pull a product line or all of the supplier's business.[29] When and if the supplier wishes to resume selling is the supplier's unilateral decision, although some cases suggest that warnings, threats, and probation short of termination support the inference that some form of agreement has been reached.

To make such a policy stick, the supplier must generally have brand or market power. Otherwise, resellers simply won't bother to follow the policy, since there are plenty of substitutes available. Ironically, it is those highly desirable products that are most susceptible to discounting anyway, so the requisite power is typically present. In addition, it is important to note that resale price policies have a vertical reach that is limited to one level down the distribution channel. If all resellers buy directly from the manufacturer, this restriction poses no problem, but if a significant amount of sales are made through multiple levels of distribution, a policy will be too porous to be effective. In other words, a manufacturer can control a direct-buying retailer's sell price by policy, but it can't reach that of a retailer that buys from a wholesaler. To address this problem, the manufacturer may "jump over" the wholesaler by making a sale directly to the retailer, or it may convert the wholesaler into an agent for the purpose of such a sale. Alternatively, the policy may be circulated to both direct- and indirect-buying resellers, while wholesalers are permitted to sell to "approved" resellers only. One way to remain on the approved list is to comply with the policy.

Resale price policies are potent, but the rules for managing them within the law are necessarily stringent. Careful implementation keeps otherwise lawful programs from going astray. This means that any form of agreement regarding resale prices must be avoided. There must be no resale pricing contracts, no assurances of compliance, and no probation. Because this area can be a legal minefield, it's crucial to carefully train supplier personnel. At the same time, many companies have adopted such programs with low risk and considerable success.

Direct Dealing Programs

Another way to control the prices charged to end users is for the supplier to sell them directly or, constructively, by the use of agents. When the supplier agrees with the end user on price, but the latter cannot handle delivery of large quantities or maintain sufficient inventory to justify direct shipments from the supplier, some suppliers look to a reseller to fill the order out of the reseller's warehouse. This can be done by consignment or by the supplier buying back inventory from the reseller immediately prior to its transfer to the end user, so, in either event, the sale runs directly from the supplier to the end user. The reseller becomes the supplier's warehousing and delivery agent and is compensated by the supplier for performing only these functions.

When the supplier has negotiated the price to the end user, but the reseller has or retains the title, the supplier has another alternative. Under the "reseller's choice" approach, the reseller may either choose to sell the product to the end user at the price set by the supplier or tell the supplier to find someone else to do so. Even if the reseller agrees to sell at the contracted price, there is no per se illegal price fixing, as this practice is seen as voluntary and, therefore, subject to the rule of reason.[30]

Resale Price Encouragement

Instead of dictating a resale price by agreement, policy, or direct sale, some suppliers encourage desirable resale pricing behavior by providing financial or other incentives, such as advertising allowances to promote certain prices. Although these practices are judged under the rule of reason because participation is voluntary, the provision of incentives is subject to the prohibitions in the Robinson-Patman Act against price and promotional discrimination.[31]

In the area of price advertising, a common practice is to use a minimum advertised price (MAP) program, although the underlying concept could also be used for maximum or exact prices. Under this approach, the reseller receives an advertising allowance (often in the form of co-op advertising funds) in return for adhering to the appropriate price in advertising, in a catalog, or over the Internet.[32] Some companies pay an explicit allowance (such as a percentage rebate on purchases), while others employ an implicit allowance stating that failure to follow program requirements results in the loss of the allowance and an increase in price. The latter is found in consumer electronics.

A variant on MAP programs is group or shared-price advertising, through which a supplier sponsors an ad, but resellers can be listed in it only if they agree to sell at the promoted price during the period indicated. Again, resellers that wish pricing freedom may decline to be in the ad, and, because of the voluntary nature of this approach, there is no per se illegality.

Another alternative is target-price rebates. Here, the supplier rewards the reseller with financial incentives the closer its resale prices are to the target set by the supplier. This practice requires point-of-sale (POS) reporting, typically easier to get in the consumer area due to the widespread use of scanners, but becoming more common in the industrial marketplace.

PRICE AND PROMOTIONAL DISCRIMINATION

Although economists maintain that the ability to charge different prices to different customers promotes efficiency by clearing the market, U.S. law on that issue has focused on maintaining the viability of numerous sellers as a means to preserve competition. Consequently, while price discrimination has been unlawful since 1914, the Robinson-Patman Act amended existing legislation in 1936, so this entire area is commonly referred to by the name of the amendment.[33]

This complex, Depression-era legislation was enacted to protect small businesses by outlawing discriminatory price and promotional allowances obtained by large businesses, while exempting sales to government or "charitable" organizations for their own use.[34] At the same time, the emergence of contemporary power buyers through internal growth or consolidation (such as Wal-Mart or W. W. Grainger), as well as supplier efforts to make discounts and allowances provided to customers more efficient, have forced or encouraged sellers to provide lawful account-specific pricing and promotions by creatively finding ways through the Robinson-Patman maze. This trend is likely to continue, as further consolidation and evolving distribution channels (brought on by e-commerce, among other things) will demand and reward more sophisticated differentiation.

As is the case with the other antitrust laws, the Department of Justice, the FTC, and private parties may each bring Robinson-Patman cases, although the enforcement agencies have not focused on this area for some time. Indeed, the Justice Department has criminal powers in this area that have gone unused for many years, while the FTC today brings few significant cases in this area after being particularly active through the 1970s. Private suits on behalf of businesses (consumers have no standing to sue under the statute) account for most of the enforcement activity.[35] Successful plaintiffs are entitled to the same remedies as those available under the antitrust laws discussed previously (injunctions, treble damages, attorneys' fees and costs).

Price Discrimination

Keep in mind that discrimination in price is not always unlawful. In order to prove illegal price discrimination under the Robinson-Patman Act and assuming that the supplier sells in interstate commerce, each of five elements must be present:[36]

1. *Discrimination.* This standard is met simply by charging different prices to different customers. However, if the reason for the difference is due to a discount or allowance made available to all or almost all customers (like a prompt payment discount), but some customers choose not to take advantage of it, the element of discrimination drops out, ending the inquiry. This is known as the "availability defense."

2. *Sales to Two or More Purchasers.* The different prices must be charged on reasonably contemporaneous sales to two or more purchasers—a rule that permits price fluctuations. In other words, it is inappropriate under the statute to compare two widely separated sales in a highly volatile market. Yet, if prices typically change annually or semiannually, a sale made in January may be compared with one made in March.

In addition, offering different prices is not enough. Actual sales or agreements to sell at different prices must exist. For example, if two electrical supply distributors seek special pricing from the manufacturer to bid on a construction job or an integrated supply contract that only one will get, the manufacturer may, if it is careful, give one a better price than the other, because in doing so, it is providing two offers, but making only one sale.[37]

3. *Goods.* Robinson-Patman applies to the sale of goods only ("commodities" in the statute), so services—such as telecommunications, banking, and transportation—are not covered.[38] When a supplier sells a bundled offering, such as repair services that include parts or computer hardware that includes maintenance services, Robinson-Patman is relevant only if the value of the goods in the bundle predominates. Also, it is possible to turn goods into services if the manufacturer procures raw materials and produces and stores the products on behalf of the customer, with the customer owning the inventory every step of the way and bearing the risk of loss.

4. *Like Grade and Quality.* The goods involved must be physically or essentially the same. Brand preferences are irrelevant, but functional variations can differentiate products. In a key case, the Supreme Court stated that a branded product and its physically and chemically identical private-label version must be priced the same by the manufacturer.[39] While the distinctions drawn in the case law sometimes appear arbitrary, meaningful functional or physical variations can result in different products that legitimize different prices. For example, two air conditioners that have significant differences in cooling capacity are distinct products, even if they otherwise are or appear physically identical.

5. *Reasonable Probability of Competitive Injury.* The law generally focuses on injury at one of two levels. The first, called "primary line," permits a supplier to sue a competitor for the latter's discriminatory pricing. But here the law also requires that the supplier's discriminatory pricing be below its cost, something designed to drive its rival out of business or otherwise injure competition in the market as a whole (called "predatory intent"), rather than to merely take some incremental market share. Moreover, the structure of the market must be such that the discriminating supplier can raise prices after it disposes of the targeted competitor or that market injury otherwise is threatened through reduced output.[40] Not surprisingly, there are few contemporary primary-line cases due to this tough standard.

Far more common is "secondary-line" injury, where a supplier's disfavored reseller or end-user customer may sue the supplier for price discrimination. However, the law is clear that only competing customers must be treated alike. To the extent that customers do not compete due to their locations or the markets they serve, different prices are appropriate under the Robinson-Patman Act. If these customer distinctions do not occur naturally, they may be introduced or formalized by contract or policy through the use of vertical nonprice restrictions.*

Defenses to Price Discrimination

Even if all five price-discrimination elements are present, there are three defenses that may be used to avoid what otherwise is unlawful discrimination.[41]

1. *Cost Justification.* This defense permits a price disparity if it is based on legitimate cost differences. For example, freight is usually less expensive on a per-case basis for a truckload shipment. However, while there is no requirement to pass on any savings, if the supplier does so, the law states that some or all of the actual savings may be passed on to the customer, but not a penny more.

One common problem area is volume discounts, particularly those that are stair-stepped with large differences between levels. Perhaps this structure reflected real cost differences many years ago when it was adopted by the supplier, but unless the underlying cost analysis is regularly updated, the discounts probably do not track today's costs. Indeed, the dynamic nature of business and the precision required to support this defense make it difficult to apply successfully, although the sophistication of activity-based costing holds a great deal of potential. Some manufacturers keep profit-and-loss statements on their customers and adjust their pricing accordingly.

2. *Meeting Competition.* Under this defense, discrimination is permissible if it is based on a good-faith belief that a discriminatory price is necessary to meet the price of a competitive supplier to the favored customer or to maintain a traditional price disparity.[42] Many managers are familiar with the application of this defense on the micro level, that is, when a buyer tells the seller that the seller's competitor offered a lower price. However, meeting competition may also be used on the macro level to justify things like volume discounts that are

---

*See "Vertical Nonprice Restrictions" on page 320.

so institutionalized in the industry that adjusting them to reflect true cost savings would result in the loss of business.

Of course, it is at the micro level where this defense is most often used. Unfortunately, this means relying on the purchaser for competitive pricing information when the buyer has every incentive to lie.[43] Some companies provide their salespeople with detailed meeting-competition forms that require competitive invoices and other documentary evidence. While this sort of evidence is helpful, it is not essential if the seller has a reasonable basis at the time of the decision to believe that the competitive price described by the buyer is legitimate, even if it turns out to be wrong later. Nevertheless, a written or electronic record of why the otherwise discriminatory price was provided is useful.

Because meeting competition is a defense, there is no obligation to provide the special price to anyone other than the customer that asked for it. Of course, smart buyers will attempt to secure "most-favored-nations" clauses in their contracts or purchase orders to automatically get the benefit of a lower price elsewhere, regardless of whether they would otherwise be entitled to it. Such clauses may cause tension between a supplier's Robinson-Patman responsibilities and those under the law of contract.

3. Changing Conditions.   Special prices may be provided to sell perishable, seasonal, obsolete, or distressed merchandise, even though the full price had been charged up to the point of offering the special prices.

Promotional Discrimination

The Robinson-Patman Act also bans promotional discrimination in an effort to deny an alternative means of achieving discriminatory pricing. The distinction between price and promotional discrimination is an important one because different legal standards apply and, while the requirements in certain respects are tougher for promotional discrimination, there is ultimately more flexibility.

Price discrimination covers the sale from the supplier to the reseller or to the direct-buying end user, while promotional discrimination usually relates only to the reseller's sale of the supplier's products.[44] Historically, promotional discrimination was largely the purview of consumer goods marketers, as industrial goods sellers concentrated on such things as volume discounts subject to price discrimination standards. However, the need for creative account-specific marketing and the desire to make supplier incentives work harder have caused many industrial sellers to face the same issues. Both consumer and industrial suppliers are now focusing on how their resellers sell their products (promotional discrimination), rather than only on how they buy them (price discrimination).

As was the case with price discrimination, each of several elements must be present to violate the law:

1. The Provision of Allowances, Services, or Facilities.   Here, the supplier grants to the reseller advertising or promotional allowances (like $5 off per case to promote a product) or provides services or facilities (such as demonstrators or free display racks), usually in return for some form of promotional performance.

2. *In Connection with the Resale of the Supplier's Goods.*   As is the case with price discrimination, the law regarding promotional discrimination does not reach service providers. In addition, promotional discrimination generally applies only to resellers. Typically, this does not cover purchasers that use or consume the supplier's product in making their own. Also, it usually does not cover the incorporation of a product, such as sugar used in baked goods or sound systems installed at the automotive factory. However, these purchasers are resellers for promotional discrimination purposes if they receive allowances or other benefits from the supplier for promoting the fact that the finished goods were made using the supplier's product or contain it, such as an ice cream producer that advertises the use of a particular brand of chocolate chip or a manufacturer that promotes the use of an axle brand in its heavy-duty trucks.

3. *Not Available to All Competing Customers on Proportionally Equal Terms.*   Once again, not all of the supplier's customers need to be treated alike, only those that compete. In addition, the services or facilities offered or the performance required to earn the allowances must be "functionally available," that is, usable or attainable in a practical sense by all competing resellers, something that may require alternatives. In other words, if a reseller could take advantage of a promotional program, but chooses not to do so, the supplier is off the legal hook.[45] For example, if a warehouse club chain could advertise in newspapers, but it decides not to do so, the supplier is under no legal obligation to offer an alternative to a newspaper-advertising allowance. On the other hand, if the supplier pays for advertising on grocery carts, but some of its retail customers can't have them due to the size of their stores, the supplier must make available an alternative means of performance, such as a poster or window sign in lieu of cart advertising.

The flexibility available under promotional discrimination standards is based on the fact that competing customers do not have to receive the same level of benefits, something contrary to the implicit mandate to do so under price discrimination rules. Instead, the promotional discrimination requirement is one of "proportional equality," and there are three ways to proportionalize what is provided: (1) on unit or dollar purchases (buy a case, get a dollar—something that lawfully favors larger resellers that buy more); (2) on the cost to the reseller of the promotional activity (a full-page ad in a national trade magazine costs more than that in a regional newsletter); or (3) on the value of the promotional activity to the supplier (salespeople dedicated exclusively to the supplier's brand have more value than those who are not).[46]

Competitive Injury, Defenses, and Indirect Purchasers

There also are other, somewhat less attractive differences between price and promotional discrimination. First, no competitive injury is necessary for illegal promotional discrimination, making it more like a per se rule.[47] Second, meeting competition is the only defense, as cost justification and changing conditions are irrelevant. Third, if the supplier provides promotional allowances to direct-buying resellers, it must also furnish them to competitive resellers that buy the promoted product through intermediaries, something that may be accomplished with ultimate reseller rebates or mandatory pass-throughs.

USING NONPRICE VARIABLES TO SUPPORT PRICING GOALS

Vertical Nonprice Restrictions

Under the standards for price and promotional discrimination, the Robinson-Patman Act requires that only competing reseller and direct-buying end-user customers be treated similarly. For this reason, or to be consistent with other price-related or marketing objectives, the supplier may wish to control the degree to which its resellers compete with each other, something known as "intrabrand competition." In 1977, the Supreme Court's *Sylvania* decision provided suppliers with considerable flexibility in this regard, by holding that vertical nonprice restrictions are subject to the rule of reason and that intrabrand competition could be reduced to promote "interbrand competition," or the rivalry between competing brands.[48]

As a result, suppliers may impose vertical restraints on resellers to help manage distribution channels and to provide considerable leeway in pricing design using the carrot approach (financial incentives), the stick approach (contractual requirements), or some combination of the two.* Historically, industrial sellers have favored the use of vertical restrictions and the more selective distribution that goes with them, while many consumer goods suppliers (except those which sell durables) have been more interested in widespread distribution without the same sort of restrictions. However, the challenges of Internet sales and other factors have focused more attention on limiting how products may be resold.

Broadly speaking, there are three types of vertical nonprice restraints, each subject to the rule of reason:

1. *Customer Restrictions.*   Rather than selling to any customer, the reseller is restricted only to particular customers or is prohibited from selling to certain customers. For example, in the industrial area, the reseller could be required to sell only to plumbing contractors or to stay away from accounts that are reserved to the supplier or another reseller. On the consumer side, the reseller could be limited to customers who order over the Internet or prohibited from selling to such customers at all.

---

*While vertical restrictions are often used with product resellers, certain restraints may also be useful in dealing with sales agents, the provision of services, and direct-buying product end users. For example, with respect to direct buyers, see the discussion of product restrictions on the next page.

2. *Territorial Restrictions.* Although generally designed to prevent or discourage selling outside of a geographic area, these can also be thought of as market restrictions. An "exclusive distributorship" is actually a restraint on the supplier, as it agrees that a particular reseller will be the exclusive outlet in the latter's territory or market (however defined) for some or all of the supplier's products. When the reseller is required to sell inside only a particular territory or market, it is subject to "absolute confinement." By combining an exclusive distributorship with absolute confinement, the result is known as an "airtight territory." In other words, if a supplier promises a dealer that the latter will be the only outlet in Oregon for a particular product, it has granted an exclusive distributorship. If the dealer is limited to selling in that state, there is absolute confinement and, when it is combined with an exclusive distributorship, the reseller has an airtight territory.

Due to some flip-flopping on the part of the Supreme Court, vertical nonprice restrictions were per se illegal from 1968 until the *Sylvania* decision in 1977. In response, a number of so-called "lesser restraints" were established that may not be as helpful in pricing as other restrictions, but still can be useful. The first of these is an "area of primary responsibility" that permits sales outside a reseller's territory, but expects the reseller to focus its efforts on its designated geographic area.[49] The second is a "profit passover" that allows the reseller to sell anywhere, but, to neutralize the "free-rider effect," the reseller must split revenue or profit for sales outside its territory with the reseller in the area encroached upon. The third is a "location clause" that restricts the reseller to approved sites only. While this last approach is ineffective if sales are made over the Internet or by phone or fax, it can be useful where a physical presence in the territory is necessary, especially in an environment where resellers are consolidating.

3. *Product Restrictions.* Suppliers have no legal obligation to sell their reseller or end-user customers any of their products, except in two instances—when the supplier has a contract to do so or in the relatively rare situation when the supplier is a monopolist with excess capacity.[50] In other words, the supplier may generally determine what products, if any, it sells to its reseller or direct-buying end-user customers, something that can be referred to as *designated products*. In this way, it may limit intrabrand competition or other conflicts by restricting what can be purchased by whom.

In addition, if the reseller or the end user is not permitted to purchase particular products or services or types of products or services from another supplier, this practice is known as *exclusive dealing*. Alternatively, it may be discouraged from doing so through financial or other incentives, often called "loyalty programs." Judged under the rule of reason, the test is whether competing suppliers are unreasonably foreclosed from the market. As long as such suppliers have reasonable access to the market through other resellers or other means, exclusive dealing is permissible.[51]

In some respects, *tying* is the other side of the coin from exclusive dealing, with the same effect.[52] In its most extreme form, tying requires that in order to purchase a desirable product or service, the customer must also buy another product or service that is less desirable. Although tying is often described as per se illegal, the analysis necessary to prove a violation is more like that required by the rule of reason.[53] Bundling is not illegal tying, as long as the products or services are available separately, even at a somewhat higher, but reasonable, cost.

Full-line forcing, judged under the rule of reason, is a variation on tying that requires a reseller to carry the supplier's entire line or a specified assortment to avoid the customer's cherry-picking of the more desirable products. Note that tying and full-line forcing can effectively crowd competitive products off the shelf.

Nonprice Incentives

To motivate desired behavior, a supplier may provide a favored reseller or end user with certain nonprice benefits, such as first access to new products or enhanced technical support. Due to their nonprice nature, this type of discriminatory reward is not covered by the Robinson-Patman Act, although the other laws still may apply.[54] At the same time, anything that the supplier does to assume or subsidize an expense that normally would be incurred by the customer triggers application of the Robinson-Patman Act.

OTHER PRICING ISSUES

Predatory Pricing

The practice of setting a price so low that a seller harms its own profitability in an attempt to do greater harm to a competitor is *predatory pricing.* The purpose of such behavior is either to discipline a competitor for competing too intensely or to drive it from the market and thus reduce or eliminate its competition.

Long-term aggressive pricing that is below marginal cost (or its measurable surrogate, average variable cost) can be attacked as monopolization or attempted monopolization under Section 2 of the Sherman Act and by the FTC under Section 5 of the FTC Act.[55] However, in 1993, the Supreme Court ruled that a successful prosecution requires proof that the price-cutting seller could likely recoup its losses with higher prices later on.[56] This heavy burden of proof severely limits claims of predation and favors the presumption that price-cutting is procompetitive.

Price Signaling

The practice of a supplier communicating its future pricing intentions to its competitors is known as *price signaling.* It is usually done to facilitate price parallelism through such means as supplying advance notice of price changes to customers or the media. In *DuPont,* the court of appeals overturned an FTC decision that such behavior violates the antitrust laws, ruling that consciously parallel pricing is not unlawful unless it is collusive, predatory, coercive, or exclusionary.[57] While signaling raises questions about the possibility of collusion, it can have legitimate business purposes as well. According to the court of appeals, signaling serves the lawful purpose of aiding buyers in their financial and purchasing planning.[58]

Summary

The development and implementation of pricing strategies and tactics that do not violate the law is an important aspect of pricing. In addition to the risk of legal actions initiated by the government, a company can be sued by private parties, usually its competitors or its customers. If the Justice Department can prove that the company's pricing violated the criminal provisions of the antitrust laws, the company is subject to fines and its managers may face both fines and imprisonment. In successful civil cases brought by the Justice Department or the FTC, the company may be enjoined from certain conduct, while in civil actions filed by private parties, defendants that lose may also be enjoined and have to pay treble damages and the attorneys' fees and court costs of the plaintiff. Even if antitrust claims are successfully defended, their defense is usually disruptive to the business and expensive in terms of monetary and management costs, as well as the effects on reputation.

At the same time, it is obvious that the law is rarely black and white, particularly in the area of pricing. Over the past several decades, U.S. courts have placed more emphasis on showing demonstrable economic effect, rather than relying on assumptions to find antitrust violations. Indeed, once the business objectives are clear, contemporary antitrust law provides considerable flexibility to develop alternative strategies and tactics, which are usually compatible with the degree of legal and trade-relations risk a business wishes to assume. While there often are no easy answers, in most cases the ends are achievable with some modification of the means.

Eugene F. Zelek, Jr. wrote The Legal Framework for Pricing section of this chapter. He is a partner and chairs the Antitrust and Trade Regulation Group at the Chicago law firm of Freeborn & Peters LLP. The author wishes to thank his colleagues, William C. Holmes, Tonita M. Helton, and Hillary P. Krantz, for their assistance.

Notes

1. Clarence C. Walton, *Ethos and the Executive* (Upper Saddle River, NJ: Prentice Hall, 1969, 209).
2. William J. Kehoe, "Ethics, Price Fixing, and the Management of Price Strategy," in *Marketing Ethics: Guidelines for Managers,* ed. Gene R. Laczniak and Patrick E. Murphy (Lexington, MA: D. C. Heath, 1985, 72).
3. Kehoe, "Ethics, Price Fixing, and the Management of Price Strategy," p. 71.
4. Manuel G. Velasquez, *Business Ethics,* 3rd ed. (Upper Saddle River, NJ: Prentice Hall, 1992, 282–283).
5. Tom L. Beaucamp and Normal E. Bowie, *Ethical Theory and Business,* 4th ed. (Upper Saddle River, NJ: Prentice Hall, 1993, 697–698).

6. Specialized or industry-specific statutes are outside the scope of this discussion. However, federal and state laws of general applicability tend to be consistent. For antitrust issues (particularly in pricing), it is wise to have the assistance of knowledgeable legal counsel. This section is not a substitute for such help.

7. See 1999 O.J. (L 336) 21 (the safe harbor is available to the supplier if its market share is 30 percent or less). The U.S. approach does not establish a numerical market-share threshold, but instead looks at economic effects as a whole under the "rule of reason" discussed in the next section. For an even more significant difference between U.S. and EU antitrust law, see note 27 *infra*.

8. Criminal violation of the Sherman Act, the country's principal antitrust statute, is a felony punishable by a $100 million fine if the perpetrator is a corporation or other entity and a $1 million fine or ten years in prison or both if the violator is an individual. 15 U.S.C. § 1 (the penalties were raised substantially in 2004). Application of the Comprehensive Crime Control Act and the Criminal Fine Improvements Acts, 18 U.S.C. §§ 3571–3572, permits an even greater financial penalty by allowing the fine to be increased to twice the gain from the illegal conduct or twice the loss to the victims, while the Federal Sentencing Guidelines can also impact the penalties imposed. See United States Sentencing Commission, 1991 Sentencing Guidelines.

9. The FTC has no authority under the Sherman Act and relies on other antitrust statutes, including Section 5 of the Federal Trade Commission Act, 15 U.S.C. § 45.

10. Since the 1980s, state attorneys general also have been active in civil antitrust enforcement at the federal level, suing on behalf of the citizens of their states and often coordinating their efforts through the National Association of Attorneys General (NAAG).

11. On July 30, 2002, the Sarbanes-Oxley Act of 2002, Pub.L. 107-204, 116 Stat. 745, enacted 15 U.S.C. § 7201, *et. seq.*, 15 U.S.C. §§ 78d-3, 78o-6, and 78kk, and 18 U.S.C. §§ 1348 to 1350, 1514A, 1519, and 1520, amended 11 U.S.C. § 523, 15 U.S.C. §§ 77h-1, 77s, 77t, 78c, 78j-1, 78l, 78m, 78o, 78o-4, 78o-5, 78p, 78q, 78q-1, 78u, 78u-1, 78u-2, 78u-3, 78ff, 80a-41, 80b-3, and 80b-9, 18 U.S.C. §§ 1341, 1343, 1512, and 1513, 28 U.S.C. § 1658, and 29 U.S.C. §§ 1021, 1131, and 1132, enacted provisions set out as notes under 15 U.S.C. §§ 78a, 78o-6, 78p and 7201, 18 U.S.C. §§ 1341 and 1501, and 28 U.S.C. § 1658, and amended provisions set out as notes under 28 U.S.C. § 994.

12. An "issuer" is defined by the act: "The term 'issuer' means an issuer (as defined in Section 3 of the Securities Exchange Act of 1934 (15 U.S.C. § 78c)), the securities of which are registered under Section 12 of that Act (15 U.S.C. § 78l), or that is required to file reports under Section 15(d) (15 U.S.C. § 78o(d)), or that files or has filed a registration statement that has not yet become effective under the Securities Act of 1933 (15 U.S.C.§ 77a et. seq.), and that it has not withdrawn." 15 U.S.C. § 7201(7).

13. See, for example, ABA Antitrust Section, Antitrust Compliance: Perspectives and Resources for Corporate Counselors 37–38 (2005).

14. 15 U.S.C. § 7241; 18 U.S.C. § 1350.

15. 18 U.S.C. §§ 1513–14.

16. Similarly, vertical price-fixing does not apply to the sale of services through intermediaries when the services are performed by the supplier for the end user (such as cellular telephone services), because

ownership of the services never passes to the intermediaries. Indeed, the role of the intermediaries is that of selling agent on behalf of the supplier.

17. 15 U.S.C. § 1.

18. This also is why sales through agents are not subject to the price-fixing prohibitions of the Sherman Act's section 1 nor are consignment sales where the supplier retains title to the goods in the reseller's possession until they are sold to the end user. These are unilateral activities on the part of the supplier, because ownership flows directly to the end user from the supplier.

19. For a discussion of "price signaling," a practice that facilitates conscious parallelism, see "Other Pricing Issues," below.

20. See *Interstate Circuit, Inc. v. United States*, 306 U.S. 208, 222 (1939) (restrictions); *American Tobacco Co. v. United States*, 328 U.S. 781, 805 (1946) (price increases). Of course, if the challenged conduct is consistent with rational individual behavior or there is little reason for the defendants to engage in a conspiracy, it is more difficult to find one.

21. See, for example, *In re Baby Food Antitrust Litig.*, 166 F.3d 112 (3d Cir. 1999). Moreover, the validity of the purported reasons for engaging in the conduct under examination is a consideration, but even a pretext for doing so does not alone establish a conspiracy.

22. For a case illustrating direct price-fixing, see *United States v. Andreas*, 216 F.3d 645 (7th Cir. 2000) (Archer Daniels Midland executives). For a situation involving indirect price-fixing, see *United States v. Container Corp.*, 393 U.S. 333 (1969).

23. 468 U.S. 85 (1984). This case validated the Court's decision in *Chicago Board of Trade v. United States*, 246 U.S. 231 (1918), which upheld an ex-change rule that after-hours trading had to be at prices at which the market most recently closed. Such a rule was supportive of the free-for-all competition that occurred during the trading day and, therefore, was reasonable even though it set prices among members.

24. *State Oil Co. v. Khan*, 522 U.S. 3 (1997); *Leegin Creative Leather Prods., Inc. v. PSKS*, 551 U.S. 877 (2007).

25. S.148, 111th Con. (2009); H.R. 3190, 111th Con. (2009); Md. Commercial Law Code Ann. § 11-204(b) (2009). Although Maryland is the only state that has addressed *Leegin* head-on, many states, such as New York and California, generally construe their antitrust laws consistently with those at the federal level, but will diverge when state policy requires. In what could have been an important showdown under *Leegin*, the attorneys general of New York, Michigan, and Illinois filed suit against Herman Miller, Inc. in 2008 under federal and state law, claiming that the company had entered into illegal minimum price-fixing agreements. However, only four days after filing, the case was settled by consent decree, so not only was there was no opportunity for the court to consider a *Leegin* defense, but the decree also has no precedential value. *New York v. Herman Miller, Inc.*, No. 08 Civ. 2977 (S.D.N.Y. March 25, 2008) (Stipulated Final Judgment and Consent Decree).

26. Ironically, amid the considerable handwringing in the U.S. over *Leegin*, Canada, which by statute banned all forms of resale price setting and treated violations as criminal, amended its laws in 2009 to drop this approach in favor of something more akin to the rule of reason. Competition Act, R.S.C., ch. C 34 (1985), § 76.

27. See *United States v. Colgate & Co.*, 250 U.S. 300 (1919); *Leegin Creative Leather Prods., Inc. v. PSKS*, 551 U.S. at 880. *Colgate* is the first Supreme Court decision that permitted this conduct, and unilateral vertical price-fixing is said to apply the *"Colgate* doctrine." Strictly speaking, the supplier is not "setting" prices. It is only "suggesting" or "recommending" them, but the result is the same if the supplier's unilateral price policy is effective. For a detailed discussion of the application of the *Colgate* doctrine, see Brian R. Henry and Eugene F. Zelek, Jr., *Establishing and Maintaining an Effective Minimum Resale Price Policy: A* Colgate *How-To, Antitrust* 8 (Summer 2003). Note that vertical price-fixing of any sort (maximum, minimum, or exact) by agreement is illegal in the EU, and there is also nothing analogous to the *Colgate* doctrine.

28. See *Business Electronics Corp. v. Sharp Electronics Corp.*, 485 U.S. 717, 726-27 (1988).

29. The flexibility under antitrust law notwithstanding, pulling all of the supplier's business may trigger reseller protective statutes at the federal or state level that are usually industry-specific (covering automobile dealers or beer wholesalers, for example), although some states have more general protections. (See, for example, Wisconsin Fair Dealership Law, Wisc. Stat. § 135.) Also, unless the deletion of one or more products is allowed by the applicable agreement, doing so under an otherwise lawful price policy could still constitute breach of contract.

30. For example, this approach is common in the area of disposable medical products. Interestingly, the supplier-negotiated sell price to a large hospital chain may be below the reseller's buy price from the supplier. However, after proof of such a sale is provided to the supplier, it rebates the difference, along with additional funds to provide the reseller with a margin. It is not clear what effect, if any, the anti-*Leegin* legislation will have on direct dealing programs or the resale price encouragement efforts discussed in the next section. However, such conduct was subject to the rule of reason pre-*Leegin* when minimum price agreements were per se illegal, so it is likely that such status will be retained.

31. 15 U.S.C. § 13. This statute is discussed in the next section. Until 1987, the FTC classified price restrictions in promotional programs as per se illegal, but then changed its mind. See 6Trade Reg. Rep. (CCH) ¶ 39,057 at 41,728 (FTC May 21, 1987).

32. Of course, practices that go too far are still subject to attack, as was the case of five major suppliers of consumer audio recordings that, faced with an FTC enforcement proceeding alleging the effective elimination of price competition, agreed to drop their MAP programs by consent order. Because such proceedings were settled in this fashion, there was no real factual determination and they are not binding as legal precedent. At the same time, they provide some guidance, especially in the rather rare situation where virtually identical MAP programs are widely used in an industry, they suppress almost all forms of price communication, they have a demonstrated adverse effect on industry pricing, and they lack any procompetitive justification. See *In re* Sony Music Entertain. Inc., No. 971-0070, 2000 WL 689147 (FTC May 10, 2000); *In re* Universal Music & Video Dist. Corp., No. 971-0070,

2000 WL 689345 (FTC May 10, 2000); *In re* BMG Music, No. 971-0070, 2000 WL 689347 (FTC May 10, 2000); *In re* Time Warner Inc., No. 971-0070, 2000 WL 689349 (FTC May 10, 2000); *In re* Capitol Records, Inc., No. 971-0070, 2000 WL 689350 (FTC May 10, 2000).

33. 15 U.S.C. § 13. Price discrimination is covered by section 2(a) of the act, while promotional discrimination is addressed under Sections 2(d) and 2(e). *Id.* §§ 13(a), (d)–(e). States tend to have laws that are comparable to that at the federal level. Canada also has a statutory prohibition on economic discrimination, which was decriminalized in 2009 and is now analyzed under abuse of dominance standards where there must be a likelihood of substantial anticompetitive effect for a violation. Competition Act, R.S.C., ch. C 34 (1985), §§ 76, 77, 79. In 2007, the Antitrust Modernization Commission chartered by Congress called for repeal of the Robinson-Patman Act, but no action has been taken. See Antitrust Modernization Commission, Report and Recommendations, iii (April 2007).

34. To be clear, direct sales by a supplier to the government or a charitable organization (such as a not-for-profit hospital) for its own use are outside the Robinson-Patman Act. However, if the supplier sells to an intermediary that resells to such an entity, the intermediary's sale is exempt, but that of the supplier to the intermediary is not.

35. For example, certain pharmaceutical companies paid more than $700 million to settle a consolidated lawsuit brought by thousands of drug resellers who alleged that health maintenance and managed care organizations received preferential pricing in violation of the Robinson-Patman Act and as part of a price-fixing conspiracy. *In re* Brand Name Prescription Drugs Litig., No. 94 C 897, 1999 WL 639173, at *2 (N.D. Ill. Aug. 17, 1999). Other companies fought the suit and succeeded in getting essential portions of it thrown out. *In re* Brand Name Prescription Drugs Litig., 1999–1 Trade Cas. (CCH) ¶ 72,446 (N.D. Ill), aff'd in part, 186 F.3d 781 (7th Cir. 1999).

36. For structuring purposes, there is no violation if one or more of the elements are missing. Often overlooked is that resellers selling to other businesses in interstate commerce are required to follow the Robinson-Patman Act with respect to their selling activities. In addition, buying activities by resellers or end users are covered by section 2(f) of the act, 15 U.S.C. § 13(f). See note 43 *infra*.

37. See *Volvo Trucks North America, Inc. v Reeder-Simco GMC, Inc.*, 546 U.S. 164 (2006). In this situation, many companies insist on treating both resellers the same, a somewhat more conservative approach that avoids the trade relations risk of the disfavored reseller finding out what occurred, as well as the legal risk that a sale will be made at the special price for the project and another of the identical goods and quantity at a higher price will be made to a second reseller at about the same time. Alternatively, if the supplier wishes to provide favorable bid pricing on a selective basis, it could implement a clearly articulated policy that each piece of bid business is discrete from every other and from everyday sales for inventory. In addition, a tiered-price program that is available to competing resellers may be a useful vehicle to permit discrimination in bid pricing by favoring those that

chose to meet certain criteria in the program over those that do not.

38. This distinction between a good and a service is not always obvious. For example, printing, advertising, and real estate are all services, even though something tangible is involved. In addition, off-the-shelf software is a good (much like a book or a music CD), while customized software is most likely a service. The courts have split as to whether electricity is a good or a service, a particularly important distinction in the era of deregulation. While service sellers are free from the Robinson-Patman Act, economic discrimination on their part may give rise to other antitrust claims or violate industry-specific statutes. Moreover, state law can cover discrimination in service pricing, such as in California. See Cal. Bus. & Prof. Code § 17045.

39. *FTC v. Borden Co.*, 383 U.S. 637 (1966) (evaporated milk). Although this result is counterintuitive, if brand preferences translate into different costs to produce or sell, these costs may be taken into account in pricing the otherwise identical products by relying on the defense known as "cost justification," which is discussed in the section titled "Defenses to Price Discrimination."

40. Consistent with its modern focus on actual economic effect, the Supreme Court substantially raised the bar in this area in *Brooke Group v. Brown & Williamson Corp.*, 509 U.S. 209 (1993). See the discussion of "Predatory Pricing" below.

41. Note that a defense shifts the burden of proof from the plaintiff to the defendant, so recordkeeping on the part of the defendant takes on added importance.

42. Sometimes a supplier provides a trade discount to a purchaser that is based on the latter's role in the supplier's distribution system and that reflects in a generalized way the services performed by the purchaser for the supplier. For example, a wholesaler may receive a lower price than a direct-buying retailer for such functions as warehousing and taking credit risk. There is no requirement or blanket Robinson-Patman exemption to differentiate between distribution levels, so if it is done, the differences may be cost-justified or legitimized as meeting competition. If either of these defenses is not available, a functional discount may still be lawful if it reflects reasonable compensation for the services provided. See *Texaco Inc. v. Hasbrouck*, 496 U.S. 543 (1990). Danger areas include (1) the use of intermediaries controlled by the ultimate customer to disguise discounts and (2) situations in which the intermediary makes some sales as a wholesaler and others as a retailer, but the supplier provides it with the wholesaler discount on all purchases.

43. Section 2(f) of the Robinson-Patman Act, 15 U.S.C. § 13(f), prohibits buyers from knowingly inducing discriminatory prices, but this provision is largely toothless, as the FTC is not as zealous in its enforcement as it once was and suppliers almost never sue their customers.

44. While it is possible that an industrial manufacturer that consumes the supplier's products could be covered under the promotional-discrimination provisions of the Robinson-Patman Act in certain situations (see the discussion below), it is far more common for these provisions to apply only to resellers. For consistency in this section, the party that purchases from a supplier will be referred to as the "reseller," unless otherwise noted.

45. Of course, the supplier may still face trade relations issues.

46. In its *Guides for Advertising Allowances and Other Merchandising Payments and Services*, 16 C.F.R. § 240, the FTC endorses the first two approaches and purposely ignores the third, although there is case support for it. Fortunately, the guides do not carry the force of law.

47. As is the case with price discrimination, it is illegal for buyers to knowingly induce discriminatory promotional allowances, but, due to a drafting quirk, only the FTC can chase lying buyers here. See 15 U.S.C. § 13(f).

48. *Continental T.V., Inc. v. GTE Sylvania Inc.*, 433 U.S. 36, 51–52 (1977).

49. The best area-of-primary-responsibility contract or policy language requires that a quantitative goal be attained before outside sales are permitted. The worst provision uses a meaningless "best efforts" clause that requires the reseller to use its best efforts to sell the supplier's products in the reseller's area. Note that if the supplier does not have written contracts with its resellers, it may use written policies to impose vertical restrictions.

50. The same rule applies to noncustomers who want to become customers and request certain products.

51. When a monopolist uses a loyalty program to entrench or extend its monopoly, it can run afoul of the prohibitions on monopolization and attempted monopolization under section 2 of the Sherman Act, 15 U.S.C. § 2. See *LePage's Inc. v. 3M (Minnesota Mining and Mfg. Co.)*, 324 F.3d 141 (3d Cir. 2003), *cert. denied*, 124 S. Ct. 2932 (2004) (use of bundled rebates) and note 55 *infra.*.

52. Both exclusive dealing and tying may be challenged under section 1 of the Sherman Act, 15 U.S.C. § 1 (goods or services); section 3 of the Clayton Act, *id.* § 14 (goods only); and section 5 of the Federal Trade Commission Act, *id.*§ 45 (goods or services).

53. The elements of unlawful tying are (1) two separate products or services; (2) the sale of one (the "tying product") is conditioned on the purchase of the other (the "tied product"); (3) there is sufficient economic power in the market for the tying product to restrain trade in the market for the tied product; (4) a not insubstantial amount of commerce in the market for the tied product is affected; and (5) there is no defense or justification available, such as proper functioning or trade secrets.

54. Under certain distributor, dealer, or franchisee protective laws at the state level, suppliers may be required to treat all intermediaries more or less the same in all business dealings, or, as in Wisconsin, not change their "competitive circumstances" without cause. See Wisconsin Fair Dealership Law, Wisc. Stat. § 135.

55. 15 U.S.C. §§ 2, 45. Monopolization requires (1) monopoly power in the relevant market and (2) the willful acquisition or maintenance of that power, while attempted monopolization consists of (1) predatory or exclusionary conduct, (2) specific or predatory intent to achieve monopoly power in the relevant market, and (3) a dangerous probability that the defendant will be successful. The presence of a conspiracy to engage in predatory pricing can violate sections 1 and 2 of the Sherman Act. *Id.* §§ 1, 2.

56. *Brooke Group v. Brown & Williamson Corp.*, 509 U.S. 209 (1993). The Supreme Court later extended this approach to predatory buying, that is, overpaying for inputs to drive out

competitors. See *Weyerhaeuser Co. v. Ross-Simmons Hardwood Lumber Co.*, 549 U.S. 312 (2007). A variation is the "price squeeze," where an integrated manufacturer with a large market share in a key input sells it at a higher price to manufacturers of competing finished goods than the input manufacturer sells its own finished products. However, the Supreme Court has held that there is no antitrust issue as long as the input manufacturer is under no obligation to sell to others and its finished goods are not priced below cost. *Pac. Bell Tel. Co. v. linkLine Communications, Inc.*, 129 S.Ct. 1109 (2009).

57. *E. I. Du Pont de Nemours & Co. v. FTC*, 729 F.2d 128, 139–40 (2d Cir. 1984).

58. *Id.* at 134. Of course, not all types of price signaling fare as well. Eight airlines and their jointly owned data collection and dissemination company settled a price-fixing case brought by the Justice Department over a computerized system that was used to communicate fare changes and promotions in advance to the participants and permitted later modification or withdrawal of such announcements. *United States v. Airline Tariff Publishing Co.*, 1994–92 Trade Cas. (CCH) ¶ 70,686 (D.D.C. 1994) (all defendants, except United Air Lines, Inc. and USAir, Inc.); 836 F. Supp. 12 (D.C.C. 1993) (United and USAir). In the government's view, the nonpublic nature of this data exchange and its method of operation were tantamount to the airlines having direct discussions in the same room.

INDEX

A

Activity-based costing, 196–197
Analytics, for pricing, 168–178

B

Benefits sought by customers
  monetary, 74–81
  psychological, 74–81, 92
Break-even analysis for pricing, 207–243
  baseline for, 223–224
  case studies, 209–212, 225–232
  derivation of formula, 233–234
  developing charts and tables for, 235–243
  fixed and sunk costs with, 224–225
  for reaction to competition 216–217
  incorporating variable costs, 212–213
  sales curves, 220–223
  with incremental fixed costs, 130–131, 213–216
Bundling, 50–55
  competition and, 55
  gains and losses, 93
  See also Unbundling
Buying process, 11, 82–87
  participants in, 86–87
Buy-response survey. *See* Price elasticity

C

Capitation price, 55
Change process, managing, 178–180
Competition, 244–267
  and price discounting, 244
  and price discrimination, 317–318
  bundling and, 55
  in growth stage of product life cycle, 149–150
  in maturity stage of product life cycle, 151
  reacting to, 251–267
  when to compete on price, 266–267
  willingness and ability to defend against, 264–265
Competitive advantage, 246–251, 255
Competitive information, 261–265
  collection and evaluation of, 261–263
  communication of, 263–265
Conjoint analysis. *See* Trade-off (conjoint) analysis
Consumer surplus, 18
Contribution margin, 197–199
Cost accounting, 189–191

Cost justification for price discrimination, 317
Cost leadership strategy, 147–149
Cost of search, 74–76, 81, 83, 103
Costs
  activity-based, 196–197
  avoidable, 186–196
  determining relevant, 182–183
  estimating relevant, 191–196
  improved control of, 152–153
  incremental, 183–186, 190–196
  opportunity, 191–196
  role in pricing, 181–182
  sunk, 186–187, 224–225
  See also Break-even analysis for pricing
Customer value modeling (CVM), 36–38

D

Decision rights, 14, 164–165
Decline, life cycle stage
  consolidation strategy in, 155
  harvesting strategy in, 154
  retrenchment strategy in, 154
Demonstration projects, 179–180
Depth interviews. *See* In-depth interviews
Differentiation, 147–148, 150–152
  product strategy, 147–148
  value, 18–19, 21, 26, 37, 103–110, 118–123
Discounts. *See* Price discounts
Distribution channels, reevaluation of, 153
Dynamic pricing models, 137–138

E

Early adopters, 144
Economic value
  cost of shortcuts, 36–38
  estimating, 21–38
  monetary, 23–32
  psychological, 32–36
  See also Benefits sought
Ethical constraints on pricing, 305–308
Everyday low price, 97
Expectations, 97–98, 111
Experience goods, 11, 74–77

F

"Fair" profit, 307
Fair-value line, 37–38
Fee-for-service, 55
Fences. *See* Price fences
Full-line forcing, 322

G

Growth, life cycle stage, 146–150
  price reductions in, 149–150

I

In-depth interviews, 286–288
Innovation, 141–146
  communicating value of with direct
      sales, 145–146
  diffusion of, 143
  marketing of through distribution
      channels, 146
  pricing in growth stage, 143–150
  strategy for pricing an, 143–146
Innovator's Dilemma, The, 49
In-store purchase experiments,
      277–279, 299–300

L

Laboratory purchase experiments, 279–280
LIFO (last-in, first-out) accounting, 187

M

Managerial judgment, 13
Market decline, pricing in, 153–155
Market-share myth, 247–248
Maturity, life cycle stage, 150–153
maintaining profits in, 151
Minimum advertised price (MAP)
      program, 314
Monetary benefits. *See* Benefits sought
Monetary value, 19, 23–32, 286
  algorithms, 25–26
  drivers. *See* Value drivers
  estimating, 23–32
  See also Value, perceptions of versus actual

N

Negative-sum game, price competition as,
      245, 260–261
Next best competitive alternative (NBCA),
      20, 26, 64
NIFO (next-in, first-out) accounting, 187

P

Panel data, to estimate price elasticity
      272–274
Penetration pricing. *See* Pricing, penetration
Perceived value. *See* Value, perceptions of
      versus actual
Performance-based rebate, 115–116
Positive-sum game, 245
Price
  discrimination, 315–320
  expectations, 97–98, 111
  fairness, 90–91, 133, 137–139, 144

increases
  policies for, 110–114
  preannouncing, 264
  integrity, 101, 105
  signaling, 322–323
Price banding analysis, 112, 172–173
Price communication, 87–93
  gain-loss framing, 91–93
  perceived fairness, 90–91, 133,
      137–139, 144
  proportional price evaluations, 87–88
  reference prices, 21–23, 87–90
Price competition. *See* Competition
Price discounts, 64–70, 92, 97, 99, 114–117,
      172–175
  in competitive markets, 244
  See also Promotional pricing
Price elasticity
  attribute rating to measure, 283
  buy-response surveys to measure, 283–286,
      299–300
  direct questioning about, 283
  measurement of, 269–301
    selecting appropriate technique,
        299–300
    using judgment, 295–297
    using Internet-based techniques,
        297–298
Price fences, 44–45, 63–70
  buyer-identification fences, 64–65
  purchase location fences, 65–66
  purchase quantity fences, 68–70
  step discounts, 68–70
  time of purchase fences, 66–68
Price level, 13, 118–140
Price metrics, 55–61
  criteria for selecting, 56–60
  performance-based, 60–61
Price promotions. *See* Promotional pricing
Price segmentation. *See* Segmentation
Price sensitivity, 13, 64–68, 149, 152
  measuring and estimating, 269–301
Price setting, 118–140
  break-even analysis case studies for,
      209–212, 225–232
  estimating customer response to, 124,
      131–136
Price structure, 9–10
  customer segments and, 47–70
  price fences, 44–45, 63–70
  price metrics, 55–61
  price-offer bundles, 50–55
  segments to distinguish within, 48–50
  step discounts, 68–70
Price waterfalls, 173–175

Price window, 121–123
Price-fixing, 310–315
    horizontal, 311–312
    resale, 312–315
    vertical, 312–314
Price-offer configuration, 50–55
    optimizing an offer bundle, 51–53
    segment specific bundles, 53–54
    unbundling strategically, 54–55
    See also Unbundling
Price-volume tradeoff, 5, 13, 47, 124, 129–131,
    152, 207–225
Pricing
    analytics, 168–178
    break-even analysis for, 130–131, 207–243
    cost-based, 9
    cost-plus, 2–3, 5, 181
    customer-driven, 3–4, 207
    ethical constraints on, 305–308
    for innovations, 143–150
    implementing strategy for, 14–15, 158–159
    legal framework for, 308–310
    life cycle. See Product life cycle pricing
    market-based, 207–208
    neutral, 129
    opportunistic, 260–263, 265
    peak, 193–194
    penetration, 13, 127–129, 147–149
    performance-based, 60–61
    predatory, 322–323
    proactive, 6, 207–216
    process, 12, 165–166
    profit-driven, 6, 61
    promotions. See Promotional pricing
    reactive, 216–217
    share-driven, 4–5
    skim, 125–127
    strategic, 5–7
        versus tactical, 98
    transfer, 199–204
    value-based, 6, 104
Pricing policy, 12, 96–117
    ad hoc negotiation, 100–102
    development of, 99–100
    for brand-driven buyers (relationship
        buyers), 103, 105–107
    for convenience-driven buyers, 103, 108
    for economic downturn, 114–115
    for outlaw customers, 112–114
    for power buyers, 108–110
    for price-driven buyers, 103, 106–108
    for value-driven buyers, 103–105, 107
    negotiation, policies for, 102–103
    "no exceptions," 99
    promotional pricing, 115–117, 144–145

    responding to objections, 100–110
    transitioning, 112–114
Pricing strategy
    and product life cycle, 141–156
    implementation of, 14–15, 158–180
    managing the change process, 178–180
    motivation for, 159–160, 166–178
    organization of pricing function, 159–166
    performance measures, 175–178
    reasons for failure, 158–159
Product life cycle pricing, 141–156
    in development stage, 143–146
    in growth stage, 146–150
    in market decline, 153–155
    in maturity stage, 150–153
Promotional discrimination, 315, 318–320
Promotional pricing, 115–117
    communicating value with, 144–145
    price-induced sampling, 145
    pulsed, 116
    See also Price discounts
Psychological benefits. See Benefits sought
Psychological value, 19, 23–24, 286
    trade-off (conjoint) analysis to estimate,
        32–36

R

Reference prices, 21–23, 87–90
Reference value, 19–21, 26, 37, 64
Regression analysis
    of prices, 172–173
    of sales data, 275–276
Resale price
    agreements, 312–315
    encouragement, 314–315
    maintenance, 146
    policies, 313
Robinson-Patman Act, 315–320, 322

S

Sales data, 271–272, 296
    analyzing, 275–276
Sarbanes-Oxley, 309–310
Search goods, 11, 74
Segmentation, 38–70, 119–121, 150
    metrics for, 44–45
    value-based, 38–45
Senior management leadership, 178–179
Services, pricing for, 57–58
Simulated purchase experiments, 288–289,
    299–300
Single-price strategy, 47–49
SPIN selling, 103
Store scanner data, 273–275
Strategic pricing. See Pricing, strategic

Strategic pricing pyramid, 6–7, 17, 160
Strategic sourcing, 98

T

Territorial restrictions, 321
Trade-off (conjoint) analysis, 289–294, 299–300
   illustration of, 32–36

U

Unbundling, 54–55, 93
   in maturity stage of product life cycle,
      151–152
   See also Bundling; Price-offer configuration

V

Value
   communication, 11–12, 72–93, 126
      adapting to purchase context, 81–82
      of innovation, 143–145

creation of, 7–9, 17–46
differentiation, 18–19, 21, 26, 37, 103–110,
   118–123
economic. *See* Economic value
exchange, 18
   See also Economic value
monetary, 19, 23–32, 286
   drivers. *See* Value drivers
   estimating, 23–32
perceptions of versus actual, 7, 20, 77,
   90, 287
psychological, 19, 23–24, 32–36, 286
reference, 19–21, 26, 37, 64
use, 18
Value drivers, 23–32, 74, 77, 83,
   algorithms, 25–26
Value equivalence line, 37–38
ValueScan Survey, 1, 14